World Intellectual Property Indicators 2019

WIPO
WORLD
INTELLECTUAL PROPERTY
ORGANIZATION

Table of contents

Patents

Trademarks

Industrial designs

Plant varieties

Geographical indications

Creative economy

Additional information

Foreword

Global intellectual property (IP) filing activity continues to grow at a rapid pace, setting new records in 2018. Patent filings around the world exceeded 3.3 million, representing a 5.2% growth on 2017 figures. Trademark filing activity totaled 14.3 million, up 15.5% on 2017. Industrial design filing activity amounted to 1.3 million. Applications for utility models grew by 21.8% to reach 2.1 million applications, while plant varieties filings reached 20,210 in 2018.

China has been the main driver of global growth in IP filings in recent years and it was once again the main source of growth in worldwide IP filings in 2018. Filing activity in China grew by 11.6% for patents, 28.3% for trademarks and 12.7% for industrial designs. The IP office of China now accounts for 46.4% of patent filings and more than half of global trademark (51.4%) and industrial design (54%) filing activity.

The United States of America (U.S.) saw a 1.6% fall in patent filings in 2018 – the first decline since 2009. However, trademark filing activity in the U.S. grew by 4.3% – a ninth successive year of growth. Patent filings and trademark filing activity in Japan declined by 1.5% and 8.6%, respectively. The Republic of Korea saw growth in both patent filings (+2.5%) and trademark filing activity (+14.5%). Another notable trend for the year were the large increases in trademark filing activity in India (+20.9%), France (+10.5%) and Brazil (+9.8%). India saw strong growth in patent filings (+7.5%), while in respect of industrial design filing activity, the United Kingdom (U.K.) (+42.4%), the Russian Federation (+21%), Italy (+16.6%) and India (+13.6%) all saw double-digit growth in 2018.

For a second year, this report includes statistics on the creative economy, reflecting the publishing industry. Considerable efforts have been made to improve the quality and geographical coverage of these statistics; as a result, this year's edition of *World Intellectual Property Indicators* includes 2018 publishing activity data for 49 countries. In addition, for the first time, data on legal deposits at national libraries covering 39 countries are included in this edition. It should be noted that, although these statistics are in many ways still partial and incomplete, they represent progress in building a more complete and comparable picture of global publishing activity worldwide.

Readers wishing to go beyond the statistics presented in this report can use the statistical tools on WIPO's website (*www.wipo.int/ipstats*), notably the IP Statistics Data Center and the Statistical Country Profiles.

As always, I would like to thank our member states, as well as national and regional IP authorities, for sharing their annual statistics with WIPO. Their invaluable cooperation makes the *World Intellectual Property Indicators* possible.

Francis GURRY
Director General

Acknowledgements

World Intellectual Property Indicators 2019 was prepared under the direction of Francis Gurry (Director General) and supervised by Carsten Fink (Chief Economist). The report was prepared by a team led by Mosahid Khan and comprising Kyle Bergquist, Ryan Lamb, Bruno Le Feuvre, Anastasiya Letnikava and Hao Zhou, all from the Economics and Statistics Division. Peter Button and Tomochika Motomura of the International Union for the Protection of New Varieties of Plants (UPOV) provided comments and suggestions for the plant varieties section. Alexandra Grazioli and Matteo Gragnani of the Brands and Designs Sector provided comments and suggestions for the geographical indications section.

Samiah Do Carmo Figueiredo, Cécile Roure and Caterina Valles Galmes provided administrative support. Gratitude is also due to the Publications Division for the editing and design and to staff in the Printing Plant for their services.

Further information

Online resources

The electronic version of this report and the underlying data can be downloaded at *www.wipo.int/ipstats*. This webpage also provides a link to the IP Statistics Data Center, offering access to WIPO's statistical data.

Contact information

Economics and Statistics Division
Website: *www.wipo.int/ipstats*
e-mail: *ipstats.mail@wipo.int*

Key numbers

Patents	2017	2018	Growth rate (%)	Share of world total (%)
Applications worldwide	**3,162,300**	**3,326,300**	**5.2**	**100.0**
China	1,381,594	1,542,002	11.6	46.4
U.S.	606,956	597,141	−1.6	18.0
Japan	318,481	313,567	−1.5	9.4

Utility models				
Applications worldwide	**1,761,440**	**2,145,960**	**21.8**	**100.0**
China	1,687,593	2,072,311	22.8	96.6
Germany	13,301	12,307	−7.5	0.6
Russian Federation	10,643	9,747	−8.4	0.5

Trademarks				
Application class counts worldwide	**12,395,700**	**14,321,800**	**15.5**	**100.0**
China	5,739,669	7,365,522	28.3	51.4
U.S.	613,895	640,181	4.3	4.5
Japan	560,265	512,156	−8.6	3.6

Industrial designs				
Application design counts worldwide	**1,242,100**	**1,312,600**	**5.7**	**100.0**
China	628,658	708,799	12.7	54.0
EUIPO (EU Office)	111,234	108,174	−2.8	8.2
Republic of Korea	67,482	68,054	0.8	5.2

Plant varieties				
Applications worldwide	**18,550**	**20,210**	**8.9**	**100.0**
China	4,465	5,760	29.0	28.5
Community Plant Variety Office (EU)	3,422	3,554	3.9	17.6
U.S.	1,557	1,609	3.3	8.0

Source: WIPO Statistics Database, August 2019.

Overview of IP filing activity

Table 1. Ranking of total (resident and abroad) IP filing activity by origin, 2018

Origin	Patents	Marks	Designs	Origin	Patents	Marks	Designs
China	1	1	1	Bulgaria	61	45	42
U.S.	2	2	4	Cyprus	62	53	37
Germany	5	4	2	Greece (b)	47	74	31
Japan	3	3	6	Colombia	57	36	67
Republic of Korea	4	11	3	Liechtenstein (a)	44	62	54
France	6	5	9	Pakistan	67	33	61
U.K.	7	8	8	Chile	48	30	86
Italy	10	12	5	Slovakia	59	51	57
Switzerland	8	14	11	Belarus	42	63	74
India	12	9	13	Saudi Arabia	25	95	64
Russian Federation	11	7	19	Slovenia	52	73	59
Iran (Islamic Republic of)	20	6	12	Bangladesh	102	55	34
Turkey	23	10	7	United Arab Emirates (c)	54	50	87
Netherlands	9	19	14	Uzbekistan	60	66	70
Spain	22	16	10	Egypt	46	115	36
Australia	19	17	15	Croatia	76	65	58
Sweden	13	21	17	Serbia	71	69	60
Canada	14	15	26	Lithuania	75	67	69
Brazil	26	13	21	Latvia	80	70	65
Austria (c)	17	27	22	Mongolia	104	56	55
Poland (c)	27	25	18	Malta (a, b, c)	64	68	84
Belgium	16	28	27	Estonia	74	75	68
Ukraine	33	23	16	Peru	91	42	85
Denmark	18	38	25	Syrian Arab Republic	96	59	63
China, Hong Kong SAR	35	26	24	Kenya (b)	72	72	80
Mexico	32	18	35	Barbados (a, b, c)	49	113	65
Thailand	38	29	20	Kazakhstan	40	96	91
Indonesia	43	24	29	Republic of Moldova	84	82	62
Singapore	24	32	41	Armenia	82	79	81
Czech Republic	34	34	30	Monaco	92	76	76
Portugal	39	31	28	Ecuador	113	57	75
Finland	21	40	38	Panama	79	61	105
Israel	15	52	32	Georgia	93	84	72
Viet Nam	51	22	33	Sudan	67	97	89
New Zealand	31	37	39	Iraq	56	106	92
Norway	28	41	40	China, Macao SAR	89	91	77
Argentina	50	20	47	Iceland (c)	73	86	99
Luxembourg	30	44	43	Mauritius	78	88	92
Malaysia	36	39	53	Algeria	83	133	46
South Africa	37	47	44	Sri Lanka	66	123	73
Romania	41	43	49	Costa Rica	95	58	110
Ireland (b)	29	54	51	Côte d'Ivoire (a, b, c)	64	108	94
Philippines	53	35	48	Tunisia (b)	76	112	79
Morocco	70	48	23	Nigeria (b)	86	146	45
Hungary	45	49	50	Cameroon (a, b, c)	55	122	104

Origin	Patents	Marks	Designs
Bosnia and Herzegovina	100	104	78
Senegal (a, b, c)	69	119	97
Azerbaijan	63	129	96
San Marino (b)	107	125	56
Cuba	87	89	116

Origin	Patents	Marks	Designs
Ghana	132	109	52
Jamaica	118	87	88
Jordan	113	81	100
Guatemala	132	64	101
Bahamas (a, b, c)	117	94	90

Note: Rankings are based on the total numbers of applications filed by origin. Patent data refer to numbers of equivalent patent applications. Trademark data refer to numbers of equivalent trademark applications based on class counts – the number of classes specified in applications. Industrial design data refer to numbers of equivalent industrial design applications based on design counts – the number of designs contained in applications. This table lists origins for which at least two types of IP filing data are available.

(a) Data on patent applications at the national IP office are not available.

(b) Data on trademark applications at the national IP office are not available.

(c) Data on industrial design applications at the national IP office are not available.

Source: WIPO Statistics Database, August 2019.

Table 2. Ranking of resident IP activity by origin, 2018

Origin	Patents	Marks	Designs
China	1	1	1
U.S.	2	2	8
Japan	3	3	7
Germany	5	7	3
Republic of Korea	4	9	2
France	7	5	10
Iran (Islamic Republic of)	11	4	11
U.K.	8	12	6
India	9	6	12
Italy	10	13	4
Turkey	14	8	5
Russian Federation	6	10	17
Brazil	16	11	18
Spain	21	16	9
Netherlands	12	22	15
Switzerland	13	24	19
Ukraine	25	21	13
Poland	17	23	..
Australia	24	17	20
Indonesia	31	19	21
Mexico	29	14	28
Sweden	15	33	23
Austria	19	32	..
Canada	18	15	44
Thailand	37	27	14

Origin	Patents	Marks	Designs
Portugal	39	25	22
Belgium	22	35	30
Viet Nam	43	18	26
Denmark	20	46	24
Czech Republic	36	36	29
Egypt	35	39	27
Argentina	51	20	38
Romania	32	38	41
Finland	23	50	40
South Africa	41	37	36
Philippines	47	29	39
China, Hong Kong SAR	57	28	31
Greece	46	..	32
Norway	26	45	46
Malaysia	33	40	48
Morocco	62	44	16
Saudi Arabia	27	41	57
New Zealand	34	42	51
Ireland	40	..	49
Singapore	28	48	58
Israel	30	71	35
Pakistan	58	30	52
Bulgaria	61	43	37
Hungary	47	52	42
Colombia	52	31	61

Origin	Patents	Marks	Designs
Nigeria	69	..	33
Luxembourg	44	63	47
Algeria	66	58	34
Slovakia	59	51	50
Bangladesh	82	55	25
Uzbekistan	49	56	59
Chile	53	26	90
Kazakhstan	38	..	80
Mongolia	80	53	45
Sri Lanka	56	57	67
Paraguay	..	47	75
Belarus	45	69	71
Slovenia	54	64	68
Peru	77	34	76
Syrian Arab Republic	71	60	56

Origin	Patents	Marks	Designs
Croatia	67	75	54
Kenya	60	..	72
Panama	67	65	..
Ecuador	85	49	65
Latvia	74	62	63
Lithuania	70	68	62
Tunisia	64	..	73
Republic of Moldova	75	78	53
Serbia	65	77	70
United Arab Emirates	76	67	..
Iraq	42	92	81
Estonia	81	69	66
Cyprus	83	82	55
Georgia	71	81	69
Liechtenstein (a)	50	108	64

Note: Rankings are based on the numbers of resident applications filed by origin. Patent data refer to numbers of equivalent patent applications. Trademark data refer to numbers of equivalent trademark applications based on class counts – the number of classes specified in applications. Industrial design data refer to numbers of equivalent industrial design applications based on design counts – the number of designs contained in applications. This table lists origins for which at least two types of IP filing data are available.

(a) Data on patent applications at the national IP office are not available.

.. indicates not available.

Source: WIPO Statistics Database, August 2019.

Patents

Highlights

Patent applications worldwide grew by 5.2% in 2018

Applicants around the world filed 3.3 million patent applications in 2018. This represents a 5.2% increase on the previous year (figure 1.1). Driving such strong growth was an exceptional number of filings in China, which received about 160,400 more filings in 2018 than it had in 2017. The next largest contributors were the European Patent Office (EPO) (7,812 additional filings) and the offices of the Republic of Korea (5,217) and India (3,473).

The long-term trend shows patent applications growing worldwide every year since 2004, with the sole exception of 2009 when they decreased by 3.8% due to the financial crisis.

Of the 3.3 million applications filed worldwide in 2018, resident applicants filed 2.4 million (71.5% of the total), while non-resident applicant filed the remaining 0.9 million (28.5%). Resident share increased from 61.6% in 2004 to 71.5% in 2018. In addition, the proportion of resident versus non-resident filings varies greatly across offices. For example, more than half of all applications filed in the United States of America (U.S.) were non-resident applications, whereas non-resident share was less than a one-tenth of all applications filed in China.

China received 1.5 million patent applications

The National Intellectual Property Administration of the People's Republic of China received 1.5 million patent applications in 2018, an amount similar in magnitude to the combined total of the offices ranked from 2 to 11. The United States Patent and Trademark Office (USPTO) ranked second, with 597,141 applications. It was followed by the Japan Patent Office (JPO), with 313,567 applications, the Korean Intellectual Property Office (KIPO), with 209,992 applications, and the EPO, with 174,397 applications. Together, the top five offices accounted for 85.3% of the world total in 2018, which is 10 percentage points higher than their combined 2008 share. China's share of the world total increased from 15% in 2008 to 46.4% in 2018, whereas that of the other four offices declined over the same period.

The composition and the ranking of the top 10 offices have both remained relatively stable since 2008. The composition of the top 10 offices has remained the same, except that in some years Australia has been among the top 10 offices, while in others it has lost its place in the list to Brazil. In addition, China moved up from third position in 2008 to take the top spot in 2011 and has continued to head the ranking for the past eight years. Figure 1.2 shows the patent applications received by the top 10 offices, broken down by resident and non-resident filings. The intellectual property (IP) offices of China (90.4%), Germany (68.7%), Japan (80.9%), the Republic of Korea (77.4%) and the Russian Federation (65.7%) received the bulk of their applications from resident applicants. In contrast, Australia (90.8%), Canada (88%) and India (67.5%) reported a high share of non-resident filings.

Patent applications filed worldwide reached 3.3 million

1.1. Patent applications worldwide, 2004–2018

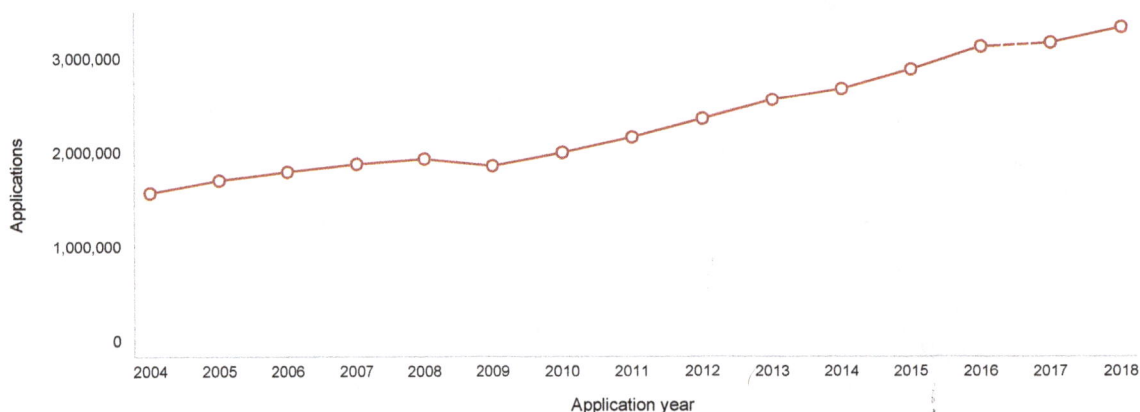

Source: Figure A1.

China received 46.4% of all patent applications filed worldwide
1.2. Patent applications at the top 10 offices, 2018

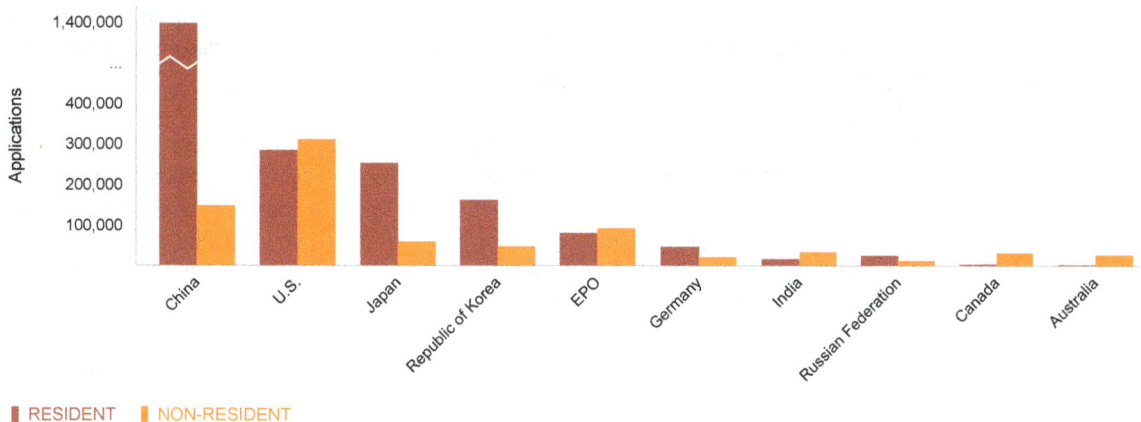

RESIDENT   NON-RESIDENT

Source: Figure A8.

Patents

Among the top five offices, China (+11.6%), the EPO (+4.7%) and the Republic of Korea (+2.5%) recorded growth in applications in 2018; in contrast, both Japan (–1.5%) and the U.S. (–1.6%) saw small declines.

The long-term trend shows that the office of China has recorded year-on-year growth for the past 23 years. The EPO saw a second consecutive year of growth in 2018, while the Republic of Korea's office returned to growth following two years of decline in applications. The patent office of Japan has experienced either a fall in applications or negligible growth since 2005, mainly as a result of a persistent fall in resident applications. The U.S. office saw its first decline in applications for nine years in 2018.

Among the top 20 offices, 13 had a greater number of patent applications in 2018 than in 2017 (figure A9). The largest increases were in China, Hong Kong SAR (+20.2%), China (+11.6%), Singapore (+8.4%) and India (+7.5%). The increases in number of applications filed at three of these four offices were driven primarily by growth in non-resident applications. The exception was China, where a strong growth in resident applications was the main driver of total growth.

Of the seven offices among the top 20 to have received fewer applications in 2018 than in 2017, the Islamic Republic of Iran (–21.1%) reported the steepest decline, due mainly to a fall in resident applications. The United Kingdom (U.K.) (–5.1%), Mexico (–4.4%) and Brazil (–3.1%) likewise recorded considerable annual drops. Applications in Brazil fell for a fifth consecutive year, while Mexico reported a third successive year of declining numbers of applications.

Looking outside the top 20 offices to selected offices of low- and middle-income countries shows that Pakistan (+27.8%), Philippines (+26.7%), Uzbekistan (+17.5%), Morocco (+14.1%) and Vietnam (+12.8%) recorded particularly rapid growth in 2018. An increase in non-resident applications was the main driver of total growth in Morocco, the Philippines and Vietnam, whereas resident applications were the primary driver in Pakistan and Uzbekistan (figure A11). The three regional offices – the African Intellectual Property Organization (OAPI), the African Regional Intellectual Property Organization (ARIPO) and the Eurasian Patent Organization (EAPO) – likewise reported strong growth in applications in 2018. Among the three, ARIPO (+11.2%) had the largest increase, followed by OAPI (+6.2%) and EAPO (+5.6%). At most of the offices of low- and middle-income countries, the bulk of applications are filed by non-resident applicants. As a result, overall increases or decreases in applications received by these offices are determined mainly by the filing behavior of non-resident applicants.

Patents

Offices located in Asia received two-thirds of all applications filed worldwide in 2018

Of the top 20 offices, nine were located in Asia, six in Europe, two each in North America and Latin America and the Caribbean (LAC), and one in Oceania. South Africa is the highest ranked African office, in 24th place. Offices located in Asia received over 2.2 million applications in 2018, representing 66.8% of the world total (figure 1.3). The combined total of Europe and North America was just below the 1 million mark. Asia's share of all applications filed worldwide increased from 50.8% in 2008 to 66.8% in 2018. This was primarily driven by strong growth in filings in China, which accounted for close to 70% of all applications filed in the region. Offices in North America accounted for just under one-fifth of the 2018 world total, while those in Europe accounted for just over one-tenth. The combined share for Africa, LAC and Oceania was 3.3%. The shares of all the world's regions except Asia have gradually declined over the past decade due to the rapid growth in applications filed in China.

Included among the top 20 list were 12 offices located in high-income, six in upper middle-income and two in lower middle-income countries.

The distribution of applications by income group shows that – for the first time – offices of upper middle-income countries received more than half of all applications filed worldwide in 2018, while offices of high-income countries accounted for 46.8% of the total (table A5). Over the past 15 years there has been a sizeable shift in the distribution of applications toward the upper middle-income group, which is largely explained by the strong growth in filings in China and a decline in Japan. The share for offices of upper middle-income countries rose from 22.6% in 2008 to 50.6% in 2018; however, excluding China from the upper middle-income group shows the share of this income group to have remained stable at around 8% over the 2008–2018 period.

Patent filings since 1883

From 1883 to 1963, the patent office of the U.S. was the leading office for world filings. Application numbers in Japan and the U.S. were stable until the early 1970s, when Japan began to see rapid growth – a pattern also observed for the U.S. from the 1980s onward. Among the top five offices, Japan surpassed the U.S. in 1968 and maintained the top position until 2005. Since the early 2000s, however, the number of applications filed in Japan has followed a downward trend. Both the EPO and the Republic of Korea have seen increases each year since the early 1980s, as has China since 1995. China surpassed the EPO and the Republic of Korea in 2005, Japan in 2010 and the U.S. in 2011 – and it now receives the largest number of applications worldwide. There has been a gradual upward trend in the combined share of the top five offices in the world total – from 75.3% in 2008 to 85.3% in 2018.

Trend in patent applications for the top five offices, 1883–2018

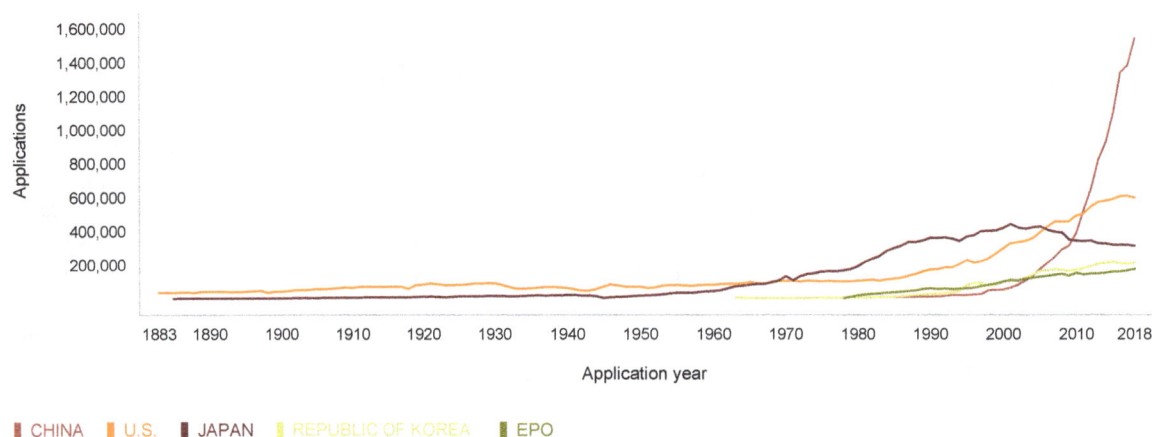

CHINA   U.S.   JAPAN   REPUBLIC OF KOREA   EPO

Note: The IP office of the Soviet Union, not represented in this figure, was the leading office in the world in terms of filings from 1964 to 1969. Like Japan and the U.S., the office of the Soviet Union saw stable application numbers until the early 1960s, after which it recorded rapid growth in the number of applications filed.

Source: Figure A7.

Offices located in Asia received 66.8% of all patent applications filed worldwide
1.3. Patent applications by region, 2008 and 2018

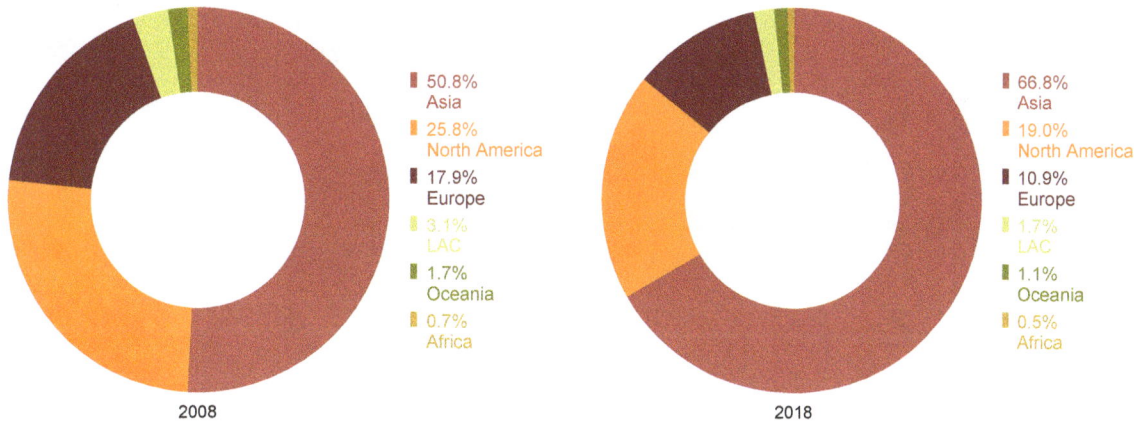

2008

- 50.8% Asia
- 25.8% North America
- 17.9% Europe
- 3.1% LAC
- 1.7% Oceania
- 0.7% Africa

2018

- 66.8% Asia
- 19.0% North America
- 10.9% Europe
- 1.7% LAC
- 1.1% Oceania
- 0.5% Africa

Source: Table A6.

Equivalent application count

Applications at regional IP offices are equivalent to multiple applications in the countries that are members of the organizations establishing those offices. In particular, to calculate the number of equivalent applications for the African Intellectual Property Organization (OAPI), the Eurasian Patent Organization (EAPO) and the Patent Office of the Cooperation Council for the Arab States of the Gulf (GCC Patent Office), each application is multiplied by the corresponding number of member states. For African Regional Intellectual Property Organization (ARIPO) and the European Patent Office (EPO) data, each application is counted as one application abroad if the applicant does not reside in a member state or as one resident application and one application abroad if the applicant resides in a member state. The equivalent application concept is used for reporting data by origin.

U.S. applicants filed around 230,000 patent applications abroad

Applications received by offices from resident and non-resident applicants are referred to as office data, whereas applications filed by applicants at a national/regional office (resident applications) or at foreign offices (applications abroad) are referred to as origin data. Here, patent statistics based on the origin of residence of the first named applicant are reported in order to complement the picture of patent activity worldwide.

Applicants from China filed around 1.46 million equivalent patent applications in 2018, followed by the U.S. (515,180), Japan (460,369), the Republic of Korea (232,020) and Germany (180,086) (figure A18). However, the distribution between resident and abroad filings differs considerably. For example, only 4.5% of all applications from China are filed abroad. In contrast, abroad filings constitute 59.3% of total applications from Germany. Among the top 20 origins, applications filed abroad made up more than 80% of the totals for Canada (82.2%), Israel (90.3%) and Switzerland (80.3%), whereas less than a fifth of total applications originating from China (4.5%), the Islamic Republic of Iran (1.4%) and the Russian Federation (17.5%) were filed abroad.

U.S. applicants filed the largest number of equivalent applications abroad (230,085) in 2018, followed by Japan (206,739), Germany (106,753), the Republic of Korea (69,459) and China (66,429) (figure 1.4). Filing abroad for Canada, France, the Netherlands, the U.K. and Switzerland ranged from around 20,000 to 44,000. Among the 10 origins reported in figure 1.4, China (+21.2%), the Republic of Korea (+4.1%), the U.K. (+2.4%) and Switzerland (+2.4%) saw a strong average annual growth in applications abroad between 2008 and 2018. For all other origins, except the Netherlands, growth ranged from 1.1% to 1.5% over the same period.

U.S. applicants filed the largest number of applications abroad
1.4. Patent applications filed abroad by the top 10 origins, 2018

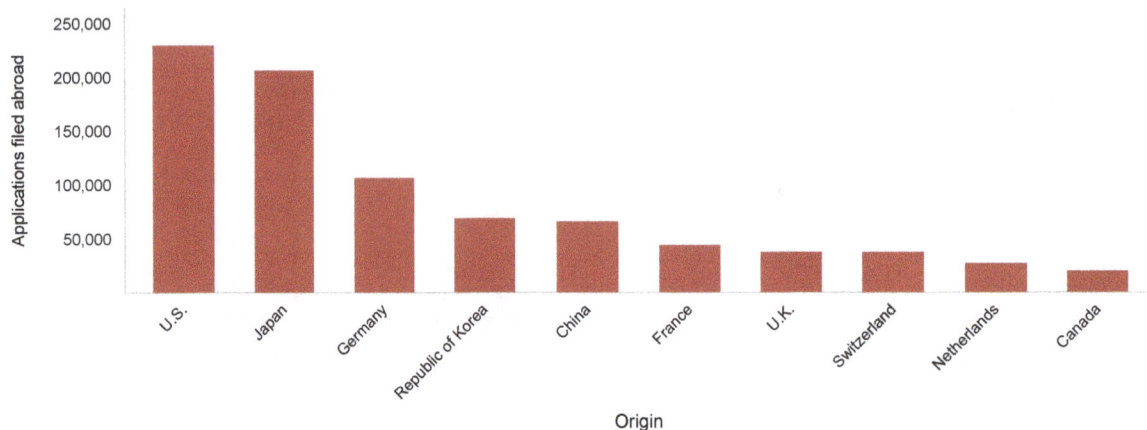

Source: Figure A18.

The flow of non-resident applications between origins and offices shows U.S. applicants accounting for a high proportion of non-resident filings in Australia (49.2%), Canada (51.8%), the EPO (47.1%) and Mexico (48.2%). Applicants residing in Japan accounted for at least a third of all non-resident applications filed in Germany (37.7%), Thailand (42.2%) and the Republic of Korea (32.9%) (table A19).

The Republic of Korea continues to file the highest number of patents per unit of GDP

Variations in patenting activity across countries reflect differences in their size and the structure of their economies. It is therefore informative to examine resident patent activity with regard to population, research and development spending, gross domestic product (GDP) and other variables.

With 8,561 resident patent applications per unit of USD 100 billion GDP, the Republic of Korea continued to file the greatest number of patent applications (figure 1.5). China (6,183) had the second highest ratio in 2018, followed by Japan (5,101), Germany (1,924) and Switzerland (1,831). However, over the past 11 years, the gap between the Republic of Korea and China has narrowed considerably, reflecting the strong growth in resident applications in China, with resident applications per unit of GDP increasing from 1,854 in 2008 to 6,183 in 2018. In contrast, the Republic of Korea's ratio fell from 9,064 in 2008 to 8,651 in 2018. Similarly, third-ranked Japan has seen its ratio fall from 7,105 to 5,101 over the same period.

A number of countries with a low number of resident patent applications, such as Denmark, Finland and New Zealand, rank among the top 20 origins when resident patent applications are adjusted by GDP (figure A37). The list of top 20 origins is predominantly comprised of high-income countries; however, three middle-income countries – China, the Russian Federation and Ukraine – also feature. Among large middle-income origins, Turkey's resident patent application to GDP ratio (371) is far higher than that of India (175), Brazil (166), Malaysia (126) and South Africa (94). India moved above Brazil in ranking in 2018, due to a rise in resident applications, whereas contrariwise, Brazil experienced a decline in resident applications.

The profile of resident applications per million population is similar to that adjusted by GDP, but shows some subtle differences. The list of top 10 origins for resident applications per GDP and population is the same, albeit with a different ranking. The Republic of Korea retains its lead when resident applications are expressed per population, Japan ranks second and Switzerland third, ahead of China and Germany (figure A38).

A second consecutive year of double-digit growth for filings for unique inventions

Patent applicants traditionally file at their national offices and then subsequently abroad. This means that some inventions are recorded more than once. To take this into account, WIPO has developed indicators for patent families, and the trend in patent families mirrors that for patent applications.

The Republic of Korea had the highest number of patent applications per unit of GDP

1.5 Resident patent applications per USD 100 billion GDP for the top 10 origins, 2008 and 2018

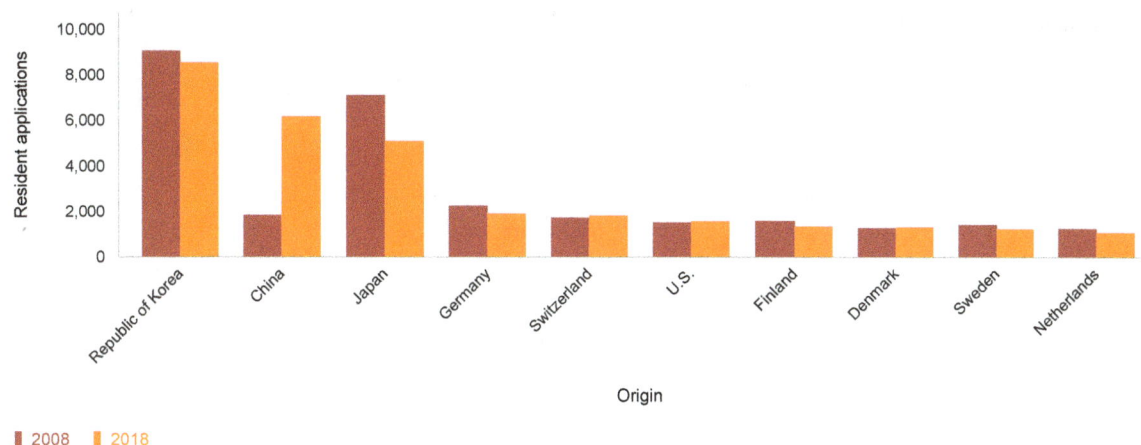

■ 2008   ■ 2018

Source: Figure A37.

Patent families worldwide grew by 12.1% in 2016, following a 10.1% growth in 2015. The total number of patent families worldwide amounted to 1.8 million in 2016, which is more than double the number reported in 2002 (figure 1.6). Applicants from China accounted for close to three-fifths of all patent families (58.2%) in 2016, followed by Japan (13%), the U.S. (9%) and the Republic of Korea (7.7%). However, for foreign-oriented patent families, the U.S. (147,964) and Japan (144,114) created by far the largest number of such families for the period 2014–2015 (figure A26), and far above that of China (40,303).

The size of a patent family (i.e., the number of offices where a patent is filed) reflects its geographical coverage. Around 83% of patent families created worldwide between 2014 and 2016 were filed at a single office (figure A24). There is considerable variation among top origins, however. For example, more than 63% of total patent families originating from the Netherlands, Sweden and Switzerland cover two or more offices, whereas only around 2% of all families for China and the Russian Federation cover two or more offices.

Patent families

A patent family is a set of interrelated patent applications filed in one or more offices to protect the same invention. The patent applications in a family are interlinked by one or more of the following: priority claim, Patent Cooperation Treaty (PCT) national phase entry, continuation, continuation-in-part, internal priority and addition or division. A special subset comprises foreign-oriented patent families – that is, those patent families that have at least one filing office which differs from the office of the applicant's country of origin. Some foreign-related patent families include only one filing office because applicants may choose to file only with a foreign office. For example, if a Canadian applicant files a patent application directly with the United States Patent and Trademark Office (USPTO) without having previously filed with the patent office of Canada, that patent family will constitute a foreign-oriented patent family with just one office.

Worldwide patent applications relating to computer technology accounted for 7.8% of all published applications worldwide in 2017

In 2017 – the latest year for which complete data are available due to the delay between application and publication – computer technology was the most frequently featured technology in published patent applications worldwide, with 229,269 published applications (table A29). It was followed by electrical machinery (197,645), measurement (148,809), digital communication (144,669) and medical technology (132,863). Together, these five fields accounted for 28.9% of all published applications worldwide, similar to their share for each of the previous six years.

Among the top 20 technology fields, food chemistry (+13.4%), other special machines (+10.1%), machine tools (+9.2%) and basic materials chemistry (+9.2%) witnessed the fastest average annual growth between 2007 and 2017. All the top 20 technology fields saw growth in published applications between 2007 and 2017, with the exceptions of audio-visual technology (–1.2%) and optics (–0.6%), both of which saw a slight decline. Among the top 10 origins in the period from 2015 to

Strong growth in patent filings for unique inventions

1.6. Patent applications and patent families worldwide, 2002–2018

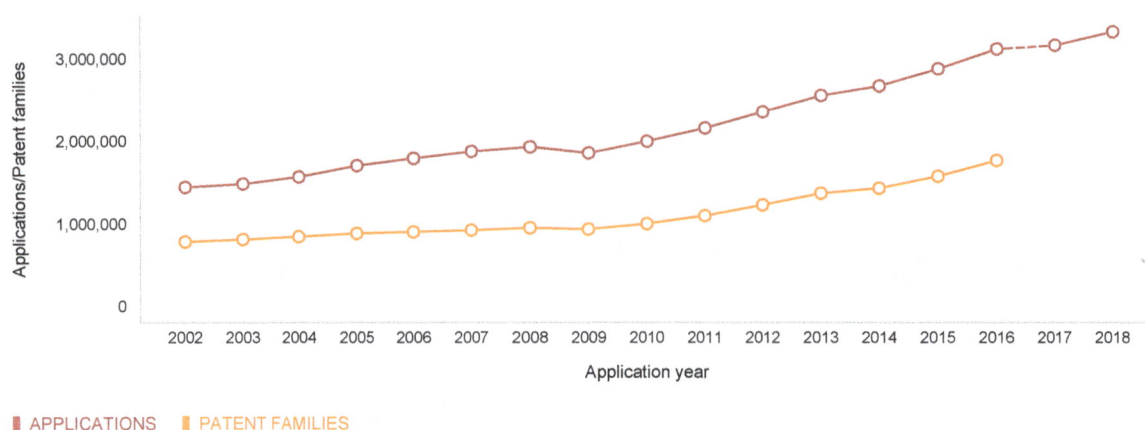

APPLICATIONS   PATENT FAMILIES

Sources: Figures A1 and A23.

2017, China and the U.S. filed most heavily in computer technology (figure A30); Japan and the Republic of Korea in electrical machinery; France and Germany in transport; Switzerland and the U.K. in pharmaceuticals; the Netherlands in medical technology; and the Russian Federation in food chemistry.

Among the large middle-income countries in the period from 2015 to 2017, applicants residing in India (16.8% of total published applications) and Mexico (10%) filed most heavily in pharmaceuticals; Argentina (10.3%) and Brazil (6.8%) in other special machines; Malaysia (8.8%) and Philippines (5.7%) in computer technology; Thailand (13.7%) in optics; and Turkey (9.7%) in other consumer goods.

The European Patent Office granted 20% more patents in 2018 than in 2017

Offices carry out a formal and substantive examination to decide whether to issue a patent. The procedure for granting a patent varies between offices, and differences in the numbers of granted patents among offices depend on factors such as examination capacity and procedural delays. For this reason, application data for a given year should not be compared with grant data from the same year.

In 2018, an estimated 1.42 million patents were granted worldwide, up 1.8% on 2017 figures (figure 1.7). China

(432,147) issued the largest number of patents in 2018, followed by the U.S. (307,759), Japan (194,525), the EPO (127,603) and the Republic of Korea (119,012) (figure A15). Among the top 10 offices, the EPO granted 20.8% more patents in 2018 than in 2017, while the office of India granted 12.3% more patents in 2018. For both the EPO and India, this was the third successive year of double-digit growth. Strong growth moved the EPO up one spot to fourth position in the ranking, while India remained in tenth position. The offices of the U.S. (–3.5%) and Japan (–2.5%), were second and third in the ranking, having issued fewer patents in 2018 than in 2017. However, Australia (–25%) was the office that saw the largest fall in the number of patents granted in 2018.

Looking beyond the top 10 offices to the top 20 list, France granted 12,249 patents in 2018. Brazil (9,966), China, Hong Kong SAR (9,651) and Mexico (8,921) each issued more than 8,900 patents (figure A15). The offices of Indonesia (+176.1%) and Brazil (+82.9%) recorded the fastest growth among the top 20 offices in 2018. In contrast, Malaysia (–15.3%), Singapore (–16.8%) and South Africa (–14.3%) all had double-digit declines.

Asia's share of worldwide patent grants was 57.1% in 2018. This is 4.7 percentage points above its 2008 share. Offices located in North America accounted for 23.3% of patent grants worldwide in 2018, while offices in Europe accounted for 15.9% of the world total. The combined share for Africa, LAC and Oceania was 3.6%.

Patents granted worldwide reached 1.42 million in 2018

1.7. Patent grants worldwide, 2004–2018

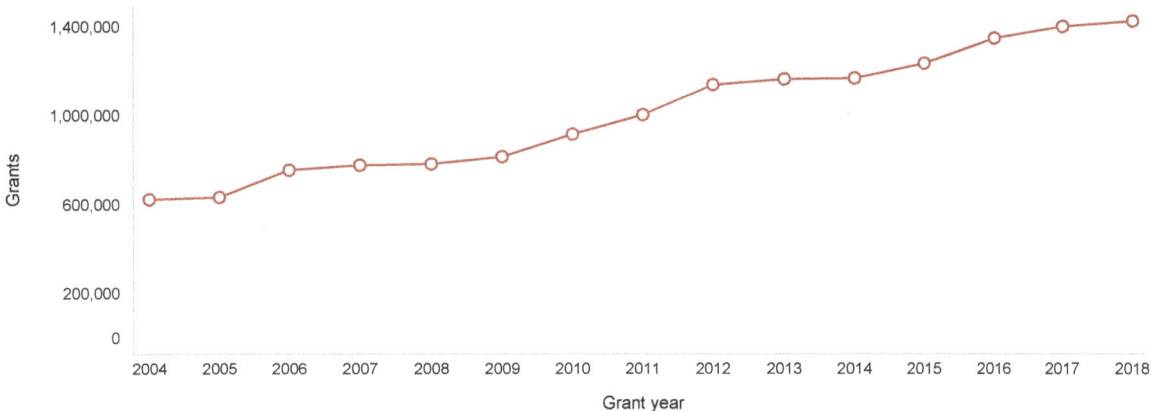

Source: Figure A3.

More than 3 million patents were in force in the U.S. in 2018

Patent rights generally last for up to 20 years from the date an application was filed. An estimated 14 million patents were in force across 125 jurisdictions in 2018, representing an increase of 6.7% on 2017 figures. In 2018, the largest number of patents in force was recorded in the U.S. (3.1 million). China (2.4 million) and Japan (2.1 million) each had around 2 million patents and the Republic of Korea had 1 million. Germany with 703,606 patents in force ranked in fifth position (figure 1.8). Half of all patents in force in the U.S. originated from non-resident applicants, while resident applicants accounted for around 70% of all patents in force in China. Non-resident applicants accounted for more than half of all patents in force in each of the top 20 offices, except for China, the Republic of Korea and the Russian Federation (figure A40).

Holders must pay maintenance/renewal fees to maintain the validity of their patents, and may opt to let a patent lapse before the end of its full term. For the 78 offices that reported their in-force data broken down by year of filing, between 42% and 44% of patents granted remained in force for at least six to nine years after the filing date, and about one-fifth lasted for the full 20 years (figure A41).

Although patents can be maintained for 20 years, the average age of patents varied across offices.

For example, the average age of all patents in force in 2018 in Thailand was 13.4 years, while in the U.K. and China it was 7.7 and 7.4 years, respectively. Along with Thailand, India (12.9 years), Viet Nam (12.1), Chile (11.8) and Germany (11.3) also had a high average age of patents in force (figure A42).

Patent examination outcomes vary greatly across offices

Patent offices examine applications and decide whether to grant patent rights. Examination processes differ across offices, which makes cross-country comparisons difficult. However, every effort has been made to compile examination outcome data based on common definitions and concepts.

The share of withdrawn or abandoned applications was highest in Argentina (60.8%), India (66.2%) and Thailand (59.3%) in 2018. More than 84% of applications examined in 2018 resulted in patents being granted at the offices of Spain and Turkey. Japan and the Russian Federation also had a high share of patents granted for applications processed. Among 10 selected offices, India, the U.K. and the U.S. granted patents for fewer than 35% of all applications processed in 2018 (figure 1.9). The shares of rejected applications were highest in the U.K. and the U.S.

3.1 million patents were in force in the U.S.

1.8. Patents in force at the top 10 offices, 2018

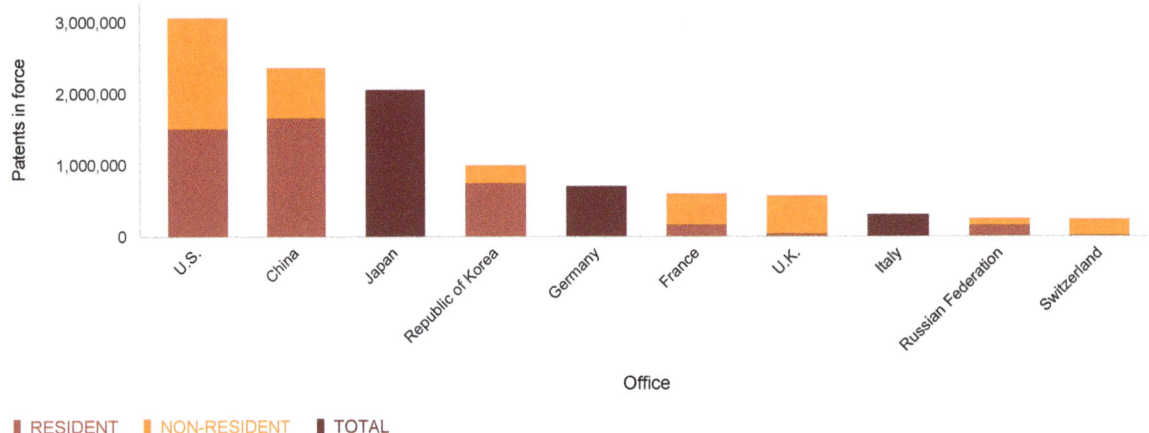

Source: Figure A40.

The offices of China and the U.S. each had around 1 million pending patent applications in 2018

Patent offices must assess whether the claims in applications meet the standards of novelty, non-obviousness and industrial applicability defined in national laws. Processing patents therefore consumes time and resources. The total number of potentially pending applications worldwide stood at 5.7 million in 2018. This estimate is based on data from 108 offices.

The USPTO had the largest number of pending applications (1.1 million) in 2018 (figure A44). It was followed by China (971,434), Japan (923,093), the EPO (621,516) and the Republic of Korea (519,965). Among these five offices, the Republic of Korea (+0.1%) had an increase in the number of pending applications in 2018 compared to 2017, whereas China (–12.4%), the EPO (–4.7%), Japan (–1.2%) and the U.S. (–0.1%) all managed to reduce their pending applications. Among selected middle-income countries, Brazil (196,354) and India (169,971) had a substantial number of pending applications. However, India reduced the number of pending applications by 25% in 2018 compared with a year earlier, while Brazil saw a 6.8% reduction.

Pending applications

Pending applications include all patent applications, at any stage in the process, awaiting a final decision by a patent office, including those applications for which applicants have not filed a request for examination (where applicable).

U.S.-based inventors filed the greatest number of PCT patent applications in 2018

An international treaty administered by WIPO, the Patent Cooperation Treaty (PCT) allows applicants to seek patent protection for an invention simultaneously in a large number of countries by filing a single PCT international application. The granting of patents remains under the control of national and regional patent offices and is carried out in what is called the "national phase" or "regional phase."

WIPO's PCT passed the record-breaking quarter-million (253,000) filing mark in 2018, a 3.9% increase over 2017. U.S.-based inventors (56,142) filed the greatest number of PCT patent applications in 2018, followed closely by applicants from China (53,345) and Japan (49,702). Germany and the Republic of Korea ranked fourth and fifth, respectively, with 19,883 and 17,014 applications (figure A50). China, India (2,013) and Turkey (1,578) are the only three middle-income countries in the top 20 origins of PCT applications.

Among the top 20 origins, India (+27.2%), Turkey (+26.1%) and Finland (+14.7%) are the only three to record double-digit annual growth in 2018. China (+9.1%) and the Republic of Korea (+8%) also saw strong growth.

More than half of all PCT applications filed in 2018 came from Asia (50.5%), with Europe (24.5%) and North America (23.2%) accounting for about a quarter each.

The shares of withdrawn applications were highest in India

1.9. Distribution of patent examination outcomes for selected offices, 2018

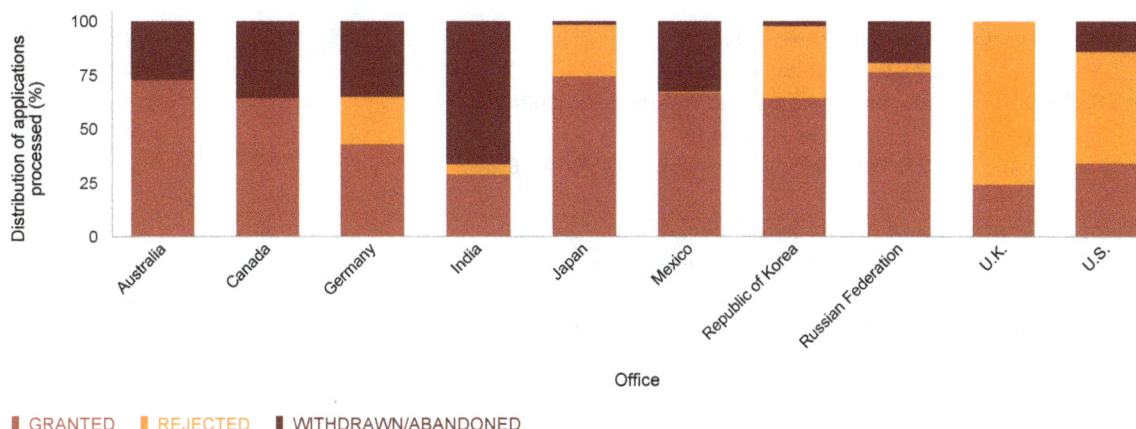

GRANTED   REJECTED   WITHDRAWN/ABANDONED

Source: Figure A43.

Women inventors accounted for only 17.1% of all inventors listed in PCT applications in 2018

In 2018, women accounted for 17.1% of all inventors listed in PCT applications and men the remaining 82.9% (figure A33). The share of women inventors increased from 12% in 2004 to 17.1% in 2018. About 94% of PCT applications named at least one man as inventor in 2018, and 32.6% named at least one woman as inventor (figure A34).

The gender gap among PCT inventors varies considerably across countries. Within the top 20 origins, China (28.9%), the Republic of Korea (26.8%) and Spain (24.4%) had the highest shares of inventors who were women in 2018 (figure A35). Conversely, Germany (10.3%), Japan (10.1%) and Austria (9.4%) had the lowest shares. Fields of technology related to the life sciences had comparatively high shares of PCT applications with women inventors in 2018. Women represented more than a quarter of inventors listed in published PCT applications in the fields of biotechnology (29.9%), pharmaceuticals (29.2%), food chemistry (28.7%), analysis of biological materials (26.7%) and organic fine chemistry (26.1%) (figure A36).

Utility model applications filed worldwide grew by 21.8% in 2018

A utility model is a special form of patent right granted by a state or jurisdiction to an inventor or the inventor's assignee for a fixed period of time. The terms and conditions for granting a utility model differ slightly from those for normal patents, including a shorter term of protection and less stringent eligibility requirements.

In 2018, the total number of utility model applications worldwide reached 2.15 million, up by over a fifth (21.8%) on 2017 (figure A53). The IP office of China received 96.6% of the world total – the other 74 offices accounted for just 3.4%. The IP office of China received 2.07 million applications in 2018, followed by Germany (12,307), the Russian Federation (9,747), Ukraine (9,120) and the Republic of Korea (6,232) (figure A54). The long-term trend shows utility model applications at the offices of Germany, Japan and the Republic of Korea declined substantially between 2008 and 2018. For example, applications at the office of Germany decreased from 17,067 in 2008 to 12,307 in 2018, while in the Republic of Korea applications declined from 17,405 in 2008 to 6,232 in 2018. In contrast, China had enormous growth over the same period – increasing from 225,586 in 2008 to 2.07 million by 2018.

Patents

Patent statistics

Patents

Patent applications and grants worldwide

A1. Trend in patent applications worldwide, 2004–2018

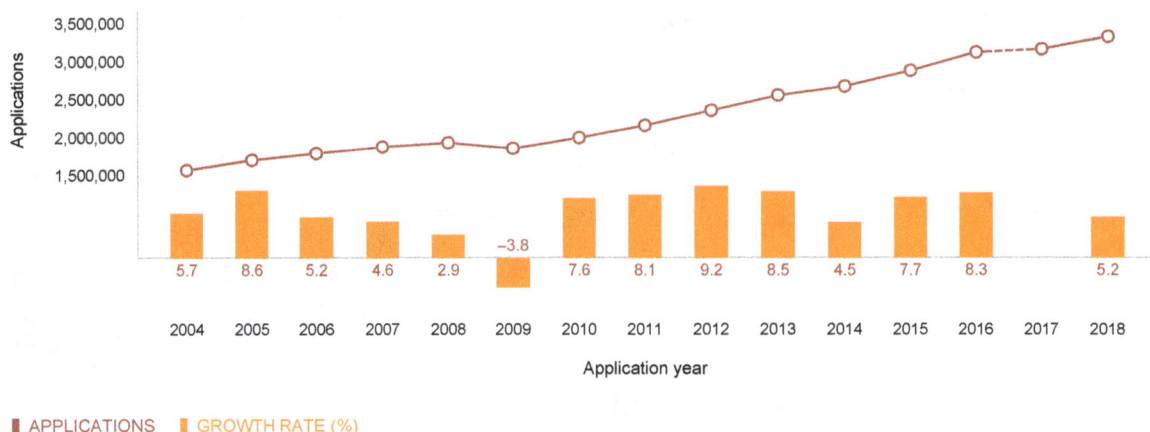

APPLICATIONS   **GROWTH RATE (%)**

Note: World totals are WIPO estimates using data covering 160 patent offices. These totals include applications filed directly with national and regional offices and applications entering offices through the Patent Cooperation Treaty national phase (where applicable). China's pre-2017 data are not comparable due to a change in methodology. Due to this break in the data series, and to the large number of filings in China, it is not possible to report an accurate 2017 growth rate at world level (see the data description section in Additional information for details).

Source: WIPO Statistics Database, August 2019.

A2. Resident and non-resident patent applications worldwide, 2004–2018

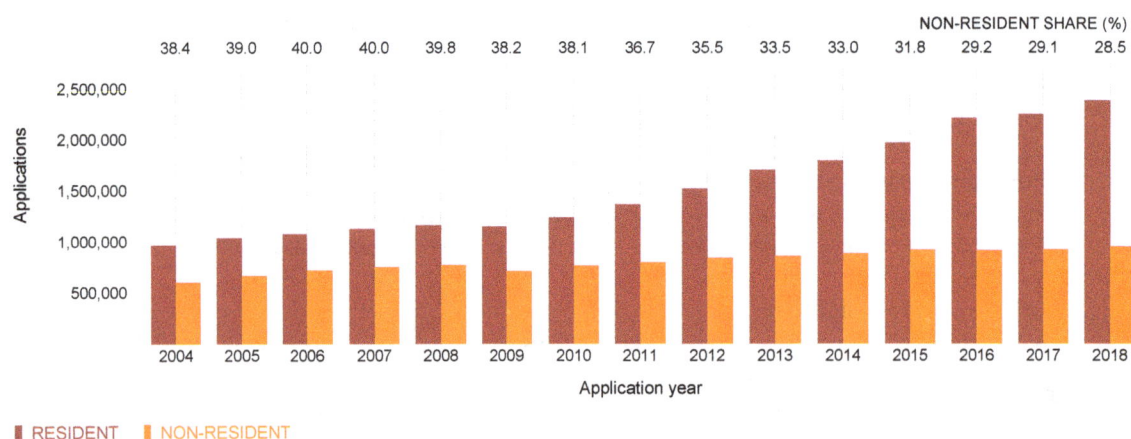

RESIDENT   **NON-RESIDENT**

Note: World totals are WIPO estimates using data covering 160 patent offices. These totals include applications filed directly with national and regional offices and applications entering offices through the Patent Cooperation Treaty national phase (where applicable). See the glossary for definitions of resident and non-resident.

Source: WIPO Statistics Database, August 2019.

A3. Trend in patent grants worldwide, 2004–2018

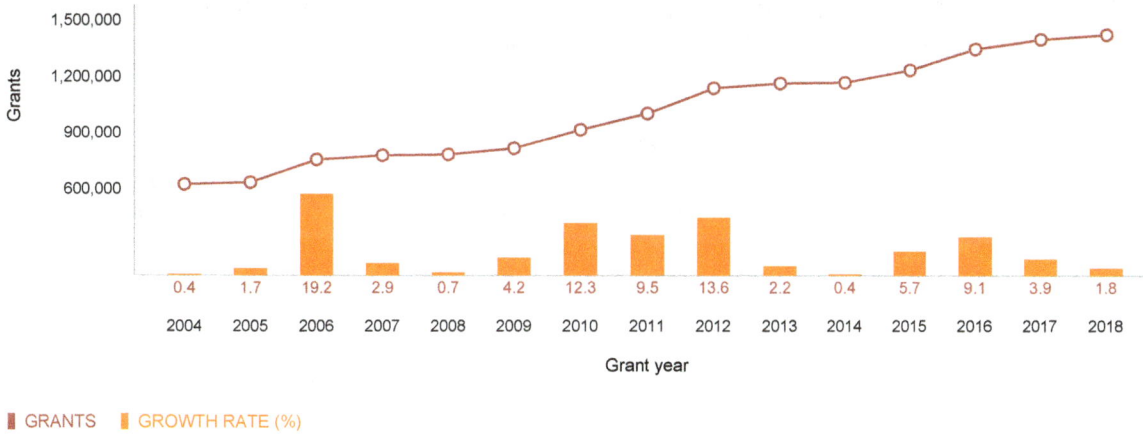

GRANTS **GROWTH RATE (%)**

Note: World totals are WIPO estimates using data covering 158 patent offices. These totals include patent grants based on applications filed directly with national and regional offices and patents granted by offices on the basis of the Patent Cooperation Treaty national phase (where applicable).

Source: WIPO Statistics Database, August 2019.

A4. Resident and non-resident patent grants worldwide, 2004–2018

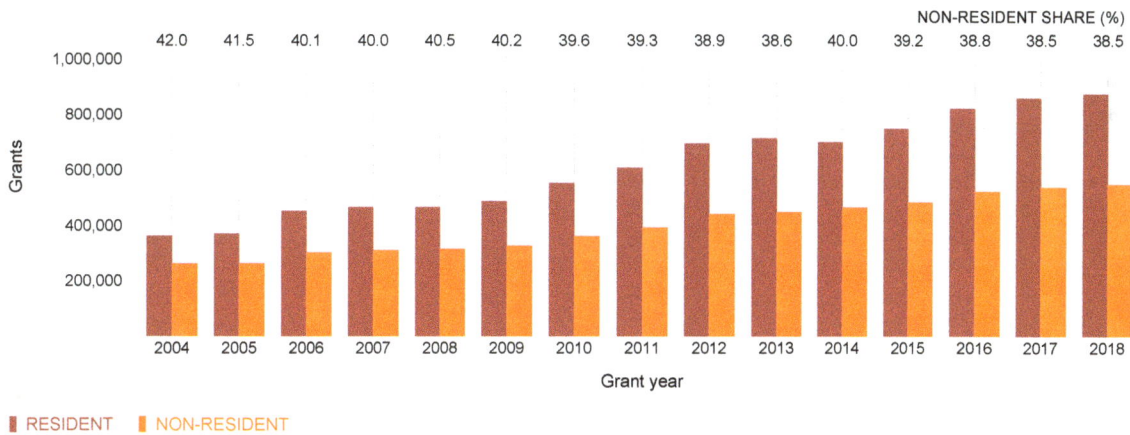

RESIDENT **NON-RESIDENT**

Note: World totals are WIPO estimates using data covering 158 patent offices. These totals include patent grants based on applications filed directly with national and regional offices and patents granted by offices on the basis of the Patent Cooperation Treaty national phase (where applicable). See the glossary for definitions of resident and non-resident.

Source: WIPO Statistics Database, August 2019.

Patent applications and grants by office

A5. Patent applications by income group, 2008 and 2018

Income group	Number of applications		Resident share (%)		Share of world total (%)		Average growth (%)
	2008	2018	2008	2018	2008	2018	2008–2018
High-income	1,422,600	1,556,000	62.4	57.9	73.7	46.8	0.9
Upper middle-income	436,100	1,683,100	58.4	86.3	22.6	50.6	14.5
Lower middle-income	62,400	84,900	19.7	28.6	3.2	2.6	3.1
Low-income	8,900	2,300	87.9	16.5	0.5	0.1	−12.7
World	**1,930,000**	**3,326,300**	**60.2**	**71.5**	**100.0**	**100.0**	**5.6**

Note: Totals by income group are WIPO estimates using data covering 160 offices. Each category includes the following number of offices: high-income countries/economies (60), upper middle-income (50), lower middle-income (32) and low-income (18). European Patent Office data are allocated to the high-income group because most of its member states are high-income countries. For a similar reason, data for the African Regional Intellectual Property Organization and the African Intellectual Property Organization are allocated to the low-income group, while those for the Eurasian Patent Organization are allocated to the lower middle-income group. For information on income group classification, see the data description section in Additional information.

Source: WIPO Statistics Database, August 2019.

A6. Patent applications by region, 2008 and 2018

Region	Number of applications		Resident share (%)		Share of world total (%)		Average growth (%)
	2008	2018	2008	2018	2008	2018	2008–2018
Africa	14,100	17,000	15.8	18.4	0.7	0.5	1.9
Asia	980,000	2,221,800	70.6	83.7	50.8	66.8	8.5
Europe	345,900	362,000	63.7	59.4	17.9	10.9	0.5
Latin America and the Caribbean	59,500	56,000	11.3	14.9	3.1	1.7	−0.6
North America	498,400	633,300	47.5	45.7	25.8	19.0	2.4
Oceania	32,100	36,200	12.7	10.4	1.7	1.1	1.2
World	**1,930,000**	**3,326,300**	**60.2**	**71.5**	**100.0**	**100.0**	**5.6**

Note: Totals by geographical region are WIPO estimates using data covering 160 offices. Each region includes the following number of offices: Africa (32), Asia (45), Europe (45), Latin America and the Caribbean (32), North America (2) and Oceania (4).

Source: WIPO Statistics Database, August 2019.

Patents

A7. Trend in patent applications for the top five offices, 1883–2018

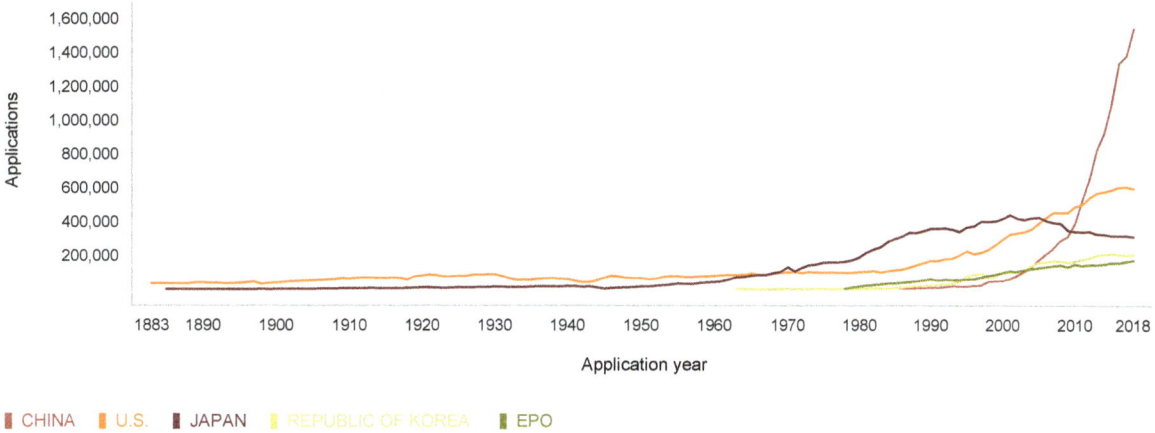

CHINA   U.S.   JAPAN   REPUBLIC OF KOREA   EPO

Note: EPO is the European Patent Office. The top five offices were selected based on their 2018 totals.

Source: WIPO Statistics Database, August 2019.

A8. Patent applications at the top 20 offices, 2018

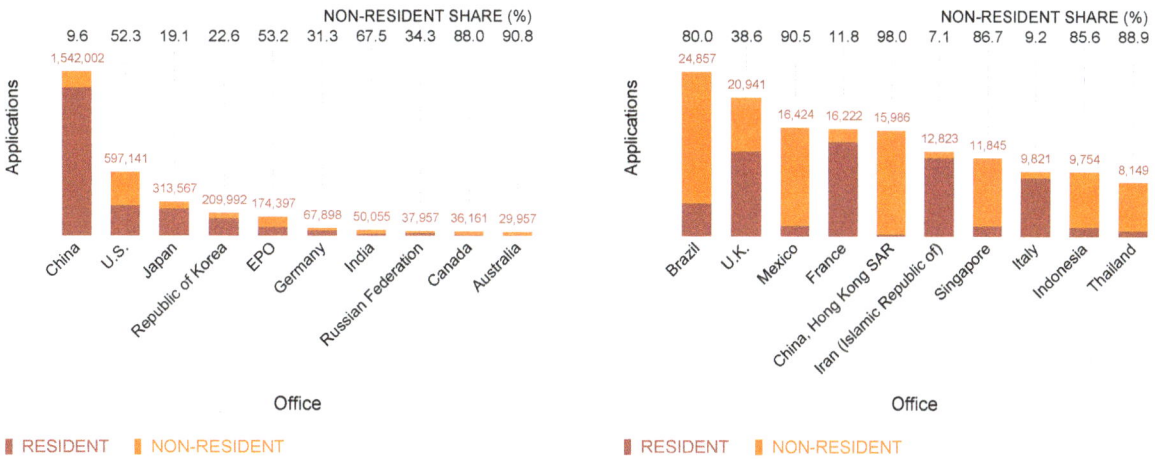

RESIDENT   NON-RESIDENT

RESIDENT   NON-RESIDENT

Note: EPO is the European Patent Office. In general, national offices of the EPO member states receive lower volumes of applications because applicants may apply via the EPO to seek protection within any EPO member state.

Source: WIPO Statistics Database, August 2019.

27

Patents

A9. Contribution of resident and non-resident applications to total growth for the top 20 offices, 2017–2018

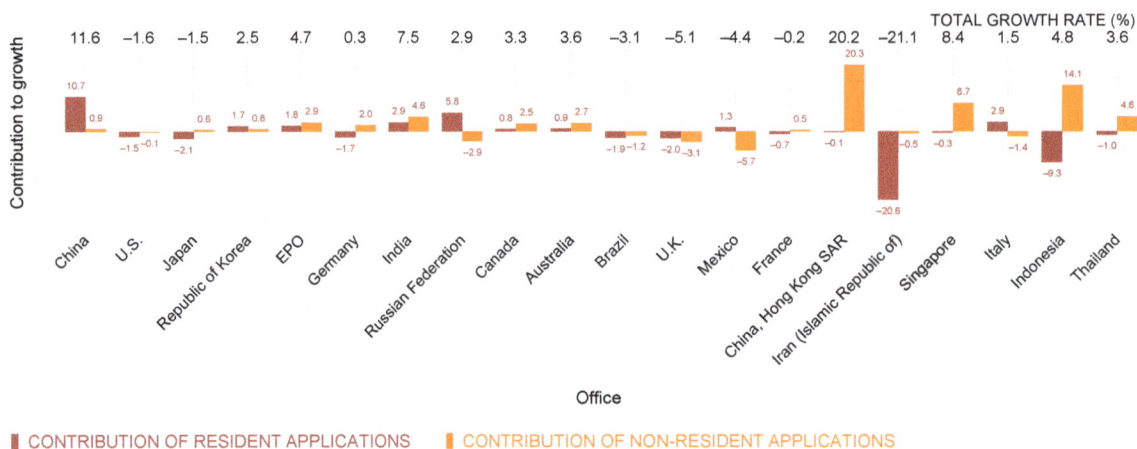

TOTAL GROWTH RATE (%)

China	U.S.	Japan	Republic of Korea	EPO	Germany	India	Russian Federation	Canada	Australia	Brazil	U.K.	Mexico	France	China, Hong Kong SAR	Iran (Islamic Republic of)	Singapore	Italy	Indonesia	Thailand
11.6	−1.6	−1.5	2.5	4.7	0.3	7.5	2.9	3.3	3.6	−3.1	−5.1	−4.4	−0.2	20.2	−21.1	8.4	1.5	4.8	3.6

Contribution to growth (data labels): China 10.7 / 0.9; U.S. −1.5/−0.1; Japan 0.6/−2.1; Rep. Korea 1.7/0.8; EPO 1.8/2.9; Germany 2.0/−1.7; India 2.9/4.6; Russian Federation 5.8/−2.9; Canada 0.8/2.5; Australia 0.9/2.7; Brazil −1.9/−1.2; U.K. −2.0/−3.1; Mexico 1.3/−5.7; France −0.7/0.5; China, Hong Kong SAR 20.3/−0.1; Iran −20.6/−0.5; Singapore 8.7/−0.3; Italy 2.9/−1.4; Indonesia 14.1/−9.3; Thailand 4.6/−1.0

CONTRIBUTION OF RESIDENT APPLICATIONS   **CONTRIBUTION OF NON-RESIDENT APPLICATIONS**

Note: EPO is the European Patent Office. This figure shows the total growth or decrease in applications at each office, broken down by the respective contributions of resident and non-resident applications. For example, applications filed at the IP office of China grew by 11.6%. Growth in resident applications accounted for 10.7 percentage points of this increase, while the remaining 0.9 percentage point reflected growth in non-resident applications.

Source: WIPO Statistics Database, August 2019.

A10. Patent applications at offices of selected low- and middle-income countries, 2018

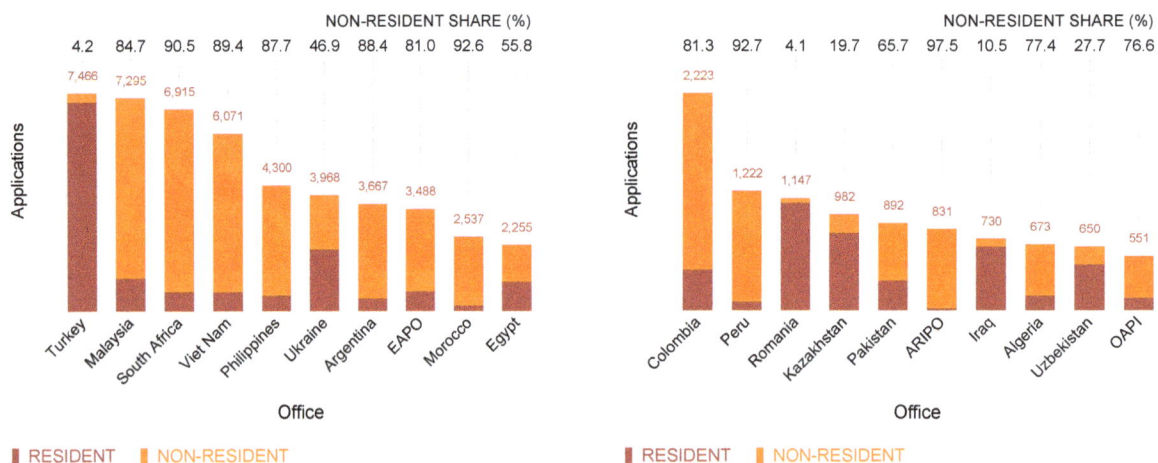

NON-RESIDENT SHARE (%)

Turkey	Malaysia	South Africa	Viet Nam	Philippines	Ukraine	Argentina	EAPO	Morocco	Egypt
4.2	84.7	90.5	89.4	87.7	46.9	88.4	81.0	92.6	55.8
7,466	7,295	6,915	6,071	4,300	3,968	3,667	3,488	2,537	2,255

NON-RESIDENT SHARE (%)

Colombia	Peru	Romania	Kazakhstan	Pakistan	ARIPO	Iraq	Algeria	Uzbekistan	OAPI
81.3	92.7	4.1	19.7	65.7	97.5	10.5	77.4	27.7	76.6
2,223	1,222	1,147	982	892	831	730	673	650	551

RESIDENT   **NON-RESIDENT**

Note: ARIPO is the African Regional Intellectual Property Organization, EAPO is the Eurasian Patent Organization and OAPI is the African Intellectual Property Organization. The selected offices are from different world regions and income groups (low-income, lower middle-income and upper middle-income). Where available, data for all offices are presented in table A58.

Source: WIPO Statistics Database, August 2019.

Patents

A11. Contribution of resident and non-resident applications to total growth for offices of selected low- and middle-income countries, 2017–2018

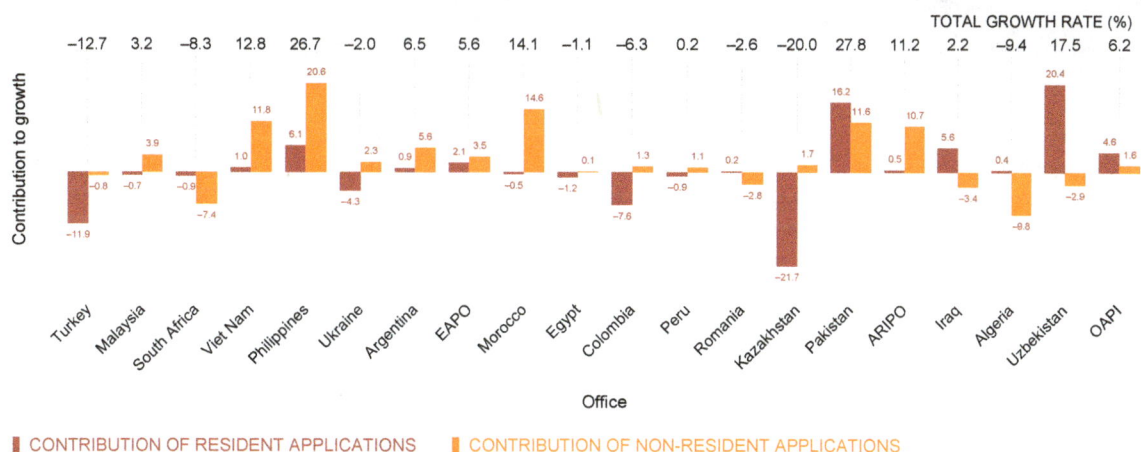

CONTRIBUTION OF RESIDENT APPLICATIONS   **CONTRIBUTION OF NON-RESIDENT APPLICATIONS**

Note: ARIPO is the African Regional Intellectual Property Organization, EAPO is the Eurasian Patent Organization and OAPI is the African Intellectual Property Organization. The selected offices are from different world regions and income groups (low-income, lower middle-income and upper middle-income). This figure shows the total growth or decrease in applications at each office, broken down by the respective contributions of resident and non-resident applications. For example, applications filed in Viet Nam grew by 12.8%. Growth in resident applications accounted for 1.0 percentage points of this increase, while the remaining 11.8 percentage points came from growth in non-resident applications.

Source: WIPO Statistics Database, August 2019.

A12. Patent grants by income group, 2008 and 2018

Income group	Number of grants		Resident share (%)		Share of world total (%)		Average growth (%)
	2008	2018	2008	2018	2008	2018	2008–2018
High-income	586,600	872,800	62.8	56.3	75.0	61.3	4.1
Upper middle-income	161,800	516,500	52.8	73.2	20.7	36.3	12.3
Lower middle-income	27,300	32,300	22.7	16.7	3.5	2.3	1.7
Low-income	6,000	1,200	88.3	16.7	0.8	0.1	−14.9
World	**781,700**	**1,422,800**	**59.5**	**61.5**	**100.0**	**100.0**	**6.2**

Note: Totals by income group are WIPO estimates using data covering 158 offices. Each category includes the following number of offices: high-income countries/economies (59), upper middle-income (48), lower middle-income (33) and low-income (18). European Patent Office data are allocated to the high-income group because most of its member states are high-income countries. For similar a reason, data for the African Regional Intellectual Property Organization and the African Intellectual Property Organization are allocated to the low-income group, while those for the Eurasian Patent Organization are allocated to the lower middle-income group. For information on income group classification, see the data description section in Additional information.

Source: WIPO Statistics Database, August 2019.

A13. Patent grants by region, 2008 and 2018

Region	Number of grants		Resident share (%)		Share of world total (%)		Average growth (%)
	2008	2018	2008	2018	2008	2018	2008–2018
Africa	5,300	8,700	28.3	16.1	0.7	0.6	5.1
Asia	409,600	812,000	68.7	73.9	52.4	57.1	7.1
Europe	157,900	226,900	63.9	54.6	20.2	15.9	3.7
Latin America and the Caribbean	17,300	24,700	5.2	8.5	2.2	1.7	3.6
North America	176,500	331,300	45.0	44.2	22.6	23.3	6.5
Oceania	15,100	19,200	9.3	5.2	1.9	1.3	2.4
World	781,700	1,422,800	59.5	61.5	100.0	100.0	6.2

Note: Totals by geographical region are WIPO estimates using data covering 158 offices. Each region includes the following number of offices: Africa (32), Asia (43), Europe (45), Latin America and the Caribbean (31), North America (2) and Oceania (5).

Source: WIPO Statistics Database, August 2019.

A14. Trend in patent grants for the top five offices, 1883–2018

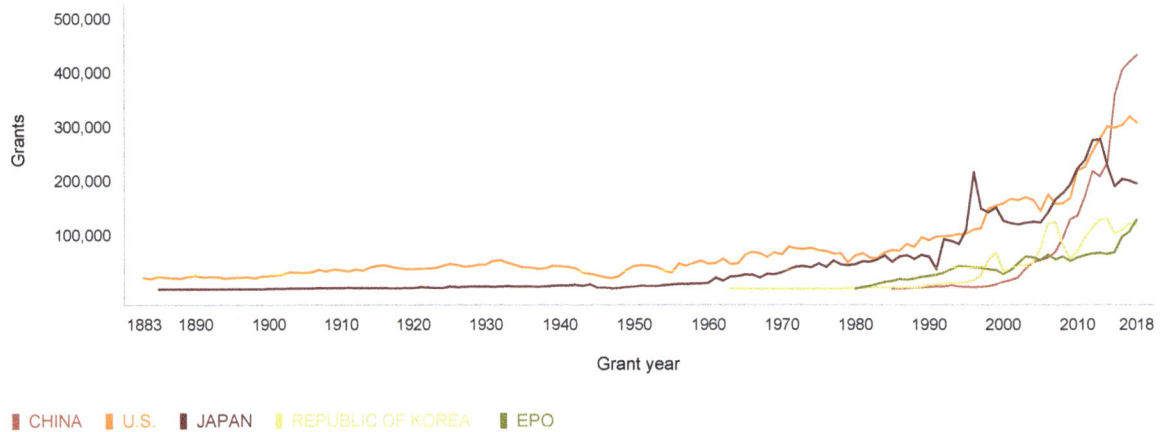

Note: EPO is the European Patent Office. The top five offices were selected based on their 2018 totals.

Source: WIPO Statistics Database, August 2019.

A15. Patent grants for the top 20 offices, 2018

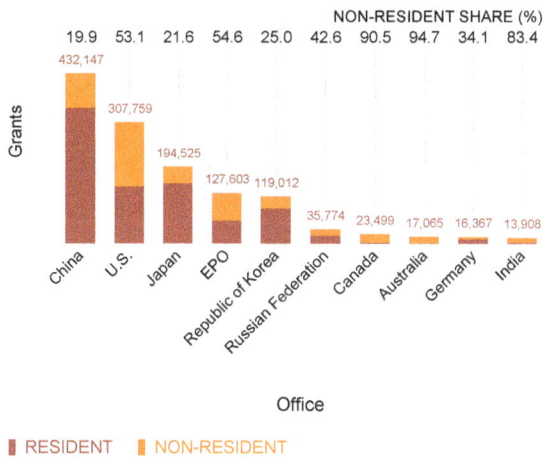

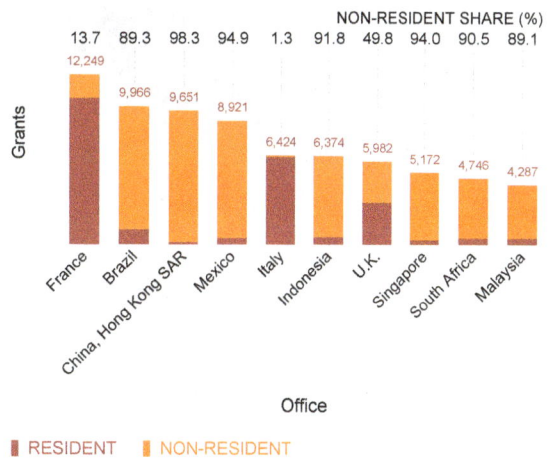

NON-RESIDENT SHARE (%)

| 19.9 | 53.1 | 21.6 | 54.6 | 25.0 | 42.6 | 90.5 | 94.7 | 34.1 | 83.4 |

Grants

- China: 432,147
- U.S.: 307,759
- Japan: 194,525
- EPO: 127,603
- Republic of Korea: 119,012
- Russian Federation: 35,774
- Canada: 23,499
- Australia: 17,065
- Germany: 16,367
- India: 13,908

Office

■ RESIDENT ■ NON-RESIDENT

NON-RESIDENT SHARE (%)

| 13.7 | 89.3 | 98.3 | 94.9 | 1.3 | 91.8 | 49.8 | 94.0 | 90.5 | 89.1 |

Grants

- France: 12,249
- Brazil: 9,966
- China, Hong Kong SAR: 9,651
- Mexico: 8,921
- Italy: 6,424
- Indonesia: 6,374
- U.K.: 5,982
- Singapore: 5,172
- South Africa: 4,746
- Malaysia: 4,287

Office

■ RESIDENT ■ NON-RESIDENT

Note: EPO is the European Patent Office. The procedure for issuing patents varies between offices, and differences in the numbers of patents granted among offices depend on factors such as examination capacity and procedural delays. The examination process can also be lengthy therefore there is a time lag between application and grant dates. For this reason, data on applications for a given year should not be compared with data on grants for the same year.

Source: WIPO Statistics Database, August 2019.

A16. Patent grants for offices of selected low- and middle-income countries, 2018

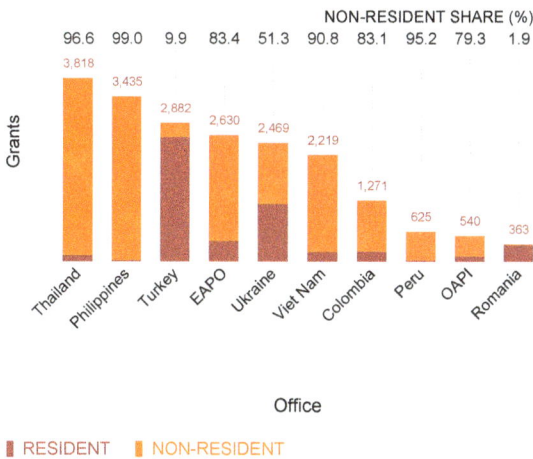

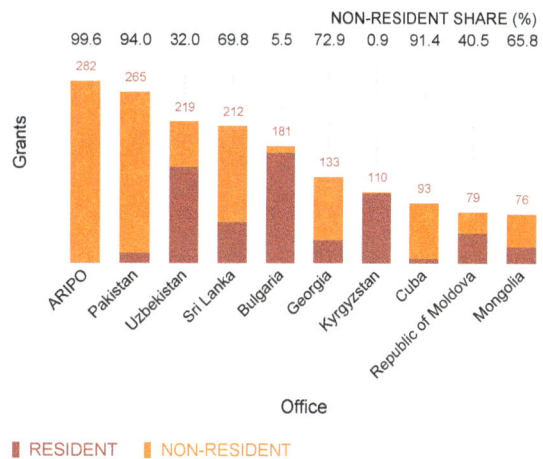

NON-RESIDENT SHARE (%)

| 96.6 | 99.0 | 9.9 | 83.4 | 51.3 | 90.8 | 83.1 | 95.2 | 79.3 | 1.9 |

Grants

- Thailand: 3,818
- Philippines: 3,435
- Turkey: 2,882
- EAPO: 2,630
- Ukraine: 2,469
- Viet Nam: 2,219
- Colombia: 1,271
- Peru: 625
- OAPI: 540
- Romania: 363

Office

■ RESIDENT ■ NON-RESIDENT

NON-RESIDENT SHARE (%)

| 99.6 | 94.0 | 32.0 | 69.8 | 5.5 | 72.9 | 0.9 | 91.4 | 40.5 | 65.8 |

Grants

- ARIPO: 282
- Pakistan: 265
- Uzbekistan: 219
- Sri Lanka: 212
- Bulgaria: 181
- Georgia: 133
- Kyrgyzstan: 110
- Cuba: 93
- Republic of Moldova: 79
- Mongolia: 76

Office

■ RESIDENT ■ NON-RESIDENT

Note: ARIPO is the African Regional Intellectual Property Organization, EAPO is the Eurasian Patent Organization and OAPI is the African Intellectual Property Organization. The selected offices are from different world regions and income groups (low-income, lower middle-income and upper middle-income). Where available, data for all offices are presented in table A59.

Source: WIPO Statistics Database, August 2019.

Patents

Patent applications and grants by origin

A17. Equivalent patent applications by origin, 2018

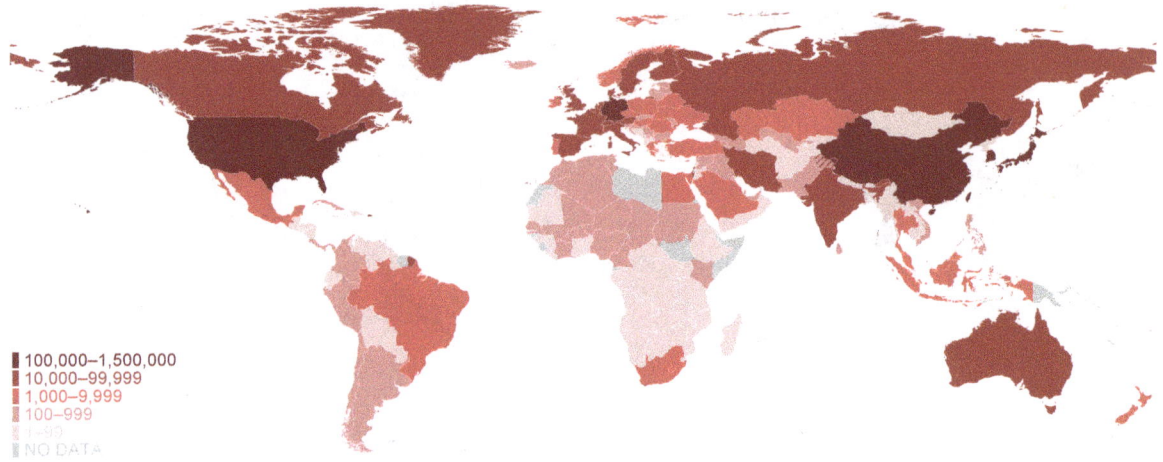

- ▌ 100,000–1,500,000
- ▌ 10,000–99,999
- ▌ 1,000–9,999
- ▌ 100–999
- ▌ 1–99
- ▌ NO DATA

Note: Patent filing activity by origin includes resident applications and applications filed abroad. The origin of a patent application is determined by the residence of the first named applicant. Applications filed at regional offices are considered equivalent to multiple applications in the relevant member states. See the glossary for the definition of equivalent application.

Source: WIPO Statistics Database, August 2019.

A18. Equivalent patent applications for the top 20 origins, 2018

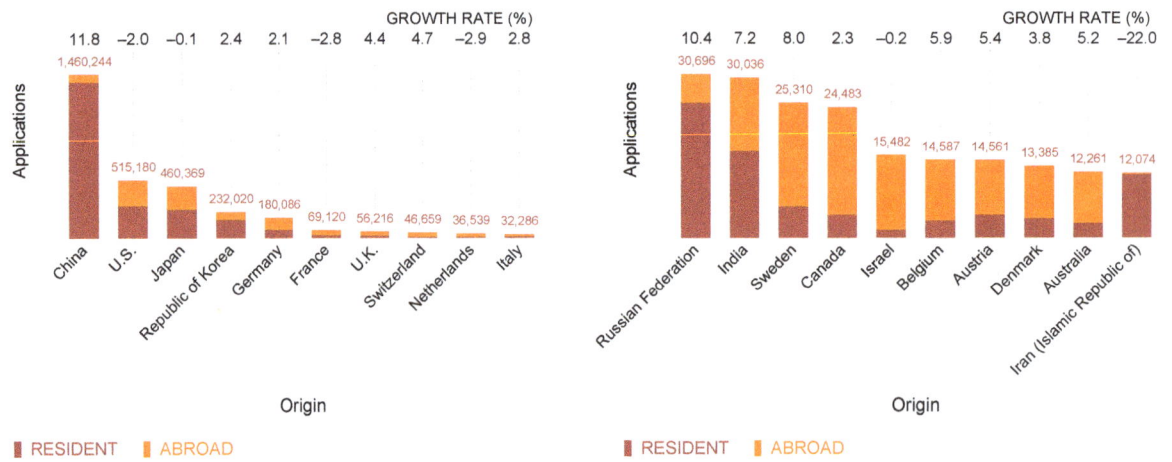

GROWTH RATE (%)

11.8	−2.0	−0.1	2.4	2.1	−2.8	4.4	4.7	−2.9	2.8

China	U.S.	Japan	Republic of Korea	Germany	France	U.K.	Switzerland	Netherlands	Italy
1,460,244	515,180	460,369	232,020	180,086	69,120	56,216	46,659	36,539	32,286

Origin

▌ RESIDENT ▌ ABROAD

GROWTH RATE (%)

10.4	7.2	8.0	2.3	−0.2	5.9	5.4	3.8	5.2	−22.0

Russian Federation	India	Sweden	Canada	Israel	Belgium	Austria	Denmark	Australia	Iran (Islamic Republic of)
30,696	30,036	25,310	24,483	15,482	14,587	14,561	13,385	12,261	12,074

Origin

▌ RESIDENT ▌ ABROAD

Note: Patent activity by origin includes resident applications and applications filed abroad. The origin of a patent application is determined by the residence of the first named applicant. Applications filed at regional offices are considered equivalent to multiple applications in the relevant member states. See the glossary for the definition of equivalent application.

Source: WIPO Statistics Database, August 2019.

A19. Patent applications for the top 20 offices and origins, 2018

Origin	Office									
	Australia	Brazil	Canada	China	China, Hong Kong SAR	EPO	France	Germany	India	Indonesia
Australia	2,757	141	464	700	184	971	14	23	281	68
Austria	199	205	299	1,029	65	2,288	9	777	281	37
Belgium	293	301	377	831	125	2,359	91	53	316	88
Canada	548	187	4,349	1,105	274	1,579	10	111	315	46
China	1,245	648	1,091	1,393,815	1,597	9,416	104	491	2,859	546
Denmark	240	234	311	935	91	2,386	11	49	370	60
France	685	1,214	1,424	4,784	338	10,438	14,303	346	1,192	236
Germany	1,462	1,970	2,147	15,427	856	26,716	475	46,617	2,728	445
India	211	155	159	327	40	701	5	17	16,289	120
Iran (Islamic Republic of)				6		7		1	1	
Israel	483	190	480	977	155	1,444	6	25	334	15
Italy	373	604	588	1,827	221	4,402	91	114	601	72
Japan	1,671	1,688	1,851	45,284	1,387	22,569		8,013	4,676	2,592
Netherlands	522	833	530	3,412	207	7,142	30	152	1,193	317
Republic of Korea	582	249	286	13,875	276	7,280	11	1,313	2,321	579
Russian Federation	27	41	72	195	16	226	1	24	76	25
Sweden	471	494	439	2,090	186	4,051	48	393	976	119
Switzerland	1,182	1,104	1,362	3,768	922	7,921	92	813	1,338	370
U.K.	1,345	741	1,349	2,836	683	5,734	57	371	1,168	218
U.S.	13,385	7,578	16,465	38,859	5,837	43,740	249	6,669	10,023	1,667
Others/Unknown	2,276	6,280	2,118	9,920	2,526	13,027	615	1,526	2,717	2,134
Total	**29,957**	**24,857**	**36,161**	**1,542,002**	**15,986**	**174,397**	**16,222**	**67,898**	**50,055**	**9,754**

Origin	Office									
	Iran (Islamic Republic of)	Italy	Japan	Mexico	Republic of Korea	Russian Federation	Singapore	Turkey	U.K.	U.S.
Australia	10	5	452	113	199	88	192	29	122	3,569
Austria	27	9	424	130	304	186	79	28	37	2,598
Belgium	19	43	570	166	311	155	97	45	165	2,614
Canada	12	3	608	234	417	93	81	15	183	13,045
China	46	28	5,325	278	3,140	763	870	271	1,007	32,615
Denmark	37	10	430	136	186	156	60	39	35	2,167
France	136	61	2,727	520	1,701	727	335	216	184	12,290
Germany	99	320	6,431	1,155	4,381	1,596	552	300	470	30,691
India	12	1	260	103	129	66	101	62	41	9,860
Iran (Islamic Republic of)	11,908		1		2				3	142
Israel		10	706	123	288	146	100	24	73	8,000
Italy	63	8,921	938	307	515	478	72	57	43	5,406
Japan	40	41	253,630	1,191	15,595	1,562	1,828	3,055	637	85,322
Netherlands	20	4	2,003	353	974	607	154	151	153	5,057
Republic of Korea	41	1	5,070	218	162,561	362	354	182	183	33,961
Russian Federation	35	1	104	16	77	24,926	13	3	7	1,100
Sweden	13	34	1,041	279	713	367	106	61	149	5,041
Switzerland	46	144	2,751	905	1,307	944	496	238	275	5,425
U.K.	29	22	1,890	423	1,228	509	412	80	12,865	13,681
U.S.	79	56	23,121	7,173	13,035	3,191	3,469	823	2,479	285,095
Others/Unknown	151	107	5,085	2,601	2,929	1,035	2,474	2,470	1,830	39,462
Total	**12,823**	**9,821**	**313,567**	**16,424**	**209,992**	**37,957**	**11,845**	**8,149**	**20,941**	**597,141**

Note: EPO is the European Patent Office. Origin data are based on absolute counts, not equivalent counts. The top 20 offices and origins are selected based on the available 2018 data, broken down by country of origin.

Source: WIPO Statistics Database, August 2019.

A20. Flows of non-resident patent applications between the top five origins and the top 10 offices, 2018

Origin **Office**

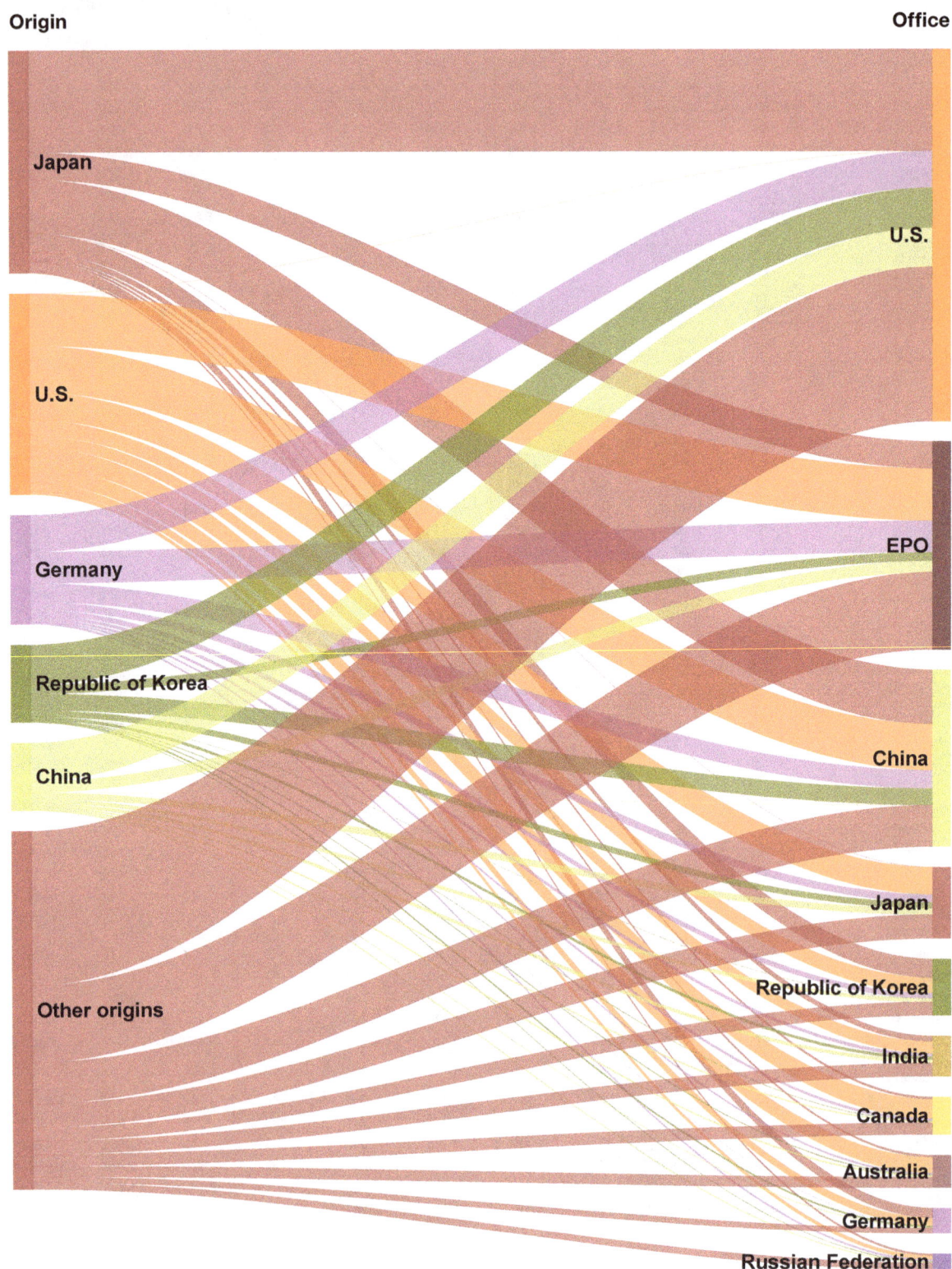

Note: EPO is the European Patent Office. Origin data are based on absolute counts, not equivalent counts.

Source: WIPO Statistics Database, August 2019.

Patents

A21. Distribution of patent applications for the top 15 offices and selected origins, 2018

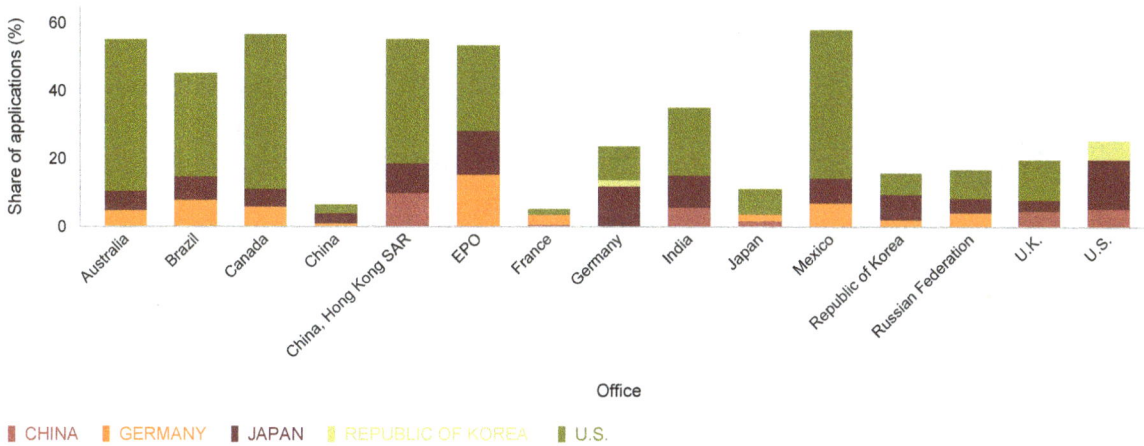

Y-axis: Share of applications (%)

X-axis: Office — Australia, Brazil, Canada, China, China, Hong Kong SAR, EPO, France, Germany, India, Japan, Mexico, Republic of Korea, Russian Federation, U.K., U.S.

Legend: CHINA, GERMANY, JAPAN, REPUBLIC OF KOREA, U.S.

Note: EPO is the European Patent Office. Origin data are based on absolute counts, not equivalent counts.

Source: WIPO Statistics Database, August 2019.

A22. Equivalent patent grants for the top 20 origins, 2018

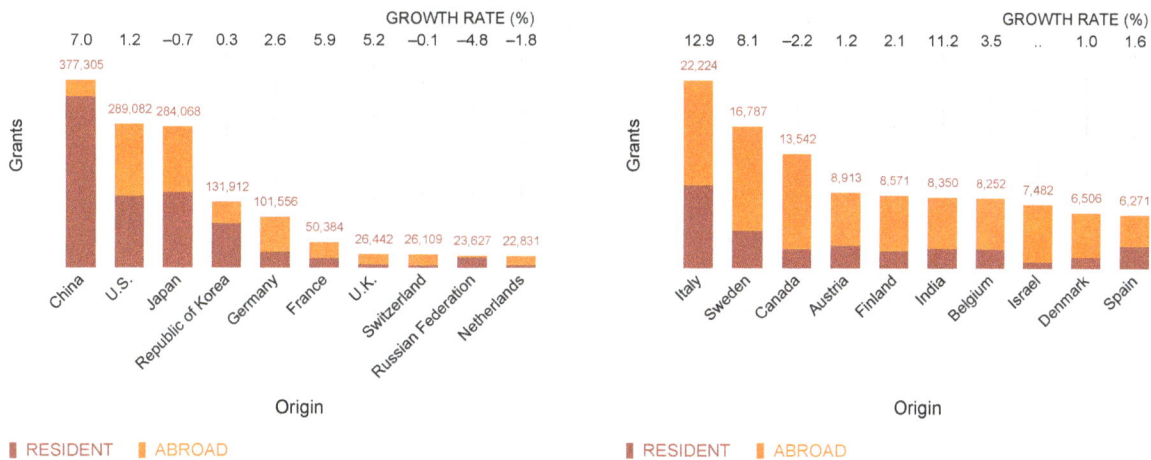

GROWTH RATE (%)

| 7.0 | 1.2 | −0.7 | 0.3 | 2.6 | 5.9 | 5.2 | −0.1 | −4.8 | −1.8 |

| China | U.S. | Japan | Republic of Korea | Germany | France | U.K. | Switzerland | Russian Federation | Netherlands |
| 377,305 | 289,082 | 284,068 | 131,912 | 101,556 | 50,384 | 26,442 | 26,109 | 23,627 | 22,831 |

Y-axis: Grants
X-axis: Origin
Legend: RESIDENT, ABROAD

GROWTH RATE (%)

| 12.9 | 8.1 | −2.2 | 1.2 | 2.1 | 11.2 | 3.5 | .. | 1.0 | 1.6 |

| Italy | Sweden | Canada | Austria | Finland | India | Belgium | Israel | Denmark | Spain |
| 22,224 | 16,787 | 13,542 | 8,913 | 8,571 | 8,350 | 8,252 | 7,482 | 6,506 | 6,271 |

Y-axis: Grants
X-axis: Origin
Legend: RESIDENT, ABROAD

Note: See the glossary for the definition of equivalent grant.

.. indicates not available.

Source: WIPO Statistics Database, August 2019.

Patent families

A23. Trend in patent families worldwide, 2002–2016

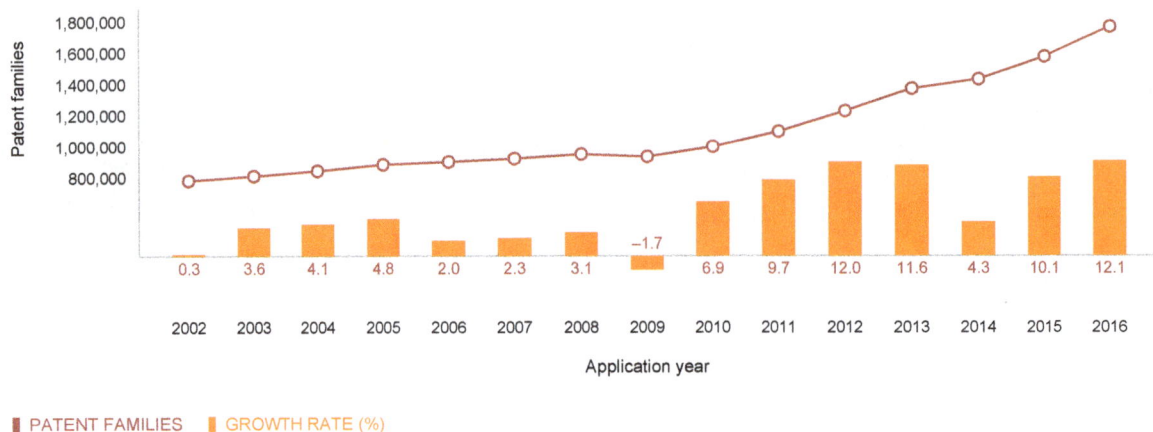

PATENT FAMILIES   GROWTH RATE (%)

Note: Applicants often file patent applications in multiple jurisdictions therefore some inventions are recorded more than once. To take this into account, WIPO has indicators related to patent families, defined as patent applications interlinked by one or more of the following: priority claim, Patent Cooperation Treaty national phase entry, continuation, continuation-in-part, internal priority and addition or division. Patent families here include only those associated with patent applications for inventions and exclude patent families associated with utility model applications.

Sources: WIPO Statistics Database and EPO PATSTAT database, August 2019.

A24. Distribution of patent families by number of offices for the top 20 origins, 2014–2016

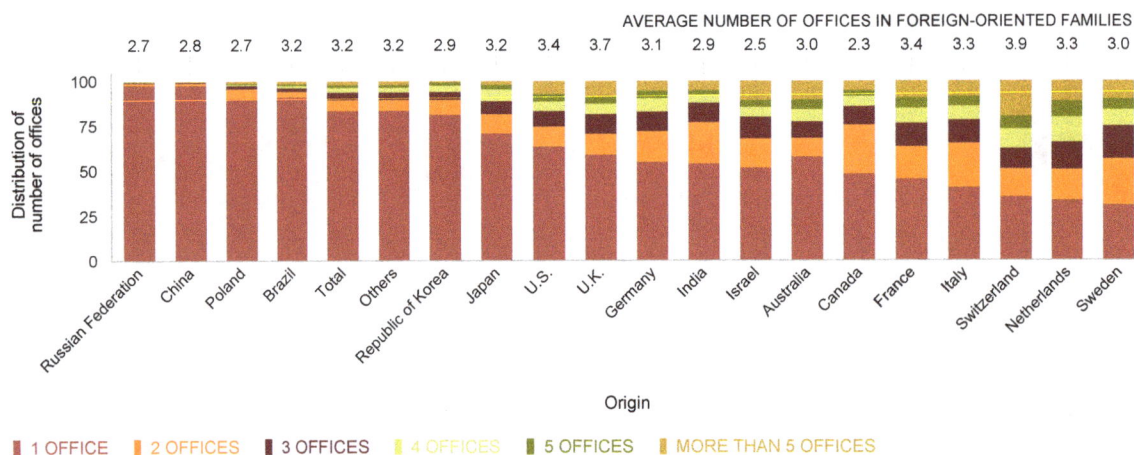

1 OFFICE   2 OFFICES   3 OFFICES   4 OFFICES   5 OFFICES   MORE THAN 5 OFFICES

Note: A patent family is defined as patent applications interlinked by one or more of the following: priority claim, Patent Cooperation Treaty national phase entry, continuation, continuation-in-part, internal priority and addition or division. Patent families here include only those associated with patent applications for inventions and exclude patent families associated with utility model applications.

Sources: WIPO Statistics Database and EPO PATSTAT database, August 2019.

A25. Trend in foreign-oriented patent families worldwide, 2002–2015

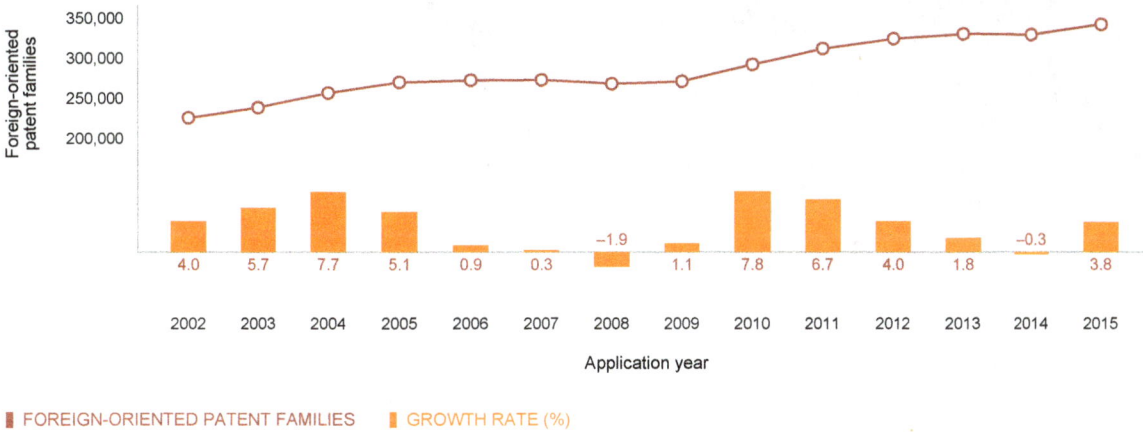

FOREIGN-ORIENTED PATENT FAMILIES   GROWTH RATE (%)

Note: A special subset of patent families comprises foreign-oriented patent families: this includes only patent families that have at least one filing office different from the office of the applicant's country of origin. Some foreign-oriented patent families include only one filing office, because applicants may choose to file directly with a foreign office. For example, if a Canadian applicant files a patent application directly with the United States Patent and Trademark Office (USPTO) without having previously filed with the patent office of Canada, that application and applications filed subsequently with the USPTO will form a foreign-oriented patent family.

Sources: WIPO Statistics Database and EPO PATSTAT database, August 2019.

A26. Foreign-oriented patent families for the top 20 origins, 2014–2015

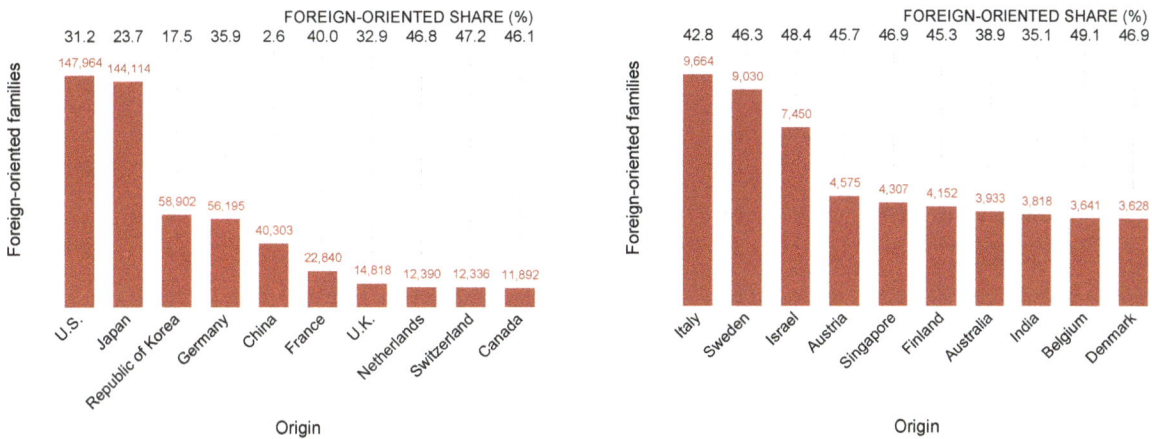

Note: A special subset of patent families comprises foreign-oriented patent families: this includes only patent families that have at least one filing office different from the office of the applicant's country of origin. Some foreign-oriented patent families include only one filing office, because applicants may choose to file directly with a foreign office. For example, if a Canadian applicant files a patent application directly with the United States Patent and Trademark Office (USPTO) without having previously filed with the patent office of Canada, that application and applications filed subsequently with the USPTO will form a foreign-oriented patent family.

Sources: WIPO Statistics Database and EPO PATSTAT database, August 2019.

Patents

A27. Distribution of technology fields for selected applicants based on patent families, 2014–2016

Field of technology	Canon Inc	Samsung Electronics	State Grid Corp of China	Mitsubishi Electric Corp	IBM	Toyota Jidosha KK	Huawei Technologies	Toshiba KK	LG Electronics Inc	Robert Bosch Gmbh
Electrical machinery, apparatus, energy	2.8	4.9	28.7	19.6	1.1	25.7	1.7	13.8	3.4	16.4
Audio-visual technology	16.7	9.4	1.9	4.8	2.8	0.9	3.3	5.5	6.4	2.7
Telecommunications	6.3	7.3	2.4	4.3	1.3	0.2	11.5	4.2	14.5	0.9
Digital communication	2.8	16.8	4.1	4.1	14.5	0.6	57.4	4.1	40.6	2.4
Basic communication processes	0.3	1.7	0.2	1.6	1.0	0.2	1.7	2.2	0.4	0.6
Computer technology	14.1	25.0	7.3	6.6	51.0	2.0	17.9	14.0	8.0	3.4
IT methods for management	0.5	1.4	11.1	1.1	5.8	0.2	0.8	2.1	0.9	0.4
Semiconductors	2.8	12.9	0.2	6.7	11.6	3.5	0.6	15.6	2.6	1.9
Optics	29.2	3.4	0.5	3.2	0.8	0.2	1.6	3.1	2.1	1.0
Measurement	2.6	3.1	20.4	6.2	2.8	3.9	1.3	6.2	1.5	10.7
Analysis of biological materials	0.0	0.2	0.3	0.0	0.2	0.0	0.0	0.2	0.1	0.3
Control	0.5	1.0	5.2	4.9	2.4	3.0	0.4	4.3	0.8	4.7
Medical technology	3.9	2.9	0.1	0.5	0.7	0.7	0.2	3.1	0.6	0.6
Organic fine chemistry	0.1	0.3	0.1	0.0	0.2	0.0	0.0	0.1	0.0	0.0
Biotechnology	0.0	0.4	0.0	0.0	0.1	0.1	0.0	0.1	0.0	0.1
Pharmaceuticals	0.0	0.2	0.2	0.0	0.1	0.0	0.0	0.0	0.0	0.0
Macromolecular chemistry, polymers	0.4	0.3	0.4	0.1	0.4	0.1	0.0	0.1	0.0	0.1
Food chemistry	0.0	0.0	0.0	0.0	0.0	0.0	0.0	0.0	0.1	0.0
Basic materials chemistry	1.0	0.6	0.5	0.2	0.2	0.2	0.3	0.3	0.1	0.1
Materials, metallurgy	0.1	0.3	0.4	0.2	0.1	1.8	0.1	1.0	0.1	0.6
Surface technology, coating	0.4	0.5	0.4	0.5	0.3	1.3	0.1	1.4	0.2	0.5
Micro-structural and nano-technology	0.1	0.1	0.0	0.0	0.1	0.0	0.0	0.2	0.0	1.4
Chemical engineering	0.2	0.5	0.8	0.5	0.3	1.0	0.0	1.3	0.7	0.7
Environmental technology	0.6	0.2	0.7	0.6	0.1	2.6	0.0	2.3	0.4	2.3
Handling	3.1	0.4	2.1	5.6	0.1	1.0	0.1	1.4	0.7	1.3
Machine tools	0.2	0.2	2.4	1.6	0.2	2.3	0.0	1.0	0.1	4.7
Engines, pumps, turbines	0.1	0.2	0.7	3.5	0.1	13.3	0.0	4.9	1.4	16.1
Textile and paper machines	9.0	0.1	0.0	0.4	0.0	0.0	0.0	0.9	0.1	0.1
Other special machines	1.4	0.4	1.0	0.5	0.3	1.3	0.0	0.5	0.3	1.3
Thermal processes and apparatus	0.0	1.4	0.7	13.2	0.2	0.4	0.1	1.5	4.4	1.3
Mechanical elements	0.5	0.3	1.1	1.3	0.1	9.9	0.1	0.8	0.4	6.7
Transport	0.1	0.3	0.9	3.8	0.6	23.1	0.2	1.6	1.2	15.6
Furniture, games	0.0	0.9	0.4	2.3	0.2	0.3	0.0	0.4	2.0	0.2
Other consumer goods	0.1	2.0	1.1	1.4	0.1	0.1	0.2	1.5	5.3	0.4
Civil engineering	0.0	0.2	3.4	0.4	0.1	0.2	0.0	0.4	0.2	0.5

Note: WIPO's International Patent Classification (IPC) technology concordance table was used to convert IPC symbols into 35 corresponding fields of technology. For an electronic version of the IPC technology concordance table, visit *www.wipo.int/ipstats*.

Sources: WIPO Statistics Database and EPO PATSTAT database, August 2019.

A28. Distribution of technology fields for selected universities and PROs based on patent families, 2014–2016

Field of technology	Applicant											
	Zhejiang University	Harbin Institute of Technology	CEA	CNRS	Fraunhofer Ges Forschung	DLR	AIST	Tokyo University	Korea Electronics Telecomm	KAIST	University of California	MIT
Electrical machinery, apparatus, energy	5.7	10.0	12.6	4.5	6.3	5.6	8.6	11.1	2.6	8.2	4.1	6.3
Audio-visual technology	0.7	1.3	1.8	0.9	5.2	0.8	1.1	1.9	7.1	3.4	0.6	2.0
Telecommunications	1.2	3.1	2.3	1.3	3.3	3.3	0.9	1.0	11.2	6.5	1.3	2.8
Digital communication	1.8	3.8	1.9	0.2	4.1	3.3	0.5	0.9	31.8	9.3	0.8	1.6
Basic communication processes	0.3	0.6	2.1	1.5	1.4	3.4	0.8	0.3	2.3	1.9	0.8	1.0
Computer technology	10.3	9.1	7.7	4.2	8.9	2.0	2.1	4.9	20.6	16.7	4.3	6.5
IT methods for management	1.7	0.6	0.2	0.0	0.2	0.7	0.6	0.6	4.2	2.4	0.3	0.4
Semiconductors	1.6	0.7	18.8	5.1	5.1	0.8	10.3	3.1	3.5	5.8	4.3	5.4
Optics	1.4	3.3	4.2	6.0	5.5	2.6	3.8	2.8	3.6	4.8	2.4	3.6
Measurement	13.1	16.5	12.6	10.7	13.3	15.0	13.0	10.0	4.3	7.2	6.1	7.6
Analysis of biological materials	1.4	0.4	1.2	4.1	1.5	0.4	2.5	4.8	0.3	1.6	5.0	3.7
Control	3.1	3.6	0.8	0.6	0.9	6.0	0.9	1.0	2.3	1.5	0.6	1.2
Medical technology	3.2	2.0	2.1	4.4	3.7	2.8	3.1	5.8	2.0	3.5	11.4	8.5
Organic fine chemistry	3.2	1.5	0.8	7.1	0.9	0.2	6.0	4.1	0.0	0.6	6.5	3.0
Biotechnology	7.1	1.5	0.9	10.3	2.9	0.0	7.8	13.3	0.1	3.5	16.9	13.8
Pharmaceuticals	3.6	0.8	0.4	10.0	1.4	0.0	2.1	8.8	0.0	1.8	16.5	9.5
Macromolecular chemistry, polymers	2.3	1.3	0.6	3.1	1.7	0.1	2.5	3.6	0.0	1.3	1.7	1.4
Food chemistry	4.2	1.6	0.1	0.3	0.6	0.0	1.2	0.6	0.0	0.1	0.6	0.7
Basic materials chemistry	2.3	1.7	1.5	2.4	2.4	1.0	2.9	2.4	0.1	1.1	1.8	1.9
Materials, metallurgy	3.6	6.2	2.6	4.8	3.6	1.9	9.1	2.6	0.1	1.9	1.5	1.3
Surface technology, coating	1.4	2.5	3.6	1.8	3.2	1.2	3.3	1.2	0.2	1.7	1.4	1.8
Micro-structural and nano-technology	1.1	1.0	2.6	2.1	1.2	0.0	1.9	1.1	0.1	0.9	1.0	1.2
Chemical engineering	3.6	3.3	3.2	6.1	2.5	0.7	5.3	1.8	0.3	2.7	3.6	4.1
Environmental technology	4.6	4.2	2.3	1.7	0.9	0.9	2.3	1.0	0.1	1.1	1.0	1.3
Handling	1.0	1.7	0.9	0.7	1.6	5.3	0.5	0.5	0.3	0.9	0.4	0.8
Machine tools	1.2	5.4	1.0	0.0	5.4	1.0	1.0	0.7	0.0	0.2	0.2	0.3
Engines, pumps, turbines	1.4	1.5	2.7	0.9	0.8	5.2	1.0	0.8	0.1	1.8	0.5	0.6
Textile and paper machines	0.5	0.8	0.2	0.4	0.9	2.3	1.1	1.3	0.1	0.2	0.4	0.5
Other special machines	3.7	1.5	1.5	1.4	4.1	9.3	2.3	3.5	0.5	1.5	1.6	3.6
Thermal processes and apparatus	2.0	1.4	3.5	0.8	1.9	7.4	0.4	0.9	0.1	0.4	0.6	0.7
Mechanical elements	1.7	1.9	1.1	0.7	1.3	3.7	0.1	0.3	0.0	0.5	0.3	0.5
Transport	1.6	2.9	1.2	0.6	1.5	12.1	0.2	0.8	1.5	2.1	0.5	1.2
Furniture, games	0.8	0.3	0.2	0.2	0.3	0.2	0.2	0.2	0.4	0.5	0.2	0.0
Other consumer goods	0.9	0.3	0.3	0.6	1.1	0.8	0.2	0.3	0.2	0.5	0.4	0.5
Civil engineering	2.8	1.6	0.5	0.4	0.6	0.2	0.4	1.9	0.1	1.7	0.4	0.5

Note: PRO means public research organization. A patent family is defined as patent applications interlinked by one or more of the following: priority claim, Patent Cooperation Treaty national phase entry, continuation, continuation-in-part, internal priority and addition or division. Patent families include only those associated with patent applications for inventions and exclude patent families associated with utility model applications. Le Centre national de la recherche scientifique (CNRS); Le Commissariat à l'énergie atomique et aux énergies alternatives (CEA); Deutsches Zentrum für Luft- und Raumfahrt E.V. (DLR); Korea Advanced Institute of Science and Technology (KAIST); Massachusetts Institute of Technology (MIT); and National Institute of Advanced Industrial Science and Technology (AIST).

Sources: WIPO Statistics Database and EPO PATSTAT database, August 2019.

Patents

Published patent applications by field of technology

A29. Published patent applications worldwide by field of technology, 2007, 2012 and 2017

Field of technology		Number of published applications			Share of total (%)	Average growth (%)
		2007	2012	2017	2017	2007–2017
Electrical engineering	Electrical machinery, apparatus, energy	102,410	146,626	197,645	6.7	6.8
	Audio-visual technology	93,742	77,319	82,888	2.8	−1.2
	Telecommunications	66,954	51,694	58,467	2.0	−1.3
	Digital communication	64,059	91,738	144,669	4.9	8.5
	Basic communication processes	17,794	16,345	16,685	0.6	−0.6
	Computer technology	125,073	150,721	229,269	7.8	6.2
	IT methods for management	20,414	28,743	53,326	1.8	10.1
	Semiconductors	80,228	85,794	83,954	2.8	0.5
Instruments	Optics	78,025	65,003	73,134	2.5	−0.6
	Measurement	66,697	94,890	148,809	5.0	8.4
	Analysis of biological materials	11,354	12,440	17,869	0.6	4.6
	Control	27,776	32,997	67,309	2.3	9.3
	Medical technology	75,479	89,164	132,863	4.5	5.8
Chemistry	Organic fine chemistry	54,696	55,306	68,901	2.3	2.3
	Biotechnology	34,623	43,222	64,012	2.2	6.3
	Pharmaceuticals	75,046	75,788	106,312	3.6	3.5
	Macromolecular chemistry, polymers	28,444	33,631	54,504	1.8	6.7
	Food chemistry	21,262	34,580	74,470	2.5	13.4
	Basic materials chemistry	39,717	54,239	95,776	3.2	9.2
	Materials, metallurgy	30,734	48,464	71,684	2.4	8.8
	Surface technology, coating	30,091	38,879	46,696	1.6	4.5
	Micro-structural and nano-technology	2,594	4,295	5,294	0.2	7.4
	Chemical engineering	33,888	44,848	80,378	2.7	9.0
	Environmental technology	21,900	32,006	55,918	1.9	9.8
Mechanical engineering	Handling	43,261	51,316	85,296	2.9	7.0
	Machine tools	37,130	56,168	89,742	3.0	9.2
	Engines, pumps, turbines	42,149	56,113	65,948	2.2	4.6
	Textile and paper machines	36,316	34,849	44,541	1.5	2.1
	Other special machines	44,917	61,862	117,901	4.0	10.1
	Thermal processes and apparatus	25,598	34,503	50,357	1.7	7.0
	Mechanical elements	44,321	54,196	77,156	2.6	5.7
	Transport	65,707	79,069	124,203	4.2	6.6
Other fields	Furniture, games	44,773	48,281	77,522	2.6	5.6
	Other consumer goods	32,227	38,997	58,809	2.0	6.2
	Civil engineering	53,279	67,884	105,322	3.6	7.1
	Unknown	40,822	30,963	22,976	0.8	−5.6
Total		**1,713,500**	**2,022,933**	**2,950,605**	**100.0**	**5.6**

Note: Data refer to published patent applications. There is a minimum delay of 18 months between the application date and the publication date. WIPO's International Patent Classification (IPC) technology concordance table was used to convert IPC symbols into 35 corresponding fields of technology. For an electronic version of the IPC technology concordance table, visit *www.wipo.int/ipstats*.

Sources: WIPO Statistics Database and EPO PATSTAT database, August 2019.

A30. Distribution of published patent applications by technology field for the top 10 origins, 2015–2017

Field of technology	China	U.S.	Japan	Republic of Korea	Germany	France	U.K.	Switzerland	Russian Federation	Netherlands
Electrical machinery, apparatus, energy	6.5	4.4	10.4	9.1	8.9	6.3	5.6	5.3	3.5	7.4
Audio-visual technology	2.1	2.9	4.7	5.4	1.5	2.3	1.7	0.9	0.6	2.7
Telecommunications	1.8	2.4	2.5	2.9	0.9	2.1	1.7	0.5	1.4	1.3
Digital communication	4.9	7.7	2.9	6.4	1.6	5.1	3.4	1.2	0.7	2.3
Basic communication processes	0.4	0.8	0.8	0.6	0.6	0.6	0.6	0.3	0.8	0.8
Computer technology	7.2	12.6	6.1	8.7	3.1	5.4	6.3	2.6	2.8	6.3
IT methods for management	1.5	2.9	1.2	3.2	0.4	1.0	1.4	0.7	0.4	0.6
Semiconductors	1.4	3.0	5.7	6.4	2.5	2.1	1.1	0.6	0.8	3.3
Optics	1.5	1.8	6.2	3.4	1.7	1.8	1.5	1.0	0.8	4.2
Measurement	6.0	4.0	4.3	3.6	5.8	5.1	5.2	7.6	7.6	5.1
Analysis of biological materials	0.4	0.9	0.3	0.4	0.6	0.9	1.3	1.3	2.2	0.7
Control	2.7	1.9	2.0	1.5	1.9	1.4	1.8	1.5	1.8	1.1
Medical technology	2.4	8.3	3.6	3.4	4.7	4.4	6.6	7.3	6.9	11.2
Organic fine chemistry	2.1	3.0	1.6	1.7	3.4	4.7	5.0	7.1	1.7	3.6
Biotechnology	1.6	3.8	1.0	1.5	1.8	3.0	4.4	6.1	1.7	3.6
Pharmaceuticals	4.0	5.8	1.3	2.0	2.5	4.2	7.2	11.0	4.2	3.5
Macromolecular chemistry, polymers	2.1	1.4	2.2	1.3	2.1	1.7	0.8	2.0	0.9	3.4
Food chemistry	4.5	1.0	0.8	1.8	0.4	0.8	1.0	3.4	12.5	3.1
Basic materials chemistry	4.4	2.9	2.2	1.7	3.4	2.2	3.1	3.1	2.8	4.9
Materials, metallurgy	3.6	1.1	2.4	1.9	2.0	2.3	1.6	1.5	4.9	0.8
Surface technology, coating	1.6	1.4	2.5	1.4	1.7	1.5	1.1	1.4	1.6	1.3
Micro-structural and nano-technology	0.2	0.2	0.1	0.1	0.2	0.2	0.2	0.1	0.8	0.1
Chemical engineering	3.4	1.9	1.4	2.1	2.7	2.5	3.1	2.4	3.6	2.6
Environmental technology	2.7	1.0	1.2	1.6	1.5	1.5	1.9	1.0	2.4	1.7
Handling	3.2	2.0	2.9	2.1	3.4	2.4	2.7	6.2	0.9	2.9
Machine tools	4.6	1.5	2.4	1.9	3.7	1.5	1.3	1.7	2.7	1.1
Engines, pumps, turbines	1.4	2.6	3.1	1.8	6.2	4.8	3.4	2.4	4.7	0.9
Textile and paper machines	1.6	0.9	2.6	0.9	1.5	0.7	0.9	2.4	0.4	1.3
Other special machines	4.8	2.7	2.8	2.9	3.7	3.8	2.6	2.6	5.7	4.9
Thermal processes and apparatus	2.1	0.8	1.8	1.9	1.7	1.6	1.2	1.1	1.6	1.0
Mechanical elements	2.2	2.0	3.2	2.2	7.3	4.1	3.3	2.0	3.6	1.5
Transport	2.7	3.5	5.7	5.2	9.9	10.5	5.2	1.8	4.4	2.4
Furniture, games	2.2	2.2	4.2	2.6	1.6	1.5	3.1	2.8	1.1	2.4
Other consumer goods	2.0	1.7	1.5	2.8	1.8	2.5	4.1	4.9	1.2	2.0
Civil engineering	4.0	3.2	2.3	3.9	3.2	3.2	4.7	2.0	6.5	3.9

Note: Data refer to published patent applications. There is a minimum delay of 18 months between the application date and the publication date. WIPO's International Patent Classification (IPC) technology concordance table was used to convert IPC symbols into 35 corresponding fields of technology. For an electronic version of the IPC technology concordance table, visit www.wipo.int/ipstats. The top 10 origins were selected based on their 2015–2017 total published applications.

Sources: WIPO Statistics Database and EPO PATSTAT database, August 2019.

Patents

A31. Trend in patent applications in energy-related technologies, 2002–2017

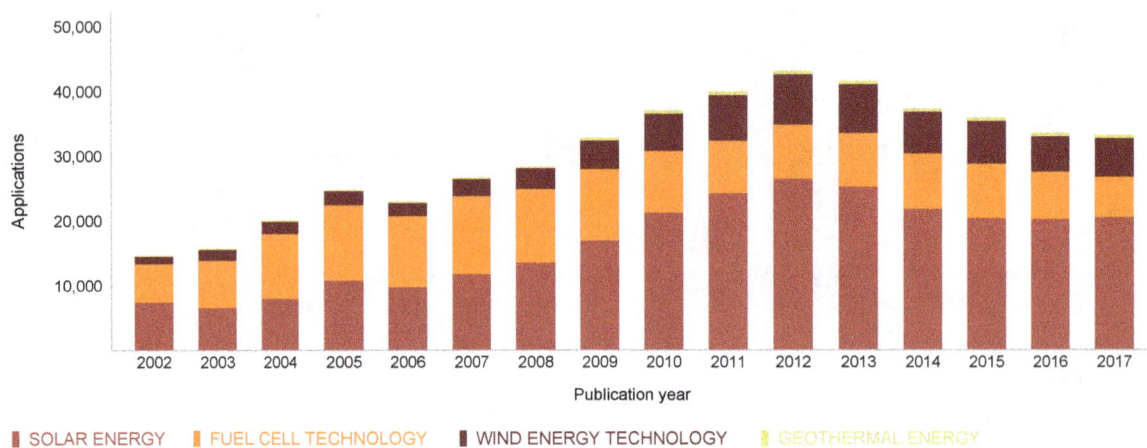

Note: For definitions of the technologies – fuel cells, geothermal, solar and wind energy – see annex A. The correspondence between International Patent Classification (IPC) symbols and technology fields is not always apparent (there is no one-to-one correspondence). It is therefore difficult to capture all patents in a specific technology field. Even so, the IPC-based definitions are likely to capture the vast majority of patent applications in these areas. Data refer to published patent applications.

Sources: WIPO Statistics Database and EPO PATSTAT database, August 2019.

A32. Relative specialization for patent applications in energy-related technologies for the top origins, 2015–2017

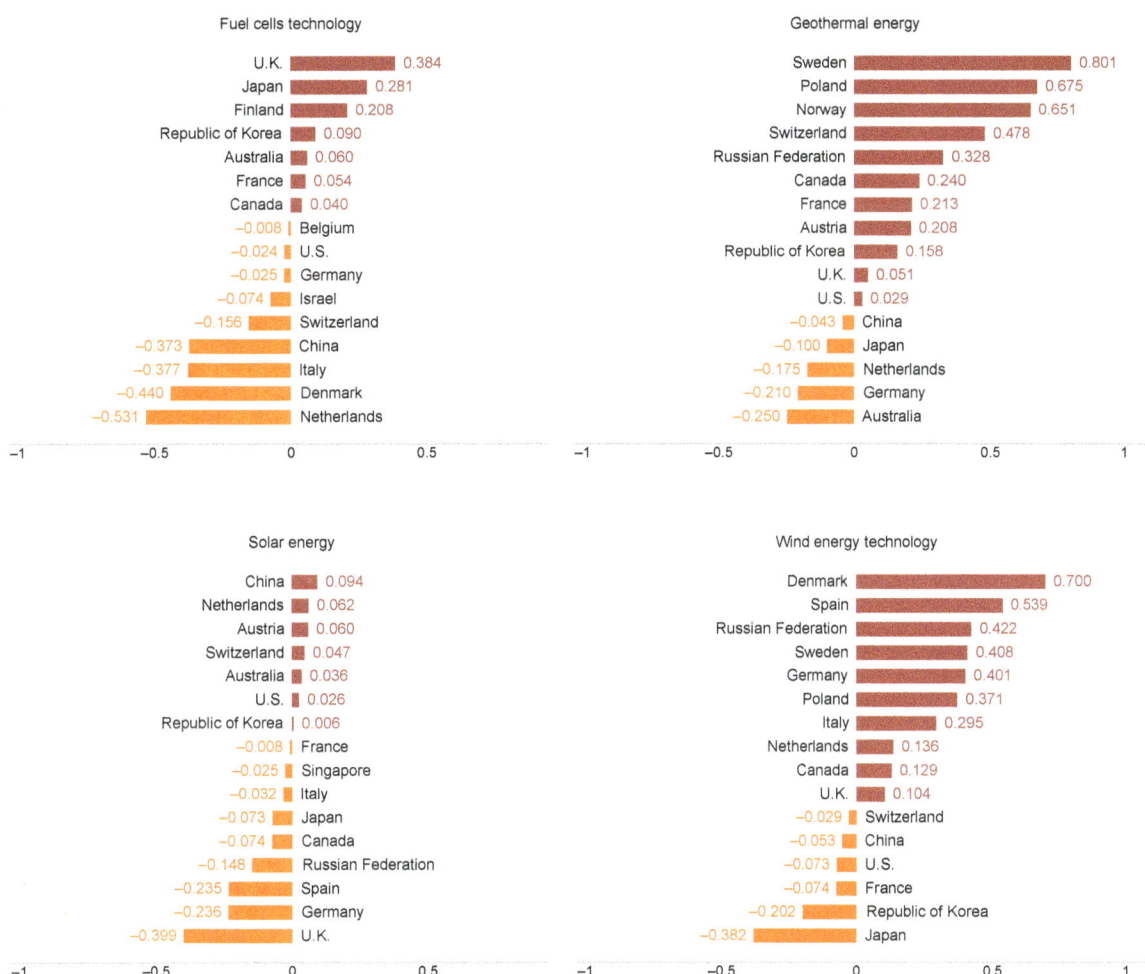

Fuel cells technology

	Value
U.K.	0.384
Japan	0.281
Finland	0.208
Republic of Korea	0.090
Australia	0.060
France	0.054
Canada	0.040
Belgium	−0.008
U.S.	−0.024
Germany	−0.025
Israel	−0.074
Switzerland	−0.156
China	−0.373
Italy	−0.377
Denmark	−0.440
Netherlands	−0.531

Geothermal energy

	Value
Sweden	0.801
Poland	0.675
Norway	0.651
Switzerland	0.478
Russian Federation	0.328
Canada	0.240
France	0.213
Austria	0.208
Republic of Korea	0.158
U.K.	0.051
U.S.	0.029
China	−0.043
Japan	−0.100
Netherlands	−0.175
Germany	−0.210
Australia	−0.250

Solar energy

China	0.094
Netherlands	0.062
Austria	0.060
Switzerland	0.047
Australia	0.036
U.S.	0.026
Republic of Korea	0.006
France	−0.008
Singapore	−0.025
Italy	−0.032
Japan	−0.073
Canada	−0.074
Russian Federation	−0.148
Spain	−0.235
Germany	−0.236
U.K.	−0.399

Wind energy technology

Denmark	0.700
Spain	0.539
Russian Federation	0.422
Sweden	0.408
Germany	0.401
Poland	0.371
Italy	0.295
Netherlands	0.136
Canada	0.129
U.K.	0.104
Switzerland	−0.029
China	−0.053
U.S.	−0.073
France	−0.074
Republic of Korea	−0.202
Japan	−0.382

Note: For definitions of the technologies – fuel cells, geothermal, solar and wind energy – see annex A. The correspondence between International Patent Classification (IPC) symbols and technology fields is not always apparent (there is no one-to-one correspondence). It is therefore difficult to capture all patents in a specific technology field. Even so, the IPC-based definitions are likely to capture the vast majority of patent applications in these areas. Data refer to published patent applications.

Sources: WIPO Statistics Database and EPO PATSTAT database, August 2019.

Patents

Participation of women inventors in PCT applications

A33. Share of women among listed inventors in PCT applications, 2004–2018

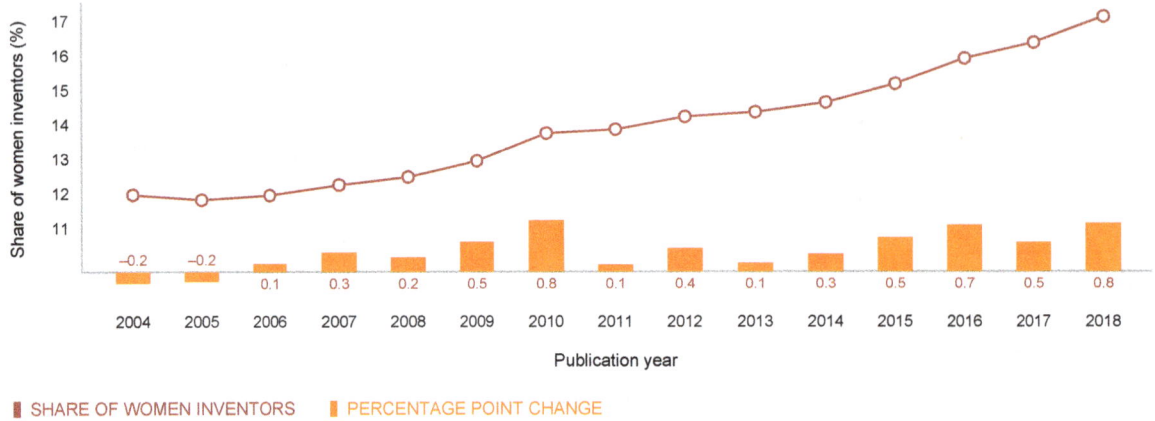

■ SHARE OF WOMEN INVENTORS   ■ PERCENTAGE POINT CHANGE

Note: In order to attribute gender to inventors' names recorded in PCT applications, WIPO produced a world gender–name dictionary based on information from 13 different public sources. Gender is attributed to a given name on a country-by-country basis because certain names can be considered male in one country but female in another.

Source: WIPO Statistics Database, August 2019.

A34. Share of PCT applications with at least one woman as inventor and with at least one man as inventor, 2004–2018

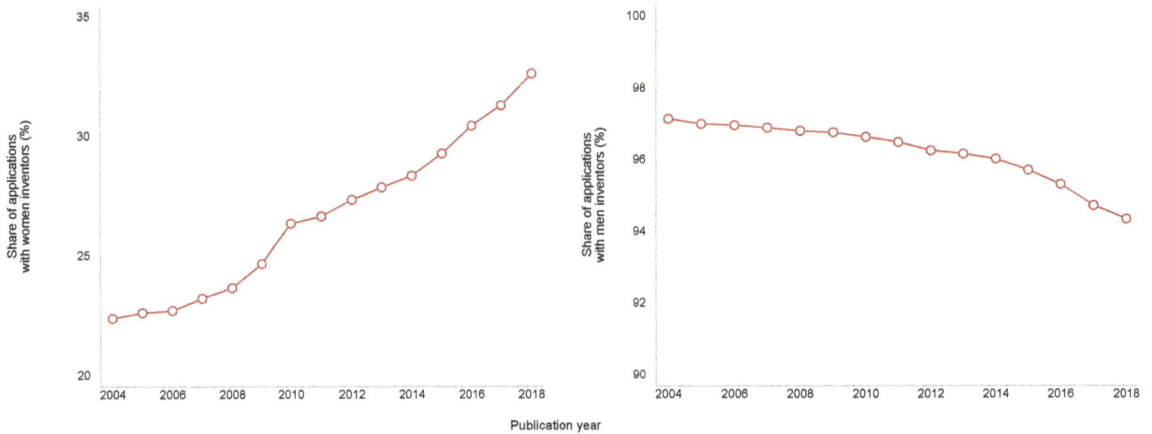

Note: In order to attribute gender to inventors' names recorded in PCT applications, WIPO produced a gender–name dictionary based on information from 13 different public sources. Gender is attributed to a given name on a country-by-country basis because certain names can be considered male in one country but female in another.

Source: WIPO Statistics Database, August 2019.

A35. Share of women among listed inventors and share of PCT applications with at least one woman as inventor for the top 20 origins, 2018

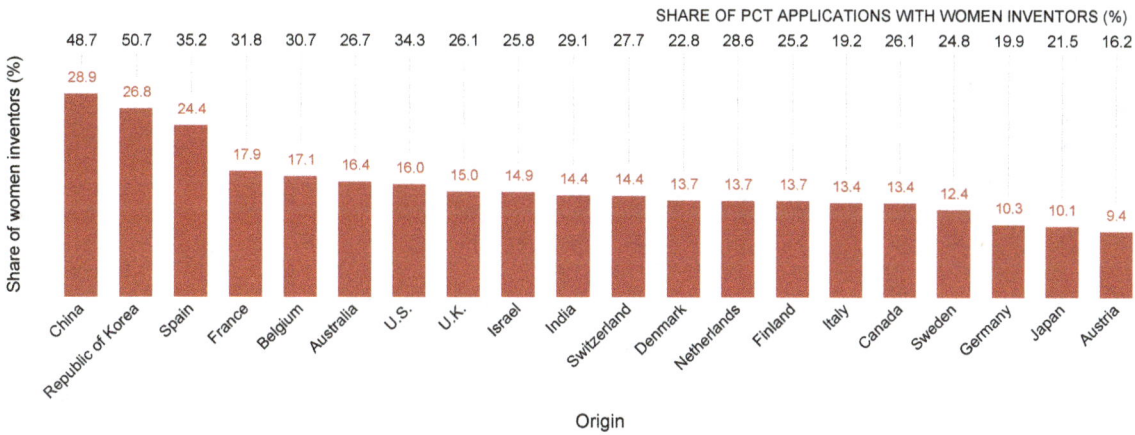

SHARE OF PCT APPLICATIONS WITH WOMEN INVENTORS (%)

| | 48.7 | 50.7 | 35.2 | 31.8 | 30.7 | 26.7 | 34.3 | 26.1 | 25.8 | 29.1 | 27.7 | 22.8 | 28.6 | 25.2 | 19.2 | 26.1 | 24.8 | 19.9 | 21.5 | 16.2 |

Share of women inventors (%)

China	Republic of Korea	Spain	France	Belgium	Australia	U.S.	U.K.	Israel	India	Switzerland	Denmark	Netherlands	Finland	Italy	Canada	Sweden	Germany	Japan	Austria
28.9	26.8	24.4	17.9	17.1	16.4	16.0	15.0	14.9	14.4	14.4	13.7	13.7	13.7	13.4	13.4	12.4	10.3	10.1	9.4

Origin

Note: In order to attribute gender to inventors' names recorded in PCT applications, WIPO produced a gender–name dictionary based on information from 13 different public sources. Gender is attributed to a given name on a country-by-country basis because certain names can be considered male in one country but female in another.

Source: WIPO Statistics Database, August 2019.

A36. Share of PCT patent applications with women inventors by field of technology, 2018

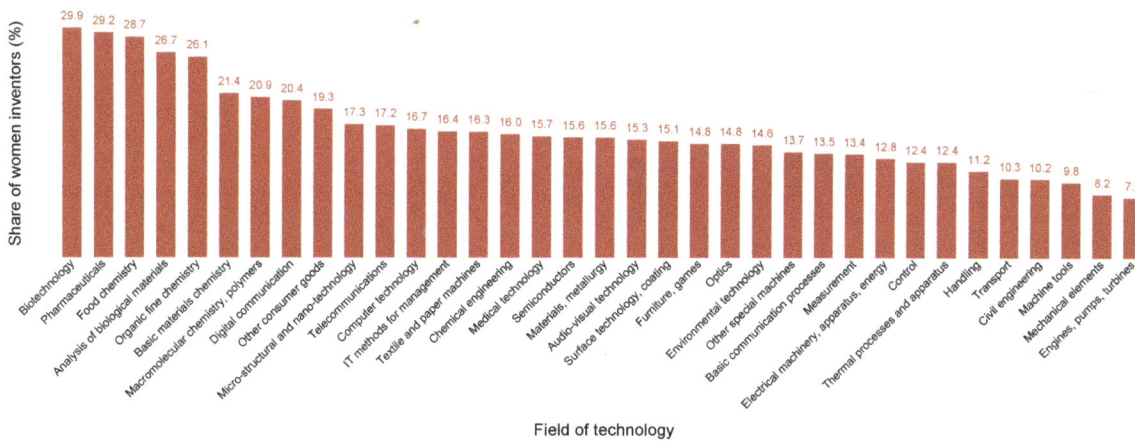

Share of women inventors (%)

Biotechnology	Pharmaceuticals	Food chemistry	Analysis of biological materials	Organic fine chemistry	Basic materials chemistry	Macromolecular chemistry, polymers	Digital communication	Other consumer goods	Micro-structural and nano-technology	Telecommunications	Computer technology	IT methods for management	Textile and paper machines	Chemical engineering	Medical technology	Semiconductors	Materials, metallurgy	Audio-visual technology	Surface technology, coating	Furniture, games	Optics	Environmental technology	Other special machines	Basic communication processes	Measurement	Electrical machinery, apparatus, energy	Control	Thermal processes and apparatus	Handling	Transport	Civil engineering	Machine tools	Mechanical elements	Engines, pumps, turbines
29.9	29.2	28.7	26.7	26.1	21.4	20.9	20.4	19.3	17.3	17.2	16.7	16.4	16.3	16.0	15.7	15.6	15.6	15.3	15.1	14.8	14.8	14.6	13.7	13.5	13.4	12.8	12.4	12.4	11.2	10.3	10.2	9.8	8.2	7.8

Field of technology

Note: In order to attribute gender to inventors' names recorded in PCT applications, WIPO produced a gender–name dictionary based on information from 13 different public sources. Gender is attributed to a given name on a country-by-country basis because certain names can be considered male in one country but female in another.

Source: WIPO Statistics Database, August 2019.

Patents

Patent applications in relation to GDP and population

A37. Resident patent applications per USD 100 billion GDP for the top 20 origins, 2008 and 2018

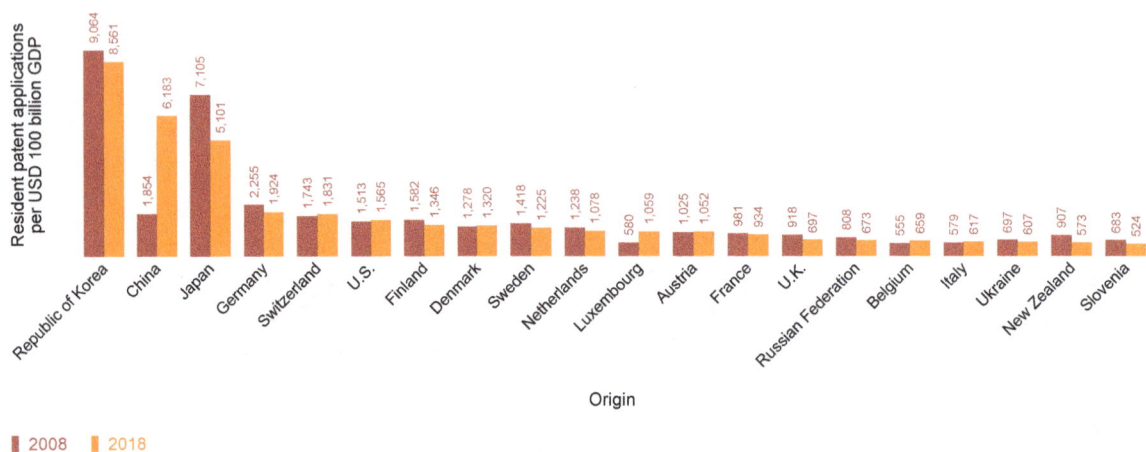

Resident patent applications per USD 100 billion GDP

Origin	2008	2018
Republic of Korea	9,064	8,561
China	1,854	6,183
Japan	7,105	5,101
Germany	2,255	1,924
Switzerland	1,743	1,831
U.S.	1,513	1,565
Finland	1,582	1,346
Denmark	1,278	1,320
Sweden	1,418	1,225
Netherlands	1,238	1,078
Luxembourg	580	1,059
Austria	1,025	1,052
France	981	934
U.K.	918	697
Russian Federation	808	673
Belgium	555	659
Italy	579	617
Ukraine	697	607
New Zealand	907	573
Slovenia	683	524

■ 2008 ■ 2018

Note: GDP data are in 2011 US purchasing power parity (PPP) dollars. The top 20 origins were included if they had a GDP greater than USD 25 billion PPP and more than 100 resident patent applications. Due to space constraints, only the top 20 origins to fulfil these criteria are presented.

Sources: WIPO Statistics Database and World Bank, August 2019.

A38. Resident patent applications per million population for the top 20 origins, 2008 and 2018

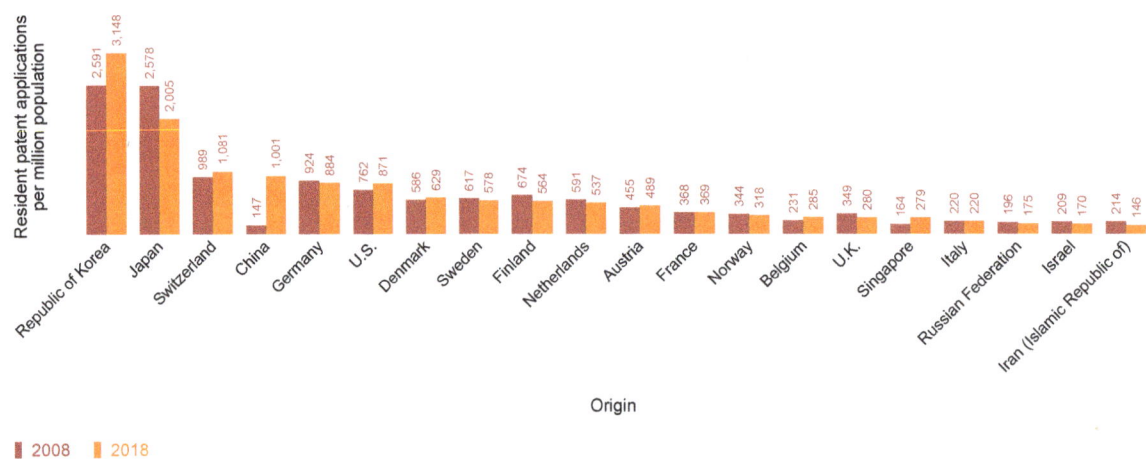

Resident patent applications per million population

Origin	2008	2018
Republic of Korea	2,591	3,148
Japan	2,578	2,005
Switzerland	989	1,081
China	147	1,001
Germany	924	884
U.S.	762	871
Denmark	586	629
Sweden	617	578
Finland	674	564
Netherlands	591	537
Austria	455	489
France	368	369
Norway	344	316
Belgium	231	285
U.K.	349	280
Singapore	164	279
Italy	220	220
Russian Federation	196	175
Israel	209	170
Iran (Islamic Republic of)	214	146

■ 2008 ■ 2018

Note: The top 20 origins were included if they had a population greater than 5 million and if they had more than 100 resident patent applications. Due to space constraints, only the top 20 origins to fulfil these criteria are presented.

Sources: WIPO Statistics Database and World Bank, August 2019.

Patents in force

A39. Trend in patents in force worldwide, 2008–2018

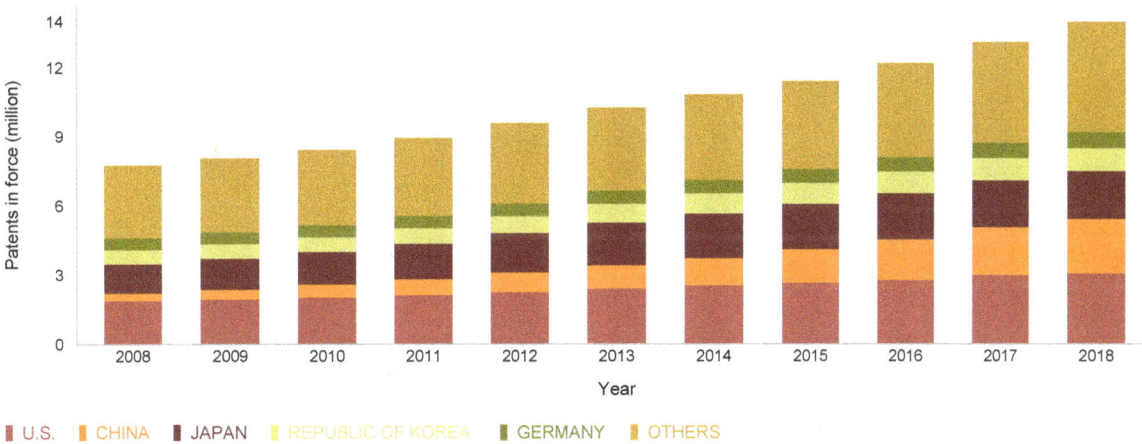

Legend: U.S. | CHINA | JAPAN | REPUBLIC OF KOREA | GERMANY | OTHERS

Note: World totals are WIPO estimates using data covering 125 offices.
Source: WIPO Statistics Database, August 2019.

A40. Patents in force at the top 20 offices, 2018

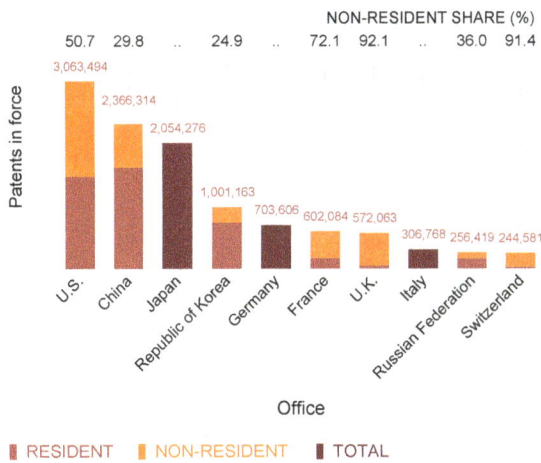

NON-RESIDENT SHARE (%)

| 50.7 | 29.8 | .. | 24.9 | .. | 72.1 | 92.1 | .. | 36.0 | 91.4 |

U.S.	3,063,494
China	2,366,314
Japan	2,054,276
Republic of Korea	1,001,163
Germany	703,606
France	602,084
U.K.	572,063
Italy	306,768
Russian Federation	256,419
Switzerland	244,581

RESIDENT | NON-RESIDENT | TOTAL

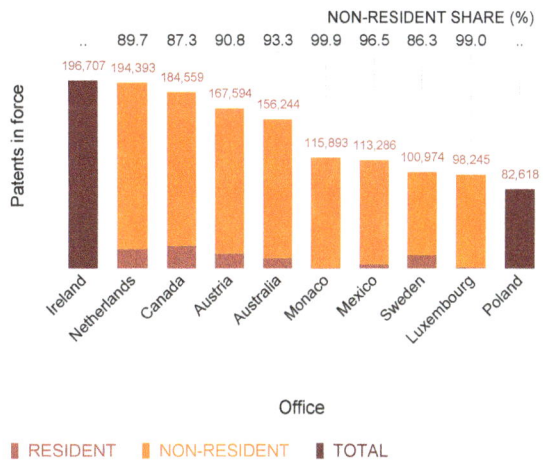

NON-RESIDENT SHARE (%)

| .. | 89.7 | 87.3 | 90.8 | 93.3 | 99.9 | 96.5 | 86.3 | 99.0 | .. |

Ireland	196,707
Netherlands	194,393
Canada	184,559
Austria	167,594
Australia	156,244
Monaco	115,893
Mexico	113,286
Sweden	100,974
Luxembourg	98,245
Poland	82,618

RESIDENT | NON-RESIDENT | TOTAL

.. indicates not available.
Source: WIPO Statistics Database, August 2019.

47

Patents

A41. Patents in force in 2018 as a percentage of total applications

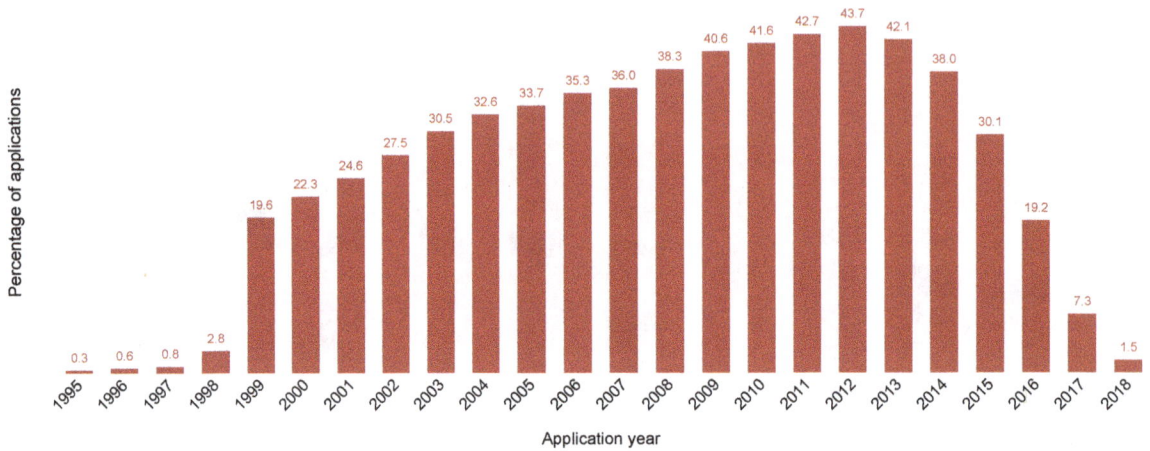

Note: Percentages are calculated as the number of patent applications filed in year *t* and in force in 2018, divided by the total number of patent applications filed in year *t*. Patent holders must pay maintenance fees to maintain the validity of their patents. Depending on technological and commercial considerations, patent holders may opt to let a patent lapse before the end of the full protection term. This figure shows the distribution of patents in force in 2018 as a percentage of total applications in the year of filing. However, not all offices provide these data. Data for 78 offices show that 43.7% of the applications for which patents were eventually granted remained in force for at least 7 years after the application date. About 19.6% of these patents lasted the full 20-year patent term.

Source: WIPO Statistics Database, August 2019.

A42. Average age of patents in force at selected offices, 2013 and 2018

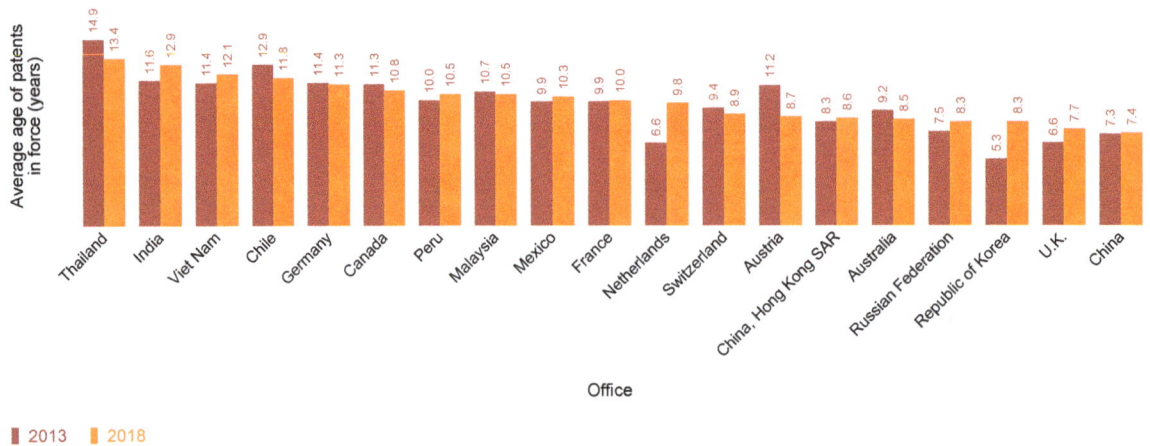

■ 2013 ■ 2018

Note: The average age of patents in force is calculated using the following formula: $\sum(p^*y)/\sum p$, where p is the number of patents in force and y the number of years between filing and reporting year.

Source: WIPO Statistics Database, August 2019.

Patent office procedural data

A43. Distribution of patent examination outcomes for selected offices, 2018

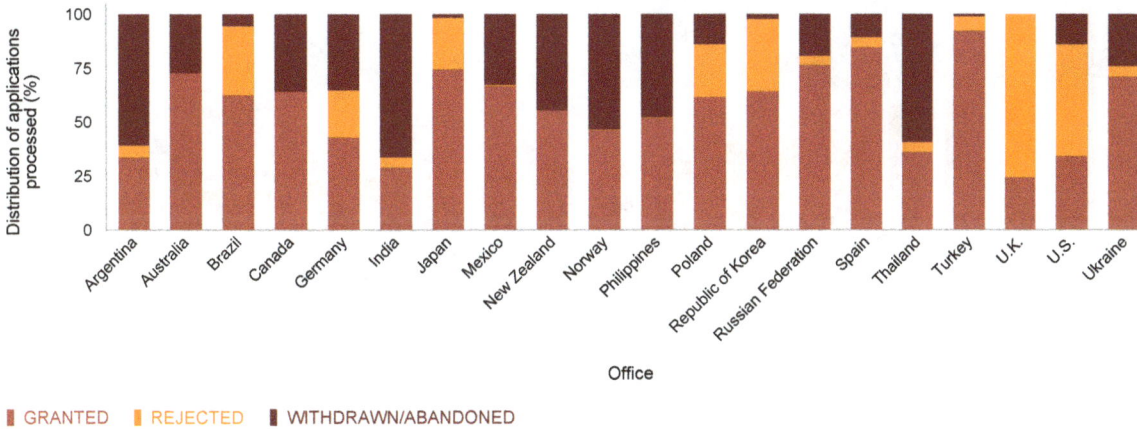

GRANTED   REJECTED   WITHDRAWN/ABANDONED

Note: The share of applications granted should not be interpreted as grant rates, as they are based on the examination date rather than the date when the application was filed. The number of grants in a given year relates to applications filed in previous years. WIPO collects data from IP offices using a common questionnaire and methodology. However, due to differences in patent procedures between offices, data cannot be fully harmonized. Therefore caution should be exercised when making comparisons across offices.

Source: WIPO Statistics Database, August 2019.

A44. Potentially pending applications at the top 20 offices, 2018

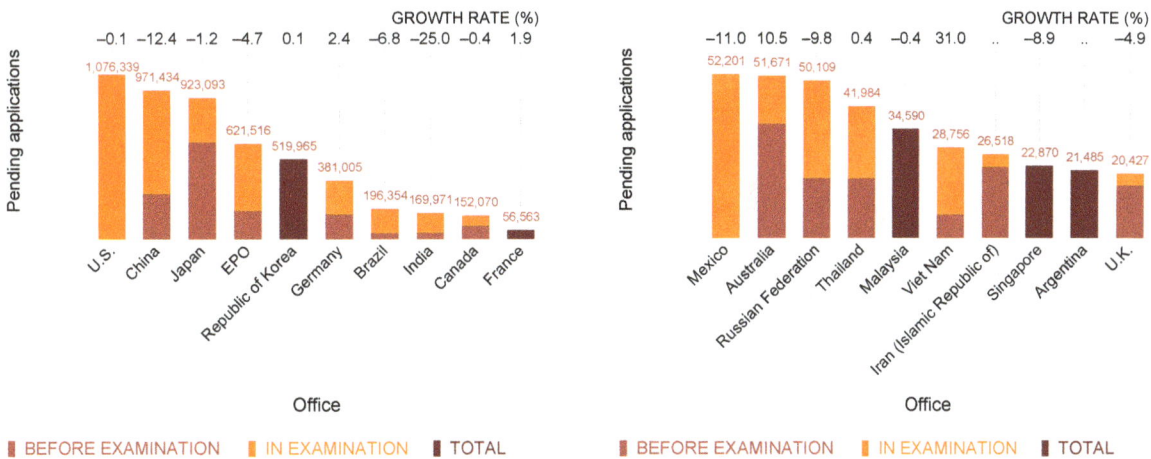

BEFORE EXAMINATION   IN EXAMINATION   TOTAL   **BEFORE EXAMINATION   IN EXAMINATION   TOTAL**

Note: EPO is the European Patent Office. Application processing varies between offices, making it difficult to measure pending applications. In some offices, patent applications automatically proceed to the examination stage unless applicants withdraw them; in others, applications do not proceed to examination unless applicants file a separate request for examination. To take account of procedural differences, pending application data are separated between (a) all patent applications, at any stage in the process, that are awaiting a final decision by a patent office, including those for which applicants have not filed a request for examination (where applicable) and (b) patent applications undergoing examination for which the applicant has requested examination (where such separate requests are necessary). Data for Brazil include both pending patent and utility model applications, and so are not comparable with other offices.

.. indicates not available.

Source: WIPO Statistics Database, August 2019.

A45. Average pendency times for first office action and final decision at selected offices, 2018

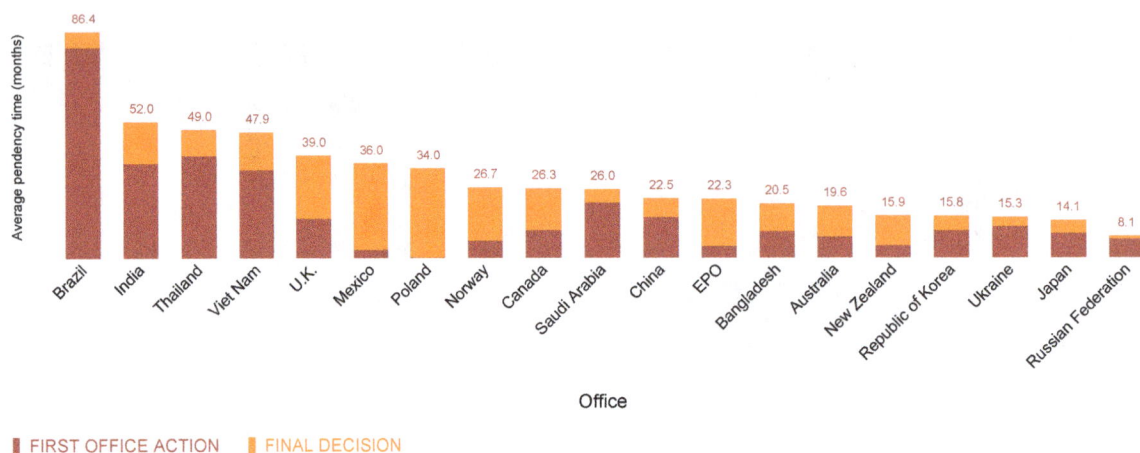

Average pendency time (months)

Brazil 86.4 · India 52.0 · Thailand 49.0 · Viet Nam 47.9 · U.K. 39.0 · Mexico 36.0 · Poland 34.0 · Norway 26.7 · Canada 26.3 · Saudi Arabia 26.0 · China 22.5 · EPO 22.3 · Bangladesh 20.5 · Australia 19.6 · New Zealand 15.9 · Republic of Korea 15.8 · Ukraine 15.3 · Japan 14.1 · Russian Federation 8.1

Office

▌ FIRST OFFICE ACTION   ▌ FINAL DECISION

Note: EPO is the European Patent Office. WIPO collects data from IP offices using a common questionnaire and methodology. However, due to differences in patent procedures between offices, data cannot be fully harmonized. Therefore caution should be exercised when making comparisons across offices.

Source: WIPO Statistics Database, August 2019.

A46. Number of patent examiners for selected offices, 2018

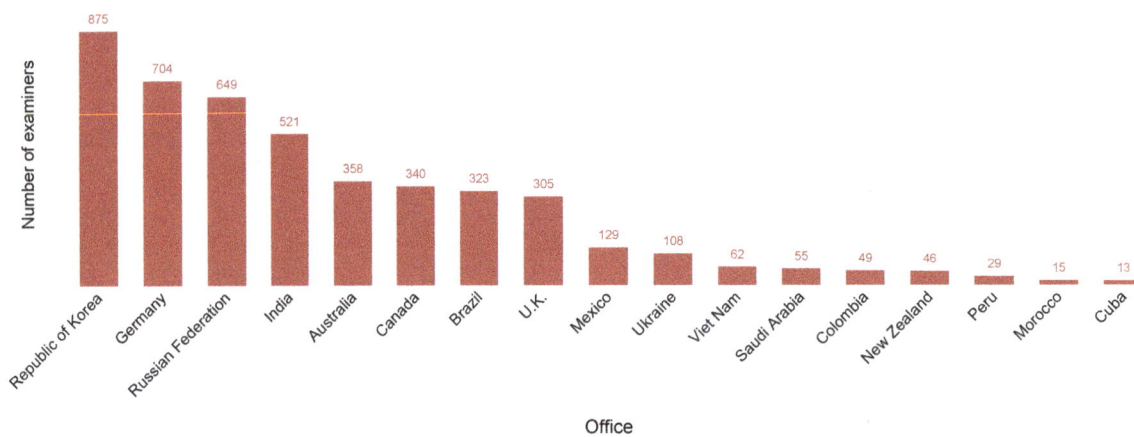

Number of examiners

Republic of Korea 875 · Germany 704 · Russian Federation 649 · India 521 · Australia 358 · Canada 340 · Brazil 323 · U.K. 305 · Mexico 129 · Ukraine 108 · Viet Nam 62 · Saudi Arabia 55 · Colombia 49 · New Zealand 46 · Peru 29 · Morocco 15 · Cuba 13

Office

Source: WIPO Statistics Database, August 2019.

A47. Average years of experience of patent examiners for selected offices, 2018

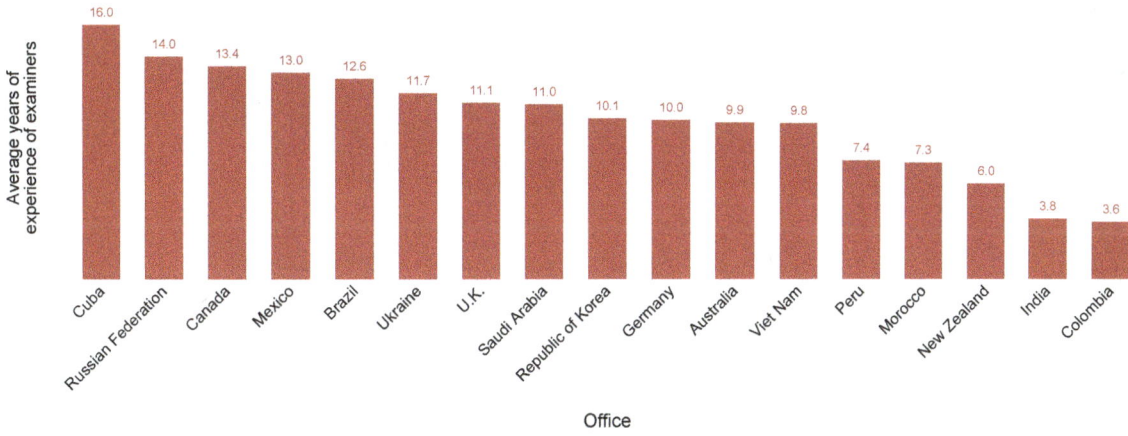

Source: WIPO Statistics Database, August 2019.

Patents

Patent applications filed through the Patent Cooperation Treaty (PCT) System

A48. Trend in PCT applications, 2004–2018

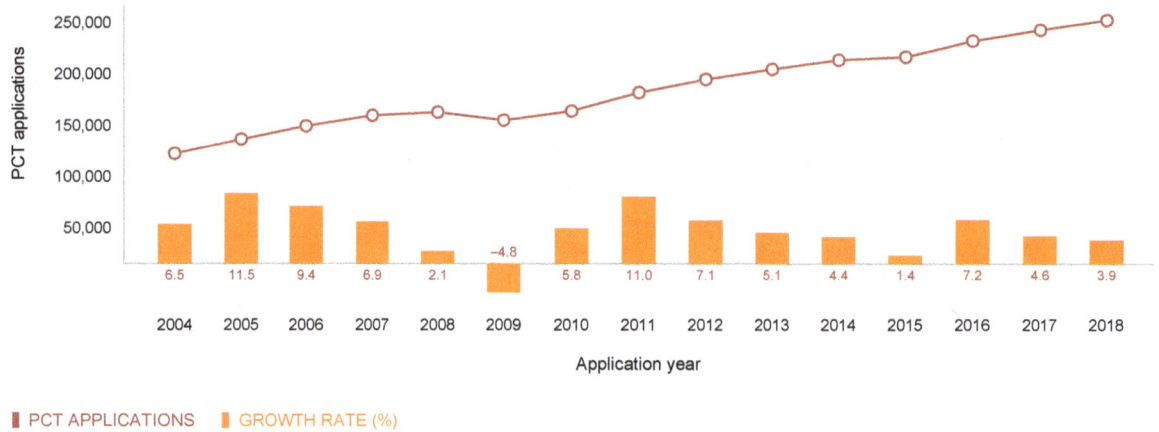

PCT APPLICATIONS   GROWTH RATE (%)

Note: Data refer to the international phase of the Patent Cooperation Treaty System. Counts are based on the international application date.
Source: WIPO Statistics Database, August 2019.

A49. PCT applications by origin, 2018

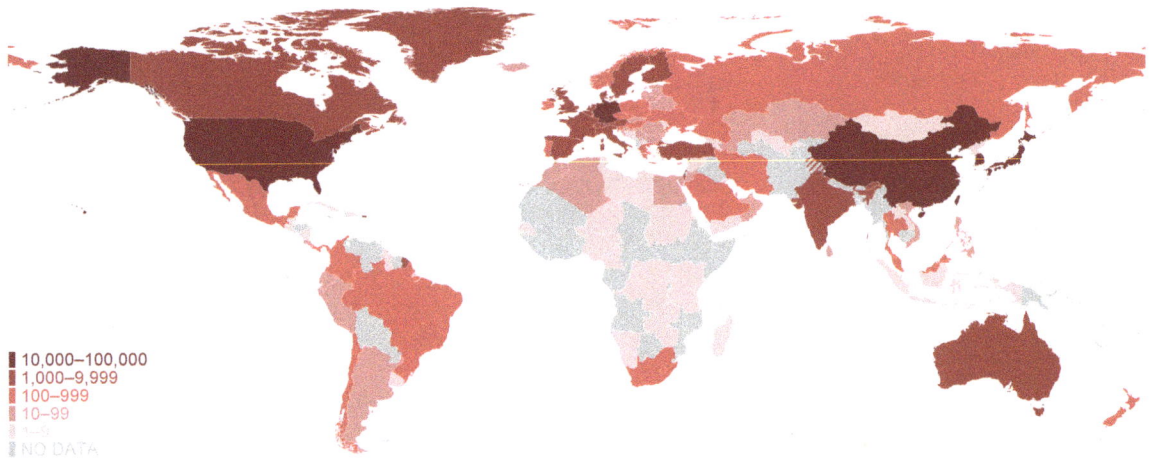

10,000–100,000
1,000–9,999
100–999
10–99
1–9
NO DATA

Note: Data refer to the international phase of the Patent Cooperation Treaty System. Counts are based on the residency of the first named applicant and the international application date.
Source: WIPO Statistics Database, August 2019.

A50. PCT applications for the top 20 origins, 2018

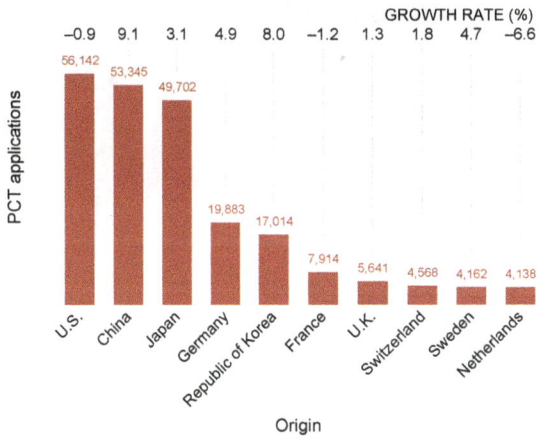

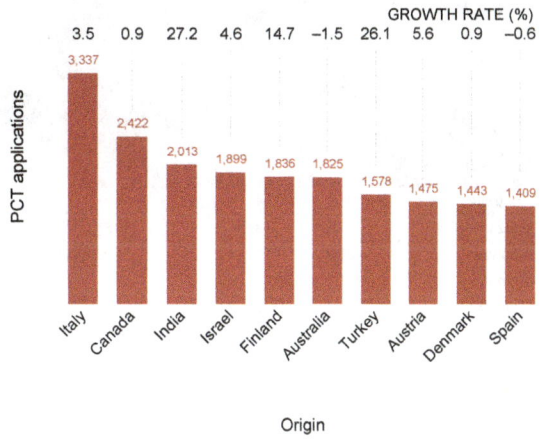

Note: Data refer to the international phase of the Patent Cooperation Treaty System. Counts are based on the residency of the first named applicant and the international application date.

Source: WIPO Statistics Database, August 2019.

Patent prosecution highway (PPH)

A51. PPH requests by office of first filing and offices of later examination, 2018

Office of later examination	U.S.	Japan	EPO	China	Republic of Korea	Canada	Australia	Germany	U.K.	Denmark	Israel	Russian Federation	Sweden	Finland	Singapore	Others/Unknown	Total
Australia	688	104	87	9	10	11	4	20	34	14		3	3	3	5	67	1,062
Brazil	69	43	17	138				2								21	290
Canada	1,885	251	429	61	34	123	85	7	9	2	17	6	2	2	7	3	2,923
China	2,151	2,326	923		302	8		73	35	41	12	25	30	9	6	2	5,943
Colombia	42	2	10			1	1	2					1			3	62
EAPO		10	11	2													23
EPO	633	585		130	80	12	25				31	14			3	3	1,516
Germany	140	872		16	4		4		21					1	1	2	1,061
Indonesia	1	269						1								1	272
Japan*	1,667	1,479	1,049	136	122	12	22	23	14	27	6	4	1	2	1	4	4,569
Mexico	269	199	130	5	8	11									1	13	636
New Zealand	29	10		1			2		4					1	2	8	57
Norway	12					3			2	1			4	2		5	29
Republic of Korea	1,580	1,150	609	101	44	10	41	14	13	38	5	4	9	8	5	3	3,634
Russian Federation	106	66	20	8	1			5	1				1			3	211
Singapore	16	26	4	2			2	1					2		1	3	57
Thailand		24															24
U.K.	125	19		31	2	1	7	3								1	189
U.S.	714	2,071	1,920	733	512	158	62	99	78	31	74	79	34	36	13	35	6,649
Viet Nam		100															100
Others/Unknown	4	20	2	4	1	1		2	1	2					3	12	52
Total	**10,131**	**9,626**	**5,211**	**1,377**	**1,120**	**351**	**255**	**252**	**212**	**156**	**147**	**135**	**85**	**67**	**45**	**189**	**29,359**

Note: EAPO is the Eurasian Patent Organization and EPO is the European Patent Office. A patent prosecution highway is a bilateral agreement between two offices that enables applicants to request a fast-track examination whereby patent examiners can use the work already undertaken by the other office.

* indicates data based on office of earlier examination rather than office of first filing.

Source: WIPO Statistics Database, August 2019.

A52. Flows of PPH requests between offices of first filing and offices of later examination, 2018

Office of first filing

Office of later examination

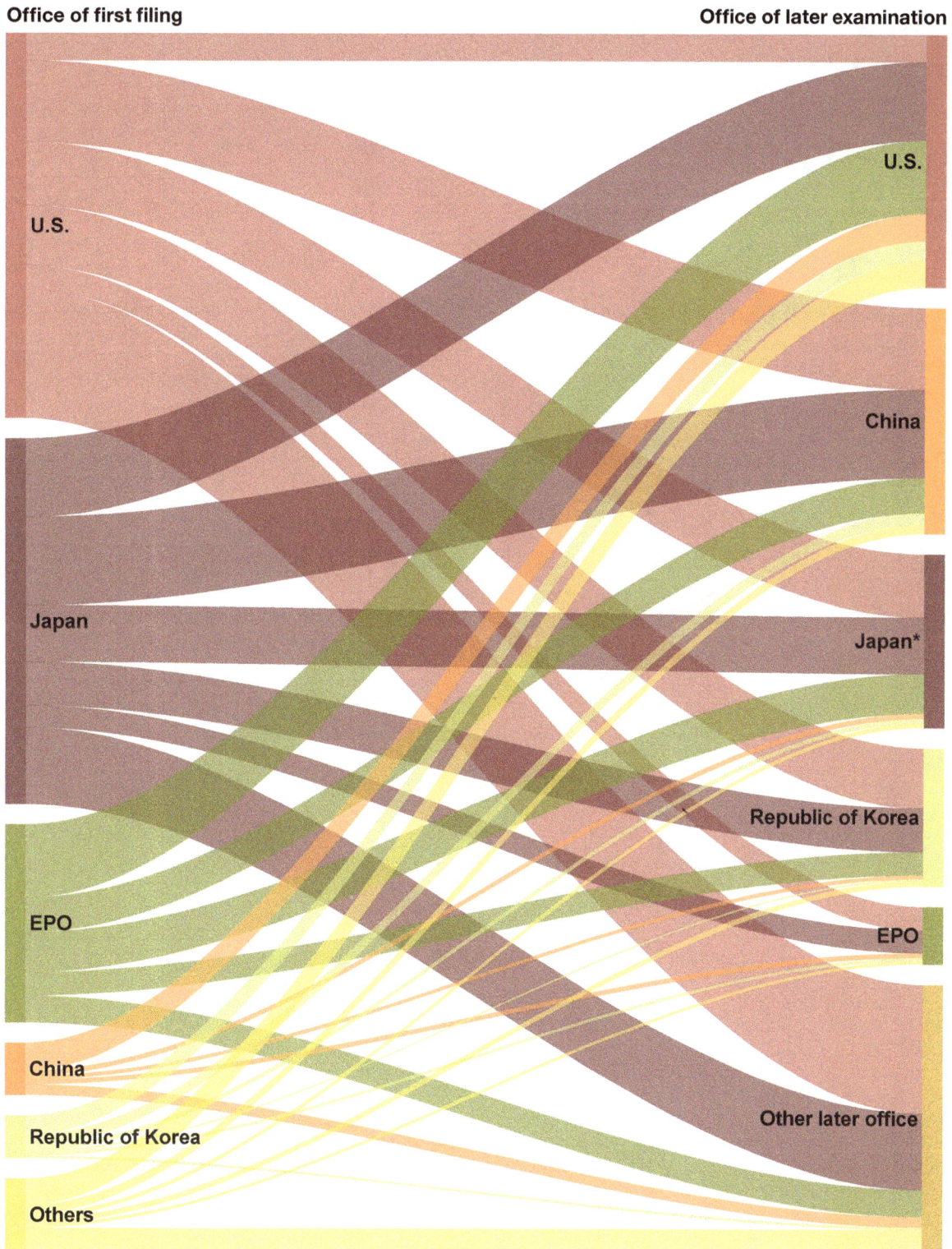

Note: EPO is the European Patent Office. Japan data refers to the office of earlier examination rather than the office of first filing. A patent prosecution highway (PPH) is a bilateral agreement between two offices that enables applicants to request a fast-track examination whereby patent examiners can use the work already undertaken by the other office. This graph shows the flows of PPH requests between offices of first filing and offices of later examination.

* indicates data based on office of earlier examination rather than office of first filing.

Source: WIPO Statistics Database, August 2019.

Utility model applications

A53. Trend in utility model applications worldwide, 2004–2018

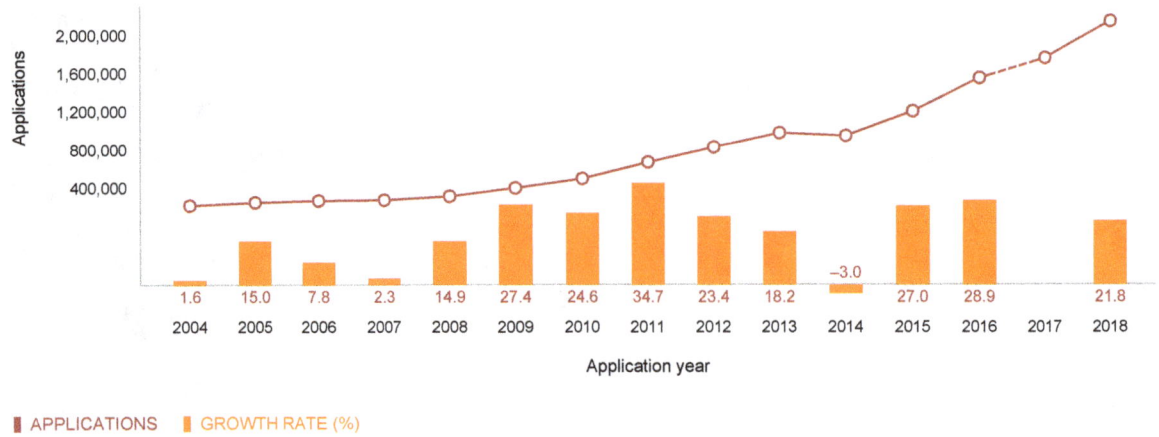

Note: World totals are WIPO estimates using data covering 75 patent offices. These totals include applications filed directly with national and regional offices and applications entering offices through the Patent Cooperation Treaty national phase (where applicable). China's pre-2017 data are not comparable due a change in methodology. Due to this break in the data series and to the large number of filings in China, it is not possible to report accurately the 2017 growth rate at world level (see the data description section in Additional information for details).

Source: WIPO Statistics Database, August 2019.

A54. Utility model applications for the top 20 offices, 2018

GROWTH RATE (%)

22.8 −7.5 −8.4 0.1 −8.5 −11.7 18.0 −16.6 10.8 −11.3

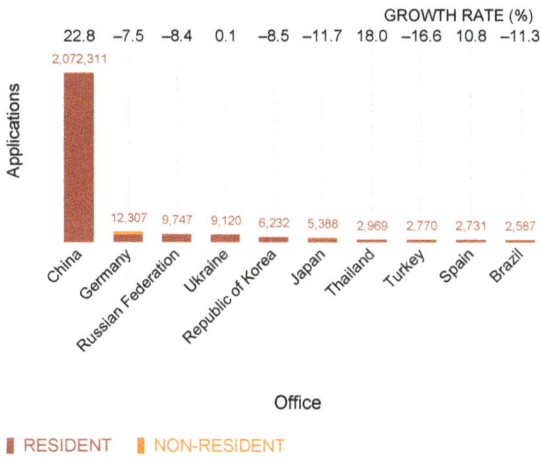

GROWTH RATE (%)

60.5 24.3 −6.2 429.1 −2.5 1.4 7.6 32.6 14.1 42.1

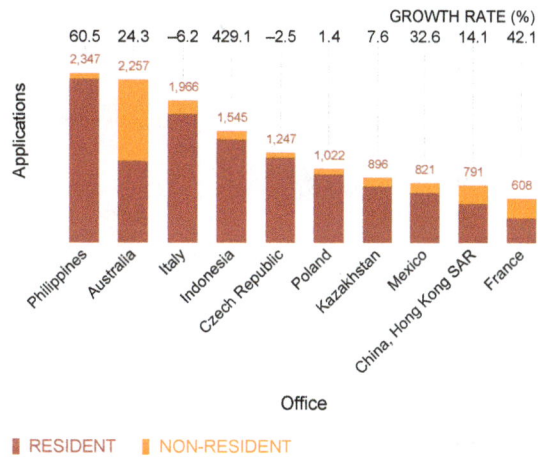

RESIDENT NON-RESIDENT

RESIDENT NON-RESIDENT

Source: WIPO Statistics Database, August 2019.

A55. Utility model applications for offices of selected low- and middle-income countries, 2018

GROWTH RATE (%)

28.3 .. 19.1 −17.9 −8.6 −12.2 41.1 −3.9 −14.7 −13.0

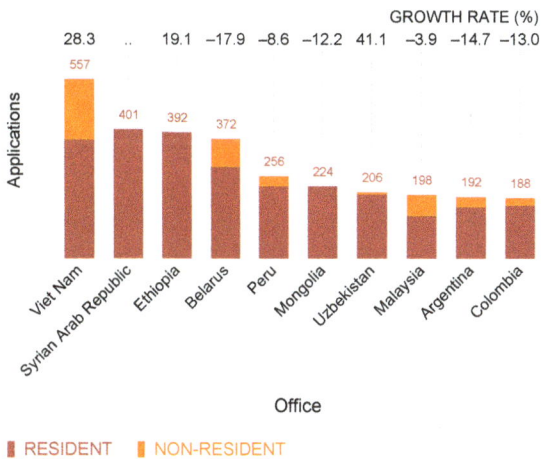

GROWTH RATE (%)

16.3 −14.1 −6.7 13.2 −3.5 −6.1 147.1 −19.2 −10.0 133.3

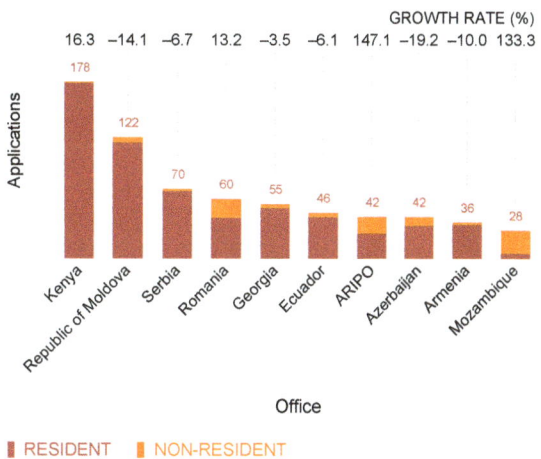

RESIDENT NON-RESIDENT

RESIDENT NON-RESIDENT

Note: ARIPO is the African Regional Intellectual Property Organization.
.. indicates not available.
Source: WIPO Statistics Database, August 2019.

Patents

Microorganisms

A56. Trend in microorganism deposits worldwide, 2004–2018

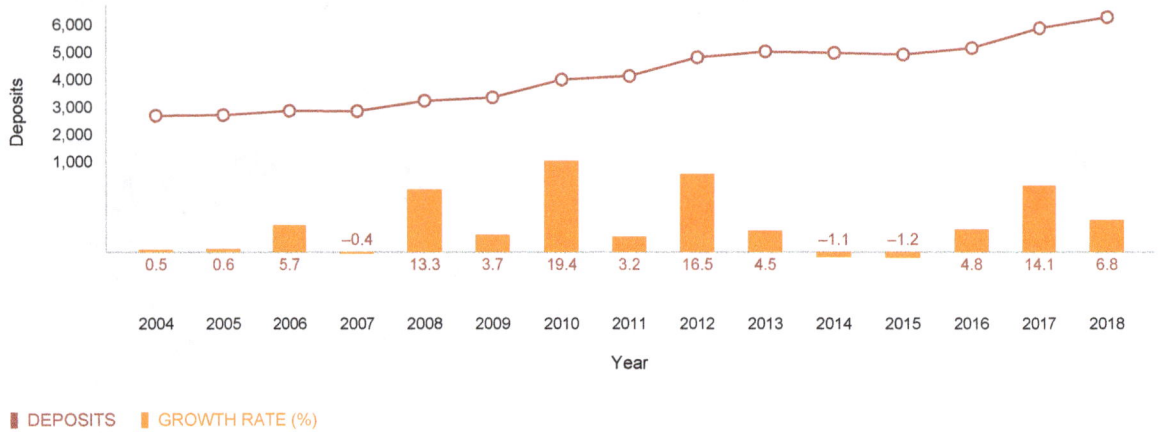

Note: Deposits of microorganisms for patent procedures are important for biotechnological inventions. Disclosing an invention is a requirement for receiving a patent.

Source: WIPO Statistics Database, August 2019.

A57. Deposits at the top international depositary authorities, 2018

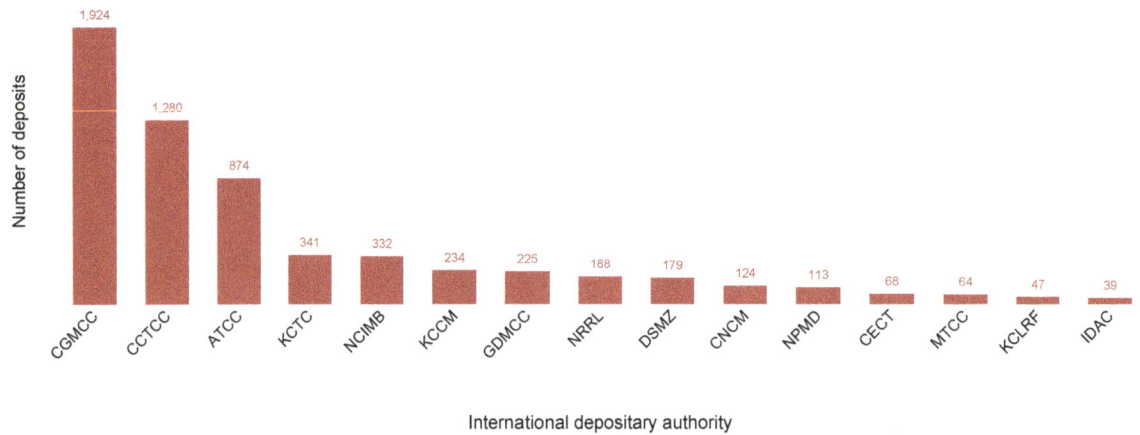

International depositary authority

Note: ATCC is the American Type Culture Collection (U.S.), CCTCC is the China Center for Type Culture Collection (China), CECT is the Colección Española de Cultivos Tipo (Spain), CGMCC is the China General Microbiological Culture Collection Center (China), CNCM is the Collection Nationale de Cultures de Micro-organismes (France), DSMZ is the Leibniz-Institut DSMZ (Deutsche Sammlung von Mikroorganismen und Zellkulturen GmbH; Germany), GDMCC is the Guangdong Microbial Culture Collection Center (China), IDAC is the International Depositary Authority of Canada (Canada), KCCM is the Korean Culture Center of Microorganisms (Republic of Korea), KCLRF is the Korean Cell Line Research Foundation (Republic of Korea), KCTC is the Korean Collection for Type Cultures (Republic of Korea), MTCC is the Microbial Type Culture Collection and Gene Bank (India), NCIMB is the National Collection of Industrial, Food and Marine Bacteria (U.K.), NPMD is the National Institute of Technology and Evaluation, Patent Microorganisms Depositary (Japan) and NRRL is the Agriculture Research Service Culture Collection (U.S.).

Source: WIPO Statistics Database, August 2019.

Statistical tables

A58. Patent applications by office and origin, 2018

Name	Applications by office			Equivalent applications by origin	PCT international applications		PCT national phase entry	
	Total	Resident	Non-resident	Total [a]	Receiving office	Origin	Office	Origin
Afghanistan (b)	..	..	..	11	n.a.	0	..	1
African Intellectual Property Organization	551	129	422	n.a.	0	n.a.	398	n.a.
African Regional Intellectual Property Organization	831	21	810	n.a.	2	n.a.	772	n.a.
Albania	18	15	3	18	0	0	3	..
Algeria	673	152	521	162	16	17	497	4
Andorra	11	1	10	22	n.a.	7	..	13
Angola (b,c)	..	..	..	8	n.a.	0	..	7
Antigua and Barbuda	10	5	5	596	0	96	5	526
Argentina	3,667	425	3,242	755	n.a.	42	..	111
Armenia	105	101	4	165	0	6	3	15
Aruba (b)	..	..	..	2	n.a.	0	..	..
Australia	29,957	2,757	27,200	12,261	1,675	1,825	20,900	7,824
Austria	2,207	2,039	168	14,561	441	1,475	427	7,473
Azerbaijan	171	155	16	414	14	15	15	27
Bahamas (b)	..	..	..	46	n.a.	4	..	22
Bahrain	230	11	219	47	0	1	213	3
Bangladesh	368	69	299	85	n.a.	0	..	1
Barbados (b,c)	..	..	..	825	n.a.	96	..	342
Belarus	547	453	94	1,479	22	23	60	75
Belgium	1,110	892	218	14,587	0	1,295	..	8,621
Belize	24	0	24	8	0	1	24	3
Benin (b,d,g)	n.a.	n.a.	n.a.	85	n.a.	0	n.a.	..
Bermuda (b)	..	..	..	74	n.a.	0	..	25
Bhutan (b)	..	..	..	6	n.a.	0	..	3
Bolivia (Plurinational State of) (b)	..	..	..	5	n.a.	0	..	3
Bosnia and Herzegovina	96	84	12	95	3	4	7	2
Botswana	3	0	3	1	0	0	..	1
Brazil	24,857	4,980	19,877	6,859	570	619	18,011	1,074
Brunei Darussalam	121	24	97	25	1	1	90	1
Bulgaria	198	180	18	459	47	60	4	145
Burkina Faso (b,d,g)	n.a.	n.a.	n.a.	120	n.a.	0	n.a.	..
Burundi (b)	..	..	..	6	n.a.	0	..	6
Cabo Verde	3	3	0	3	n.a.	0	..	..
Cambodia	159	0	159	10	0	0	26	9
Cameroon (b,d,g)	n.a.	n.a.	n.a.	708	n.a.	1	n.a.	7
Canada	36,161	4,349	31,812	24,483	1,914	2,422	28,396	9,450
Central African Republic (b,d,g)	n.a.	n.a.	n.a.	51	n.a.	0	n.a.	..
Chad (b,d,g)	n.a.	n.a.	n.a.	136	n.a.	0	n.a.	..
Chile	3,100	406	2,694	946	204	245	2,578	422
China	1,542,002	1,393,815	148,187	1,460,244	55,211	53,345	84,297	36,789
China, Hong Kong SAR	15,986	314	15,672	2,205	n.a.	0	..	511
China, Macao SAR	55	1	54	136	n.a.	0	..	28
Colombia	2,223	415	1,808	637	26	163	1,707	162
Congo (b,d,g)	n.a.	n.a.	n.a.	19	n.a.	0	n.a.	..
Cook Islands (b)	..	..	..	3	n.a.	0	..	..

Name	Applications by office			Equivalent applications by origin	PCT international applications		PCT national phase entry	
	Total	Resident	Non-resident	Total [a]	Receiving office	Origin	Office	Origin
Costa Rica	498	7	491	115	11	13	486	42
Côte d'Ivoire (b,d,g)	n.a.	n.a.	n.a.	394	n.a.	0	n.a.	2
Croatia	136	121	15	201	24	40	2	58
Cuba	155	29	126	148	7	7	120	111
Curaçao (b)	..	..	..	5	n.a.	0	..	1
Cyprus	4	4	0	432	2	40	..	247
Czech Republic	732	678	54	2,251	124	180	24	740
Democratic People's Republic of Korea (b)	..	..	..	63	2	2	..	40
Democratic Republic of the Congo (b)	..	..	..	2	n.a.	1	..	..
Denmark	1,501	1,262	239	13,385	457	1,443	93	7,496
Dominica	4	0	4	..	n.a.	0	4	..
Dominican Republic	228	17	211	40	4	4	208	8
Ecuador	405	34	371	51	2	31	364	14
Egypt	2,255	997	1,258	1,174	42	44	1,226	47
El Salvador	139	3	136	14	0	1	128	2
Eritrea (b)	..	..	..	2	n.a.	0	..	..
Estonia	30	24	6	270	4	48	4	113
Eswatini (b,f)	..	..	..	95	n.a.	0	..	93
Ethiopia	62	13	49	13	n.a.	0	..	..
Eurasian Patent Organization	3,488	664	2,824	n.a.	11	n.a.	2,643	n.a.
European Patent Office	174,397	81,565	92,832	n.a.	37,975	n.a.	102,196	n.a.
Fiji (b)	..	..	..	1	n.a.	1	..	..
Finland	1,487	1,387	100	11,572	1,007	1,836	24	6,507
France	16,222	14,303	1,919	69,120	3,555	7,914	..	35,439
Gabon (b,d,g)	n.a.	n.a.	n.a.	52	n.a.	0	n.a.	..
Gambia (b,f)	..	..	..	2	n.a.	0	..	1
Georgia	260	103	157	128	5	6	151	11
Germany	67,898	46,617	21,281	180,086	1,430	19,883	7,027	73,318
Ghana	52	13	39	15	0	0	26	..
Greece	579	430	149	1,137	60	115	..	357
Guatemala	234	6	228	15	0	1	220	3
Guinea (b,d,g)	n.a.	n.a.	n.a.	17	n.a.	0	n.a.	..
Guyana	20	2	18	2	n.a.	1	..	..
Haiti (b)	..	..	..	2	n.a.	0	..	..
Honduras	156	8	148	9	0	0	144	..
Hungary	443	407	36	1,340	113	153	11	672
Iceland	66	56	10	281	14	49	7	134
India	50,055	16,289	33,766	30,036	920	2,013	27,688	4,296
Indonesia	9,754	1,407	8,347	1,451	3	7	7,127	21
International Bureau (b)	..	..	..	n.a.	12,259	n.a.	..	n.a.
Iran (Islamic Republic of)	12,823	11,908	915	12,074	27	176	..	21
Iraq	730	653	77	664	n.a.	0	..	2
Ireland	108	76	32	6,334	16	620	..	2,863
Israel	7,363	1,506	5,857	15,482	1,437	1,899	6,158	7,281
Italy	9,821	8,921	900	32,286	434	3,337	..	14,887

Name	Applications by office			Equivalent applications by origin	PCT international applications		PCT national phase entry	
	Total	Resident	Non-resident	Total [a]	Receiving office	Origin	Office	Origin
Jamaica	79	26	53	42	n.a.	0	..	5
Japan	313,567	253,630	59,937	460,369	48,630	49,702	64,013	133,414
Jordan	133	24	109	51	9	13	16	7
Kazakhstan	982	789	193	1,633	15	18	..	33
Kenya	286	244	42	293	3	8	38	10
Kuwait	257	1	256	160	n.a.	6	256	5
Kyrgyzstan (b)	..	..	..	4	0	0	..	..
Lao People's Democratic Republic (c)	59	1	58	1	n.a.	3	40	..
Latvia	110	86	24	175	0	31	..	50
Lebanon (b)	..	..	..	76	n.a.	6	..	35
Liberia (b)	..	..	..	1	0	0	..	..
Libya (b)	..	..	..	..	0	2	..	..
Liechtenstein (b,e)	..	..	..	1,353	n.a.	263	..	749
Lithuania	105	81	24	230	0	37	..	95
Luxembourg	395	152	243	3,199	0	392	..	2,186
Madagascar (c)	46	9	37	9	n.a.	1	37	..
Malawi (b)	..	..	..	2	0	0	..	1
Malaysia	7,295	1,116	6,179	2,060	138	143	5,072	444
Mali (b,d,g)	n.a.	n.a.	n.a.	142	n.a.	0	n.a.	2
Malta (b)	..	..	..	394	0	45	..	228
Marshall Islands (b)	..	..	..	1	n.a.	0	..	1
Mauritania (b,d,g)	n.a.	n.a.	n.a.	1	n.a.	0	n.a.	..
Mauritius	29	16	13	192	n.a.	4	..	86
Mexico	16,424	1,555	14,869	2,695	196	274	12,637	643
Monaco	15	4	11	134	0	21	..	38
Mongolia	161	82	79	83	0	2	69	..
Montenegro (c)	3	3	0	16	0	8	..	8
Morocco	2,537	187	2,350	337	44	49	1,963	128
Mozambique (f)	47	34	13	34	n.a.	0	13	..
Myanmar (b)	..	..	..	1	n.a.	0	..	..
Namibia (f)	36	21	15	24	n.a.	3	7	2
Nepal (b)	..	..	..	6	n.a.	0	..	..
Netherlands	2,505	2,111	394	36,539	917	4,138	..	22,691
Netherlands Antilles (b)	..	..	..	1	n.a.	0	..	1
New Zealand	6,238	1,017	5,221	3,039	186	278	4,084	1,453
Nicaragua (b)	..	..	..	2	1	1	..	..
Niger (b,d,g)	n.a.	n.a.	n.a.	103	n.a.	1	n.a.	1
Nigeria (c)	338	120	218	153	n.a.	2	148	9
North Macedonia (b)	..	..	..	1	5	6	..	..
Norway	1,674	1,082	592	6,511	346	766	544	4,000
Oman (b,c)	..	..	..	19	11	14	..	..
Pakistan	892	306	586	350	n.a.	0	..	8
Panama	497	135	362	183	22	185	347	10
Paraguay	350	..	..	20	n.a.	0	..	5
Patent Office of the Cooperation Council for the Arab States of the Gulf	2,220	667	1,553	n.a.	n.a.	n.a.	..	n.a.

Patents

Name	Applications by office			Equivalent applications by origin	PCT international applications		PCT national phase entry	
	Total	Resident	Non-resident	Total (a)	Receiving office	Origin	Office	Origin
Peru	1,222	89	1,133	135	39	38	1,065	43
Philippines	4,300	529	3,771	736	14	18	3,182	57
Poland	4,322	4,207	115	6,757	201	335	53	1,219
Portugal	690	661	29	1,643	68	250	10	631
Qatar (b)	..	..	..	167	7	15	..	70
Republic of Korea	209,992	162,561	47,431	232,020	17,002	17,014	38,239	28,990
Republic of Moldova	113	92	21	160	5	5	20	44
Romania	1,147	1,100	47	1,501	16	28	20	151
Russian Federation	37,957	24,926	13,031	30,696	993	963	10,159	2,496
Rwanda	7	6	1	6	0	1	..	..
Saint Kitts and Nevis	4	0	4	10	0	4	4	8
Saint Lucia (c)	2	2	0	3	n.a.	0	..	..
Saint Vincent and the Grenadines (c)	4	0	4	..	n.a.	0	4	..
Samoa	1	1	0	62	n.a.	1	..	2
San Marino	695	14	681	68	0	3	..	30
Sao Tome and Principe (c)	408	0	408	3	n.a.	0	408	1
Saudi Arabia	3,399	1,078	2,321	6,910	40	661	2,464	1,104
Senegal (b,d,g)	n.a.	n.a.	n.a.	341	n.a.	4	n.a.	..
Serbia	174	163	11	308	20	20	7	92
Seychelles	17	0	17	106	0	2	16	50
Singapore	11,845	1,575	10,270	7,415	654	930	7,740	2,897
Slovakia	231	217	14	560	28	50	3	203
Slovenia	278	255	23	738	63	116	..	219
South Africa	6,915	657	6,258	1,861	67	274	5,706	1,081
Spain	1,674	1,525	149	10,292	948	1,409	96	5,062
Sri Lanka (c)	603	343	260	382	n.a.	18	234	18
Sudan	380	349	31	350	6	6	..	..
Sweden	2,280	1,838	442	25,310	1,406	4,162	73	17,371
Switzerland	1,615	1,283	332	46,659	78	4,568	82	26,856
Syrian Arab Republic	148	103	45	112	1	1	..	7
Tajikistan (b)	..	..	..	56	0	0	..	..
Thailand	8,149	904	7,245	1,685	61	105	6,290	499
Togo (b,d,g)	n.a.	n.a.	n.a.	52	n.a.	0	n.a.	..
Trinidad and Tobago	139	4	135	11	2	5	134	1
Tunisia	451	180	271	201	6	7	271	8
Turkey	7,466	7,156	310	9,360	1,292	1,578	215	1,461
Turkmenistan (b)	..	..	..	9	0	0	..	1
Uganda (f)	6	6	0	10	n.a.	1	..	..
Ukraine	3,968	2,107	1,861	2,541	143	156	1,613	206
United Arab Emirates (c)	1,783	56	1,727	734	n.a.	92	1,664	201
United Kingdom	20,941	12,865	8,076	56,216	3,887	5,641	2,573	28,914
United Republic of Tanzania (f)	25	25	0	27	n.a.	2	9	9
United States of America	597,141	285,095	312,046	515,180	55,330	56,142	155,322	189,054
Uruguay (b)	..	..	..	110	n.a.	8	..	79
Uzbekistan	650	470	180	480	1	2	157	4

Name	Applications by office			Equivalent applications by origin	PCT international applications		PCT national phase entry	
	Total	Resident	Non-resident	Total [a]	Receiving office	Origin	Office	Origin
Vanuatu (b)	..	..	..	10	n.a.	0	..	10
Venezuela (Bolivarian Republic of) (b)	..	..	..	21	n.a.	0	..	8
Viet Nam	6,071	646	5,425	749	8	22	4,567	50
Yemen (b)	..	..	..	7	n.a.	1	..	..
Zambia (b)	..	..	..	2	0	2	..	1
Zimbabwe (b)	..	..	..	4	0	1	..	2
Others/Unknown	..	..	..	40,480	n.a.	289	..	7,524
Total (2018 estimates)	**3,326,300**	**2,378,400**	**947,900**	**n.a.**	**253,000**	**253,000**	**647,700**	**n.a.**

(a) Equivalent applications by origin data are incomplete because some offices do not report by origin.

(b) The office did not report resident applications therefore the equivalent applications by origin data may be incomplete.

(c) The International Bureau acts as the receiving office for PCT applications.

(d) The African Intellectual Property Organization (OAPI) acts as the receiving office for PCT applications.

(e) The Swiss Federal Institute of Intellectual Property (IFPI) acts as the receiving office for PCT applications.

(f) The African Regional Intellectual Property Organization (ARIPO) acts as the receiving office for PCT applications.

(g) The African Intellectual Property Organization (OAPI) acts as the national office for patent applications.

.. indicates not available.

n.a. indicates not applicable.

Source: WIPO Statistics Database, August 2019.

Patents

A59. Patent grants by office and origin, and patents in force, 2018

Name	Total	Grants by office Resident	Grants by office Non-resident	Equivalent grants by origin Total [a]	In force by office Total
Afghanistan	..	..	..	7	..
African Intellectual Property Organization	540	112	428	n.a.	..
African Regional Intellectual Property Organization	282	1	281	n.a.	3,572
Albania	12	9	3	12	5,021
Algeria	162	27	135	35	2,084
Andorra	6	0	6	11	10
Angola	..	..	..	1	..
Antigua and Barbuda	..	..	..	9	78
Argentina	1,525	129	1,396	290	..
Armenia	100	98	2	128	209
Aruba	..	..	..	1	..
Australia	17,065	905	16,160	5,624	156,244
Austria	1,189	1,005	184	8,913	167,594
Azerbaijan	64	53	11	341	253
Bahamas	..	..	..	55	..
Bahrain	15	0	15	7	60
Bangladesh	138	..	..	17	990
Barbados	..	..	..	406	..
Belarus	627	524	103	1,467	1,991
Belgium	1,019	867	152	8,252	..
Belize	..	..	..	8	1,409
Benin (b)	n.a.	n.a.	n.a.	51	..
Bermuda	..	..	..	107	..
Bolivia (Plurinational State of)	..	..	..	2	..
Bosnia and Herzegovina	5	0	5	3	234
Botswana	..	..	..	..	2,038
Brazil	9,966	1,066	8,900	1,976	31,977
Brunei Darussalam	..	..	..	1	113
Bulgaria	181	171	10	310	13,393
Burkina Faso (b)	n.a.	n.a.	n.a.	153	..
Burundi	28	9	19	27	..
Cabo Verde	1	0	1	..	1
Cambodia	56	0	56	1	..
Cameroon (b)	n.a.	n.a.	n.a.	629	..
Canada	23,499	2,221	21,278	13,542	184,559
Chad (b)	n.a.	n.a.	n.a.	103	..
Chile	1,599	172	1,427	383	13,795
China	432,147	345,959	86,188	377,305	2,366,314
China, Hong Kong SAR	9,651	161	9,490	1,140	49,922
China, Macao SAR	27	1	26	59	387
Colombia	1,271	215	1,056	301	7,403
Congo (b)	n.a.	n.a.	n.a.	69	..
Cook Islands	..	..	..	2	..
Costa Rica	168	4	164	31	925
Côte d'Ivoire (b)	n.a.	n.a.	n.a.	528	..

Name	Total	Resident	Grants by office Non-resident	Equivalent grants by origin Total [a]	In force by office Total
Croatia	21	9	12	52	8,945
Cuba	93	8	85	116	727
Curaçao	..	..	..	14	..
Cyprus	..	..	..	213	12
Czech Republic	512	455	57	1,391	45,016
Democratic People's Republic of Korea	..	..	..	31	..
Denmark	322	195	127	6,506	62,408
Dominican Republic	95	11	84	16	635
Ecuador	10	2	8	7	65
Egypt	690	160	530	240	5,706
El Salvador	36	1	35	2	..
Estonia	14	13	1	137	10,452
Eswatini	..	..	..	5	..
Ethiopia	10	1	9	1	..
Eurasian Patent Organization	2,630	436	2,194	n.a.	n.a.
European Patent Office	127,603	57,882	69,721	n.a.	n.a.
Finland	533	472	61	8,571	52,140
France	12,249	10,574	1,675	50,384	602,084
Gabon (b)	n.a.	n.a.	n.a.	18	..
Gambia	..	..	..	..	16
Georgia	133	36	97	50	1,312
Germany	16,367	10,789	5,578	101,556	703,606
Ghana	9	9	0	10	..
Greece	240	229	11	561	27,426
Grenada	..	..	..	1	..
Guatemala	30	0	30	18	914
Guinea (b)	n.a.	n.a.	n.a.	18	..
Guyana	6	1	5	1	..
Holy See	..	..	..	1	..
Honduras	88	0	88	1	1,765
Hungary	156	85	71	641	28,677
Iceland	16	6	10	218	7,380
India	13,908	2,311	11,597	8,350	60,865
Indonesia	6,374	521	5,853	552	22,584
Iran (Islamic Republic of)	3,367	2,993	374	3,057	48,859
Iraq	426	398	28	400	2,784
Ireland	52	28	24	3,170	196,707
Israel	4,107	742	3,365	7,482	33,951
Italy	6,424	6,340	84	22,224	306,768
Jamaica	..	..	..	4	..
Japan	194,525	152,440	42,085	284,068	2,054,276
Jordan	167	16	151	85	532
Kazakhstan	778	589	189	945	..
Kenya	26	26	0	39	..
Kiribati	..	..	..	1	..

Name	Total	Grants by office Resident	Grants by office Non-resident	Equivalent grants by origin Total [a]	In force by office Total
Kuwait	..	..	..	68	..
Kyrgyzstan	110	109	1	151	253
Lao People's Democratic Republic	5	0	5	..	..
Latvia	51	48	3	135	9,475
Lebanon	..	..	..	29	..
Liechtenstein	..	..	..	670	..
Lithuania	92	68	24	150	474
Luxembourg	423	59	364	2,171	98,245
Madagascar	31	3	28	5	229
Malaysia	4,287	469	3,818	985	26,572
Mali (b)	n.a.	n.a.	n.a.	121	..
Malta	..	..	..	309	..
Marshall Islands	..	..	..	7	..
Mauritania (b)	n.a.	n.a.	n.a.	51	..
Mauritius	7	0	7	37	53
Mexico	8,921	457	8,464	1,170	113,286
Monaco	28	3	25	78	115,893
Mongolia	76	26	50	26	1,030
Montenegro	11	11	0	11	..
Morocco	600	126	474	207	8,364
Mozambique	..	..	..	..	2,531
Myanmar	..	..	..	1	..
Namibia	4	0	4	4	623
Nepal	..	..	..	3	..
Netherlands	1,972	1,635	337	22,831	194,393
Netherlands Antilles	..	..	..	5	..
New Zealand	2,039	82	1,957	1,236	33,331
Niger (b)	n.a.	n.a.	n.a.	102	..
Nigeria	842	200	642	204	..
North Macedonia	..	..	..	5	..
Norway	1,548	545	1,003	3,705	37,434
Oman	..	..	..	3	..
Pakistan	265	16	249	35	1,835
Panama	147	2	145	33	1,338
Paraguay	13	..	..	15	347
Patent Office of the Cooperation Council for the Arab States of the Gulf	2,660	353	2,307	n.a.	7,350
Peru	625	30	595	54	3,098
Philippines	3,435	33	3,402	141	23,405
Poland	2,980	2,906	74	3,973	82,618
Portugal	69	61	8	503	38,193
Qatar	..	..	..	73	..
Republic of Korea	119,012	89,227	29,785	131,912	1,001,163
Republic of Moldova	79	47	32	78	324
Romania	363	356	7	521	22,732
Russian Federation	35,774	20,526	15,248	23,627	256,419
Rwanda	..	..	..	..	309
Saint Kitts and Nevis	..	..	..	7	..

Name	Total	Grants by office		Equivalent grants by origin Total [a]	In force by office Total
		Resident	Non-resident		
Saint Vincent and the Grenadines	8	0	8	1	8
Samoa	..	..	..	30	52
San Marino	686	11	675	48	..
Sao Tome and Principe	8	0	8	..	19
Saudi Arabia	569	123	446	3,488	3,383
Serbia	44	36	8	424	5,685
Seychelles	11	0	11	60	209
Sierra Leone	..	..	..	1	..
Singapore	5,172	312	4,860	3,337	48,105
Slovakia	109	86	23	221	19,247
Slovenia	232	222	10	534	1,343
South Africa	4,746	451	4,295	1,443	73,270
Spain	1,760	1,638	122	6,271	81,957
Sri Lanka	212	64	148	75	850
Sudan	204	180	24	181	204
Sweden	1,063	885	178	16,787	100,974
Switzerland	614	420	194	26,109	244,581
Syrian Arab Republic	37	25	12	26	..
Tajikistan	..	..	..	32	..
Thailand	3,818	128	3,690	348	15,696
Togo (b)	n.a.	n.a.	n.a.	68	..
Trinidad and Tobago	26	1	25	10	..
Tunisia	451	..	..	6	..
Turkey	2,882	2,597	285	3,703	75,363
Turkmenistan	..	..	..	1	..
Uganda	2	2	0	2	..
Ukraine	2,469	1,203	1,266	1,498	22,977
United Arab Emirates	451	1	450	320	1,302
United Kingdom	5,982	3,005	2,977	26,442	572,063
United Republic of Tanzania	6	6	0	24	..
United States of America	307,759	144,413	163,346	289,082	3,063,494
Uruguay	..	..	..	34	..
Uzbekistan	219	149	70	164	966
Vanuatu	..	..	..	2	..
Venezuela (Bolivarian Republic of)	..	..	..	16	..
Viet Nam	2,219	205	2,014	248	12,965
Yemen	8	1	7	9	35
Zambia	..	..	..	1	..
Zimbabwe	..	..	..	1	..
Others/Unknown	..	..	..	19,262	..
Total (2018 estimates)	1,422,800	875,200	547,600	n.a.	13,950,543

(a) Equivalent grants by origin data are incomplete because some offices do not report by origin.
(b) The African Intellectual Property Organization (OAPI) acts as the national office for patent grants.
.. indicates not available.
n.a. indicates not applicable.
Source: WIPO Statistics Database, August 2019.

A60. Patent office procedural data, 2018

Office	Total applications processed	Granted	Rejected	Withdrawn or abandoned	Number of examiners (FTE)	First office action (months)	Final office decision (months)
Albania	..	826	8	..	1.0	2.5	12.0
Algeria	430	169	80	181	4.0	14.0	48.0
Argentina	4,750	1,608	256	2,886	63.0	..	..
Armenia	100	88	4	8	8.0	1.4	3.2
Australia	23,410	17,065	31	6,314	358.2	8.0	19.6
Azerbaijan	146	85	7	54	17.0	13.0	17.0
Bahrain	..	15	..	49	5.0	..	..
Bangladesh	344	138	204	2	10.0	10.0	20.5
Belarus	784	590	188	6	14.0	15.0	19.0
Belize	..	..	..	..	1.0	..	..
Bosnia and Herzegovina	..	..	..	..	7.0	2.0	30.0
Brazil	15,908	9,968	5,081	859	323.0	80.4	86.4
Brunei Darussalam	..	..	..	..	3.0	..	..
Cambodia	..	..	..	..	4.0	..	..
Canada	..	23,499	..	13,040	340.8	10.6	26.3
China	..	..	..	..	..	15.4	22.5
China, Macao SAR	..	29	35	..	..	5.0	11.9
Colombia	2,071	1,271	230	570	49.0	7.1	13.9
Costa Rica	674	168	176	330	21.0	48.0	60.0
Croatia	54	21	25	8	6.0	41.0	66.0
Cuba	158	93	3	62	13.0	24.0	32.0
Czech Republic	1,144	512	261	371	32.0	..	..
Denmark	2,057	322	3	1,732	65.4	5.5	22.6
Dominica	..	..	..	..	1.0	..	..
Ecuador	745	17	693	35	4.0	24.0	60.0
Egypt	825	594	46	185	100.0	6.0	18.0
El Salvador	..	..	..	..	2.0	24.0	36.0
Estonia	42	15	7	20	9.0	10.1	23.6
Ethiopia	..	..	..	..	25.0	..	..
European Patent Office	..	127,603	..	..	4,276.0	4.4	22.3
Finland	1,475	533	10	932	116.0	6.7	27.6
Georgia	260	133	32	95	18.0	15.0	21.0
Germany	38,087	16,367	8,375	13,345	704.3	..	..
Greece	..	..	..	..	7.0	..	..
Guyana	..	..	..	..	1.0	..	..
Honduras	325	102	115	108	4.0	1.0	36.0
Hungary	756	156	40	560	46.0	6.0	20.0
Iceland	..	16	..	19	..	4.0	84.0
India	48,755	14,130	2,325	32,300	521.0	36.0	52.0
Iran (Islamic Republic of)	1,772	1,116	88	568	..	..	..
Japan	238,482	177,852	56,701	3,929	1,690.0	9.3	14.1
Jordan	366	195	167	4	6.0	12.0	24.0
Kuwait	..	..	..	..	13.0	..	..
Latvia	78	51	15	12	6.0	..	..
Lithuania	105	98	2	5	5.0	1.0	5.0
Madagascar	..	31	..	6	2.0	30.0	30.0
Mexico	13,310	8,904	79	4,327	129.0	3.0	36.0
Monaco	..	28	4	..	2.0	4.0	7.0
Mongolia	120	76	17	27	3.0	..	..
Montenegro	..	239	..	2	3.0	2.0	20.0
Morocco	1,226	650	347	229	15.0	7.9	22.0

Office	Total applications processed	Granted	Rejected	Withdrawn or abandoned	Number of examiners (FTE)	First office action (months)	Final office decision (months)
Namibia	..	..	..	..	1.0	..	..
New Zealand	..	1,740	..	1,388	46.0	4.7	15.9
Nigeria	..	..	..	..	4.0	..	..
Norway	3,343	1,548	8	1,787	76.0	6.5	26.7
Pakistan	..	265	..	30	9.0	18.0	36.0
Panama	..	..	..	..	4.0	..	..
Patent Office of the Cooperation Council for the Arab States of the Gulf	2,812	2,660	143	9	35.0	12.9	41.8
Peru	..	1,255	359	..	29.0	22.4	35.6
Philippines	5,152	2,682	12	2,458	107.0	6.1	48.0
Poland	5,243	3,240	1,273	730	79.0	0.1	34.0
Portugal	154	60	87	7	19.0	..	32.5
Republic of Korea	165,902	106,716	55,631	3,555	875.0	10.3	15.8
Republic of Moldova	129	69	26	34	15.0	4.0	12.0
Romania	929	363	287	279	34.0	35.0	50.0
Russian Federation	45,405	34,756	1,951	8,698	649.0	7.1	8.1
Rwanda	..	..	..	..	1.0	..	..
Saint Vincent and the Grenadines	12	8	1	3	2.0	6.0	6.0
Samoa	..	..	..	..	..	3.0	12.0
Sao Tome and Principe	..	..	..	..	4.0	..	..
Saudi Arabia	2,090	569	998	523	55.0	21.0	26.0
Serbia	200	44	48	108	13.0	12.0	18.0
Seychelles	..	..	..	..	5.0	..	..
Slovakia	259	109	55	95	25.0	..	..
Spain	11,291	9,557	534	1,200	173.0	1.1	9.6
Sri Lanka	1,015	212	787	16	8.0	0.5	24.0
Sudan	..	204	18	..	16.0	..	..
Sweden	2,442	1,063	28	1,351	120.3	7.9	30.3
Thailand	10,536	3,818	471	6,247	120.0	39.0	49.0
Trinidad and Tobago	..	..	..	..	6.0	..	..
Turkey	3,784	3,496	250	38	112.0	4.8	18.2
Uganda	..	2	..	..	2.0	15.0	18.0
Ukraine	3,522	2,507	172	843	108.0	11.9	15.3
United Arab Emirates	..	451	..	..	13.0	38.7	..
United Kingdom	..	5,982	18,386	..	305.0	15.0	39.0
United Republic of Tanzania	..	6	2	..	2.0	1.0	6.0
United States of America	897,281	307,757	466,070	123,454	7,984.0	15.4	21.8
Uzbekistan	787	341	342	104	9.0	..	..
Viet Nam	203	69	70	64	62.0	33.6	47.9

Note: FTE is full time equivalent. Grant data differ slightly from grant data reported elsewhere in this report due to different dates of extraction. Every effort has been made to compile procedural data based on common definitions and concepts, but procedural differences make it extremely difficult to fully harmonize such data. For instance, "rejection" is not recorded as a final decision in Canada. Applicants are informed of the action that they must take or questions that they must answer in order for their application to be considered, and if an applicant cannot provide the required information, they are regarded as having abandoned the application. A similar situation exists in Australia.

.. indicates not available.

Source: WIPO Statistics Database, August 2019.

A61. Utility model applications and grants by office and origin, 2018

Name	Applications by office			Equivalent applications by origin	Grants by office		
	Total	Resident	Non-resident	Total [a]	Total	Resident	Non-resident
African Regional Intellectual Property Organization	42	25	17	n.a.	2	1	1
Albania	2	1	1	1	2	1	1
Algeria	..	..	..	1	..	..	..
Andorra	..	..	..	3	..	..	..
Argentina	192	161	31	190	82	67	15
Armenia	36	34	2	36	35	34	1
Australia	2,257	1,133	1,124	1,230	2,023	1,072	951
Austria	537	380	157	748	521	369	152
Azerbaijan	42	33	9	33	16	15	1
Barbados	..	..	..	10	..	..	..
Belarus	372	285	87	367	293	242	51
Belgium	..	..	..	122	..	..	..
Belize	1	1	0	1	..	..	..
Bolivia (Plurinational State of)	..	..	..	1	..	..	..
Bosnia and Herzegovina	..	..	..	1	..	..	..
Botswana	12	12	0	12	6	6	0
Brazil	2,587	2,493	94	2,537	1,098	1,052	46
Bulgaria	..	..	..	9	..	..	..
Cambodia	13	0	13	..	3	0	3
Canada	..	..	..	91	..	..	..
Chile	139	113	26	151	72	52	20
China	2,072,311	2,063,860	8,451	2,066,904	1,479,062	1,471,759	7,303
China, Hong Kong SAR	791	536	255	618	763	485	278
China, Macao SAR	28	7	21	70	2	0	2
Colombia	188	166	22	179	..	..	..
Costa Rica	20	17	3	40	6	3	3
Croatia	70	66	4	67	50	48	2
Cuba	3	1	2	1	..	..	..
Cyprus	..	..	..	244	..	..	..
Czech Republic	1,247	1,179	68	1,381	1,130	1,081	49
Democratic People's Republic of Korea	..	..	..	1	..	..	..
Denmark	92	70	22	129	108	78	30
Dominican Republic	21	12	9	12	11	7	4
Ecuador	46	42	4	45	6	2	4
Egypt	..	..	..	1	..	..	..
El Salvador	4	3	1	3	2	2	0
Estonia	31	28	3	45	30	28	2
Eswatini	..	..	..	1	..	..	..
Ethiopia	392	392	0	392	41	41	0
Fiji	..	..	..	4	..	..	..
Finland	400	370	30	572	368	340	28
France	608	341	267	835	..	..	..
Gambia	2	2	0	2	2	2	0
Georgia	55	51	4	51	42	38	4
Germany	12,307	8,800	3,507	9,967	11,295	7,765	3,530
Ghana	2	2	0	2	..	..	..

Name	Applications by office			Equivalent applications by origin	Grants by office		
	Total	Resident	Non-resident	Total [a]	Total	Resident	Non-resident
Greece	22	13	9	17	19	16	3
Guatemala	13	12	1	12	4	3	1
Honduras	4	2	2	2	4	2	2
Hungary	226	205	21	228	96	84	12
Iceland	..	..	..	1	..	..	..
India	..	..	..	34	..	..	..
Indonesia	1,545	1,432	113	1,435	331	275	56
Iran (Islamic Republic of)	..	..	..	2	..	..	..
Ireland	533	117	416	142	35	27	8
Israel	..	..	..	118	..	..	..
Italy	1,966	1,781	185	2,192	1,420	1,395	25
Japan	5,388	3,810	1,578	6,395	1,507	827	680
Jordan	..	..	..	4	..	..	..
Kazakhstan	896	778	118	795	950	862	88
Kenya	178	177	1	177	32	32	0
Kuwait	..	..	..	1	..	..	..
Kyrgyzstan	..	..	..	..	22	19	3
Lao People's Democratic Republic	7	1	6	2	..	..	..
Latvia	..	..	..	8	..	..	..
Lebanon	..	..	..	2	..	..	..
Liberia	..	..	..	1	..	..	..
Liechtenstein	..	..	..	19	..	..	..
Lithuania	..	..	..	4	..	..	..
Luxembourg	..	..	..	41	..	..	..
Malaysia	198	132	66	168	95	58	37
Mali	..	..	..	2	..	..	..
Malta	..	..	..	5	..	..	..
Mexico	821	688	133	707	199	144	55
Monaco	..	..	..	1	..	..	..
Mongolia	224	224	0	224	152	152	0
Morocco	..	..	..	1	..	..	..
Mozambique	28	5	23	5	28	5	23
Netherlands	..	..	..	211	..	..	..
New Zealand	..	..	..	23	..	..	..
Norway	..	..	..	21	..	..	..
Oman	..	..	..	1	..	..	..
Pakistan	..	..	..	2	..	..	..
Panama	5	4	1	5	7	5	2
Peru	256	225	31	232	207	186	21
Philippines	2,347	2,272	75	2,279	1,224	1,147	77
Poland	1,022	943	79	1,009	816	769	47
Portugal	99	66	33	81	48	32	16
Republic of Korea	6,232	5,768	464	6,889	2,715	2,521	194
Republic of Moldova	122	117	5	123	106	105	1
Romania	60	41	19	41	40	28	12
Russian Federation	9,747	9,262	485	9,484	9,869	9,391	478

Patents

Name	Applications by office			Equivalent applications by origin	Grants by office		
	Total	Resident	Non-resident	Total [a]	Total	Resident	Non-resident
Rwanda	6	6	0	6	5	5	0
Samoa	1	1	0	12	1	1	0
Sao Tome and Principe	10	0	10	..	1	0	1
Saudi Arabia	..	..	..	9	..	..	..
Serbia	70	68	2	69	53	49	4
Seychelles	..	..	..	17	..	..	..
Singapore	..	..	..	763	..	..	..
Slovakia	388	320	68	365	337	262	75
Slovenia	..	..	..	5	..	..	..
South Africa	..	..	..	34	..	..	..
Spain	2,731	2,571	160	2,882	2,208	2,062	146
Sweden	..	..	..	109	..	..	..
Switzerland	..	..	..	483	..	..	..
Syrian Arab Republic	401	401	0	401	..	..	..
Thailand	2,969	2,832	137	2,889	1,372	1,248	124
Trinidad and Tobago	1	1	0	1	..	..	..
Turkey	2,770	2,698	72	2,741	335	307	28
Ukraine	9,120	8,980	140	9,134	8,620	8,471	149
United Arab Emirates	11	1	10	23	1	0	1
United Kingdom	..	..	..	263	..	..	..
United Republic of Tanzania	3	3	0	3	3	3	0
United States of America	..	..	..	2,799	..	..	..
Uruguay	..	..	..	6	..	..	..
Uzbekistan	206	200	6	201	82	81	1
Venezuela (Bolivarian Republic of)	..	..	..	1	..	..	..
Viet Nam	557	370	187	372	355	290	65
Yemen	..	..	..	1	..	..	..
Others/Unknown	..	..	..	2,188	..	..	..
Total (2018 estimates)	**2,145,960**	**2,127,450**	**18,510**	**n.a.**	**..**	**..**	**..**

(a) Equivalent applications by origin data are incomplete because some offices do not report by origin.

.. indicates not available.

n.a. indicates not applicable.

Source: WIPO Statistics Database, August 2019.

Trademarks

Highlights

Applications increased by 19.2% in 2018

An estimated 10.9 million trademark applications were filed worldwide in 2018 – about 1.7 million more than in 2017 – corresponding to growth of 19.2% (figure 2.1). This marks a ninth consecutive year of growth, but is almost 11 percentage points lower than the extraordinary increase of nearly 30% seen in 2017. There are now twice as many trademark applications filed than in 2014 due to the high annual growth rates recorded in recent years. In fact, seven of the last 15 years have seen double-digit growth, with only two in which the number of applications decreased over this period.

When differences in filing systems across national and regional offices are harmonized using the application class count, trademark filing activity in 2018 also saw a double-digit increase, up 15.5% on the previous year. The total number of classes specified in applications – known as the application class count – reached an estimated 14.3 million (figure 2.2). Excluding the high 2018 application class count for China, trademark filing activity grew by 4.5% in the rest of the world.

An estimated 10.9 million trademark applications were filed worldwide

2.1. Trademark applications worldwide, 2004–2018

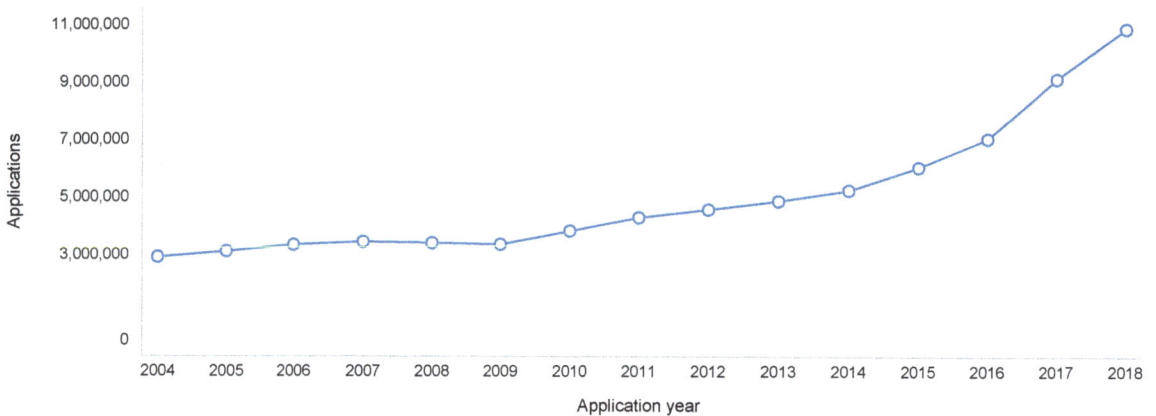

Source: Figure B1.

The total number of classes specified in trademark applications grew by 15.5%

2.2. Trademark application class counts worldwide, 2004–2018

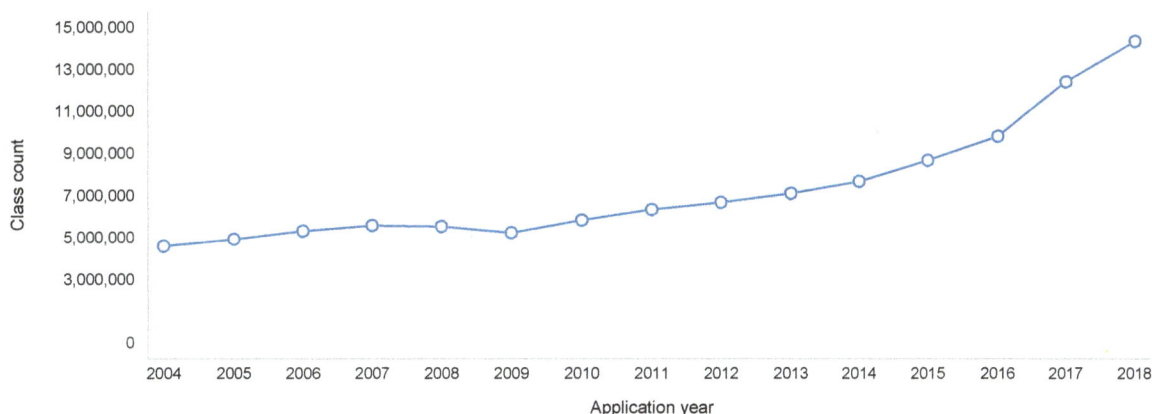

Source: Figure B2.

Class count

A trademark application may refer to different classes of goods or services. Many offices use the Nice Classification, an international classification of goods and services for registering trademarks and service marks. Applications received by these offices are classified in one or more of the 45 Nice classes (see *www.wipo.int/classifications/nice*). Some offices allow single-class filing only, meaning that applicants have to file a separate application for each class. Others permit multi-class filings, enabling applicants to file a single application in which a number of classes can be specified. To improve international comparisons of the numbers of applications received, it helps to compare class counts across offices. Class counts are also used to make trademark registration activity internationally comparable. This method for comparing offices began in 2004, the first year for which complete class count data are available.

Offices with the most filing activity

As with other forms of intellectual property (IP), the increase in trademark filing activity (measured in application class counts) largely reflects the strong growth in the number of trademark applications filed in China. In 2018, the trademark office of China accounted for 84.4% of the annual increase in global trademark filing activity using this measure. It was followed by the offices of India (3.1%) the Republic of Korea (1.7%), France (1.5%) and the United States of America (U.S.) (1.4%), each accounting for considerably smaller portions of total growth.

The office of China's class count of almost 7.4 million was followed by a count of 640,181 at the office of the U.S. (figure 2.3). These have been the two top offices since the early 2000s, but since 2006 China's class count has grown from about twice that of the U.S. to almost 12 times as much, due in large part to the high number of trademark applications filed by Chinese residents in China. These two offices were followed by that of Japan (512,156), the European Union Intellectual Property Office (EUIPO) (392,925) and that of the Islamic Republic of Iran (384,338). The top five offices in 2018 were the same as in 2017 and they accounted for almost 65% of all trademark filing activity, up from the 33% shared by the top five offices a decade earlier, in 2008.

Of the top 20 offices, 16 had higher levels of trademark filing activity in 2018 than in 2017, seven of which recorded growth exceeding 10%. The largest increases were in Indonesia (+29.1%) and China (+28.3%), followed by India (+20.9%), the Republic of Korea (+14.5%) and the United Kingdom (U.K.) (+12.4%). In contrast, the offices of the Russian Federation (–9.7%) and Japan (–8.6%) saw the two largest annual decreases, while the offices of Germany (–2.6%) and Turkey (–1.2%) recorded smaller declines (figure B11).

For offices located in selected low- and middle-income countries, annual growth was particularly high in South Africa (+46.8%) – rebounding from a considerable decrease in 2017 – Suriname (+34.6%), Angola (+23.6%) and Ecuador (+23.5%) (figure B13). The office of Algeria, however, witnessed a double-digit decrease of 10.3% in trademark filing activity from 2017 to 2018, while those of Argentina (–4.0%) and Pakistan (–1.2%) saw lesser decreases.

At most offices, trademark applications are filed mainly by residents seeking protection within their domestic

Non-resident applicants accounted for 30.4% of total trademark filing activity in the U.S.

2.3. Trademark application class counts for the top 10 offices, 2018

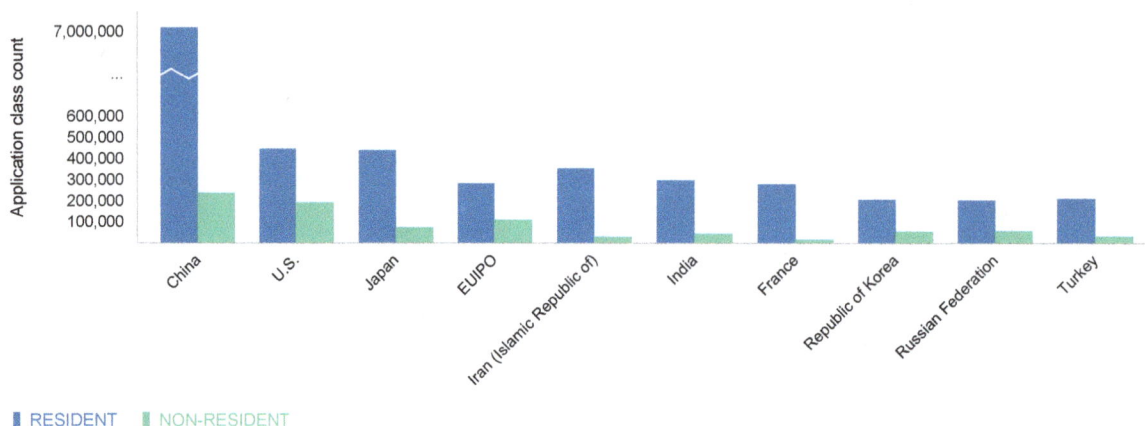

RESIDENT ■ NON-RESIDENT

Source: Figure B10.

jurisdiction. In 2018, residents accounted for 83.8% of global filing activity. In fact, domestic filing is becoming an increasingly pronounced share of total filing activity, with the world resident application class count in 2018 having increased by 16.6% on the previous year's total. The increase in the application class count for non-residents of 10.8% was less strong in comparison.

Due largely to the high number of resident trademark applications filed in China, the global non-resident share of filing activity declined by about 17 percentage points, from a peak of 33.1% in 2004 to 16.2% in 2018. However, when the figures for China are excluded, the non-resident share fell by only around six percentage points over this period.

Five of the top 20 offices received a third or more of their total filing activity from non-residents, with Australia (43.3%), Canada (43.3%), Indonesia (33.3%), Switzerland (56.8%) and Viet Nam (35.5%) recording the highest shares. The lowest non-resident shares were recorded at the offices of China (3.2%), France (6.4%) and the Islamic Republic of Iran (7.8%). The low non-resident shares for France and other European Union (EU) member state offices, such as those of Germany and Italy, can be explained by the fact that many non-resident applicants file for protection in these countries via the EUIPO.

Resident filing activity overwhelmingly drove the double-digit growth in China, France, India and the Republic of Korea in 2018, whereas non-resident fil-

ing activity accounted for most of the total growth in Australia, Indonesia, Mexico and the U.K. (figure B11). In Germany, Japan, the Russian Federation and Turkey, declines in total filing activity can be attributed entirely to a drop in resident applications.

The list of top 20 offices in 2018 is largely similar to that for 2017, but ranked somewhat differently. In addition, the office of Indonesia's high growth rate propelled it from 24th position in 2017 up to the 20th spot in 2018. The Republic of Korea moved up two places to rank 8th in terms of trademark filing activity. In contrast, the Russian Federation saw its ranking slip from 6th in 2017 to 9th in 2018, as France and India each moved up one spot from their previous year's rankings.

Total application class counts at offices of high-income economies grew by 3% between 2008 and 2018. This is lower than the average annual growth rates for all other income groups. The highest growth (+16.9%) over this 11-year period was recorded for offices of upper middle-income countries. Offices of lower middle-income (+6%) and low-income (+3.8%) countries also saw growth over the same period.

Eleven of the top 20 offices are in high-income economies, six are in upper middle-income countries (Brazil, China, the Islamic Republic of Iran, Mexico, the Russian Federation and Turkey) and three are in lower middle-income countries (India, Indonesia and Viet Nam). In 2018, the offices of high-income countries together received 27.7% of total global filing activity, down

The share for offices of high-income countries declined from 53.6% in 2008 to 27.7% in 2018

2.4. Trademark application class counts by income group, 2008 and 2018

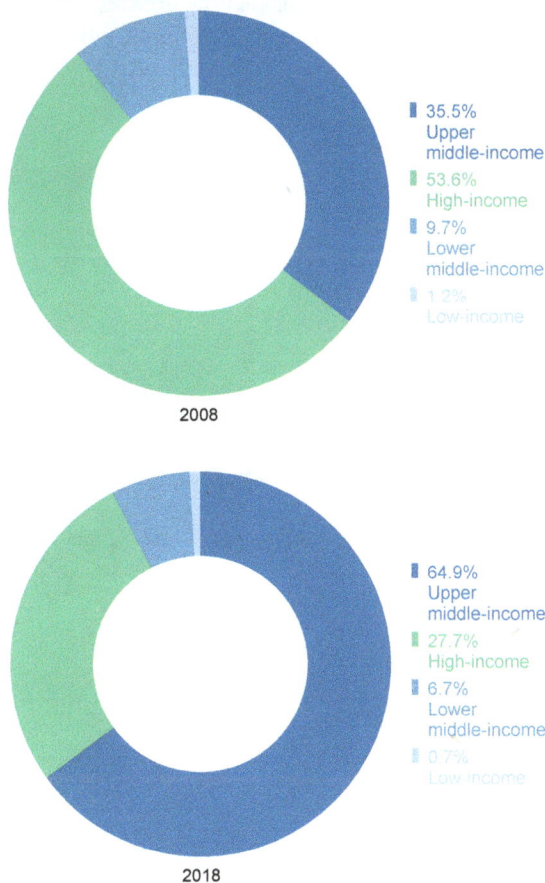

- 35.5% Upper middle-income
- 53.6% High-income
- 9.7% Lower middle-income
- 1.2% Low-income

2008

- 64.9% Upper middle-income
- 27.7% High-income
- 6.7% Lower middle-income
- 0.7% Low-income

2018

Source: Table B7.

Offices located in Asia accounted for 70% of all trademark filing activity in 2018

2.5. Trademark application class counts by region, 2008 and 2018

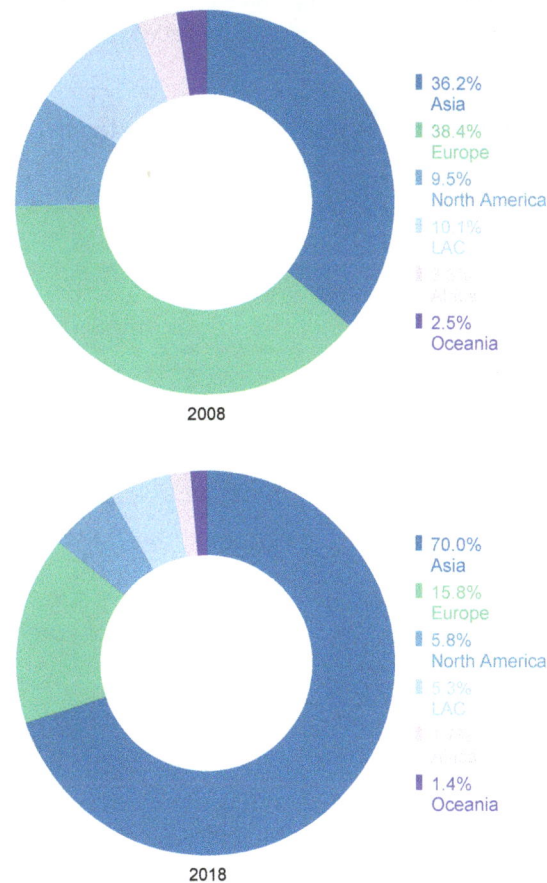

- 36.2% Asia
- 38.4% Europe
- 9.5% North America
- 10.1% LAC
- 2.5% Oceania

2008

- 70.0% Asia
- 15.8% Europe
- 5.8% North America
- 5.3% LAC
- 1.4% Oceania

2018

Source: Table B8.

from 53.6% in 2008. In contrast, the share for offices of upper middle-income countries rose from 35.5% in 2008 to 64.9% in 2018, due to a combined high average annual growth rate (figure 2.4). When China's statistics are removed from the upper middle-income group, the application class count for the other countries in this group still grew between 2008 and 2018, but at a lower rate of 4.3%. However, the combined share of the world total claimed by this group of upper middle-income countries actually decreased from 23% to 13.5% over this period. The shares of total filing activity for lower middle-income (6.7% in 2018) and low-income countries (0.7%) also fell between 2008 and 2018, albeit to a lesser extent.

Eight of the top 20 offices in 2018 were located in Asia, seven in Europe, two each in Latin America and the Caribbean (LAC) and North America, and one in Oceania. Offices in Asia accounted for 70% of all trademark filing activity, almost double their share of 36.2% in 2008. This partly explains the decline in overall shares for the other five geographical regions over the same period (figure 2.5). Offices in Europe accounted for 15.8% of the world total in 2018, followed by North America (5.8%), LAC (5.3%), Africa (1.7%) and Oceania (1.4%).

77

Trademark filings since 1883

Trademark filings were fairly low and stable up until the mid-1980s. Filings at China's office took off in the 1990s, and in 2001 exceeded those received by the U.S. office, making it the largest in terms of the number of applications received. Even so, filings at the U.S. office have more than doubled since the mid-1990s, despite declines in 2001 and 2002 at the end of the dot-com era and again during the financial crisis in 2008 and 2009. Having remained below 100,000 until 2006, India's trademark annual filings now exceed 320,000. Similar numbers of trademark applications are now filed in both Brazil and the Republic of Korea, where the volumes are around 200,000.

Trend in trademark applications for the top five offices, 1883–2018

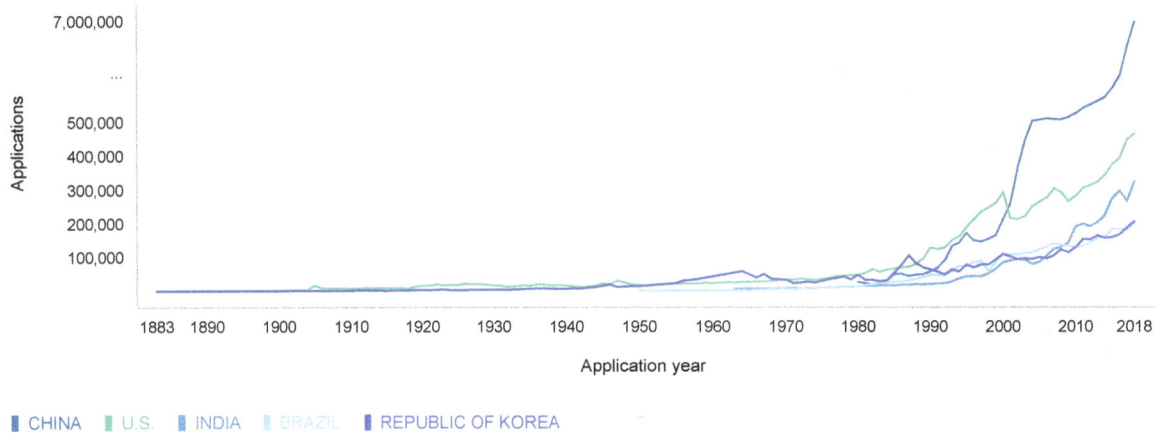

■ CHINA ■ U.S. ■ INDIA ■ BRAZIL ■ REPUBLIC OF KOREA

Source: Figure B9.

Trademark filing activity was concentrated in a few origins
2.6. Equivalent trademark application class counts by origin, 2018

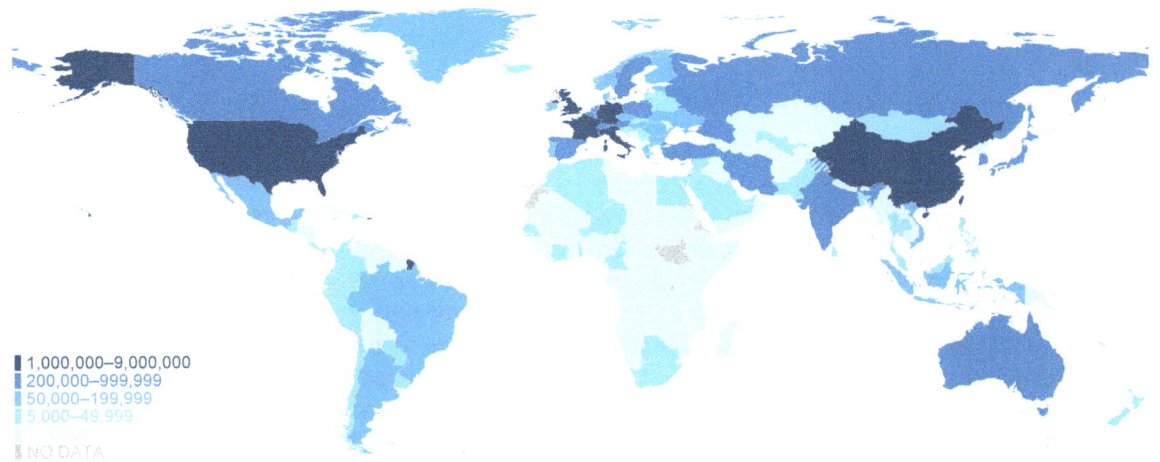

■ 1,000,000–9,000,000
■ 200,000–999,999
■ 50,000–199,999
■ 5,000–49,999

■ NO DATA

Source: Map B19.

Equivalent application class count

Applications at some regional IP offices are equivalent to multiple applications in the countries that are members of the organizations establishing those offices. For example, to calculate the number of equivalent applications for the EUIPO, each application is multiplied by the corresponding number of EU member states. So, an application filed with the EUIPO by an applicant residing outside the EU is counted as 28 applications abroad – equivalent to the 28 member countries of the EU in 2018. An application filed by an applicant residing in an EU country is counted as 1 resident application and 27 applications abroad. The same multiplier is applied to the classes specified in these applications. The equivalent application class count concept is used for reporting data by origin.

German applicants continue to file the greatest number of applications abroad

Trademark applications received by offices from resident and non-resident applicants are referred to as office data, whereas applications filed by applicants at a national/regional office (resident applications) or at foreign offices (applications abroad) are referred to as origin data. Here, trademark statistics based on the origin of the residence of the applicant are reported in order to complement the picture of trademark filing activity worldwide.

In terms of filing activity abroad based on equivalent class count, a greater number of applicants from Germany than from any other origin seek protection for their trademarks outside their country, a position Germany has held since 2006. In 2018, German filing activity abroad recorded an equivalent application class count of about 2.1 million, followed by applicants from the U.S. (1.3 million), the U.K. (1 million) and China (990,944) (figure B22).[1] The high equivalent class counts for applications abroad from these origins can be explained not only by their high application class counts at numerous offices abroad, but also by their frequent use of the EUIPO – with its multiplier effect – to seek protection within the EU as a whole.

Looking at absolute counts – and so removing the EUIPO's multiplier effect – 96% of all filing activity (application class counts) by China-based applicants was in China alone, with only 4% attributed to those seeking protection abroad. The shares for resident filing – between 70% and 76% – and filing abroad – between 24% and 30% – were similar for applicants from Canada, France, the Republic of Korea and Spain. However, applicants residing in many low- and middle-income countries, such as Argentina, Egypt, India and Romania, dedicated less than 10% of their trademark filing activity to seeking protection abroad. For applicants based in the Islamic Republic of Iran, only 0.3% of their total filing activity was directed abroad.

Among the top 20 origins, about 73% of filing activity by Switzerland-based applicants occurred outside the country. This top ranking share of applications abroad as a proportion of total filing activity was followed by that of applicants from the U.S. (46%), Germany (43%) and the U.K. (42%).

Between a quarter and half of all trademark filing activity by applicants from the middle-income countries Armenia (26%), Bulgaria (38%), Malaysia (27%) and Mauritius (48%) occurred abroad. For middle-income countries Colombia, El Salvador and South Africa, this share was only 10–14%.

When deciding where to seek trademark protection, applicants consider such factors as the appeal of various foreign markets in which to sell their goods and services, geographical proximity to these markets or well-established historical ties between the trademark holder's country of residence and the destination country. For example, 19% of all non-resident filing activity in India in 2018 came from U.S. applicants, followed by 13% from China and 11% from Germany (figure 2.7). Applicants from China (29%) and the U.K. (9%) accounted for the largest shares of non-resident trademark filing activity in the U.S., followed by applicants from Canada (8%). In China, the three origins that accounted for the largest shares of non-resident filing activity were the U.S. (21%), Japan (11%) and the Republic of Korea (8%). For non-resident filing activity at the EUIPO, applicants from the U.S. (31%), China (22%) and Switzerland (11%) constituted the largest shares.

In addition to being the most active foreign filers in the U.S., applicants from China were also the most active foreign filers at the IP offices of France, Germany, Indonesia, Italy, Spain, Thailand and Viet Nam, accounting for between 16% and 29% of application class counts in filings received by these offices from abroad.

Adjusting for GDP and population

Differences in trademark filing activity across countries may reflect both the size of their economies and their level of economic development. To compare trademark filing intensity across countries, it helps to measure resident application class counts relative to GDP or population level.

When resident trademark applications are viewed as class counts and adjusted by GDP, countries with a relatively lower number of classes specified in resident applications, such as Australia, Portugal and Switzerland, may rank higher than some countries that otherwise show higher class counts (for example, Germany, India and the U.S.). Of selected origins, China (31,615), Portugal (11,193), the Republic of Korea (10,951), Turkey (10,142), Switzerland (8,250) and Australia (7,365) exhibited among the highest ratios of resident application class count to GDP in 2018 (figure 2.8). China (+25,989), the U.K. (+2,665) and Portugal (+2,304) saw particularly large increases in resident application class count per unit of GDP between 2008 and 2018. In contrast, Finland (–1,794), Sweden (–1,659) and Germany (–1,138) saw, among selected origins, the largest decreases in their class count to GDP ratio over the same period.

The data reflecting application class count per million population show that China, with a population of about 1.4 billion, has a resident application class count of 5,117 per million population – one of the most intensive among all countries of origin in 2018. Switzerland, with a population of only 8.5 million, had a comparable resident application class count of 4,869 per million population. Among other selected origins, the resident application class count per million population exceeded 4,000 for the Republic of Korea (4,027) and was between 2,000 and 3,000 for the Czech Republic (2,165), the Netherlands (2,795) and the U.K. (2,600). Chile, Paraguay, the Russian Federation and the U.S. each had ratios of about 1,300–1,800, while the ratios for Egypt, India and Thailand were each between 200 and 500 (figure B34).

Which classes and industries saw the most filing activity by applicants filing abroad?

Trademarks are registered in relation to particular classes of goods or services. The Nice Classification of goods and services is used in the international trademark system and at certain national and regional offices. Nice Classification statistics offer insights into the relative importance of different goods and services. In 2018, goods class 9, which includes scientific, photographic, measuring instruments, recording equipment, computers and software, was represented in 11.5% of all reported non-resident trademark filing activity by class. Nice class 9 is followed by services class 35 (7.6%), which covers advertising, business management, business administration and office functions; services class 42 (5.7%),

Applicants from the U.S. were the most active foreign filers in Brazil, China, India and at the EUIPO

2.7. Share of total non-resident filing activity by origin at selected offices, 2018

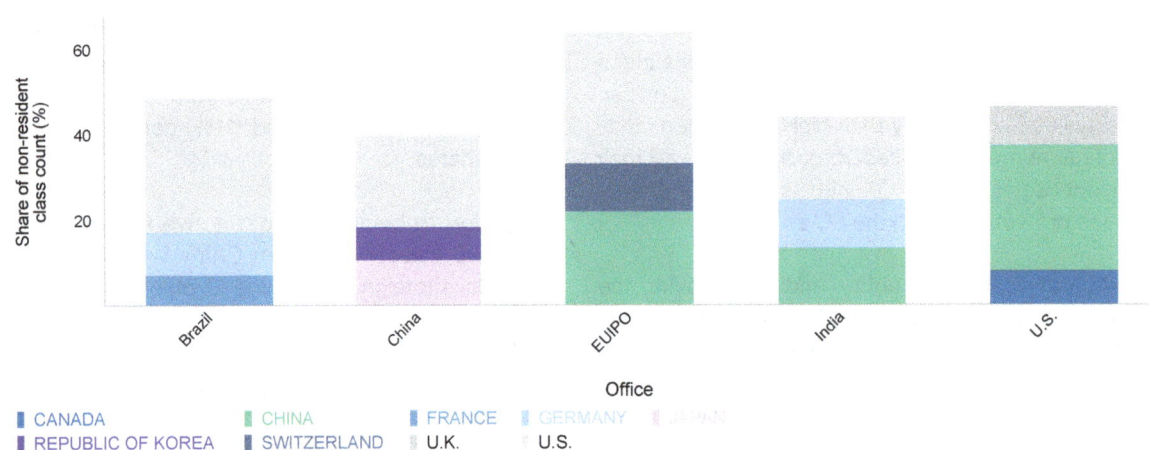

Source: Figure B25.

which includes scientific and technological services, design and development of computer hardware and software; and goods class 5 (5.3%), which relates to pharmaceutical preparations, baby food, dietary supplements for humans and animals, disinfectants, fungicides and herbicides (figure B26).

The 11 service-related classes accounted for 31.1% of all Nice classes specified in applications filed abroad in 2018, up from 24.2% in 2004. Services classes accounted for between 29% and 35% of all filing activity in Canada, India and Indonesia, and over 50% at the offices of Brazil, France and Japan.

It is useful to group the 45 Nice classes into 10 industry sectors. Research and technology, health, clothing and accessories, and agriculture were the top four sectors for applicants seeking trademark protection abroad in 2018, each accounting for between 11% and about 20% of global reported non-resident trademark filing activity. In contrast, industries relating to chemicals (3.2%) and construction (5.7%) accounted for the smallest shares of filing activity abroad (figure B28). Research and technology was the top sector at the EUIPO (21%), and at the offices of France (19%), Germany (18%), Japan (25%) and the U.S. (20%) (figure B29). Agriculture was the top sector in the Islamic Republic of Iran (21%), the Republic of Korea (19%) and the Russian Federation (16%). Filing activity for marks relating to health saw the largest share of applications filed in India (24%). In Turkey, business

services topped the list of industry sectors, accounting for 21% of all trademark filing activity. The business services sector was among the top three at eight of the top 10 offices. Only the office of the Islamic Republic of Iran (19%) included the transportation sector among its top three sectors.

A total of 7.7 million trademark registrations were recorded worldwide in 2018

After concluding the examination process, an office may decide to register a trademark. The number of registrations issued can fluctuate greatly from year to year, due in part to the resources dedicated by offices to examining trademark applications. For this reason, it is not possible to accurately compare the number of applications filed at an office in any given year with the number of registrations issued by that office in the same year.

The estimated 7.7 million trademark registrations recorded worldwide in 2018 represents an increase of 41.8%, or about 2.3 million additional registrations, on the previous year's total.

Just as class counts make application activity internationally comparable, they also permit a more meaningful comparison of registrations. In 2018, an estimated 10.1 million classes were specified in trademark registra-

Brazil, China, Portugal, the Russian Federation and the U.K. saw large increases in resident application class count per unit of GDP between 2008 and 2018

2.8. Resident trademark application class count per USD 100 billion GDP for selected origins, 2008 and 2018

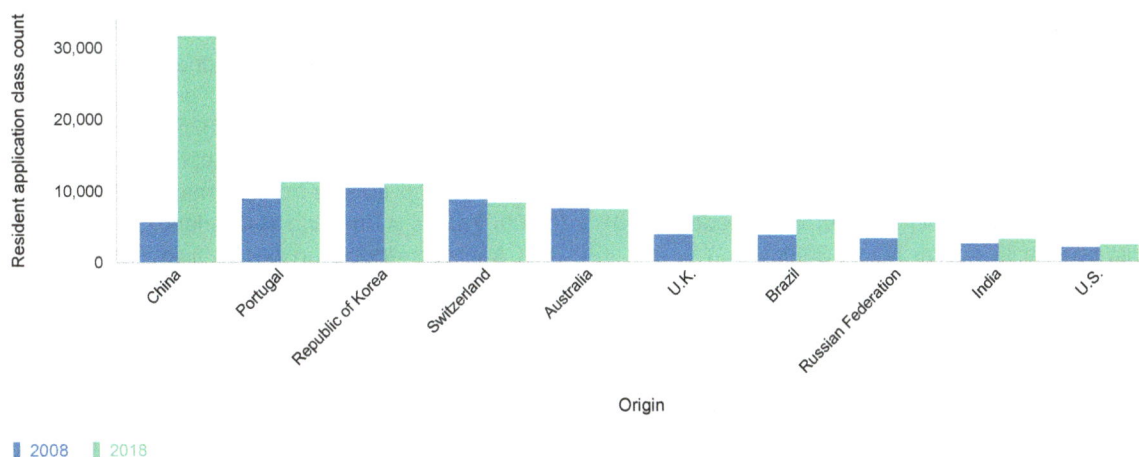

■ 2008 ■ 2018

Source: Figure B33.

tions. The 32.6% growth recorded in 2018 is more than twice the 16.1% increase in 2017. China's office saw growth of 77.3% in trademark registration activity in 2018, accounting for 88% of the total global annual increase.

China's office registered trademarks in which about 5 million classes were specified, or almost half of the worldwide total, followed by the offices of the U.S. (384,716), India (359,793) and the EUIPO (345,379) (figure B17).

Along with the high annual growth in China, several other offices among the top 20 experienced large increases in registration activity, including Italy (+70.7%), Brazil (+55.5%), the Russian Federation (+18.5%) and the U.K. (+13.5%). In contrast, the office of Canada (−20.4%) and the Benelux Office for Intellectual Property (BOIP) (−10.3%) saw the most significant declines among the top 20.

Active trademarks increased by 13.8%

Unlike most forms of IP, trademarks can be maintained indefinitely by the payment of renewal fees at defined time intervals. In 2018, there were an estimated 49.3 million active trademark registrations at 143 IP offices worldwide, representing an increase of 13.8% on 2017 figures.

Once again, the office of China accounted for the greatest number of trademark registrations in force in 2018, with about 19.6 million – a 31.1% increase on its 2017 total. It was followed by the offices of the U.S., with almost 2.4 million, and India and Japan, with approximately 1.9 million each. Reporting between 1 and 1.4 million trademark registrations in force, the EUIPO and each of the offices of Brazil, Mexico, the Republic of Korea and Turkey also recorded high numbers of active trademarks. The BOIP (623,195) – representing the Benelux countries of Belgium, the Netherlands and Luxembourg – had almost the same number of trademark registrations in force as the Russian Federation (623,712), while Australia (591,880) and Canada (581,561) also had similar figures (figure B38).

About 15.4 million trademark registrations in force at 69 offices in 2018 can be distributed according to the year in which they were initially registered. This represents 58% of a total of approximately 26.6 million trademark registrations recorded at these offices between 1994 and 2018.

About one-fifth of those trademarks registered in 1994 remained in force in 2018, a testimony to the enduring value of marks. For those registered in 2009 and later, the percentage rises above 60%. Almost half of the 15.4 million registrations in force have a recent registration date, dating back only to 2013.

Demand for Madrid international trademark registrations continues to grow

To obtain trademark protection in multiple countries or jurisdictions, applicants can either file their applications directly at each individual office – known as the "Paris route" – or file an application for international registration through the Madrid System – the "Madrid route" (see the glossary). In 2018, the Madrid System offered trademark holders the ability to obtain protection for their branded products and services in an area covering a total of 119 countries. Combined, Madrid members represent about 60% of all countries, home to over 70% of the world's population, and in which just over 80% of global GDP occurs, with the potential to increase these shares as membership grows.

Applicants filed a record-setting estimated 61,200 international trademark applications[2] under the WIPO-administered Madrid System in 2018 (figure B47). The resultant 6.4% increase represents a ninth year of uninterrupted expansion. Strong growth in Madrid applications from Japan (+22.8%), the U.S. (+11.9%) and China (+7.9%) drove this increase. The rise in filings from applicants based in the U.S. alone accounted for a quarter (25 percentage points) of total growth, while those for Japan (16) and China (14) each contributed a similar share to total growth.

For a fifth consecutive year, applicants based in the U.S. filed the largest number of international applications via the Madrid System. A strong year-on-year growth of 11.9% resulted in an estimated 8,825 Madrid applications being filed by U.S.-based applicants. This was followed by applications from Germany (7,495), China (6,900), France (4,490) and Switzerland (3,364) (figure B49). Applicants located in the U.S. filed over 900 more Madrid applications in 2018 than in 2017, increasing the gap between that country and Germany and consolidating the U.S.'s top spot among the largest origins of Madrid applications. For comparison, applicants in China filed around 500 more Madrid applications than in the previous year, while for those based in Germany, the year-on-year increase was approximately 175.

For the second year in a row, the EU (25,030) attracted the highest number of designations in Madrid applications in 2018, followed by China (24,289) and the U.S. (22,827) (figure B50). This shows that Madrid applicants sought to extend protection for their marks to the 28 EU member countries as a whole more than they did to any other Madrid member jurisdiction. Like China, half of the top 20 designated Madrid members were middle-income countries, notably the Russian Federation (15,627), India (12,254), Mexico (10,080) and Turkey (8,881). Among top destinations for international trademark registration via the Madrid System, the U.K. saw the largest surge in annual growth of 21.9%, albeit lower than its extraordinary increase of 60.6% from 2016 to 2017. For further information and statistics, see WIPO's *Madrid Yearly Review 2019*.

Trademarks

1. Equivalent application class counts differ from absolute class counts, which are presented in figure B20, and do not take into the account the multiplying effect of regional offices.
2. Because of the time lag in transmittal of applications from offices of origin to the International Bureau (IB) of WIPO, Madrid applications are estimated.

Trademark statistics

Trademarks

Trademarks

Trademark applications and registrations worldwide

B1. Trend in trademark applications worldwide, 2004–2018

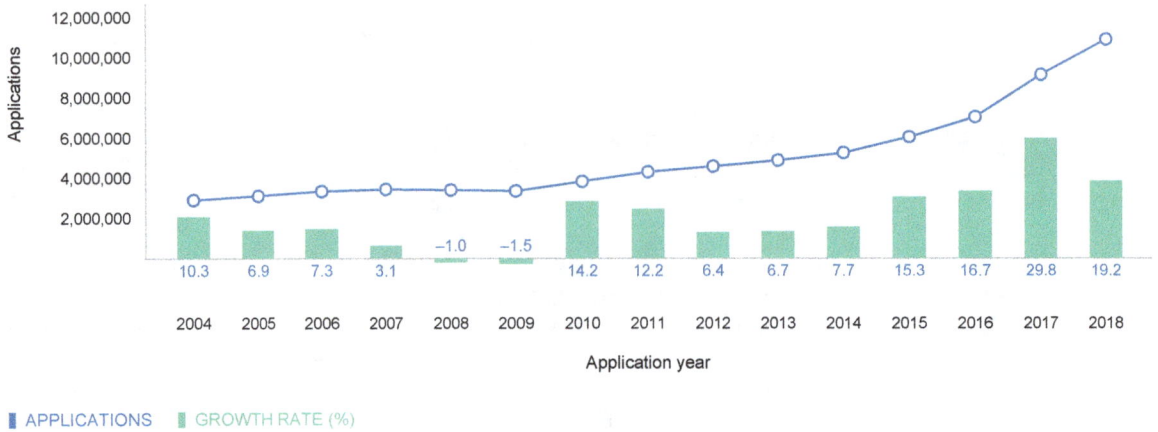

	2004	2005	2006	2007	2008	2009	2010	2011	2012	2013	2014	2015	2016	2017	2018
Growth rate (%)	10.3	6.9	7.3	3.1	−1.0	−1.5	14.2	12.2	6.4	6.7	7.7	15.3	16.7	29.8	19.2

Application year

▌ APPLICATIONS ▌ GROWTH RATE (%)

Note: World totals are WIPO estimates using data covering 169 IP offices. Each total includes the number of applications filed directly with national and regional offices (the "Paris route") as well as the number of designations received by offices via the Madrid System (where applicable).

Source: WIPO Statistics Database, August 2019.

B2. Trend in trademark application class counts worldwide, 2004–2018

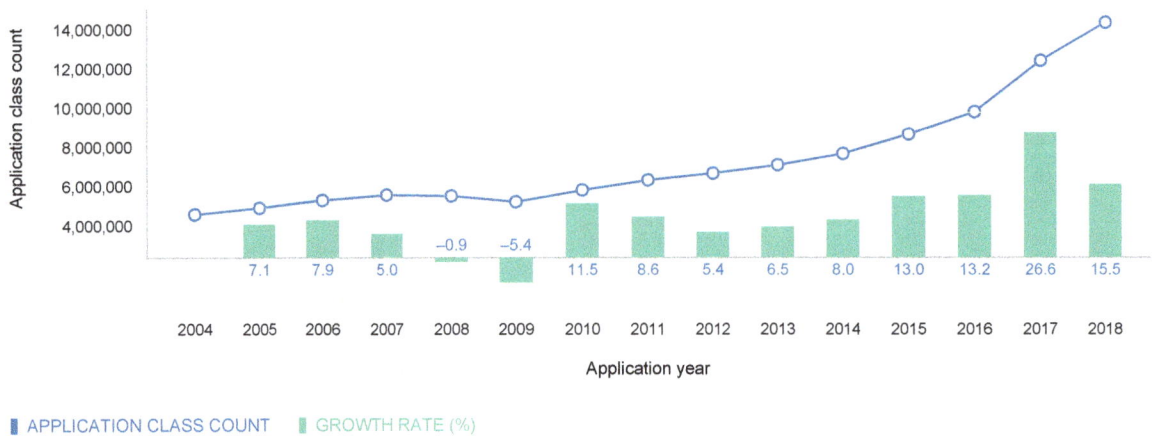

	2004	2005	2006	2007	2008	2009	2010	2011	2012	2013	2014	2015	2016	2017	2018
Growth rate (%)		7.1	7.9	5.0	−0.9	−5.4	11.5	8.6	5.4	6.5	8.0	13.0	13.2	26.6	15.5

Application year

▌ APPLICATION CLASS COUNT ▌ GROWTH RATE (%)

Note: World totals are WIPO estimates using data covering 169 IP offices. These totals include class counts in applications filed directly with national and regional offices (the "Paris route") as well as class counts in designations received by offices via the Madrid System (where applicable). See the glossary for the definition of class count.

Source: WIPO Statistics Database, August 2019.

86

B3. Resident and non-resident trademark application class counts worldwide, 2004–2018

NON-RESIDENT SHARE (%)

| 33.1 | 31.2 | 31.7 | 32.0 | 32.2 | 27.7 | 26.7 | 26.7 | 25.9 | 25.4 | 23.5 | 21.5 | 20.2 | 16.9 | 16.2 |

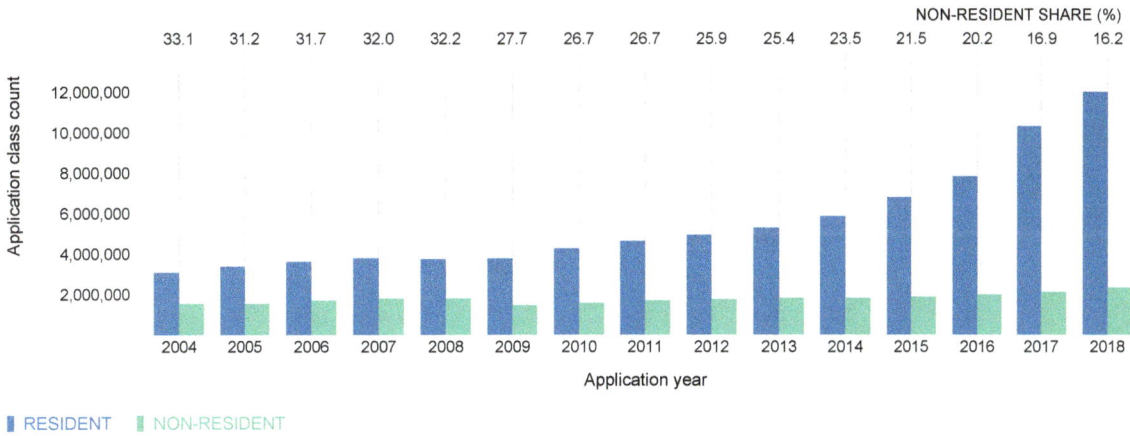

Application class count / Application year

■ RESIDENT   ■ NON-RESIDENT

Note: World totals are WIPO estimates using data covering 169 IP offices. These totals include class counts in applications filed directly with national and regional offices (the "Paris route") as well as class counts in designations received by offices via the Madrid System (where applicable). See the glossary for definitions of class count, resident and non-resident.

Source: WIPO Statistics Database, August 2019.

B4. Trend in trademark registrations worldwide, 2004–2018

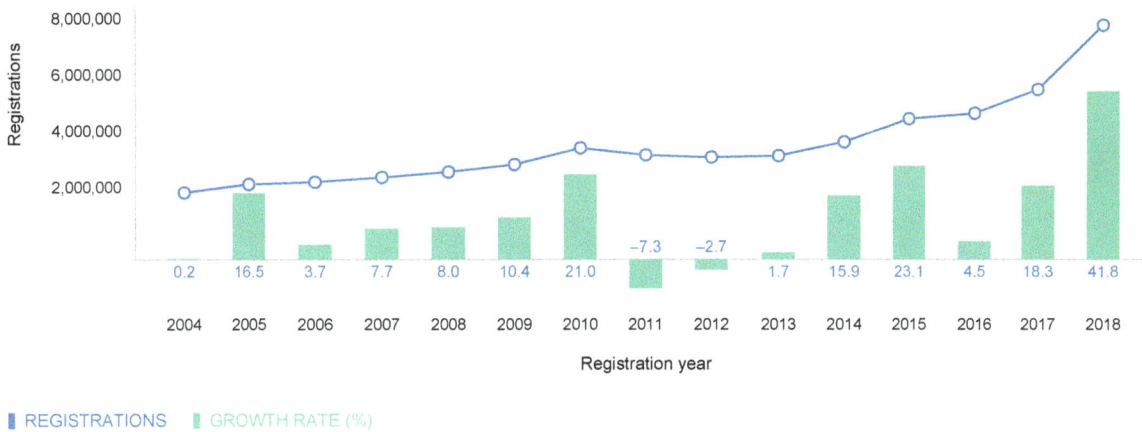

| 0.2 | 16.5 | 3.7 | 7.7 | 8.0 | 10.4 | 21.0 | −7.3 | −2.7 | 1.7 | 15.9 | 23.1 | 4.5 | 18.3 | 41.8 |

Registrations / Registration year

■ REGISTRATIONS   ■ GROWTH RATE (%)

Note: World totals are WIPO estimates using data covering 166 IP offices. Each total includes the number of registrations issued by national and regional offices for applications filed directly with offices (the "Paris route") as well as the number of designations received by offices via the Madrid System (where applicable).

Source: WIPO Statistics Database, August 2019.

Trademarks

Trademarks

B5. Trend in trademark registration class counts worldwide, 2004–2018

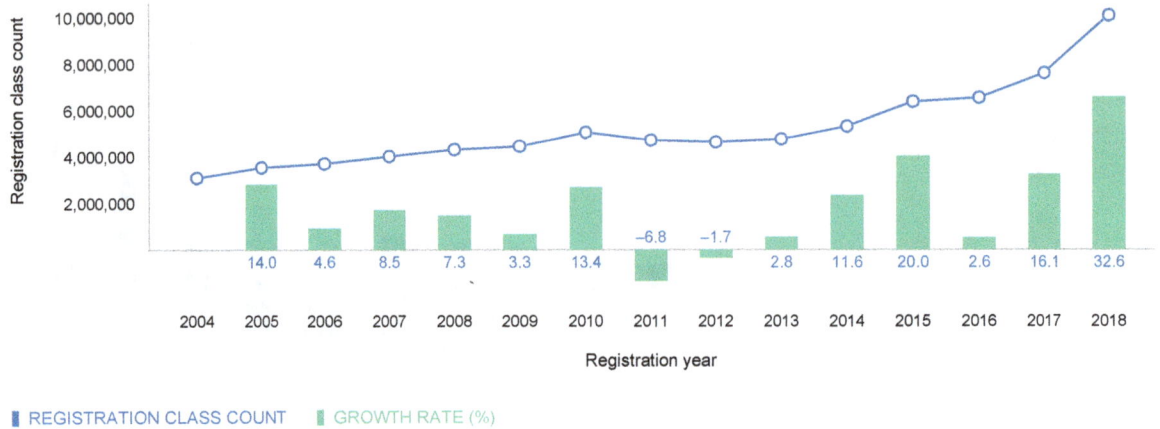

Registration class count

10,000,000
8,000,000
6,000,000
4,000,000
2,000,000

2004	2005	2006	2007	2008	2009	2010	2011	2012	2013	2014	2015	2016	2017	2018
	14.0	4.6	8.5	7.3	3.3	13.4	−6.8	−1.7	2.8	11.6	20.0	2.6	16.1	32.6

Registration year

▌ REGISTRATION CLASS COUNT   ▌ GROWTH RATE (%)

Note: World totals are WIPO estimates using data covering 166 IP offices. These totals include class counts in registrations issued by national and regional offices for applications filed directly with offices (the "Paris route") as well as designations received by offices via the Madrid System (where applicable). See the glossary for the definition of class count.

Source: WIPO Statistics Database, August 2019.

B6. Resident and non-resident trademark registration class counts worldwide, 2004–2018

NON-RESIDENT SHARE (%)

42.1	42.0	41.8	42.2	40.6	35.1	30.3	33.5	33.5	34.0	31.2	28.6	26.6	26.0	20.9

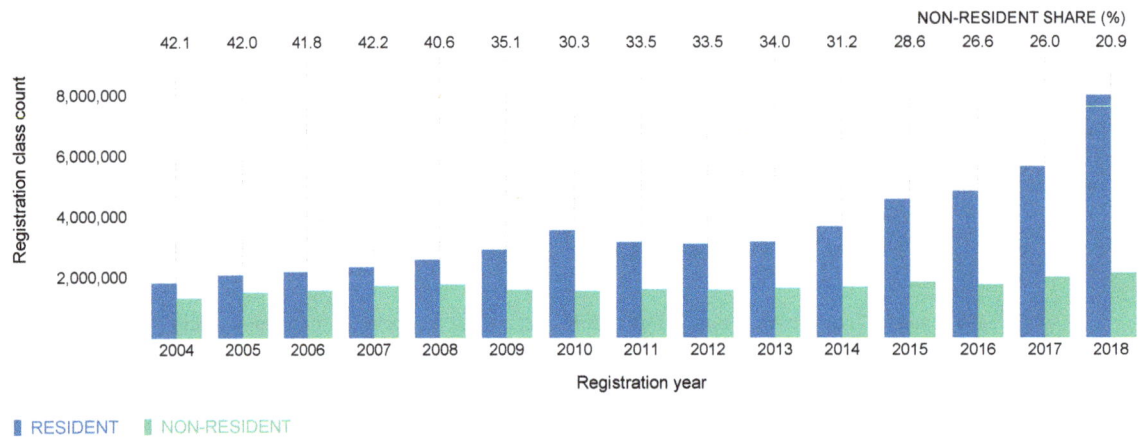

Registration class count

8,000,000
6,000,000
4,000,000
2,000,000

| 2004 | 2005 | 2006 | 2007 | 2008 | 2009 | 2010 | 2011 | 2012 | 2013 | 2014 | 2015 | 2016 | 2017 | 2018 |

Registration year

▌ RESIDENT   ▌ NON-RESIDENT

Note: World totals are WIPO estimates using data covering 166 IP offices. These totals include class counts in registrations issued by national and regional offices for applications filed directly with offices (the "Paris route") as well as for designations received by offices via the Madrid System (where applicable). See the glossary for definitions of class count, resident and non-resident.

Source: WIPO Statistics Database, August 2019.

Trademark applications and registrations by office

B7. Trademark application class counts by income group, 2008 and 2018

Income group	Application class count		Resident share (%)		Share of world total (%)		Average growth (%)
	2008	2018	2008	2018	2008	2018	2008–2018
High-income	2,953,200	3,966,400	68.2	69.8	53.6	27.7	3.0
Upper middle-income	1,957,900	9,300,300	70.4	91.7	35.5	64.9	16.9
Upper middle-income without China	*1,265,200*	*1,934,800*	*62.3*	*72.3*	*23.0*	*13.5*	*4.3*
Lower middle-income	534,900	960,000	59.8	67.0	9.7	6.7	6.0
Low-income	65,200	95,100	41.0	43.8	1.2	0.7	3.8
World	**5,511,200**	**14,321,800**	**67.8**	**83.8**	**100.0**	**100.0**	**10.0**

Note: Totals by income group are WIPO estimates using data covering 169 IP offices. Each category includes the following number of offices: high-income (63), upper middle-income (51), lower middle-income (35) and low-income (20). Data for the European Union Intellectual Property Office are allocated to the high-income group because most EU member states are high-income countries. For a similar reason, data for the African Regional Intellectual Property Organization and the African Intellectual Property Organization are allocated to the low-income group. For information on income group classification, see the data description section in Additional information.

Source: WIPO Statistics Database, August 2019.

B8. Trademark application class counts by region, 2008 and 2018

Region	Application class count		Resident share (%)		Share of world total (%)		Average growth (%)
	2008	2018	2008	2018	2008	2018	2008–2018
Africa	179,600	245,500	43.0	44.9	3.3	1.7	3.2
Asia	1,996,800	10,045,700	71.8	90.6	36.2	70.0	17.5
Europe	2,116,800	2,252,200	66.7	72.8	38.4	15.8	0.6
Latin America and the Caribbean	557,400	751,000	63.9	69.0	10.1	5.3	3.0
North America	521,200	827,800	72.4	66.7	9.5	5.8	4.7
Oceania	139,400	199,600	57.5	50.9	2.5	1.4	3.7
World	**5,511,200**	**14,321,800**	**67.8**	**83.8**	**100.0**	**100.0**	**10.0**

Note: Totals by geographical region are WIPO estimates using data covering 169 IP offices. Each region includes the following number of offices: Africa (34), Asia (48), Europe (43), Latin America and the Caribbean (37), North America (2) and Oceania (5).

Source: WIPO Statistics Database, August 2019.

B9. Trend in trademark applications for the top five offices, 1883–2018

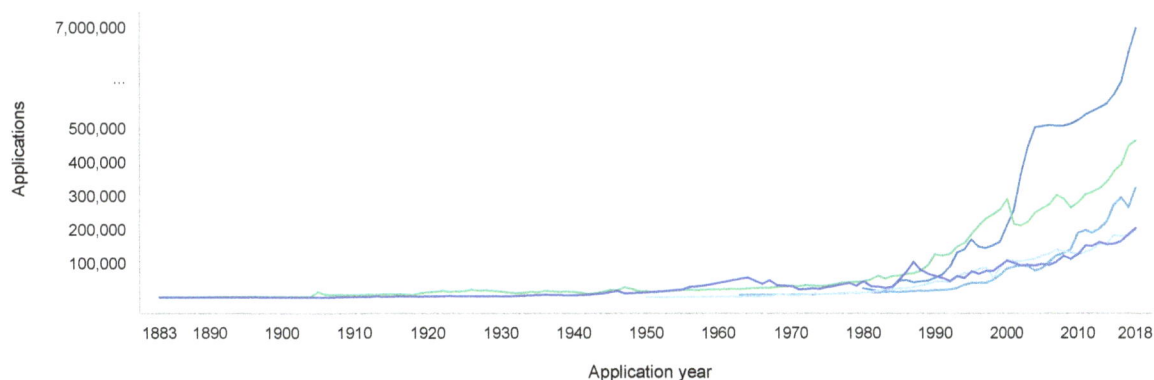

CHINA   U.S.   INDIA   BRAZIL   REPUBLIC OF KOREA

Note: Data are based on the numbers of applications filed; that is, differences between single-class and multi-class filing systems across IP offices are not taken into account. The top five offices were selected based on their 2018 application totals.

Source: WIPO Statistics Database, August 2019.

B10. Trademark application class counts for the top 20 offices, 2018

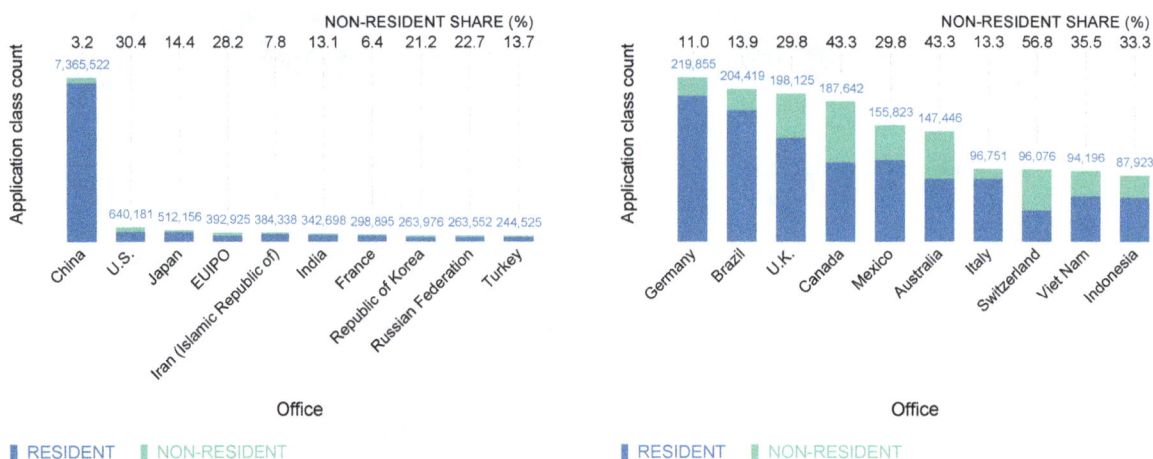

Left chart:

NON-RESIDENT SHARE (%)

| 3.2 | 30.4 | 14.4 | 28.2 | 7.8 | 13.1 | 6.4 | 21.2 | 22.7 | 13.7 |

Application class count

- China: 7,365,522
- U.S.: 640,181
- Japan: 512,156
- EUIPO: 392,925
- Iran (Islamic Republic of): 384,338
- India: 342,698
- France: 298,895
- Republic of Korea: 263,976
- Russian Federation: 263,552
- Turkey: 244,525

Office

█ RESIDENT █ NON-RESIDENT

Right chart:

NON-RESIDENT SHARE (%)

| 11.0 | 13.9 | 29.8 | 43.3 | 29.8 | 43.3 | 13.3 | 56.8 | 35.5 | 33.3 |

Application class count

- Germany: 219,855
- Brazil: 204,419
- U.K.: 198,125
- Canada: 187,642
- Mexico: 155,823
- Australia: 147,446
- Italy: 96,751
- Switzerland: 96,076
- Viet Nam: 94,196
- Indonesia: 87,923

Office

█ RESIDENT █ NON-RESIDENT

Note: EUIPO is the European Union Intellectual Property Office.

Source: WIPO Statistics Database, August 2019.

B11. Contribution of resident and non-resident application class counts to total growth for the top 20 offices, 2017–2018

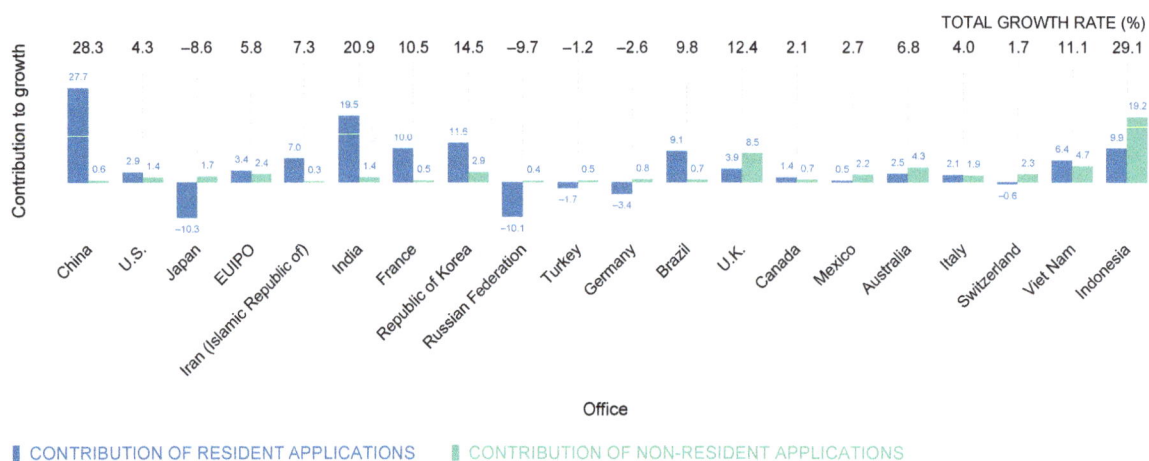

TOTAL GROWTH RATE (%)

| 28.3 | 4.3 | −8.6 | 5.8 | 7.3 | 20.9 | 10.5 | 14.5 | −9.7 | −1.2 | −2.6 | 9.8 | 12.4 | 2.1 | 2.7 | 6.8 | 4.0 | 1.7 | 11.1 | 29.1 |

Contribution to growth

- China: 27.7 / 0.6
- U.S.: 2.9 / 1.4
- Japan: −10.3 / 1.7
- EUIPO: 3.4 / 2.4
- Iran (Islamic Republic of): 7.0 / 0.3
- India: 19.5 / 1.4
- France: 10.0 / 0.5
- Republic of Korea: 11.6 / 2.9
- Russian Federation: −10.1 / 0.4
- Turkey: −1.7 / 0.5
- Germany: −3.4 / 0.8
- Brazil: 9.1 / 0.7
- U.K.: 3.9 / 8.5
- Canada: 1.4 / 0.7
- Mexico: 0.5 / 2.2
- Australia: 2.5 / 4.3
- Italy: 2.1 / 1.9
- Switzerland: −0.6 / 2.3
- Viet Nam: 6.4 / 4.7
- Indonesia: 9.9 / 19.2

Office

█ CONTRIBUTION OF RESIDENT APPLICATIONS █ CONTRIBUTION OF NON-RESIDENT APPLICATIONS

Note: EUIPO is the European Union Intellectual Property Office. This figure shows for each office the total growth or decrease in application class counts, broken down by the respective contributions of resident and non-resident filing activity. For example, the total number of classes specified in trademark applications in India grew by 20.9%. Growth in resident filing activity accounted for 19.5 percentage points of this increase, while the remaining 1.4 percentage points came from non-resident filing activity.

Source: WIPO Statistics Database, August 2019.

B12. Trademark application class counts for offices of selected low- and middle-income countries, 2018

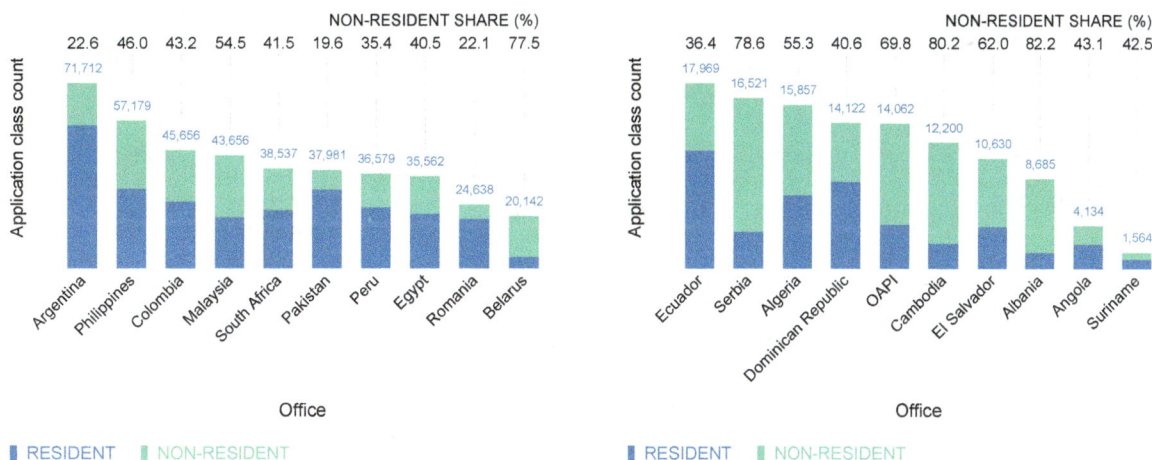

NON-RESIDENT SHARE (%)

| 22.6 | 46.0 | 43.2 | 54.5 | 41.5 | 19.6 | 35.4 | 40.5 | 22.1 | 77.5 |

Application class count

- Argentina: 71,712
- Philippines: 57,179
- Colombia: 45,656
- Malaysia: 43,656
- South Africa: 38,537
- Pakistan: 37,981
- Peru: 36,579
- Egypt: 35,562
- Romania: 24,638
- Belarus: 20,142

Office

NON-RESIDENT SHARE (%)

| 36.4 | 78.6 | 55.3 | 40.6 | 69.8 | 80.2 | 62.0 | 82.2 | 43.1 | 42.5 |

Application class count

- Ecuador: 17,969
- Serbia: 16,521
- Algeria: 15,857
- Dominican Republic: 14,122
- OAPI: 14,062
- Cambodia: 12,200
- El Salvador: 10,630
- Albania: 8,685
- Angola: 4,134
- Suriname: 1,564

Office

▮ RESIDENT ▮ NON-RESIDENT

▮ RESIDENT ▮ NON-RESIDENT

Note: The selected offices are from different world regions and income groups (low-income, lower middle-income and upper middle-income). OAPI is the African Intellectual Property Organization, which receives applications on behalf of its 17 member states. Where available, data for all offices are presented in statistical table B51 at the end of this section.

Source: WIPO Statistics Database, August 2019.

B13. Contribution of resident and non-resident application class counts to total growth for offices of selected low- and middle-income countries, 2017–2018

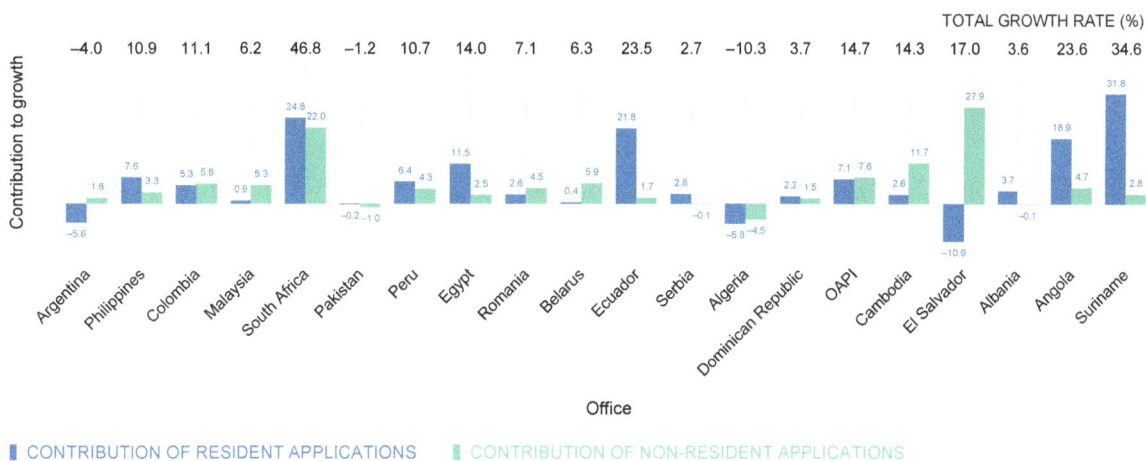

TOTAL GROWTH RATE (%)

| −4.0 | 10.9 | 11.1 | 6.2 | 46.8 | −1.2 | 10.7 | 14.0 | 7.1 | 6.3 | 23.5 | 2.7 | −10.3 | 3.7 | 14.7 | 14.3 | 17.0 | 3.6 | 23.6 | 34.6 |

Contribution to growth

- Argentina: −5.6, 1.6
- Philippines: 7.6, 3.3
- Colombia: 5.3, 5.8
- Malaysia: 0.9, 5.3
- South Africa: 24.8, 22.0
- Pakistan: −0.2, −1.0
- Peru: 6.4, 4.3
- Egypt: 11.5, 2.5
- Romania: 2.6, 4.5
- Belarus: 0.4, 5.9
- Ecuador: 21.8, 1.7
- Serbia: 2.8, −0.1
- Algeria: −5.8, −4.5
- Dominican Republic: 2.2, 1.5
- OAPI: 7.1, 7.6
- Cambodia: 2.6, 11.7
- El Salvador: −10.9, 27.9
- Albania: 3.7, −0.1
- Angola: 18.9, 4.7
- Suriname: 31.8, 2.8

Office

▮ CONTRIBUTION OF RESIDENT APPLICATIONS ▮ CONTRIBUTION OF NON-RESIDENT APPLICATIONS

Note: The selected offices are from different world regions and income groups (low-income, lower middle-income and upper middle-income). OAPI is the African Intellectual Property Organization, which receives applications on behalf of its 17 member states. Where available, data for all offices are presented in statistical table B51 at the end of this section. This figure shows for each office the total growth or decrease in application class counts, broken down by the respective contributions of resident and non-resident applications. For example, the total number of classes specified in trademark applications at the IP office of Peru grew by 10.7%. Growth in resident filing activity accounted for 6.4 percentage points of this increase, whereas the remaining 4.3 percentage points came from non-resident filing activity.

Source: WIPO Statistics Database, August 2019.

Trademarks

B14. Trademark registration class counts by income group, 2008 and 2018

Income group	Registration class count		Resident share (%)		Share of world total (%)		Average growth (%)
	2008	2018	2008	2018	2008	2018	2008–2018
High-income	2,490,200	2,896,900	62.8	63.6	57.6	28.7	1.5
Upper middle-income	1,348,700	6,351,400	59.1	88.9	31.2	62.9	16.8
Upper middle-income without China	*926,400*	*1,355,600*	*49.1*	*62.6*	*21.4*	*13.4*	*3.9*
Lower middle-income	430,600	779,400	46.3	60.9	10.0	7.7	6.1
Low-income	55,400	71,700	21.5	30.7	1.3	0.7	2.6
World	**4,324,900**	**10,099,400**	**59.4**	**79.1**	**100.0**	**100.0**	**8.9**

Note: Totals by income group are WIPO estimates using data covering 166 IP offices. Each category includes the following number of offices: high-income (61), upper middle-income (50), lower middle-income (35) and low-income (20). Data for the European Union Intellectual Property Office are allocated to the high-income group because most EU member states are high-income countries. For a similar reason, data for the African Regional Intellectual Property Organization and the African Intellectual Property Organization are allocated to the low-income group. For information on income group classification, see the data description section in Additional information.

Source: WIPO Statistics Database, August 2019.

B15. Trademark registration class counts by region, 2008 and 2018

Region	Registration class count		Resident share (%)		Share of world total (%)		Average growth (%)
	2008	2018	2008	2018	2008	2018	2008–2018
Africa	152,000	210,500	29.5	33.0	3.4	3.5	3.3
Asia	1,398,000	6,741,300	60.6	87.2	30.6	32.3	17.0
Europe	1,916,900	1,931,200	60.6	68.5	44.4	44.3	0.1
Latin America and the Caribbean	404,500	594,700	57.0	62.2	11.4	9.4	3.9
North America	339,300	446,800	68.1	59.6	7.9	7.8	2.8
Oceania	114,200	174,900	49.7	44.4	2.3	2.7	4.4
World	**4,324,900**	**10,099,400**	**59.4**	**79.1**	**100.0**	**100.0**	**8.9**

Note: Totals by geographical region are WIPO estimates based on data covering 166 offices. Each region includes the following number of offices: Africa (34), Asia (48), Europe (42), Latin America and the Caribbean (35), North America (2) and Oceania (5).

Source: WIPO Statistics Database, August 2019.

B16. Trend in trademark registrations for the top five offices, 1883–2018

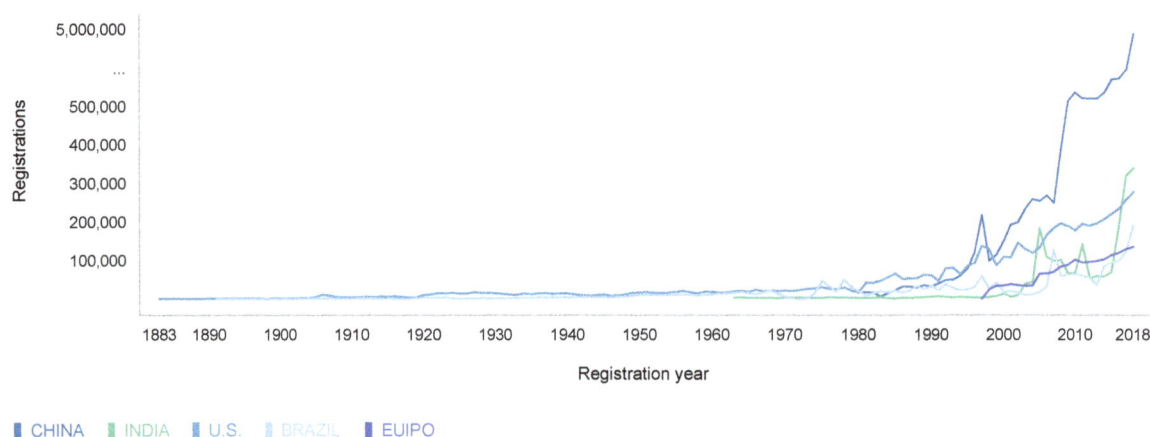

Note: EUIPO is the European Union Intellectual Property Office. Data are based on the numbers of registrations recorded; that is, differences between single-class and multi-class registration systems across IP offices are not taken into account. The top five offices were selected based on their 2018 registration totals.

Source: WIPO Statistics Database, August 2019.

B17. Trademark registration class counts for the top 20 offices, 2018

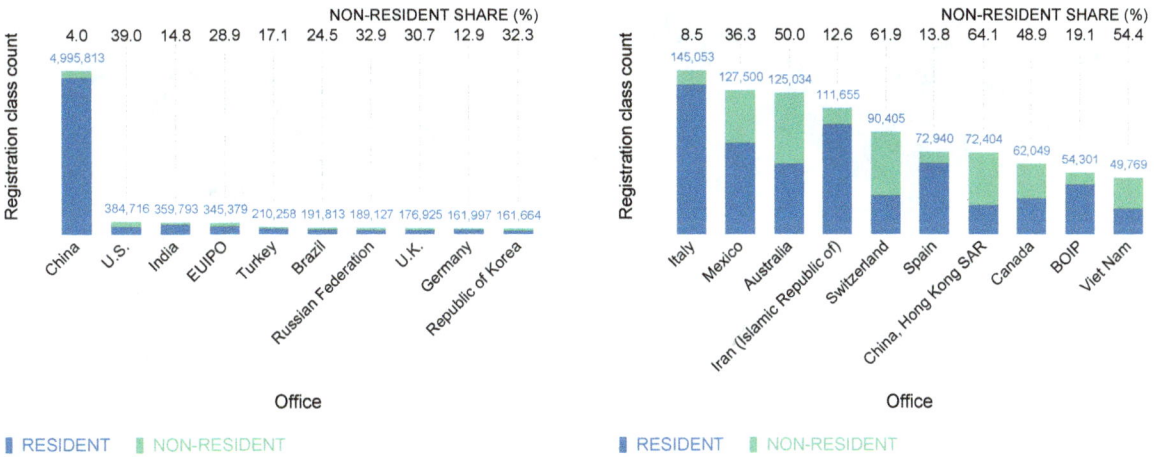

NON-RESIDENT SHARE (%)

4.0	39.0	14.8	28.9	17.1	24.5	32.9	30.7	12.9	32.3

Registration class count

- China: 4,995,813
- U.S.: 384,716
- India: 359,793
- EUIPO: 345,379
- Turkey: 210,258
- Brazil: 191,813
- Russian Federation: 189,127
- U.K.: 176,925
- Germany: 161,997
- Republic of Korea: 161,664

Office

NON-RESIDENT SHARE (%)

8.5	36.3	50.0	12.6	61.9	13.8	64.1	48.9	19.1	54.4

Registration class count

- Italy: 145,053
- Mexico: 127,500
- Australia: 125,034
- Iran (Islamic Republic of): 111,655
- Switzerland: 90,405
- Spain: 72,940
- China, Hong Kong SAR: 72,404
- Canada: 62,049
- BOIP: 54,301
- Viet Nam: 49,769

Office

■ RESIDENT   ■ NON-RESIDENT

Note: EUIPO is the European Union Intellectual Property Office and BOIP is the Benelux Office for Intellectual Property. Figures for the office of France are not presented here because the data are not available. On the basis of an examination, a registration may be issued for a trademark application. The number of registrations issued may fluctuate greatly from one year to the next, in part reflecting the resources that IP offices dedicate to examining trademark applications.

Source: WIPO Statistics Database, August 2019.

B18. Trademark registration class counts for offices of selected low- and middle-income countries, 2018

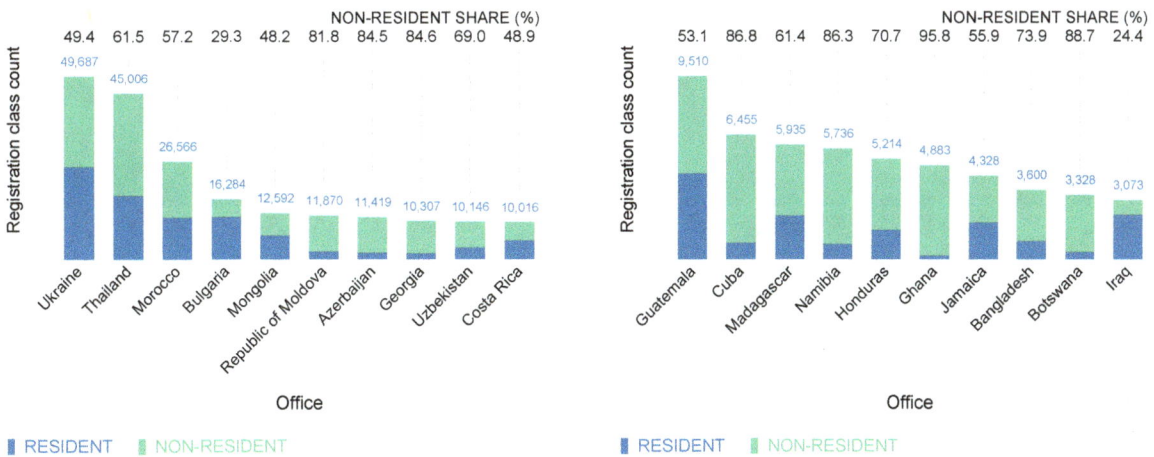

NON-RESIDENT SHARE (%)

49.4	61.5	57.2	29.3	48.2	81.8	84.5	84.6	69.0	48.9

Registration class count

- Ukraine: 49,687
- Thailand: 45,006
- Morocco: 26,566
- Bulgaria: 16,284
- Mongolia: 12,592
- Republic of Moldova: 11,870
- Azerbaijan: 11,419
- Georgia: 10,307
- Uzbekistan: 10,146
- Costa Rica: 10,016

Office

NON-RESIDENT SHARE (%)

53.1	86.8	61.4	86.3	70.7	95.8	55.9	73.9	88.7	24.4

Registration class count

- Guatemala: 9,510
- Cuba: 6,455
- Madagascar: 5,935
- Namibia: 5,736
- Honduras: 5,214
- Ghana: 4,883
- Jamaica: 4,328
- Bangladesh: 3,600
- Botswana: 3,328
- Iraq: 3,073

Office

■ RESIDENT   ■ NON-RESIDENT

Note: The selected offices are from different world regions and income groups (low-income, lower middle-income and upper middle-income). Where available, data for all offices are presented in statistical table B52 at the end of this section.

Source: WIPO Statistics Database, August 2019.

Trademarks

Trademark applications by origin

B19. Equivalent trademark application class counts by origin, 2018

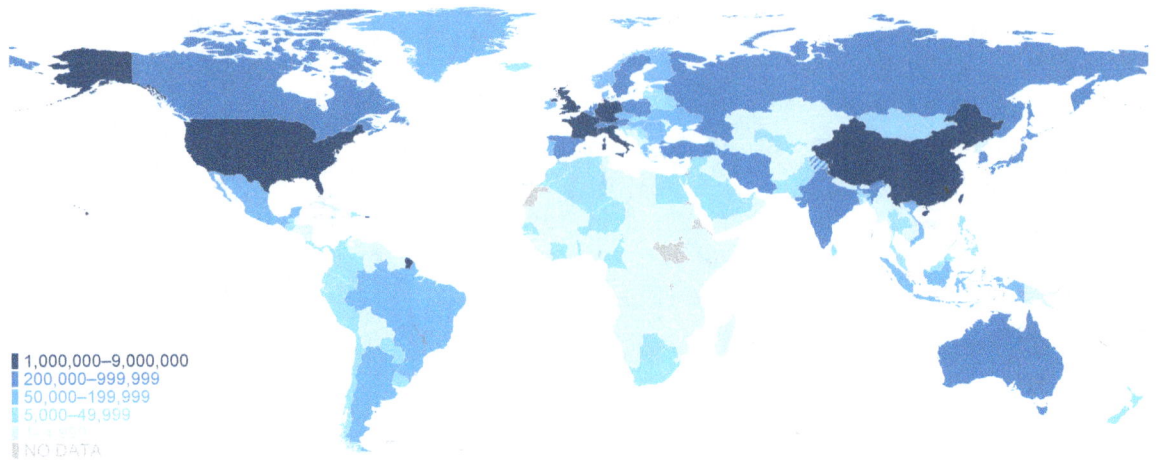

1,000,000–9,000,000
200,000–999,999
50,000–199,999
5,000–49,999
NO DATA

Note: Trademark filing activity by origin includes the number of classes specified in resident applications and in applications filed abroad. The origin of a trademark application is determined by the residence of the applicant. Applications filed at regional offices are considered equivalent to multiple applications in the relevant member states and the classes specified in these applications are multiplied accordingly. See the glossary for the definition of equivalent application.

Source: WIPO Statistics Database, August 2019.

B20. Trademark application class counts for the top 20 origins, 2018

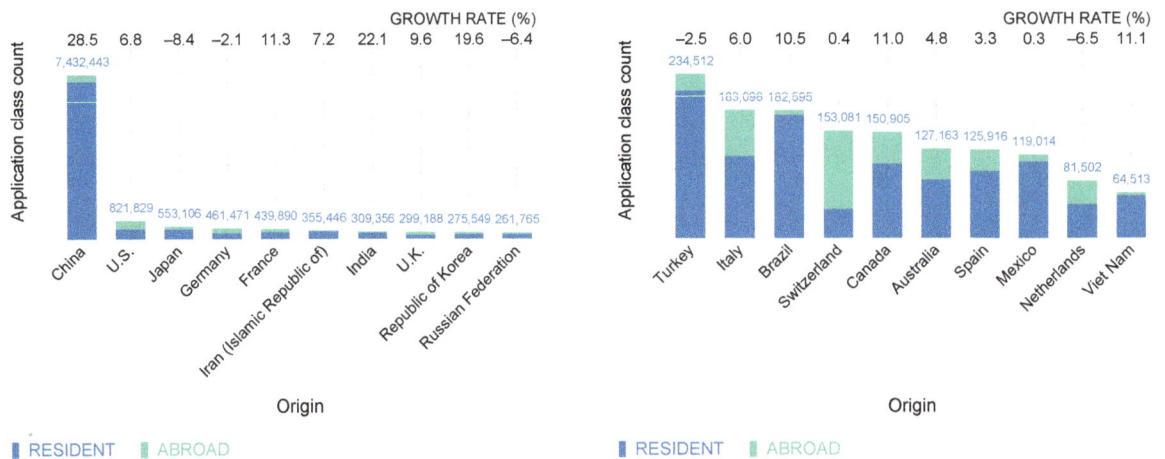

GROWTH RATE (%)

	28.5	6.8	−8.4	−2.1	11.3	7.2	22.1	9.6	19.6	−6.4
	7,432,443	821,829	553,106	461,471	439,890	355,446	309,356	299,188	275,549	261,765
	China	U.S.	Japan	Germany	France	Iran (Islamic Republic of)	India	U.K.	Republic of Korea	Russian Federation

Application class count — Origin

RESIDENT   ABROAD

GROWTH RATE (%)

	−2.5	6.0	10.5	0.4	11.0	4.8	3.3	0.3	−6.5	11.1
	234,512	183,096	182,595	153,081	150,905	127,163	125,916	119,014	81,502	64,513
	Turkey	Italy	Brazil	Switzerland	Canada	Australia	Spain	Mexico	Netherlands	Viet Nam

Application class count — Origin

RESIDENT   ABROAD

Note: In this figure, trademark application filing activity by origin includes the number of classes specified in resident applications and in applications filed abroad and is based on absolute count, not equivalent count. The origin of a trademark application is determined by the residence of the applicant. An application filed at a regional office is considered a resident filing if the applicant is a resident of one of the relevant member states.

Source: WIPO Statistics Database, August 2019.

B21. Trademark application class counts for selected low- and middle-income origins, 2018

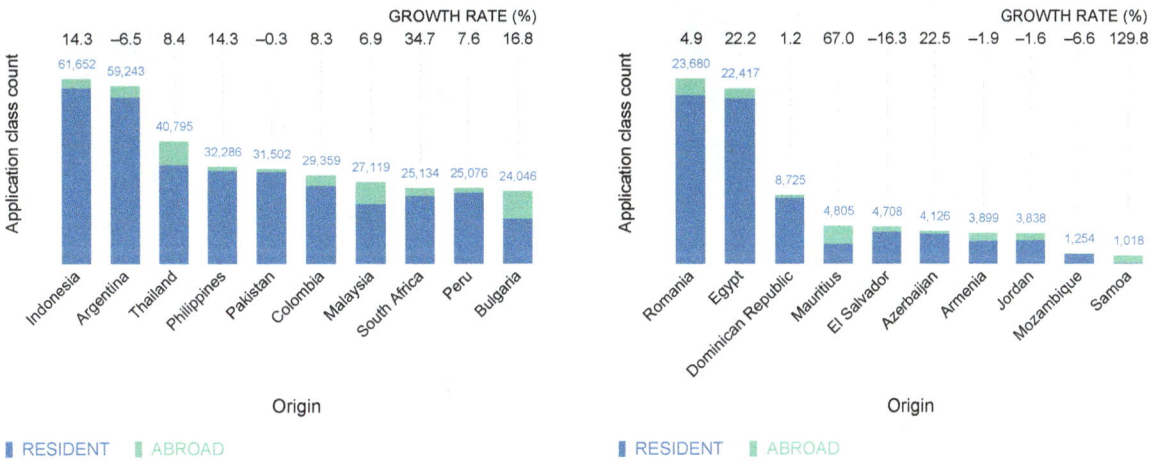

GROWTH RATE (%)

| 14.3 | −6.5 | 8.4 | 14.3 | −0.3 | 8.3 | 6.9 | 34.7 | 7.6 | 16.8 |

Application class count

- Indonesia: 61,652
- Argentina: 59,243
- Thailand: 40,795
- Philippines: 32,286
- Pakistan: 31,502
- Colombia: 29,359
- Malaysia: 27,119
- South Africa: 25,134
- Peru: 25,076
- Bulgaria: 24,046

Origin

■ RESIDENT ■ ABROAD

GROWTH RATE (%)

| 4.9 | 22.2 | 1.2 | 67.0 | −16.3 | 22.5 | −1.9 | −1.6 | −6.6 | 129.8 |

Application class count

- Romania: 23,680
- Egypt: 22,417
- Dominican Republic: 8,725
- Mauritius: 4,805
- El Salvador: 4,708
- Azerbaijan: 4,126
- Armenia: 3,899
- Jordan: 3,838
- Mozambique: 1,254
- Samoa: 1,018

Origin

■ RESIDENT ■ ABROAD

Note: In this figure, trademark application filing activity by origin includes the number of classes specified in resident applications and in applications filed abroad and is based on absolute count, not equivalent count. The origin of a trademark application is determined by the residence of the applicant. The selected origins are from different world regions and income groups (low-income, lower middle-income and upper middle-income). Where available, data for all origins are presented in statistical table B51 at the end of this section.

Source: WIPO Statistics Database, August 2019.

B22. Trademark application class counts abroad for the top 20 origins, 2018

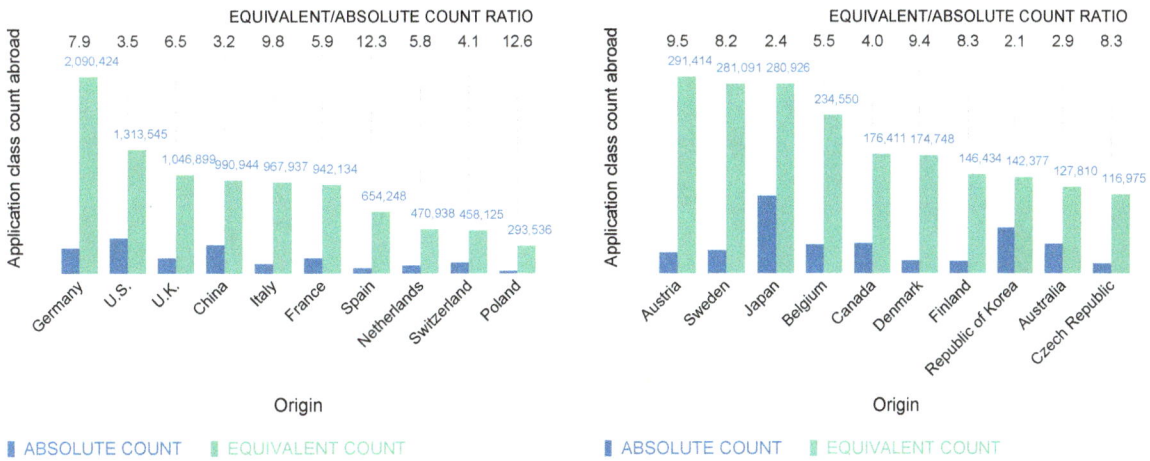

EQUIVALENT/ABSOLUTE COUNT RATIO

| 7.9 | 3.5 | 6.5 | 3.2 | 9.8 | 5.9 | 12.3 | 5.8 | 4.1 | 12.6 |

Application class count abroad

- Germany: 2,090,424
- U.S.: 1,313,545
- U.K.: 1,046,899
- China: 990,944
- Italy: 967,937
- France: 942,134
- Spain: 654,248
- Netherlands: 470,938
- Switzerland: 458,125
- Poland: 293,536

Origin

■ ABSOLUTE COUNT ■ EQUIVALENT COUNT

EQUIVALENT/ABSOLUTE COUNT RATIO

| 9.5 | 8.2 | 2.4 | 5.5 | 4.0 | 9.4 | 8.3 | 2.1 | 2.9 | 8.3 |

Application class count abroad

- Austria: 291,414
- Sweden: 281,091
- Japan: 280,926
- Belgium: 234,550
- Canada: 176,411
- Denmark: 174,748
- Finland: 146,434
- Republic of Korea: 142,377
- Australia: 127,810
- Czech Republic: 116,975

Origin

■ ABSOLUTE COUNT ■ EQUIVALENT COUNT

Note: This figure distinguishes between absolute counts and equivalent counts for filing activity abroad; that is, resident applications are excluded. Based on equivalent application class counts, applicants from Germany had the highest level of trademark filing activity abroad. This was due not only to their high application class counts at numerous foreign offices, but also to their frequent use of the European Union Intellectual Property Office – with its multiplier effect – to seek trademark protection within the entire EU. See the glossary for the definition of equivalent application. The origin of a trademark application is determined by the residence of the applicant.

Source: WIPO Statistics Database, August 2019.

Trademarks

Trademarks

B23. Trademark application class counts for the top 25 offices and origins, 2018

Origin	Office												
	China	U.S.	Japan	EUIPO	Iran (Islamic Republic of)	India	France	Republic of Korea	Russian Federation	Turkey	Germany	Brazil	U.K.
Argentina	291	262	17	167	3	20	9	23	118	2	8	335	47
Australia	7,802	7,068	1,372	3,064	136	927	155	877	390	166	170	238	2,606
Brazil	428	821	72	472	34	74	44	27	88	65	7	176,063	71
Canada	4,542	15,797	843	4,804	112	352	244	736	440	168	751	647	1,733
China	7,127,191	57,125	15,328	24,356	4,324	6,027	3,655	9,415	6,333	2,672	5,799	1,988	10,942
China, Hong Kong SAR	3	4,507	1,320	2,787		432	381	38	373	95	362	240	971
France	12,140	8,460	4,241	28,603	2,648	2,602	279,882	3,120	4,481	2,365	1,190	2,003	3,021
Germany	18,072	14,187	6,499	69,749	4,542	5,140	1,177	5,070	7,916	6,090	195,623	2,906	5,426
India	718	1,333	217	743	130	297,751	44	63	252	86	47	77	504
Indonesia	886	108	101	128	12	29	9	123	15	9	7	6	75
Iran (Islamic Republic of)	273	25	2	54	354,343	10	33	3	49	80	37		28
Italy	7,820	5,803	2,624	33,290	2,348	1,523	412	1,899	3,587	1,772	320	972	925
Japan	25,307	8,262	438,338	6,026	944	2,287	532	7,377	2,050	1,178	397	1,222	1,607
Mexico	548	2,287	67	494	11	54	34	60	53	26	35	345	40
Netherlands	3,585	3,159	942	13,554	407	806	528	663	953	964	834	470	706
Poland	1,001	682	153	10,313	309	230	93	117	647	331	374	34	170
Republic of Korea	18,609	5,420	3,915	2,655	504	1,186	367	207,953	1,237	735	301	557	793
Russian Federation	3,585	1,271	367	1,294	975	665	873	468	203,854	816	1,202	56	922
Spain	2,727	2,810	824	22,982	715	607	382	617	815	633	394	684	477
Switzerland	7,767	6,415	3,697	12,564	1,483	2,224	2,288	2,606	2,922	2,011	3,212	1,232	2,535
Turkey	846	1,219	226	1,755	2,017	239	400	169	836	211,109	694	49	621
U.K.	17,722	17,497	4,082	33,711	1,183	3,584	1,073	3,138	2,381	2,120	1,770	1,304	139,155
U.S.	50,908	445,872	15,669	33,998	1,777	8,696	1,752	11,625	4,236	4,613	1,663	8,928	13,936
Ukraine	427	488	87	402	21	55	102	52	536	131	201	5	133
Viet Nam	367	317	105	122	47	54	39	128	78	16	46	4	63
Others	51,957	28,986	11,048	84,838	5,313	7,124	4,387	7,609	18,912	6,272	4,411	4,054	10,618
Total	**7,365,522**	**640,181**	**512,156**	**392,925**	**384,338**	**342,698**	**298,895**	**263,976**	**263,552**	**244,525**	**219,855**	**204,419**	**198,125**

Origin	Canada	Mexico	Australia	Italy	Switzerland	Viet Nam	Indonesia	China, Hong Kong SAR	Spain	Thailand	Ukraine	Argentina
Argentina	39	190	13	8	4	6	8	9	58	6	4	55,492
Australia	1,817	368	83,641	123	271	743	668	1,300	76	915	91	119
Brazil	154	533	57	14	17	15	21	22	15	46	12	602
Canada	106,328	957	2,007	568	661	138	142	500	232	140	112	465
China	6,674	3,587	8,264	2,331	2,292	5,531	5,284	15,103	1,780	7,750	2,358	1,125
China, Hong Kong SAR	933	108	1,026	127	199	680	577	31,718	18	478	69	74
France	4,224	2,271	2,675	1,400	6,631	1,878	1,325	2,130	1,431	2,234	1,790	1,104
Germany	4,944	3,969	5,195	1,116	18,382	1,906	1,595	1,976	739	3,768	3,256	1,378
India	307	248	357	34	59	273	203	102	32	229	216	71
Indonesia	21	5	66	11	5	138	58,659	75	5	112	8	2
Iran (Islamic Republic of)	22		9	54	30	1	2		2	5	18	
Italy	1,861	1,221	1,645	83,863	2,963	753	577	1,152	290	1,003	946	328
Japan	2,355	1,403	2,760	256	1,261	4,011	3,443	5,971	149	7,124	468	451
Mexico	254	109,355	55	13	19	8	23	74	79	11	18	377
Netherlands	1,394	721	994	237	1,533	471	460	429	215	721	364	316
Poland	111	164	164	82	348	233	63	75	78	92	686	15
Republic of Korea	996	783	1,101	200	396	3,212	1,627	1,900	178	2,410	363	278
Russian Federation	125	363	224	969	419	513	232	155	811	445	2,466	86
Spain	610	1,959	610	135	648	228	219	276	72,710	396	299	621
Switzerland	2,554	2,255	2,272	1,242	41,468	1,101	1,156	1,501	677	1,837	1,511	868
Turkey	151	171	181	374	280	110	174	61	295	196	475	37
U.K.	5,200	2,244	6,415	547	2,320	1,338	1,328	2,452	548	2,247	1,229	592
U.S.	38,134	17,010	16,914	938	6,062	4,132	4,008	8,041	850	6,325	2,459	4,467
Ukraine	32	38	60	106	95	29	12	2	77	12	51,195	3
Viet Nam	59	31	148	14	16	60,731	102	32	6	253	48	
Others	8,343	5,869	10,593	1,989	9,697	6,017	6,015	9,529	1,485	39,526	6,057	2,841
Total	**187,642**	**155,823**	**147,446**	**96,751**	**96,076**	**94,196**	**87,923**	**84,585**	**82,836**	**78,281**	**76,518**	**71,712**

Note: EUIPO is the European Union Intellectual Property Office. The office and origin data shown here consist of absolute application class counts rather than equivalent application class counts.

Source: WIPO Statistics Database, August 2019.

Trademarks

B24. Flows of non-resident trademark application class counts between selected top origins and offices, 2018

Non-resident origin   **Office**

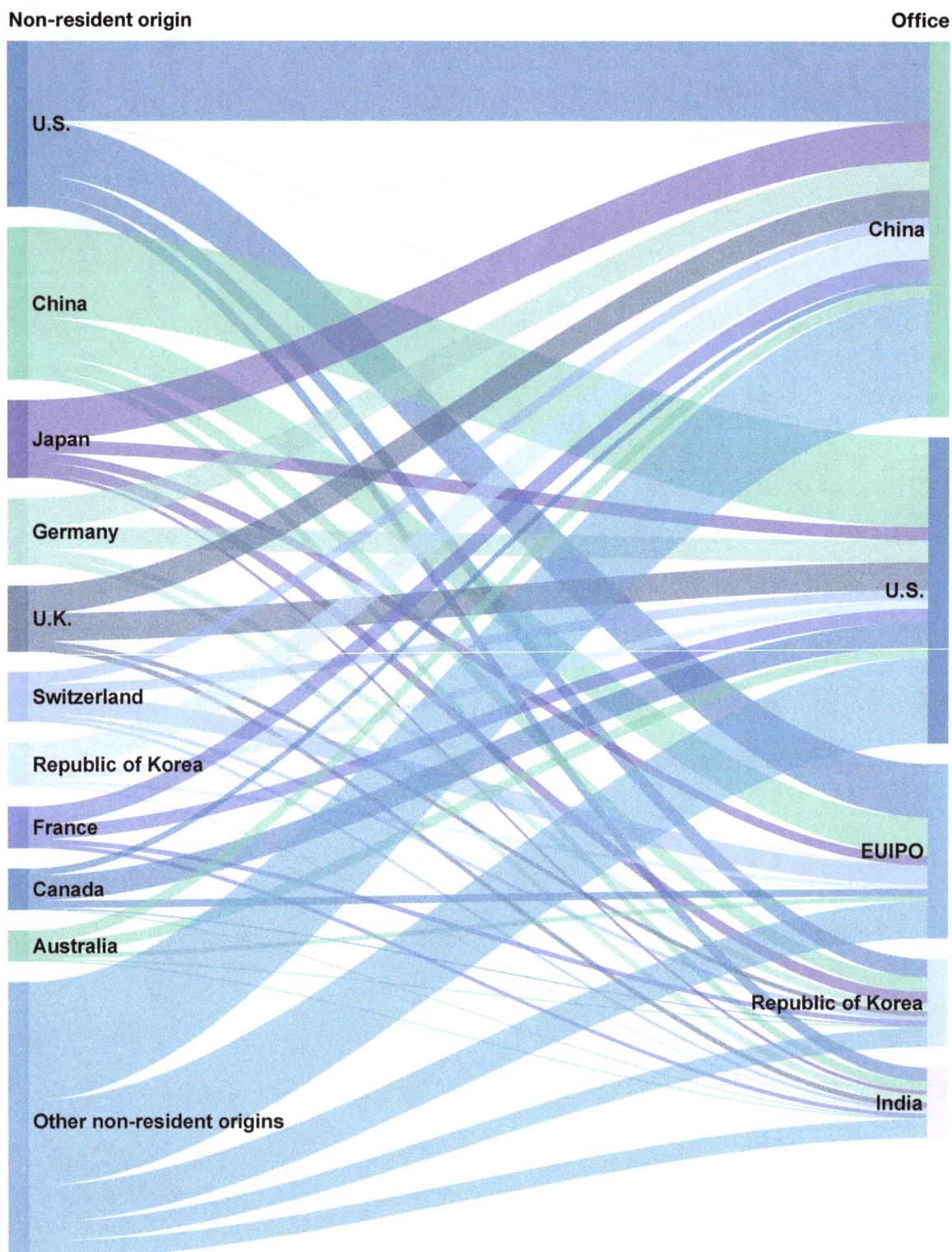

Note: EUIPO is the European Union Intellectual Property Office. The office and non-resident origin data shown here consist of absolute application class counts rather than equivalent application class counts.

Source: WIPO Statistics Database, August 2019.

B25. Distribution of trademark application class counts for the top 15 offices and selected non-resident origins, 2018

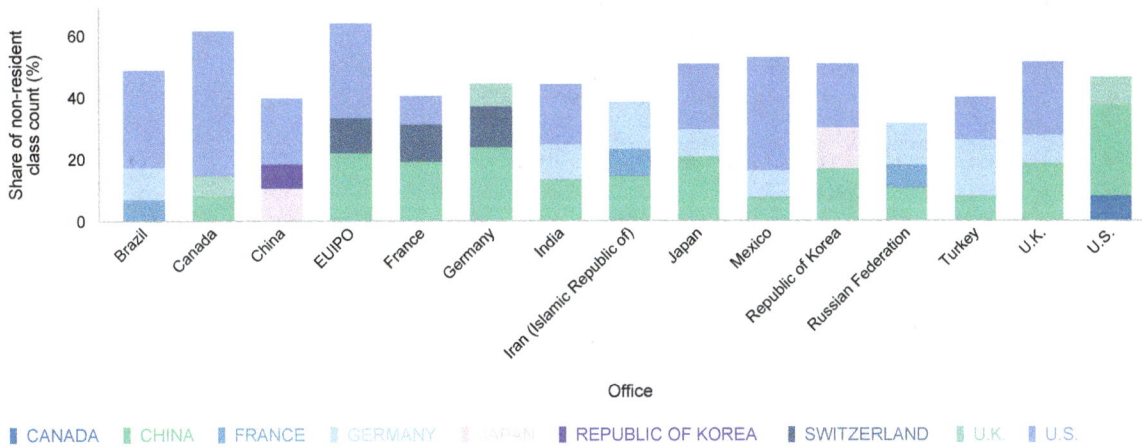

Note: EUIPO is the European Union Intellectual Property Office. The office and origin data shown here consist of absolute application class counts rather than equivalent application class counts.

Source: WIPO Statistics Database, August 2019.

Trademark applications by Nice class and industry sector

B26. Distribution of non-resident trademark applications by top Nice classes, 2018

Rank		Class	Class share (%)
1	9	Scientific, photographic, measuring instruments; recording equipment; computers and software	11.5
2	35	Advertising, business management, business administration and office functions	7.6
3	42	Scientific and technological services, design and development of computer hardware and software	5.7
4	5	Pharmaceutical preparations, baby food, dietary supplements for humans and animals, disinfectants, fungicides and herbicides	5.3
5	3	Bleaching preparations and other substances for laundry use; cleaning and abrasive preparations; soaps, perfumery and cosmetics	4.8
6	25	Clothing, footwear, headgear	4.5
7	41	Education, entertainment, and sporting activities	4.5
8	30	Coffee, tea, cocoa, rice, flour, bread, pastry and confectionery, sugar, honey, yeast, salt, mustard, vinegar, sauces (condiments) and spices	3.0
9	7	Machines and machine tools; motors and engines; agricultural implements	2.7
10	11	Apparatus for lighting, heating, steam generating, cooking, refrigerating, drying, ventilating, water supply and sanitary purposes	2.6
		Remaining classes	**47.8**

Note: These figures are based on non-resident filing data from 133 IP offices. Some classes listed are abbreviated. See *www.wipo.int/classifications/nice* for a complete list of all classes.

Source: WIPO Statistics Database, August 2019.

B27. Non-resident trademark applications by goods and services classes, 2018

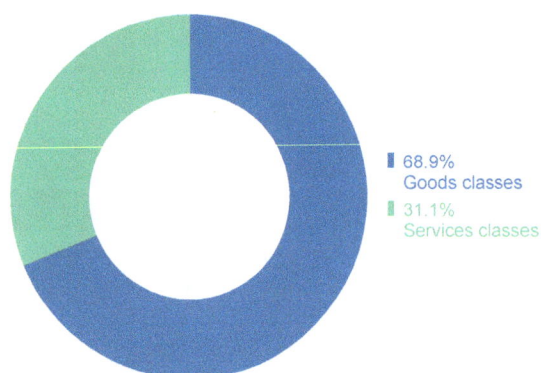

- 68.9% Goods classes
- 31.1% Services classes

Note: In the 45-class Nice Classification, the first 34 classes indicate goods and the remaining 11 refer to services. See *www.wipo.int/classifications/nice* for a complete list of all classes. These figures are based on non-resident filing data from 133 IP offices.

Source: WIPO Statistics Database, August 2019.

B28. Non-resident trademark applications by industry sector, 2018

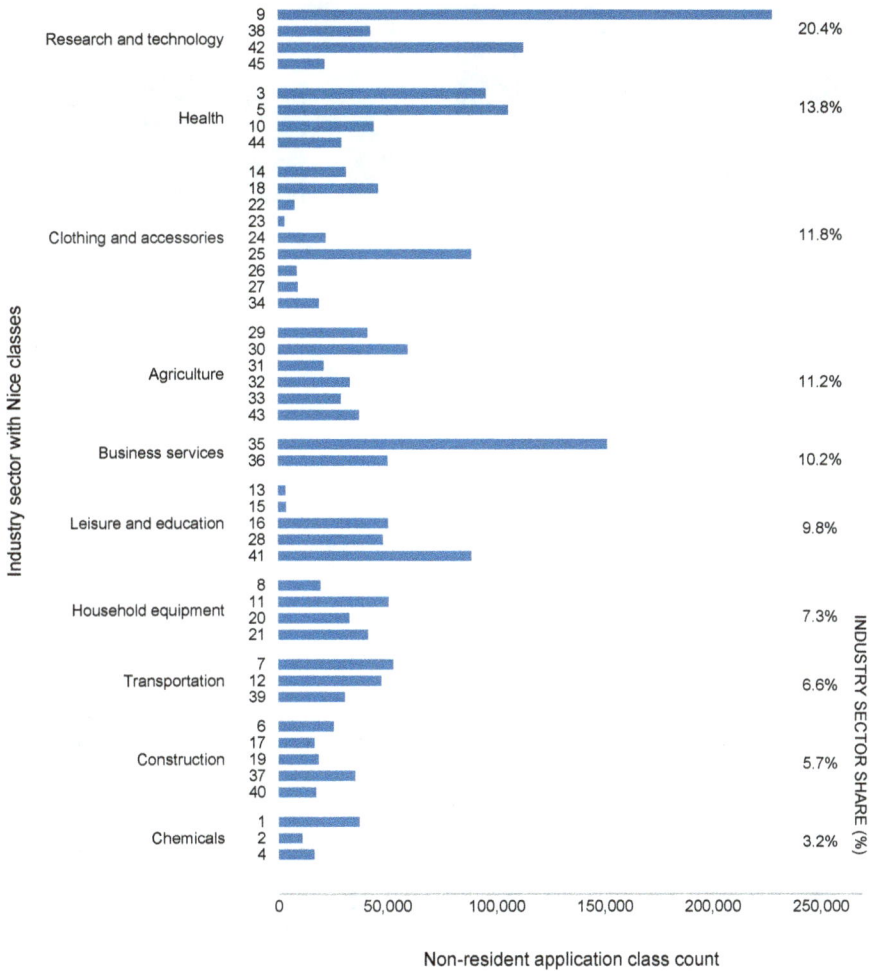

Industry sector with Nice classes

Industry sector	Nice classes	Industry sector share (%)
Research and technology	9, 38, 42, 45	20.4%
Health	3, 5, 10, 44	13.8%
Clothing and accessories	14, 18, 22, 23, 24, 25, 26, 27, 34	11.8%
Agriculture	29, 30, 31, 32, 33, 43	11.2%
Business services	35, 36	10.2%
Leisure and education	13, 15, 16, 28, 41	9.8%
Household equipment	8, 11, 20, 21	7.3%
Transportation	7, 12, 39	6.6%
Construction	6, 17, 19, 37, 40	5.7%
Chemicals	1, 2, 4	3.2%

Non-resident application class count

Note: Industry sectors based on class groups are those defined by Edital. Some industry sectors are abbreviated. See annex B for full definitions and composition of Nice goods and services classes. These figures are based on non-resident filing data from 133 IP offices.

Source: WIPO Statistics Database, August 2019.

Trademarks

Trademarks

B29. Trademark applications by top three sectors at the top offices, 2018

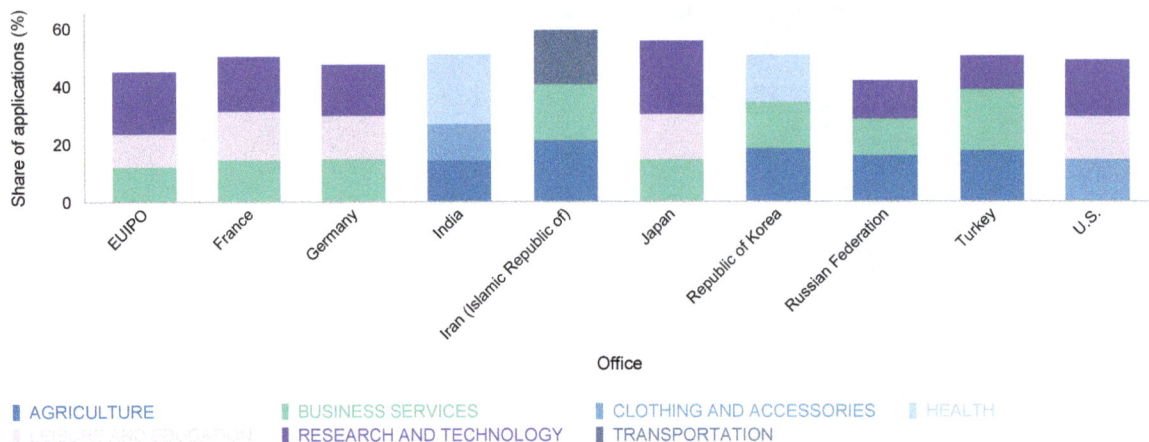

Legend:
- AGRICULTURE
- BUSINESS SERVICES
- CLOTHING AND ACCESSORIES
- HEALTH
- LEISURE AND EDUCATION
- RESEARCH AND TECHNOLOGY
- TRANSPORTATION

Note: EUIPO is the European Union Intellectual Property Office. Industry sectors based on class groups are those defined by Edital. Some industry sectors are abbreviated. See *www.wipo.int/classifications/nice* for a complete list of all classes. The top three sectors and top offices were selected based on their 2018 totals. China is not presented here due to the incompleteness of 2018 Chinese Nice Class data.

Source: WIPO Statistics Database, August 2019.

B30. Distribution of trademark applications by goods and services at the top offices, 2018

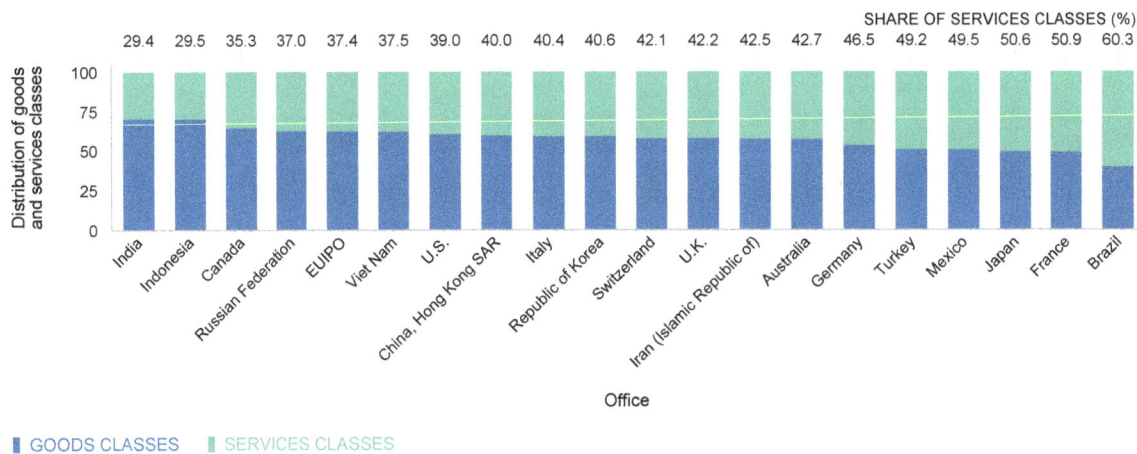

Legend:
- GOODS CLASSES
- SERVICES CLASSES

Note: EUIPO is the European Union Intellectual Property Office. China is not presented here due to incompleteness of 2018 Chinese Nice Class data.

Source: WIPO Statistics Database, August 2019.

B31. Trademark applications by top three sectors for the top origins, 2018

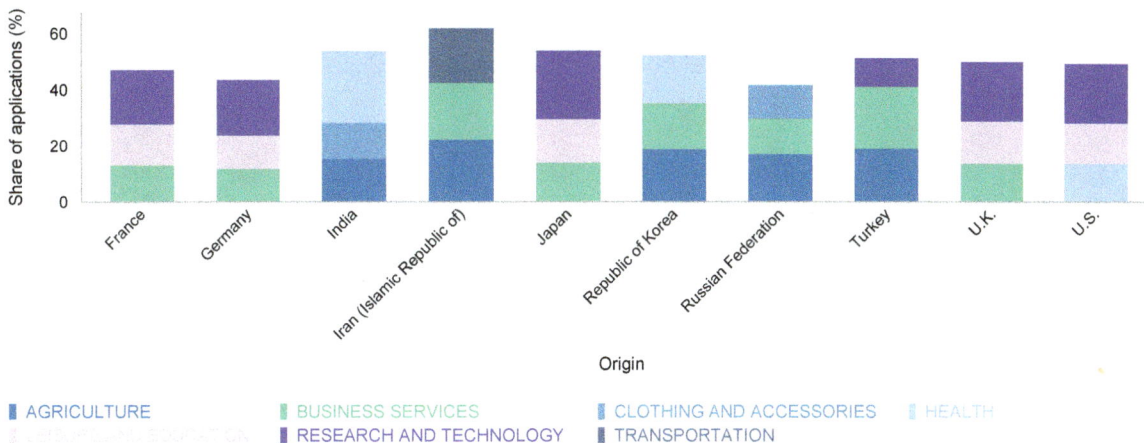

Note: Industry sectors based on class groups are those defined by Edital. Some industry sectors are abbreviated. See annex B for full definitions. The top three sectors and top origins were selected based on their 2018 totals. China is not presented here due to the incompleteness of 2018 Chinese Nice Class data.

Source: WIPO Statistics Database, August 2019.

B32. Distribution of trademark applications by goods and services for the top origins, 2018

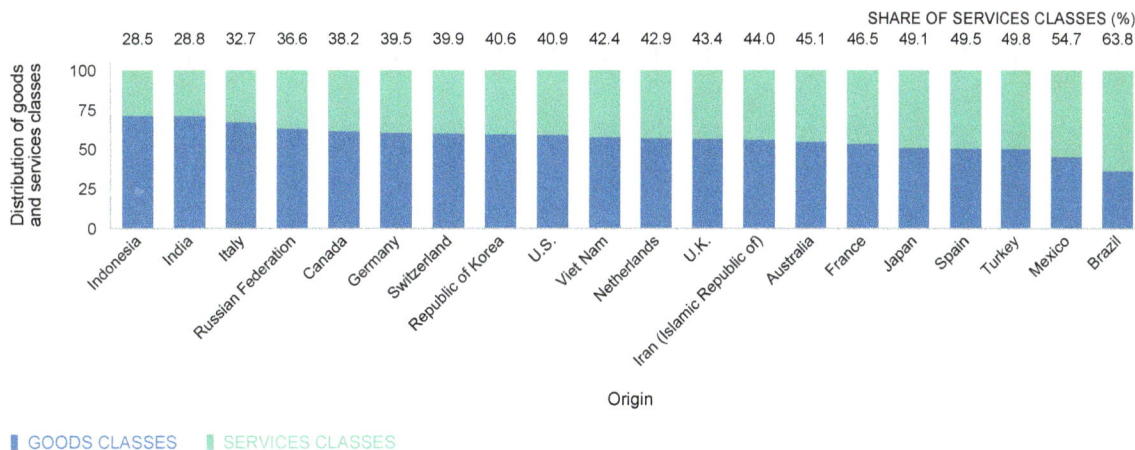

Note: China is not presented here due to the incompleteness of 2018 Chinese Nice Class data.

Source: WIPO Statistics Database, August 2019.

Trademark application class count in relation to GDP and population

B33. Resident trademark application class count per USD 100 billion GDP for selected origins, 2008 and 2018

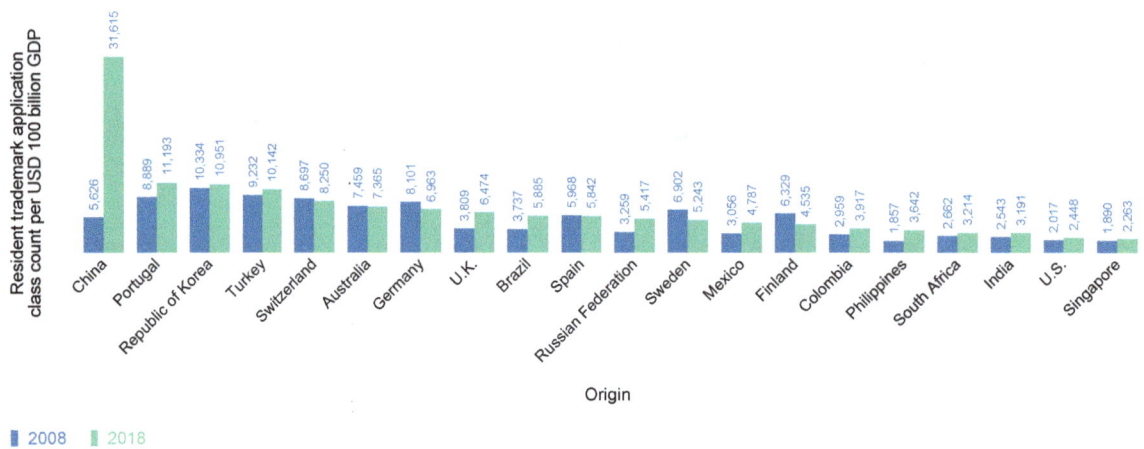

Resident trademark application class count per USD 100 billion GDP

Origin	2008	2018
China	5,626	31,615
Portugal	8,889	11,193
Republic of Korea	10,334	10,951
Turkey	9,232	10,142
Switzerland	8,697	8,250
Australia	7,459	7,365
Germany	8,101	6,963
U.K.	3,809	6,474
Brazil	3,737	5,885
Spain	5,968	5,842
Russian Federation	3,259	5,417
Sweden	6,902	5,243
Mexico	3,056	4,787
Finland	6,329	4,535
Colombia	2,959	3,917
Philippines	1,857	3,642
South Africa	2,662	3,214
India	2,543	3,191
U.S.	2,017	2,448
Singapore	1,890	2,263

■ 2008 ■ 2018

Note: GDP data are in constant 2011 U.S. PPP dollars. This figure does not provide an overall ranking of all origins; rather, it shows a selection across geographical regions and income groups.

Sources: WIPO Statistics Database and World Bank, August 2019.

B34. Resident trademark application class count per million population for selected origins, 2008 and 2018

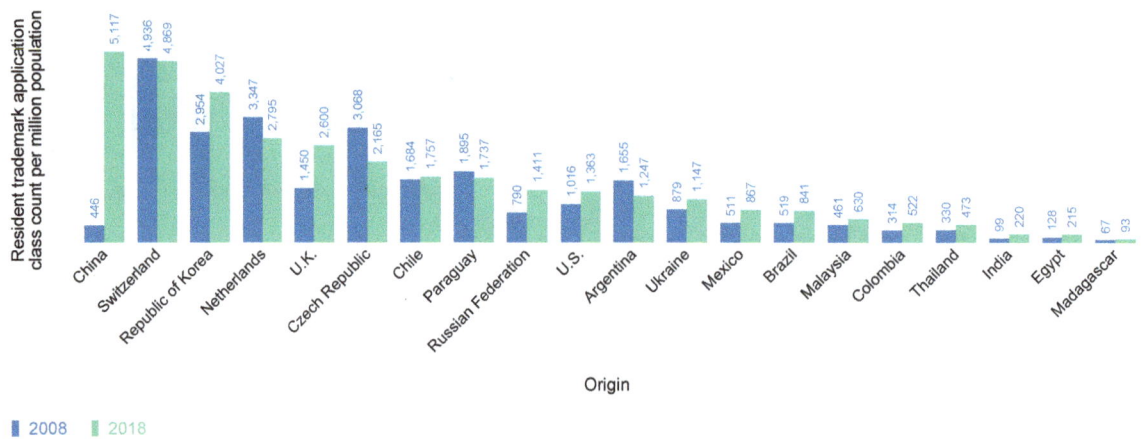

Resident trademark application class count per million population

Origin	2008	2018
China	446	5,117
Switzerland	4,936	4,869
Republic of Korea	2,954	4,027
Netherlands	3,347	2,795
U.K.	1,450	2,600
Czech Republic	3,068	2,165
Chile	1,684	1,757
Paraguay	1,895	1,737
Russian Federation	790	1,411
U.S.	1,016	1,363
Argentina	1,655	1,247
Ukraine	879	1,147
Mexico	511	867
Brazil	519	841
Malaysia	461	630
Colombia	314	522
Thailand	330	473
India	99	220
Egypt	128	215
Madagascar	67	93

■ 2008 ■ 2018

Note: This figure does not provide an overall ranking of all origins; rather, it shows a selection across geographical regions and income groups.

Sources: WIPO Statistics Database and World Bank, August 2019.

Collective and certification trademark applications by office

B35. Collective trademark applications for the top 20 offices, 2018

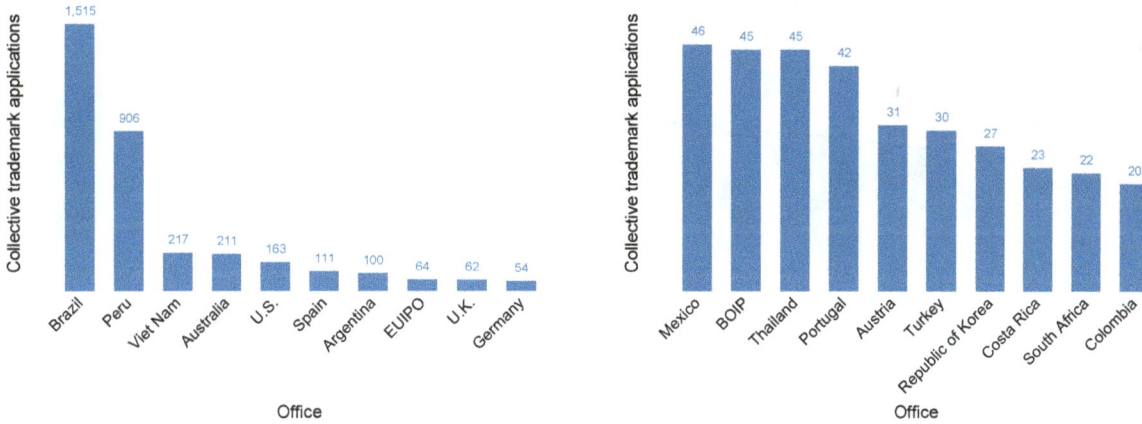

Collective trademark applications (left chart)

Office	Value
Brazil	1,515
Peru	906
Viet Nam	217
Australia	211
U.S.	163
Spain	111
Argentina	100
EUIPO	64
U.K.	62
Germany	54

Collective trademark applications (right chart)

Office	Value
Mexico	46
BOIP	45
Thailand	45
Portugal	42
Austria	31
Turkey	30
Republic of Korea	27
Costa Rica	23
South Africa	22
Colombia	20

Note: EUIPO is the European Union Intellectual Property Office and BOIP is the Benelux Office for Intellectual Property. The 2018 total for the office of China is not presented here because the data are not available.

Source: WIPO Statistics Database, August 2019.

B36. Certification trademark applications for the top 20 offices, 2018

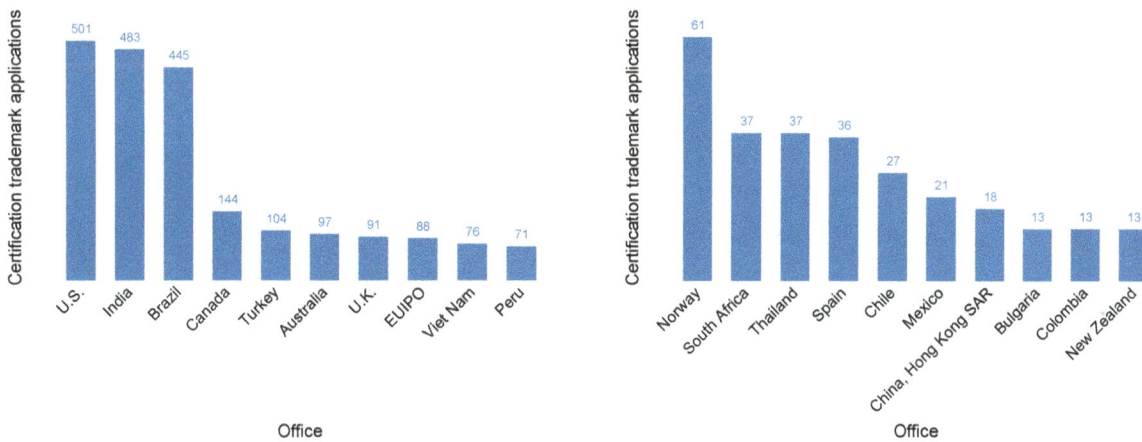

Certification trademark applications (left chart)

Office	Value
U.S.	501
India	483
Brazil	445
Canada	144
Turkey	104
Australia	97
U.K.	91
EUIPO	88
Viet Nam	76
Peru	71

Certification trademark applications (right chart)

Office	Value
Norway	61
South Africa	37
Thailand	37
Spain	36
Chile	27
Mexico	21
China, Hong Kong SAR	18
Bulgaria	13
Colombia	13
New Zealand	13

Note: EUIPO is the European Union Intellectual Property Office. The 2018 total for the office of China is not presented here because the data are not available.

Source: WIPO Statistics Database, August 2019.

Trademarks

Trademark registrations in force

B37. Trend in trademark registrations in force worldwide, 2010–2018

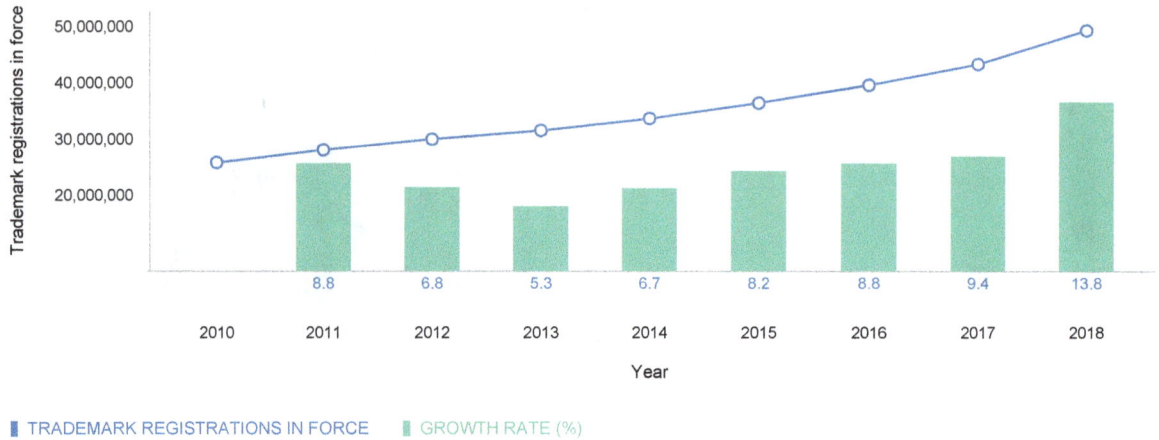

| | 8.8 | 6.8 | 5.3 | 6.7 | 8.2 | 8.8 | 9.4 | 13.8 |
| 2010 | 2011 | 2012 | 2013 | 2014 | 2015 | 2016 | 2017 | 2018 |

Year

▌ TRADEMARK REGISTRATIONS IN FORCE   ▌ GROWTH RATE (%)

Note: World totals are WIPO estimates using data covering 143 IP offices. Data refer to the number of trademark registrations in force, not the number of classes specified in those registrations. Trademark rights can be maintained indefinitely by paying renewal fees at defined time intervals. Trademarks in force provide information on the volume of trademark registrations currently active as well as the historical trademark life cycle.

Source: WIPO Statistics Database, August 2019.

B38. Trademark registrations in force for the top 20 offices, 2018

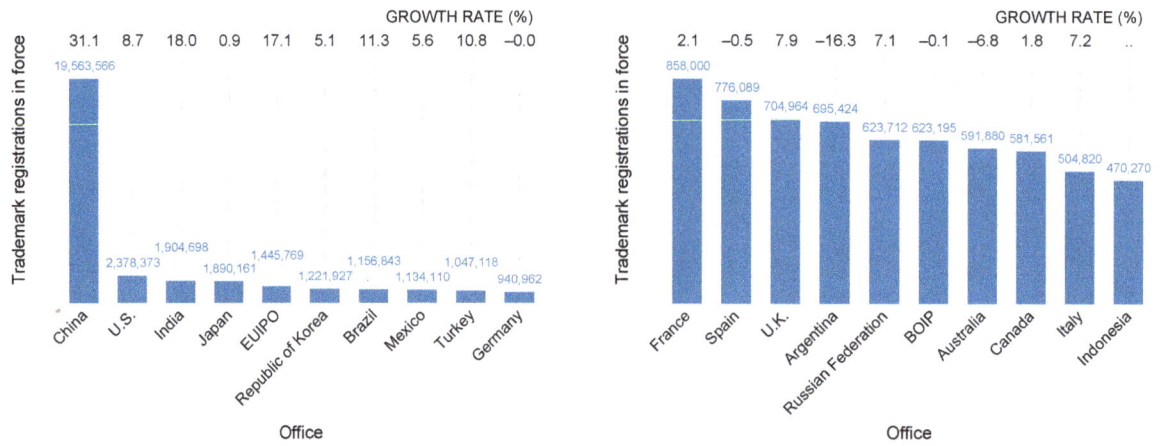

.. indicates not available.

Note: EUIPO is the European Union Intellectual Property Office and BOIP is the Benelux Office for Intellectual Property. Data refer to the number of trademark registrations in force, not the number of classes specified in those registrations.

Source: WIPO Statistics Database, August 2019.

B39. Trademark registrations in force in 2018 as a percentage of total registrations recorded between 1994 and 2018

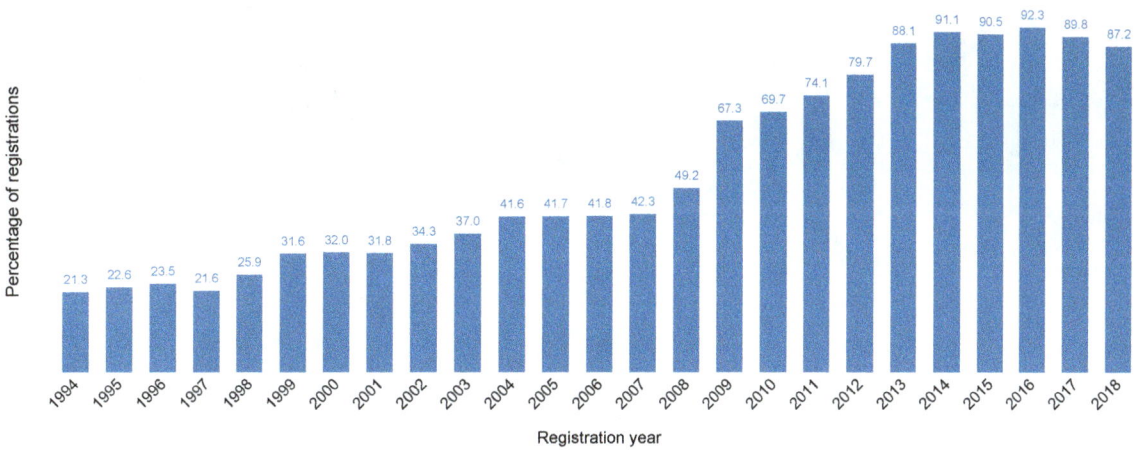

Note: Percentages are calculated as follows: the number of trademark registrations issued in year *t* and in force in 2018 divided by the total number of trademark registrations issued in year *t*. Trademark holders must pay renewal fees to maintain the validity of their marks, which in most cases can be maintained indefinitely. This figure is based on about 15.4 million active trademark registrations reported by the 69 offices that provided a breakdown by year of registration. Detailed data for several larger offices, such as those of China, France and Japan, are not available.

Source: WIPO Statistics Database, August 2019.

B40. Average age of trademarks in force at selected offices, 2013 and 2018

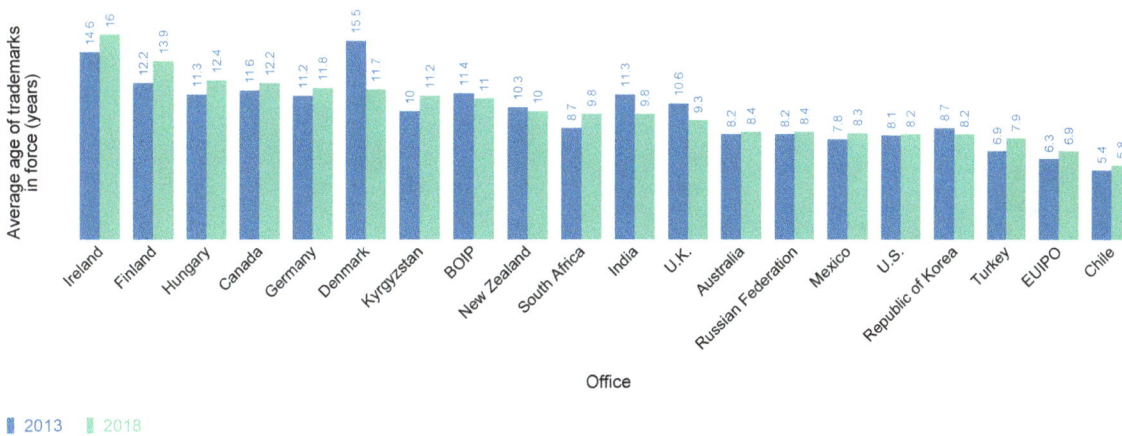

2013 **2018**

Note: EUIPO is the European Union Intellectual Property Office and BOIP is the Benelux Office for Intellectual Property.

Source: WIPO Statistics Database, August 2019.

Trademark office procedural data

B41. Distribution of trademark examination outcomes for selected offices, 2018

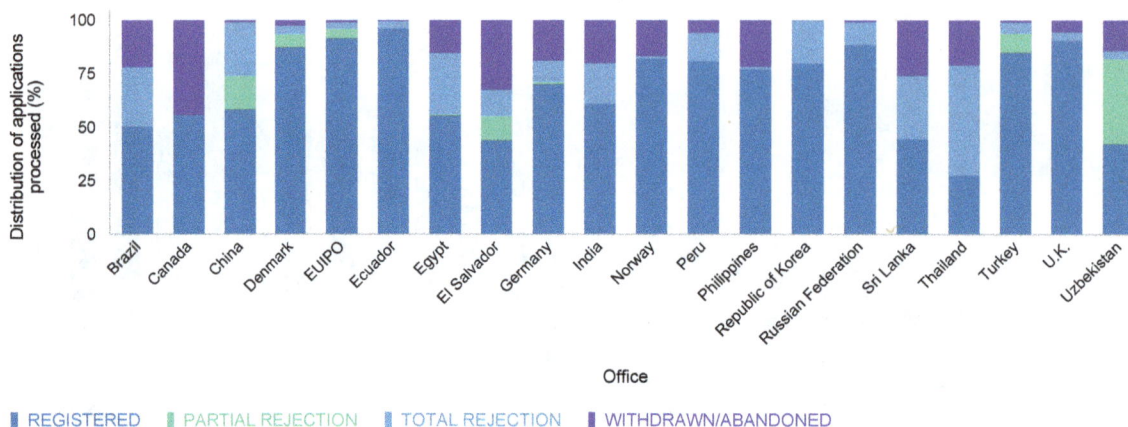

REGISTERED PARTIAL REJECTION TOTAL REJECTION WITHDRAWN/ABANDONED

Note: EUIPO is the European Union Intellectual Property Office. WIPO collects data from IP offices using a common questionnaire and methodology. However, due to differences in application processing procedures between offices, data cannot be fully harmonized. Therefore caution should be exercised when making comparisons across offices.

Source: WIPO Statistics Database, August 2019.

B42. Trademark applications pending for selected offices, 2018

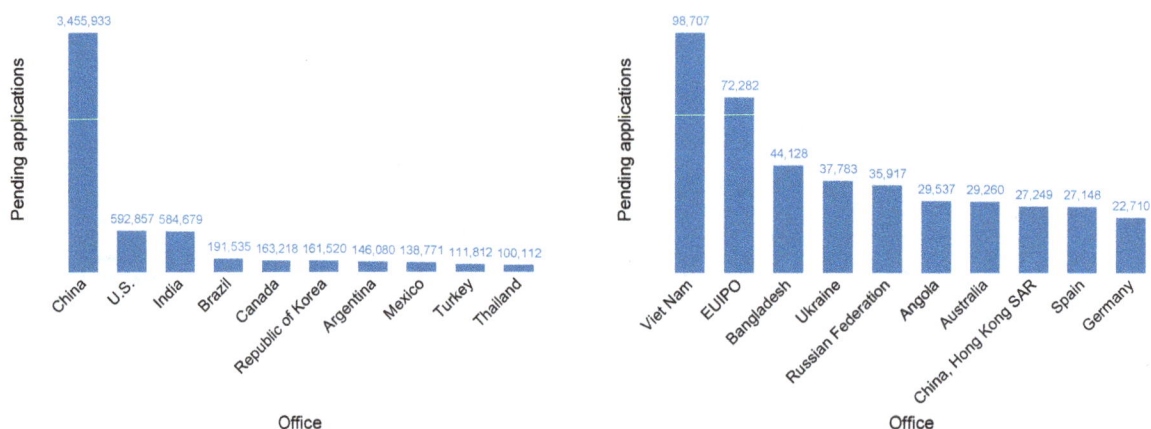

Note: EUIPO is the European Union Intellectual Property Office. WIPO collects data from IP offices using a common questionnaire and methodology. However, due to differences in application processing procedures between offices, data cannot be fully harmonized. Therefore caution should be exercised when making comparisons across offices.

Source: WIPO Statistics Database, August 2019.

B43. Number of trademark examiners for selected offices, 2018

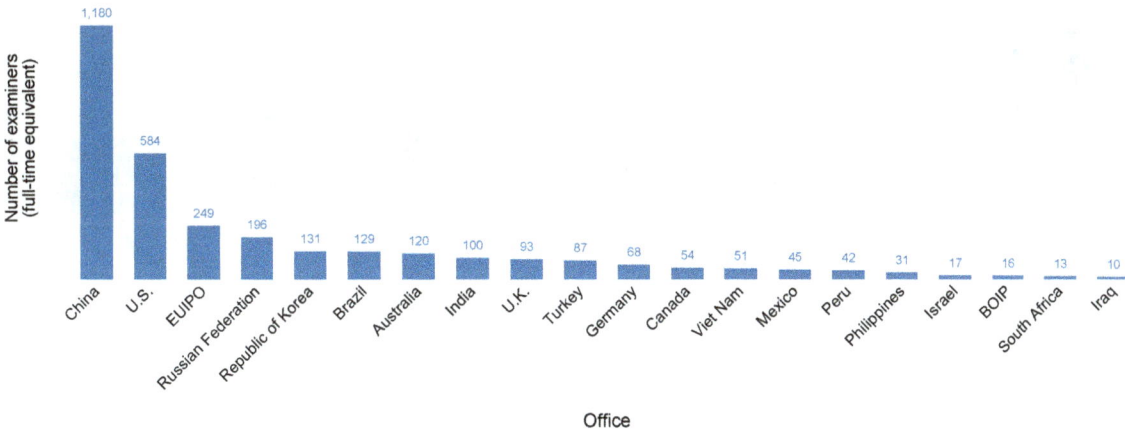

Number of examiners (full-time equivalent)

China 1,180 · U.S. 584 · EUIPO 249 · Russian Federation 196 · Republic of Korea 131 · Brazil 129 · Australia 120 · India 100 · U.K. 93 · Turkey 87 · Germany 68 · Canada 54 · Viet Nam 51 · Mexico 45 · Peru 42 · Philippines 31 · Israel 17 · BOIP 16 · South Africa 13 · Iraq 10

Office

Note: EUIPO is the European Union Intellectual Property Office and BOIP is the Benelux Office for Intellectual Property.
Source: WIPO Statistics Database, August 2019.

B44. Duration of trademark examination for selected offices, 2018

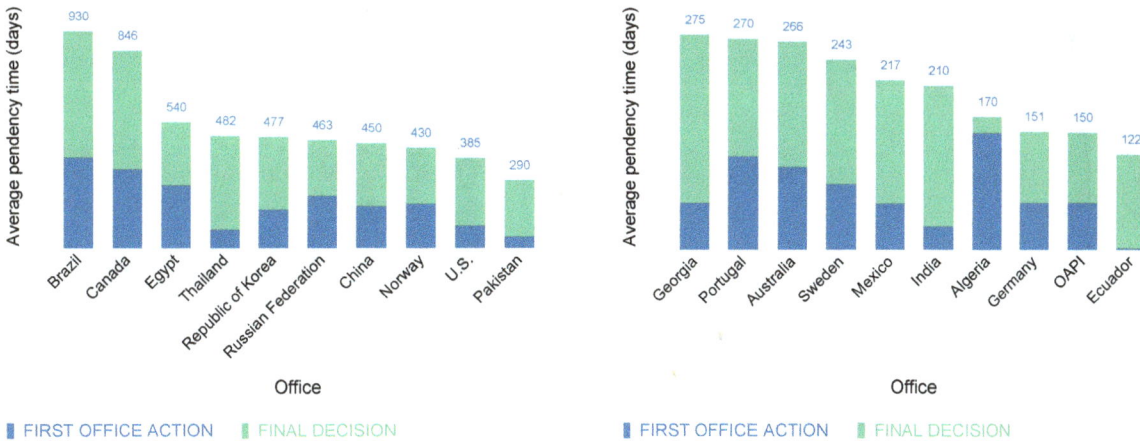

Average pendency time (days)

Brazil 930 · Canada 846 · Egypt 540 · Thailand 482 · Republic of Korea 477 · Russian Federation 463 · China 450 · Norway 430 · U.S. 385 · Pakistan 290

Average pendency time (days)

Georgia 275 · Portugal 270 · Australia 266 · Sweden 243 · Mexico 217 · India 210 · Algeria 170 · Germany 151 · OAPI 150 · Ecuador 122

Office

■ FIRST OFFICE ACTION ■ FINAL DECISION

■ FIRST OFFICE ACTION ■ FINAL DECISION

Note: OAPI is the African Intellectual Property Organization, which receives applications on behalf of its 17 member states. WIPO collects data from IP offices using a common questionnaire and methodology. However, due to differences in application processing procedures between offices, data cannot be fully harmonized. Therefore caution should be exercised when making comparisons across offices.
Source: WIPO Statistics Database, August 2019.

B45. Third party oppositions for selected offices, 2018

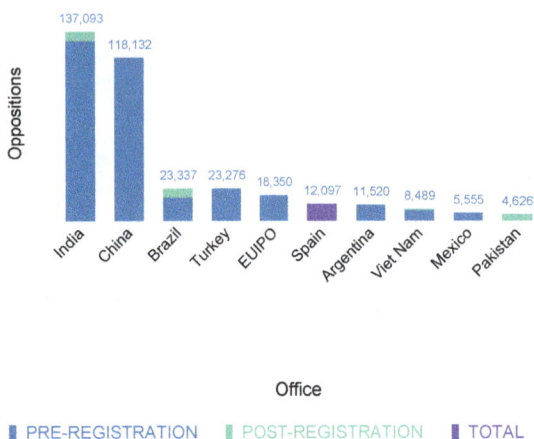

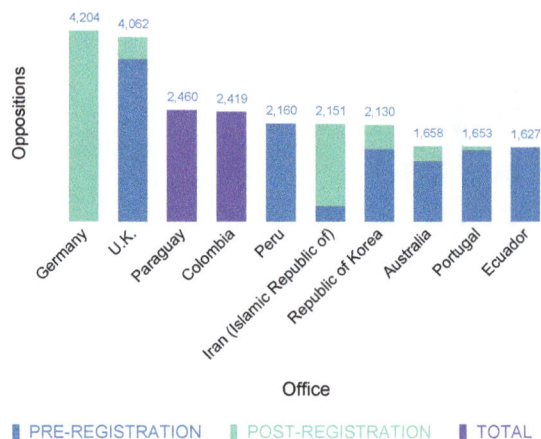

Left chart:
Oppositions (y-axis) / Office (x-axis)

- India: 137,093
- China: 118,132
- Brazil: 23,337
- Turkey: 23,276
- EUIPO: 18,350
- Spain: 12,097
- Argentina: 11,520
- Viet Nam: 8,489
- Mexico: 5,555
- Pakistan: 4,626

Right chart:
Oppositions (y-axis) / Office (x-axis)

- Germany: 4,204
- U.K.: 4,062
- Paraguay: 2,460
- Colombia: 2,419
- Peru: 2,160
- Iran (Islamic Republic of): 2,151
- Republic of Korea: 2,130
- Australia: 1,658
- Portugal: 1,653
- Ecuador: 1,627

PRE-REGISTRATION   POST-REGISTRATION   TOTAL

Note: EUIPO is the European Union Intellectual Property Office.
Source: WIPO Statistics Database, August 2019.

B46. Appeals to decisions by selected offices, 2018

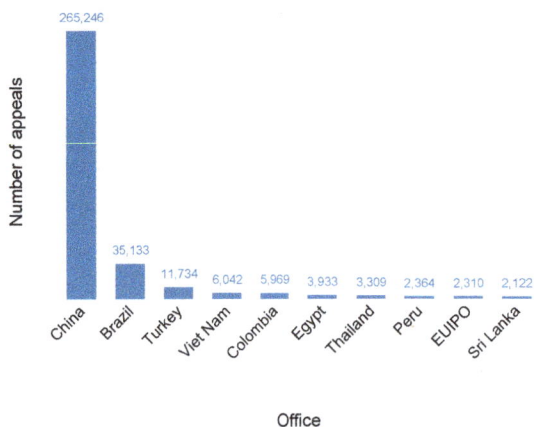

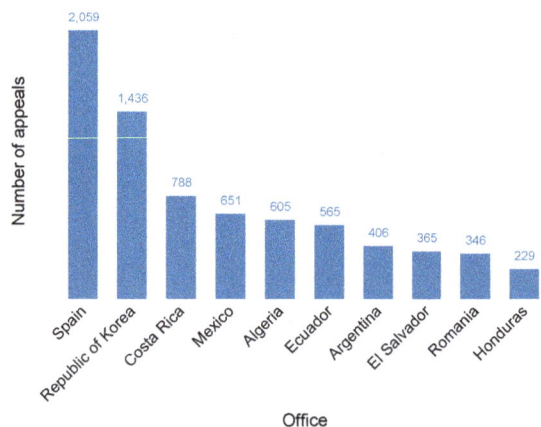

Left chart:
Number of appeals (y-axis) / Office (x-axis)

- China: 265,246
- Brazil: 35,133
- Turkey: 11,734
- Viet Nam: 6,042
- Colombia: 5,969
- Egypt: 3,933
- Thailand: 3,309
- Peru: 2,364
- EUIPO: 2,310
- Sri Lanka: 2,122

Right chart:
Number of appeals (y-axis) / Office (x-axis)

- Spain: 2,059
- Republic of Korea: 1,436
- Costa Rica: 788
- Mexico: 651
- Algeria: 605
- Ecuador: 565
- Argentina: 406
- El Salvador: 365
- Romania: 346
- Honduras: 229

Note: EUIPO is the European Union Intellectual Property Office.
Source: WIPO Statistics Database, August 2019.

Trademark applications and registrations through the Madrid System

B47. Trend in Madrid international applications, 2004–2018

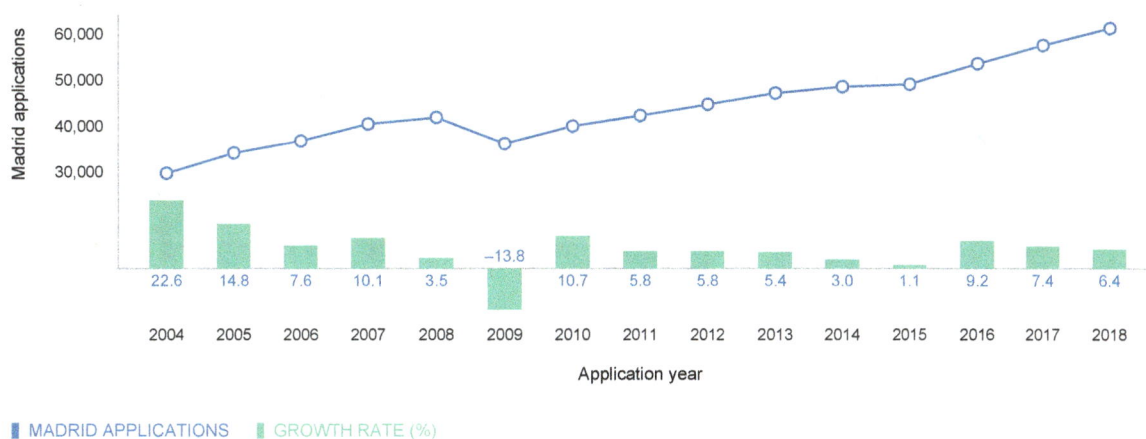

Year	Growth rate (%)
2004	22.6
2005	14.8
2006	7.6
2007	10.1
2008	3.5
2009	−13.8
2010	10.7
2011	5.8
2012	5.8
2013	5.4
2014	3.0
2015	1.1
2016	9.2
2017	7.4
2018	6.4

■ MADRID APPLICATIONS   ■ GROWTH RATE (%)

Source: WIPO Statistics Database, August 2019.

B48. Madrid international applications by origin, 2018

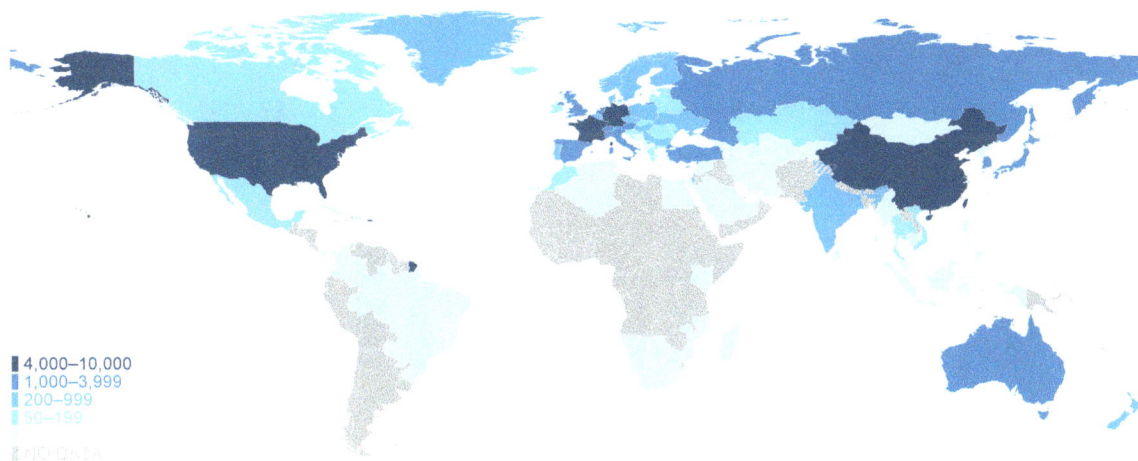

■ 4,000–10,000
■ 1,000–3,999
■ 200–999
■ 50–199
■ NO DATA

Note: Counts are based on the country of the applicant's address, not the office of origin.
Source: WIPO Statistics Database, August 2019.

Trademarks

B49. Madrid applications for the top 20 origins, 2018

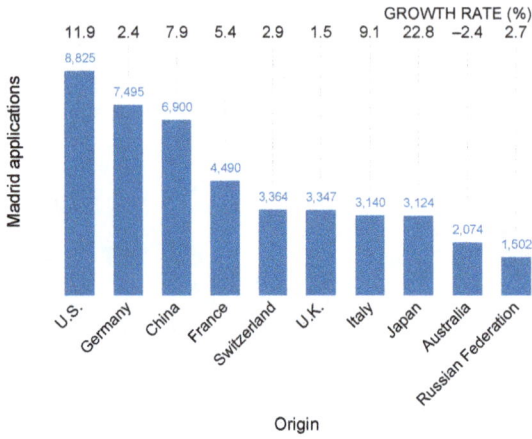

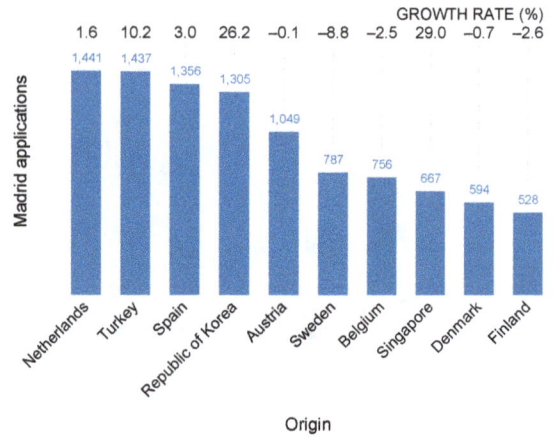

GROWTH RATE (%)

11.9	2.4	7.9	5.4	2.9	1.5	9.1	22.8	−2.4	2.7

Madrid applications

U.S.	Germany	China	France	Switzerland	U.K.	Italy	Japan	Australia	Russian Federation
8,825	7,495	6,900	4,490	3,364	3,347	3,140	3,124	2,074	1,502

Origin

GROWTH RATE (%)

1.6	10.2	3.0	26.2	−0.1	−8.8	−2.5	29.0	−0.7	−2.6

Madrid applications

Netherlands	Turkey	Spain	Republic of Korea	Austria	Sweden	Belgium	Singapore	Denmark	Finland
1,441	1,437	1,356	1,305	1,049	787	756	667	594	528

Origin

Note: Origin data are based on the country of the applicant's address.
Source: WIPO Statistics Database, August 2019.

B50. Designations in Madrid international applications for the top 20 designated Madrid members, 2018

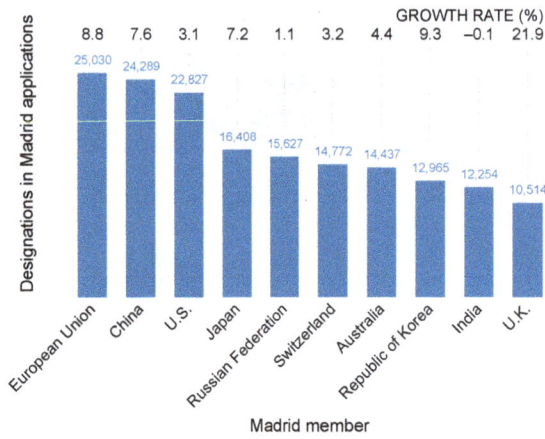

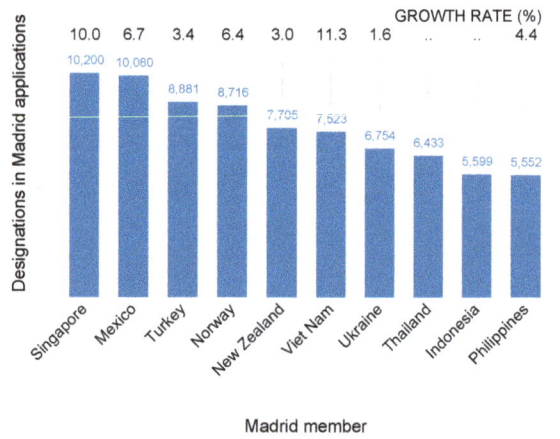

GROWTH RATE (%)

8.8	7.6	3.1	7.2	1.1	3.2	4.4	9.3	−0.1	21.9

Designations in Madrid applications

European Union	China	U.S.	Japan	Russian Federation	Switzerland	Australia	Republic of Korea	India	U.K.
25,030	24,289	22,827	16,408	15,627	14,772	14,437	12,965	12,254	10,514

Madrid member

GROWTH RATE (%)

10.0	6.7	3.4	6.4	3.0	11.3	1.6	..	..	4.4

Designations in Madrid applications

Singapore	Mexico	Turkey	Norway	New Zealand	Viet Nam	Ukraine	Thailand	Indonesia	Philippines
10,200	10,080	8,881	8,716	7,705	7,523	6,754	6,433	5,599	5,552

Madrid member

Note: The numbers of designations in applications for all Madrid members are reported in statistical table B51.
.. indicates not available.
Source: WIPO Statistics Database, August 2019.

Statistical tables

B51. Trademark applications by office and origin, 2018

Name	Application class count by office			Application class count by origin	Equivalent application class count by origin	Madrid international applications	
	Total	Resident	Non-resident	Total [a]	Total [a]	Origin [f]	Designated Madrid member
Afghanistan (b)	..	..	..	229	229	..	255
African Intellectual Property Organization	14,062	4,247	9,815	n.a.	n.a.	n.a.	2,095
African Regional Intellectual Property Organization	653	309	344	n.a.	n.a.	n.a.	n.a.
Albania	8,685	1,542	7,143	1,775	2,427	13	2,304
Algeria	15,857	7,082	8,775	7,336	8,246	5	2,621
Andorra	3,298	822	2,476	1,314	9,441	5	n.a.
Angola	4,134	2,354	1,780	2,388	2,495	..	n.a.
Antigua and Barbuda (b)	..	..	..	130	427	2	514
Argentina	71,712	55,492	16,220	59,243	63,776	..	n.a.
Armenia	10,705	2,897	7,808	3,899	4,517	35	2,458
Australia	147,446	83,641	63,805	127,163	211,451	2,074	14,437
Austria	25,394	15,663	9,731	46,205	317,075	1,049	2,573
Azerbaijan	13,059	3,791	9,268	4,126	4,265	5	2,861
Bahamas (b)	..	..	..	2,183	8,177	13	n.a.
Bahrain	12,500	305	12,195	624	953	1	1,790
Bangladesh	12,080	7,960	4,120	8,114	8,141	..	n.a.
Barbados (b)	..	..	..	1,272	3,306	3	n.a.
Belarus	20,142	4,529	15,613	7,822	9,652	157	4,481
Belgium (c)	n.a.	n.a.	n.a.	42,949	258,020	756	n.a.
Belize (b)	..	..	..	1,570	2,812	17	n.a.
Benelux Office for Intellectual Property (d)	65,163	53,519	11,644	n.a.	n.a.	n.a.	2,681
Benin (b,h)	n.a.	n.a.	n.a.	193	3,107	..	n.a.
Bermuda (b)	..	..	..	480	831	11	n.a.
Bhutan (b)	..	..	..	5	5	..	814
Bolivia (Plurinational State of) (b)	..	..	..	149	257	..	n.a.
Bonaire, Sint Eustatius and Saba (b)	..	..	..	4	4	1	441
Bosnia and Herzegovina	10,321	989	9,332	1,835	3,001	29	2,850
Botswana	3,172	606	2,566	2,032	5,709	3	770
Brazil	204,419	176,063	28,356	182,595	195,715	6	n.a.
Brunei Darussalam	4,243	189	4,054	298	352	2	951
Bulgaria	17,929	13,107	4,822	24,046	75,095	245	1,375
Burkina Faso (b,h)	n.a.	n.a.	n.a.	207	3,519	..	n.a.
Cabo Verde	344	133	211	179	195	..	n.a.
Cambodia	12,200	2,416	9,784	2,565	2,705	5	2,353
Cameroon (b,h)	n.a.	n.a.	n.a.	651	10,011	..	n.a.
Canada	187,642	106,328	81,314	150,905	282,739	95	n.a.
Central African Republic (b,h)	n.a.	n.a.	n.a.	45	157	..	n.a.
Chad (b,h)	n.a.	n.a.	n.a.	15	239	..	n.a.
Chile	47,414	32,909	14,505	36,438	38,507	..	n.a.
China	7,365,522	7,127,191	238,331	7,432,443	8,118,135	6,900	24,289
China, Hong Kong SAR	84,585	31,718	52,867	53,715	129,916	6	n.a.
China, Macao SAR	16,466	2,438	14,028	2,977	3,425	..	n.a.
Colombia	45,656	25,930	19,726	29,359	31,940	29	3,990
Comoros (b)	..	..	..	12	204	..	n.a.
Congo (b,h)	n.a.	n.a.	n.a.	92	1,196	..	n.a.

Trademarks

Name	Application class count by office			Application class count by origin	Equivalent application class count by origin	Madrid international applications	
	Total	Resident	Non-resident	Total [a]	Total [a]	Origin [f]	Designated Madrid member
Cook Islands (b)	..	..	..	50	131	..	n.a.
Costa Rica	13,563	7,034	6,529	8,081	8,999	..	n.a.
Côte d'Ivoire (b,h)	n.a.	n.a.	n.a.	1,232	20,032	..	n.a.
Croatia	7,720	3,307	4,413	5,741	18,349	129	1,375
Cuba	7,129	2,459	4,670	3,041	4,125	11	1,537
Curaçao	2,110	0	2,110	313	859	16	524
Cyprus	4,089	1,114	2,975	13,573	58,063	208	890
Czech Republic	24,796	19,065	5,731	33,122	139,981	280	1,751
Democratic People's Republic of Korea (b)	..	..	..	204	420	8	1,175
Democratic Republic of the Congo (b)	..	..	..	17	285	..	n.a.
Denmark	10,979	6,366	4,613	25,014	187,105	594	1,152
Djibouti (b)	..	..	..	7	7	..	n.a.
Dominica	178	8	170	28	55	..	n.a.
Dominican Republic	14,122	8,393	5,729	8,725	9,377	1	n.a.
Ecuador	17,969	11,435	6,534	12,407	13,613	..	n.a.
Egypt	35,562	21,158	14,404	22,417	25,088	13	4,030
El Salvador	10,630	4,040	6,590	4,708	4,735	..	n.a.
Equatorial Guinea (b,h)	n.a.	n.a.	n.a.	33	594	..	n.a.
Estonia	6,158	2,655	3,503	7,284	57,992	102	1,044
Eswatini (b)	..	..	..	86	86	..	636
Ethiopia	1,027	542	485	917	917	..	n.a.
European Union Intellectual Property Office (e)	392,925	282,032	110,893	n.a.	n.a.	n.a.	25,030
Fiji (b)	..	..	..	44	44	..	n.a.
Finland	9,429	5,556	3,873	23,208	156,919	528	929
France	298,895	279,882	19,013	439,890	1,250,619	4,490	3,422
Gabon (b,h)	n.a.	n.a.	n.a.	216	1,640	..	n.a.
Gambia	2,065	54	2,011	54	54	..	835
Georgia	10,615	2,776	7,839	3,193	3,333	19	2,497
Germany	219,855	195,623	24,232	461,471	2,355,796	7,495	4,332
Ghana	5,348	833	4,515	864	1,008	..	1,206
Greece (b)	..	..	..	4,935	71,148	118	1,117
Grenada	436	19	417	31	31	..	n.a.
Guatemala	12,321	6,513	5,808	8,194	8,977	..	n.a.
Guinea (b,h)	n.a.	n.a.	n.a.	181	2,731	..	n.a.
Guinea-Bissau (b,h)	n.a.	n.a.	n.a.	6	86	..	n.a.
Guyana	826	204	622	214	214	..	n.a.
Haiti (b)	..	..	..	22	81	..	n.a.
Honduras	7,228	2,551	4,677	2,959	3,067	..	n.a.
Hungary	12,132	7,168	4,964	17,045	61,253	256	1,482
Iceland	10,141	1,952	8,189	3,084	7,848	59	2,395
India	342,698	297,751	44,947	309,356	333,441	308	12,254
Indonesia	87,923	58,659	29,264	61,652	65,206	47	5,599
Iran (Islamic Republic of)	384,338	354,343	29,995	355,446	357,026	14	3,281
Iraq	11,832	1,832	10,000	2,652	2,953	..	n.a.
Ireland (g)	8,600	..	..	10,976	92,540	188	993

Name	Application class count by office			Application class count by origin	Equivalent application class count by origin	Madrid international applications	
	Total	Resident	Non-resident	Total [a]	Total [a]	Origin [f]	Designated Madrid member
Israel	21,198	4,142	17,056	11,598	41,422	385	4,931
Italy	96,751	83,863	12,888	183,098	1,085,090	3,140	3,232
Jamaica	10,659	5,035	5,624	5,128	5,263	..	n.a.
Japan	512,156	438,338	73,818	553,106	719,264	3,124	16,408
Jordan	7,475	2,981	4,494	3,838	6,179	..	n.a.
Kazakhstan	16,900	1	16,899	2,332	2,418	74	4,835
Kenya (b)	..	..	..	197	709	9	1,937
Kuwait	10,738	3,543	7,195	4,371	5,775	..	n.a.
Kyrgyzstan	8,297	552	7,745	609	609	2	2,438
Lao People's Democratic Republic	5,258	249	5,009	277	277	..	1,445
Latvia	9,157	5,241	3,916	7,486	22,986	101	1,275
Lebanon (b)	..	..	..	890	3,763	2	n.a.
Lesotho	2,204	68	2,136	80	107	..	666
Liberia (b)	..	..	..	51	51	..	806
Libya (b)	..	..	..	42	69	..	n.a.
Liechtenstein	8,479	527	7,952	3,566	11,966	79	2,238
Lithuania	7,952	3,769	4,183	6,151	29,487	120	1,314
Luxembourg (c)	n.a.	n.a.	n.a.	18,191	121,282	379	n.a.
Madagascar	5,923	2,448	3,475	2,490	2,813	1	1,053
Malawi (b)	..	..	..	40	40	..	2
Malaysia	43,656	19,863	23,793	27,119	30,932	9	n.a.
Maldives (b)	..	..	..	17	17	..	n.a.
Mali (b,h)	n.a.	n.a.	n.a.	220	3,308	..	n.a.
Malta (b)	..	..	..	4,995	63,044	68	n.a.
Marshall Islands (b)	..	..	..	201	1,485	1	n.a.
Mauritania (b,h)	n.a.	n.a.	n.a.	93	861	..	n.a.
Mauritius	5,227	2,523	2,704	4,805	10,923	12	n.a.
Mexico	155,823	109,355	46,468	119,014	132,420	98	10,080
Monaco	9,341	1,351	7,990	8,703	26,277	115	2,274
Mongolia	14,285	8,703	5,582	8,928	9,360	9	1,871
Montenegro	8,871	522	8,349	726	1,401	9	2,580
Morocco	28,894	14,609	14,285	15,874	22,952	71	3,880
Mozambique	5,128	1,247	3,881	1,254	1,254	1	1,106
Myanmar (b)	..	..	..	91	118	1	n.a.
Namibia	5,435	2,060	3,375	2,211	2,778	4	958
Nepal (b)	..	..	..	94	310	..	n.a.
Netherlands (c)	n.a.	n.a.	n.a.	81,502	519,092	1,441	n.a.
Netherlands Antilles (b)	..	..	..	14	110	..	0
New Zealand	50,325	17,806	32,519	28,259	47,971	495	7,705
Nicaragua (b)	..	..	..	159	402	..	n.a.
Niger (b,h)	n.a.	n.a.	n.a.	378	6,426	..	n.a.
Nigeria (g)	11,115	..	..	128	662	..	n.a.
North Macedonia (b)	..	..	..	690	1,446	29	2,579
Norway	45,288	13,935	31,353	25,536	78,641	333	8,716
Oman (b)	..	..	..	260	503	..	1,855
Pakistan	37,981	30,543	7,438	31,502	32,977	..	n.a.

Name	Application class count by office			Application class count by origin	Equivalent application class count by origin	Madrid international applications	
	Total	Resident	Non-resident	Total [a]	Total [a]	Origin [f]	Designated Madrid member
Palau (b)	..	..	..	4	4	..	n.a.
Panama	12,073	5,201	6,872	9,234	13,125	5	n.a.
Papua New Guinea (b)	..	..	..	49	49	..	n.a.
Paraguay	17,459	12,085	5,374	12,434	12,725	1	n.a.
Peru	36,579	23,644	12,935	25,076	26,851	..	n.a.
Philippines	57,179	30,853	26,326	32,286	33,210	49	5,552
Poland	38,905	31,215	7,690	54,601	335,064	395	2,247
Portugal	34,820	29,087	5,733	38,285	145,313	253	1,588
Qatar (b)	..	..	..	931	3,048	..	n.a.
Republic of Korea	263,976	207,953	56,023	275,549	350,330	1,305	12,965
Republic of Moldova	11,915	3,023	8,892	3,681	4,013	58	2,689
Romania	24,638	19,182	5,456	23,680	88,956	80	1,668
Russian Federation	263,552	203,854	59,698	261,765	299,577	1,502	15,627
Rwanda	2,876	318	2,558	327	381	..	867
Saint Kitts and Nevis	474	11	463	223	1,767	..	n.a.
Saint Lucia	385	33	352	302	572	..	n.a.
Saint Vincent and the Grenadines	466	84	382	119	119	..	n.a.
Samoa	405	68	337	1,018	1,693	..	0
San Marino (b)	..	..	..	421	2,554	11	1,087
Sao Tome and Principe	1,760	10	1,750	10	10	..	484
Saudi Arabia	31,892	18,563	13,329	21,495	26,032	3	n.a.
Senegal (b,h)	n.a.	n.a.	n.a.	633	8,864	..	n.a.
Serbia	16,521	3,530	12,991	10,351	17,275	207	4,035
Seychelles	757	67	690	1,859	3,300	3	n.a.
Sierra Leone	2,487	130	2,357	194	194	..	828
Singapore	52,895	11,496	41,399	38,728	71,997	667	10,200
Sint Maarten (Dutch Part) (b)	..	..	..	..	..	..	494
Slovakia	13,398	8,323	5,075	11,846	47,497	90	1,272
Slovenia	8,242	4,344	3,898	9,524	41,444	188	1,209
Solomon Islands (b)	..	..	..	30	30	..	n.a.
Somalia (b)	..	..	..	12	39	..	n.a.
South Africa	38,537	22,550	15,987	25,134	34,028	2	n.a.
Spain	82,836	72,710	10,126	125,916	749,940	1,356	2,850
Sri Lanka	11,483	7,356	4,127	8,065	9,161	1	n.a.
Sudan	5,345	1,780	3,565	1,961	1,961	..	1,179
Suriname	1,564	899	665	966	1,113	..	n.a.
Sweden	21,029	15,756	5,273	49,841	306,290	787	1,272
Switzerland	96,076	41,468	54,608	153,081	499,593	3,364	14,772
Syrian Arab Republic	13,616	6,993	6,623	8,625	10,148	10	873
Tajikistan (b)	..	..	..	23	23	1	2,102
Thailand	78,281	32,826	45,455	40,795	46,086	140	6,433
Timor-Leste (b)	..	..	..	91	91	..	n.a.
Togo (b,h)	n.a.	n.a.	n.a.	674	11,154	..	n.a.
Tonga	547	3	544	3	3	..	n.a.
Trinidad and Tobago	2,508	622	1,886	880	961	..	n.a.
Tunisia (b)	..	..	..	843	2,934	30	2,263

Name	Application class count by office			Application class count by origin	Equivalent application class count by origin	Madrid international applications	
	Total	Resident	Non-resident	Total [a]	Total [a]	Origin [f]	Designated Madrid member
Turkey	244,525	211,109	33,416	234,512	285,843	1,437	8,881
Turkmenistan (b)	..	..	..	141	141	1	1,739
Tuvalu (b)	..	..	..	39	39	..	n.a.
Uganda (g)	1,506	..	..	23	151	..	n.a.
Ukraine	76,518	51,195	25,323	58,190	69,302	401	6,754
United Arab Emirates	18,450	4,711	13,739	13,779	32,797	32	n.a.
United Kingdom	198,125	139,155	58,970	299,188	1,219,765	3,347	10,514
United Republic of Tanzania (g)	4,127	..	..	101	101	..	n.a.
United States of America	640,181	445,872	194,309	821,829	1,759,417	8,825	22,827
Uruguay (b)	..	..	..	6,428	8,183	..	n.a.
Uzbekistan	14,468	7,412	7,056	7,993	7,993	8	2,100
Vanuatu (b)	..	..	..	97	151	1	n.a.
Venezuela (Bolivarian Republic of) (b)	..	..	..	341	719	..	n.a.
Viet Nam	94,196	60,731	33,465	64,513	67,975	159	7,523
Yemen	5,799	4,044	1,755	4,447	4,852	..	n.a.
Zambia (b)	..	..	..	32	32	..	1,012
Zimbabwe (b)	..	..	..	39	71	..	1,075
Others/Unknown	1	0	1	101,093	215,739	18	2
Total (2018 estimates)	**14,321,800**	**12,000,000**	**2,321,800**	**14,321,800**	**n.a.**	**61,200**	**399,556**

(a) Data on application class count by origin are incomplete because some offices do not report detailed statistics containing the origin of application class counts.

(b) Only Madrid designation data are available therefore application class count by office and origin data may be incomplete.

(c) This country does not have a national trademark office. All applications for trademark protection are filed at the Benelux Office for Intellectual Property or the European Union Intellectual Property Office.

(d) Resident applications include those filed by residents of Belgium, Luxembourg and the Netherlands.

(e) Resident applications include those filed by residents of EU member states.

(f) Origin is defined as the country/territory of the stated residence of the applicant in an international application.

(g) Total includes an aggregate direct application class count that cannot be broken down into direct and non-resident components.

(h) The African Intellectual Property Office (OAPI) is the competent office for processing applications.

n.a. indicates not applicable.

.. indicates not available.

Source: WIPO Statistics Database, August 2019.

Trademarks

B52. Trademark registrations by office and origin, and trademarks in force, 2018

Name	Registration class count by office			Registration class count by origin	Equivalent registration class count by origin	Madrid international registrations	In force by office
	Total	Resident	Non-resident	Total [a]	Total [a]	Origin [f]	Total
Afghanistan (b)	..	..	..	107	134	..	..
African Intellectual Property Organization	15,087	4,063	11,024	n.a.	n.a.	n.a.	46,705
African Regional Intellectual Property Organization	589	249	340	n.a.	n.a.	n.a.	2,086
Albania	8,954	843	8,111	918	1,404	7	33,946
Algeria	14,278	4,034	10,244	4,397	5,428	17	40,055
Andorra	3,300	824	2,476	1,158	8,826	1	21,286
Angola	2,121	483	1,638	520	568	..	23,369
Antigua and Barbuda (b)	..	..	..	35	440	1	8,801
Argentina	33,204	24,572	8,632	27,595	31,776	2	695,424
Armenia	10,625	1,950	8,675	3,104	3,625	39	20,204
Australia	125,034	62,550	62,484	103,099	191,593	2,142	591,880
Austria	25,560	15,665	9,895	49,210	284,833	1,052	100,946
Azerbaijan	11,419	1,765	9,654	2,215	2,493	9	72,843
Bahamas (b)	..	..	..	1,067	3,767	2	..
Bahrain	13,228	199	13,029	368	762	..	..
Bangladesh	3,600	940	2,660	1,055	1,055	..	..
Barbados (b)	..	..	..	699	2,760	3	..
Belarus	18,734	2,922	15,812	6,171	8,646	135	125,961
Belgium (c)	n.a.	n.a.	n.a.	35,129	227,287	750	n.a.
Belize (b)	..	..	..	1,585	2,260	34	11,853
Benelux Office for Intellectual Property (d)	54,301	43,955	10,346	n.a.	n.a.	1	623,195
Benin (b,h)	n.a.	n.a.	n.a.	223	3,890	..	..
Bermuda (b)	..	..	..	475	799	11	..
Bhutan (b)	..	..	..	2	2	..	..
Bolivia (Plurinational State of) (b)	..	..	..	92	146	..	..
Bonaire, Sint Eustatius and Saba (b)	..	..	..	4	4	1	..
Bosnia and Herzegovina	10,901	565	10,336	1,144	2,257	38	16,964
Botswana	3,328	377	2,951	1,834	5,511	3	18,667
Brazil	191,813	144,723	47,090	149,377	161,152	3	1,156,843
Brunei Darussalam	3,145	59	3,086	141	195	1	..
Bulgaria	16,284	11,512	4,772	20,669	62,271	190	53,385
Burkina Faso (b,h)	n.a.	n.a.	n.a.	254	4,270	..	..
Burundi	420	24	396	24	24	..	..
Cabo Verde	177	21	156	30	262	..	..
Cambodia	10,710	1,572	9,138	1,626	1,680	1	..
Cameroon (b,h)	n.a.	n.a.	n.a.	559	9,386	..	..
Canada	62,049	31,709	30,340	55,111	144,455	82	581,561
Central African Republic (b,h)	n.a.	n.a.	n.a.	5	85	..	..
Chad (b,h)	n.a.	n.a.	n.a.	13	221	..	..
Chile	28,812	18,202	10,610	21,519	24,218	..	369,270
China	4,995,813	4,797,018	198,795	5,021,301	5,633,138	6,840	19,563,566
China, Hong Kong SAR	72,404	25,966	46,438	41,378	108,534	5	423,036
China, Macao SAR	14,450	2,107	12,343	2,508	3,091	..	116,725
Colombia	40,957	20,947	20,010	23,882	26,496	19	322,193
Comoros (b)	..	..	..	7	103	..	..

Name	Registration class count by office			Registration class count by origin	Equivalent registration class count by origin	Madrid international registrations	In force by office
	Total	Resident	Non-resident	Total [a]	Total [a]	Origin [f]	Total
Congo (b,h)	n.a.	n.a.	n.a.	41	553	..	..
Cook Islands (b)	..	..	..	24	51	..	..
Costa Rica	10,016	5,118	4,898	5,870	6,626	..	120,081
Côte d'Ivoire (b,h)	n.a.	n.a.	n.a.	983	16,535	..	..
Croatia	8,550	3,577	4,973	5,862	16,275	98	27,424
Cuba	6,455	853	5,602	1,250	2,303	7	40,379
Curaçao	2,319	0	2,319	255	528	11	21,745
Cyprus	3,346	444	2,902	11,300	52,738	181	44,241
Czech Republic	27,708	21,427	6,281	32,380	108,755	276	124,226
Democratic People's Republic of Korea (b)	..	..	..	397	640	10	..
Democratic Republic of the Congo (b)	..	..	..	15	187	..	..
Denmark	10,817	6,020	4,797	24,938	147,257	567	45,849
Djibouti (b)	..	..	..	2	2	..	..
Dominica (b)	..	..	..	12	39	..	80
Dominican Republic	11,639	6,559	5,080	6,936	7,466	1	131,667
Ecuador	15,409	8,822	6,587	9,285	9,822	..	110,985
Egypt	20,467	6,401	14,066	7,152	10,241	15	96,666
El Salvador	5,787	2,379	3,408	2,830	2,857	..	89,582
Equatorial Guinea (b,h)	n.a.	n.a.	n.a.	6	49	..	..
Eritrea (b)	..	..	..	1	1	..	..
Estonia	5,907	1,975	3,932	5,775	44,264	95	54,220
Eswatini (b)	..	..	..	38	38	..	..
Ethiopia	1,186	489	697	495	495	..	..
European Union Intellectual Property Office (e)	345,379	245,633	99,746	n.a.	n.a.	n.a.	1,445,769
Fiji (b)	..	..	..	42	42	..	..
Finland	8,950	4,955	3,995	23,614	141,546	537	100,346
France (b)	..	..	..	150,471	887,648	4,396	858,000
Gabon (b,h)	n.a.	n.a.	n.a.	66	1,074	..	..
Gambia	2,154	54	2,100	74	394	..	..
Georgia	10,307	1,591	8,716	2,045	2,392	24	60,493
Germany	161,997	141,022	20,975	430,648	2,133,584	7,872	940,962
Ghana	4,883	203	4,680	225	417	..	..
Greece (b)	..	..	..	4,856	60,437	116	..
Grenada	508	8	500	17	17	..	289
Guatemala	9,510	4,459	5,051	5,475	5,912	..	136,019
Guinea (b,h)	n.a.	n.a.	n.a.	134	2,214	..	..
Guinea-Bissau (b,h)	n.a.	n.a.	n.a.	34	578	..	..
Guyana	722	119	603	130	130	..	1,551
Haiti (b)	..	..	..	15	47	..	..
Honduras	5,214	1,528	3,686	1,703	1,703	..	..
Hungary	12,449	7,178	5,271	14,545	50,964	251	54,321
Iceland	10,017	1,287	8,730	2,240	6,533	42	59,771
India	359,793	306,469	53,324	314,824	333,584	225	1,904,698
Indonesia	40,218	19,833	20,385	21,716	23,026	22	470,270
Iran (Islamic Republic of)	111,655	97,567	14,088	98,854	100,693	21	196,219

Trademarks

Name	Registration class count by office			Registration class count by origin	Equivalent registration class count by origin	Madrid international registrations	In force by office
	Total	Resident	Non-resident	Total [a]	Total [a]	Origin [f]	Total
Iraq	3,073	2,322	751	2,875	3,122	..	..
Ireland (g)	6,513	..	..	8,910	78,800	161	75,948
Israel	25,154	4,490	20,664	10,834	37,024	337	135,883
Italy	145,053	132,793	12,260	237,767	1,022,280	3,109	504,820
Jamaica	4,328	1,907	2,421	1,977	2,247	..	68,155
Japan (b)	..	..	..	108,424	276,273	2,976	1,890,161
Jordan	5,253	1,643	3,610	2,296	4,166	..	..
Kazakhstan	25,647	8,133	17,514	9,747	9,828	76	44,232
Kenya (b)	..	..	..	218	985	7	..
Kiribati (b)	..	..	..	10	10	..	..
Kuwait (b)	..	..	..	603	2,487	..	..
Kyrgyzstan	8,262	549	7,713	626	626	3	10,458
Lao People's Democratic Republic	4,691	168	4,523	179	179	..	..
Latvia	8,325	3,928	4,397	6,187	19,420	92	25,383
Lebanon (b)	..	..	..	669	2,582	2	..
Lesotho	1,909	15	1,894	19	19	..	4,383
Liberia (b)	..	..	..	12	93	..	..
Libya (b)	..	..	..	15	58	..	..
Liechtenstein (b)	..	..	..	3,104	10,587	69	..
Lithuania	8,510	3,707	4,803	6,259	31,184	140	70,810
Luxembourg (c)	n.a.	n.a.	n.a.	18,533	110,303	388	n.a.
Madagascar	5,935	2,290	3,645	2,329	2,603	3	..
Malawi (b)	..	..	..	5	5	..	..
Malaysia	34,566	13,804	20,762	18,957	22,116	9	347,839
Maldives (b)	..	..	..	8	8	..	..
Mali (b,h)	n.a.	n.a.	n.a.	181	2,965	..	..
Malta (b)	..	..	..	4,444	52,902	69	..
Marshall Islands (b)	..	..	..	178	793	2	..
Mauritania (b,h)	n.a.	n.a.	n.a.	86	1,094	..	..
Mauritius	4,864	2,315	2,549	3,720	9,652	9	..
Mexico	127,500	81,210	46,290	89,110	100,773	80	1,134,110
Monaco	9,840	1,327	8,513	5,265	15,664	64	10,322
Mongolia	12,592	6,520	6,072	6,801	7,125	8	18,370
Montenegro	9,331	414	8,917	1,359	2,817	16	57,955
Morocco	26,566	11,377	15,189	12,566	19,615	73	..
Mozambique	4,809	962	3,847	1,024	1,174	5	25,876
Myanmar (b)	..	..	..	77	110	1	..
Namibia	5,736	788	4,948	881	1,070	1	1,955
Nauru (b)	..	..	..	8	8	..	..
Nepal (b)	..	..	..	41	230	..	..
Netherlands (c)	n.a.	n.a.	n.a.	82,099	459,904	1,497	n.a.
Netherlands Antilles (b)	..	..	..	48	144	..	..
New Zealand	48,254	14,995	33,259	24,611	42,024	463	267,256
Nicaragua (b)	..	..	..	108	189	..	..
Niger (b,h)	n.a.	n.a.	n.a.	399	6,511	..	..
Nigeria (g)	17,229	..	..	147	969	..	..
North Macedonia (b)	..	..	..	687	1,829	31	..

| Name | Registration class count by office | | | Registration class count by origin | Equivalent registration class count by origin | Madrid international registrations | In force by office |
	Total	Resident	Non-resident	Total [a]	Total [a]	Origin [f]	Total
Norway	43,138	10,289	32,849	19,562	65,142	333	221,209
Oman (b)	..	..	..	231	555	1	..
Pakistan	25,498	17,414	8,084	17,944	18,791	..	162,315
Panama	9,896	3,552	6,344	6,601	9,665	2	154,116
Papua New Guinea (b)	..	..	..	60	60	..	..
Paraguay	15,263	8,308	6,955	8,585	8,720	..	155,884
Peru	31,768	20,629	11,139	21,736	23,705	..	351,146
Philippines	45,054	18,689	26,365	19,923	21,061	46	..
Poland	34,484	26,118	8,366	44,023	274,970	406	233,118
Portugal	27,892	21,786	6,106	30,026	114,918	253	215,621
Qatar (b)	..	..	..	944	3,370	1	..
Republic of Korea	161,664	109,385	52,279	163,159	234,230	1,210	1,221,927
Republic of Moldova	11,870	2,165	9,705	2,671	3,017	54	72,121
Romania	19,590	14,370	5,220	18,023	65,163	89	73,032
Russian Federation	189,127	126,944	62,183	192,689	232,800	1,503	623,712
Rwanda	2,906	299	2,607	299	299	..	..
Saint Kitts and Nevis (b)	..	..	..	91	577	..	6,093
Saint Lucia	285	33	252	132	186	..	..
Saint Vincent and the Grenadines	77	0	77	22	49	..	..
Samoa	283	22	261	589	1,129	..	4,372
San Marino (b)	..	..	..	379	2,803	8	..
Sao Tome and Principe	1,628	10	1,618	11	11	..	1,810
Saudi Arabia (b)	..	..	..	1,831	6,367	1	..
Senegal (b,h)	n.a.	n.a.	n.a.	608	10,080	..	..
Serbia	18,529	3,573	14,956	9,453	14,638	218	31,807
Seychelles	621	14	607	1,370	2,567	4	..
Sierra Leone	2,447	130	2,317	145	145	..	..
Singapore	48,315	8,537	39,778	30,224	57,245	582	331,782
Sint Maarten (Dutch Part) (b)	..	..	..	..	..	..	..
Slovakia	13,019	7,424	5,595	10,942	40,821	109	47,024
Slovenia	8,428	3,826	4,602	9,364	39,456	191	24,797
Solomon Islands (b)	..	..	..	8	8	..	..
Somalia (b)	..	..	..	3	57	..	..
South Africa	31,992	16,745	15,247	18,822	27,360	2	363,736
South Sudan (b)	..	..	..	3	3	..	..
Spain	72,940	62,870	10,070	111,196	649,921	1,218	776,089
Sri Lanka	5,189	1,998	3,191	2,384	3,102	1	35,048
Sudan	4,663	794	3,869	815	815	..	24,402
Suriname	979	472	507	516	654	1	12,491
Sweden	17,225	12,304	4,921	48,401	296,063	830	128,436
Switzerland	90,405	34,448	55,957	142,480	461,154	3,223	238,386
Syrian Arab Republic	8,991	6,474	2,517	6,946	8,346	5	..
Tajikistan (b)	..	..	..	2	2	..	..
Thailand	45,006	17,340	27,666	22,492	27,283	101	432,876
Timor-Leste (b)	..	..	..	1	1	..	..
Togo (b,h)	n.a.	n.a.	n.a.	625	10,569	..	..
Tonga	519	1	518	1	1	..	..

Name	Registration class count by office			Registration class count by origin	Equivalent registration class count by origin	Madrid international registrations	In force by office
	Total	Resident	Non-resident	Total (a)	Total (a)	Origin (f)	Total
Trinidad and Tobago	2,768	544	2,224	597	651	..	21,094
Tunisia (b)	..	..	..	917	3,240	35	..
Turkey	210,258	174,262	35,996	199,426	253,736	1,129	1,047,118
Turkmenistan (b)	..	..	..	42	42	1	..
Tuvalu (b)	..	..	..	1	1	..	..
Uganda (g)	1,505	..	..	22	150	..	..
Ukraine	49,687	25,165	24,522	31,934	41,634	376	182,120
United Arab Emirates	22,422	4,744	17,678	11,513	29,222	27	246,235
United Kingdom	176,925	122,530	54,395	251,393	1,036,505	3,211	704,964
United Republic of Tanzania (g)	4,194	..	..	62	332	..	41,800
United States of America	384,716	234,771	149,945	555,523	1,413,967	8,923	2,378,373
Uruguay (b)	..	..	..	1,205	2,231	..	..
Uzbekistan	10,146	3,148	6,998	3,453	3,453	12	22,088
Vanuatu (b)	..	..	..	46	100	1	..
Venezuela (Bolivarian Republic of) (b)	..	..	..	342	720	..	..
Viet Nam	49,769	22,699	27,070	25,271	27,169	99	233,122
Yemen	2,430	1,600	830	1,782	2,133	..	..
Zambia (b)	..	..	..	17	17	..	..
Zimbabwe (b)	..	..	..	15	15	..	..
Others/Unknown	..	..	..	67,099	166,539	18	..
Total (2018 estimates)	**10,099,400**	**7,984,000**	**2,115,400**	**10,099,400**	**n.a.**	**60,071**	**49,253,500**

(a) Data on registration class count by origin are incomplete because some offices do not report detailed statistics containing the origin of registration class counts.

(b) Only Madrid designation data are available therefore registration class count by office and origin data may be incomplete.

(c) This country does not have a national trademark office. All trademark registrations for this country are issued by the Benelux Office for Intellectual Property or the European Union Intellectual Property Office.

(d) Resident registrations include those issued to residents of Belgium, Luxembourg and the Netherlands.

(e) Resident registrations include those issued to residents of EU member states.

(f) Origin is defined as the country/territory of the stated residence of the holder of an international registration.

(g) Total includes an aggregate direct registration class count that cannot be broken down into direct and non-resident components.

(h) The African Intellectual Property Office (OAPI) is the competent office for issuing registrations.

n.a. indicates not applicable.

.. indicates not available.

Source: WIPO Statistics Database, August 2019.

B53. Trademark office procedural data, 2018

Office	Total applications processed	Registered	Partial rejections	Total rejections	Withdrawn or abandoned	Applications pending	Number of examiners (FTE)	First office action (days)	Final office decision (days)
African Intellectual Property Organization	3,726	3,726	..	..	..	..	2.0	60.0	90.0
Albania	1,721	1,530	20	155	16	..	4.0	35.0	270.0
Algeria	4,016	1,751	2,066	150	49	6,722	4.0	150.0	20.0
Andorra	9	..	..	7	2	..	2.0	2.0	7.0
Angola	..	..	..	..	..	29,537	9.0	..	..
Antigua and Barbuda	..	..	..	..	..	..	2.0	..	..
Argentina	50,867	33,492	..	16,430	945	146,080	13.0	..	510.0
Armenia	2,220	1,453	567	173	27	1,021	10.0	10.0	120.0
Australia	52,546	50,494	..	31	2,021	29,260	120.1	106.0	160.0
Austria	6,774	5,645	30	653	446	376	10.9	3.0	..
Bangladesh	..	..	..	..	..	44,128	15.0	45.0	60.0
Belarus	2,396	2,156	..	..	240	2,968	19.0	90.0	365.0
Belize	..	..	..	..	..	274	2.0	..	..
Benelux Office for Intellectual Property	19,230	16,991	38	1,194	1,007	..	16.0	..	..
Bosnia and Herzegovina	664	581	6	37	40	1,342	3.0	8.0	500.0
Botswana	..	..	..	..	..	369	3.0	..	..
Brazil	379,767	191,813	..	105,379	82,575	191,535	129.0	390.0	540.0
Brunei Darussalam	..	..	..	..	..	73	4.0	..	..
Bulgaria	4,921	3,784	..	153	984	..	7.0	7.0	220.0
Cabo Verde	..	..	..	..	..	335	5.0	..	..
Cambodia	..	..	..	..	..	2,723	12.0	..	..
Canada	43,760	24,376	7	52	19,325	163,218	54.0	338.0	508.0
China	8,120,316	4,757,773	1,272,390	2,012,478	77,675	3,455,933	1,180.0	180.0	270.0
China, Hong Kong SAR	38,573	33,985	..	3,490	1,098	27,249	53.0	36.0	60.0
China, Macao SAR	15,259	14,309	100	807	43	6,084	5.0	199.0	199.0
Colombia	28,136	20,273	295	7,185	383	9,373	30.0	36.7	291.0
Costa Rica	10,134	8,158	..	101	1,875	..	16.0	5.0	10.0
Croatia	965	773	34	91	67	362	2.0	48.0	48.0
Cuba	1,352	877	99	225	151	2,927	7.0	60.0	940.0
Curaçao	389	388	..	1	..	40	6.0	60.0	60.0
Cyprus	25	24	..	..	1	1,370	7.0	5.0	90.0
Czech Republic	6,979	6,192	135	546	106	4,883	20.0	..	297.0
Denmark	3,003	2,632	180	120	71	746	22.0	53.0	149.0
Dominica	..	..	..	..	..	70	1.0	..	..
Dominican Republic	534	..	..	10	524	..	..	27.0	16.5
Ecuador	16,014	15,409	..	543	62	6,080	13.0	2.0	120.0
Egypt	28,975	16,136	156	8,297	4,386	11,867	10.0	270.0	270.0
El Salvador	11,753	5,171	1,366	1,405	3,811	2,073	12.0	6.0	6.0
Estonia	1,543	1,099	104	9	331	1,416	11.0	4.0	178.0
Ethiopia	..	..	..	..	..	..	22.0	..	..
European Union Intellectual Property Office	120,503	110,626	5,372	3,470	1,035	72,282	249.0	..	14.0
Gambia	..	..	..	..	..	..	3.0	..	..
Georgia	1,267	901	101	235	30	209	13.0	60.0	215.0
Germany	71,959	50,565	808	7,081	13,505	22,710	68.0	60.0	91.0
Ghana	..	..	..	..	..	2,112	6.0	..	..
Greece	..	..	..	..	..	..	4.0	..	30.0
Grenada	289	289	..	..	..	..	1.0	3.0	70.0
Guyana	..	..	..	..	..	..	1.0	..	..
Honduras	5,261	5,261	..	..	..	..	5.0	5.0	15.0
Hungary	4,040	3,177	..	72	791	2,601	12.0	15.0	195.0
Iceland	4,153	3,360	398	150	245	2,520	6.0	70.0	80.0
India	533,767	326,232	..	101,073	106,462	584,679	100.0	30.0	180.0
Iran (Islamic Republic of)	74,668	24,618	40,593	9,245	212	4,055	..	..	..
Iraq	..	..	..	..	..	5,300	10.0	..	..
Israel	..	..	..	..	..	12,869	17.0	231.0	497.0
Jamaica	..	..	..	..	..	..	2.0	..	..

Trademarks

Office	Total applications processed	Registered	Partial rejections	Total rejections	Withdrawn or abandoned	Applications pending	Number of examiners (FTE)	First office action (days)	Final office decision (days)
Kuwait	..	..	..	..	..	..	6.0	..	..
Kyrgyzstan	838	771	2	45	20	20	5.0	30.0	365.0
Latvia	1,890	1,565	15	177	133	154	6.0	1.0	132.0
Lesotho	..	..	..	..	..	366	7.0		..
Lithuania	3,181	2,632	..	281	268	459	7.0	96.0	98.0
Mexico	117,777	106,486	8,165	..	3,126	138,771	45.0	59.0	158.0
Monaco	47	..	..	20	27	..	2.0	..	36.0
Mongolia	1,826	1,557	59	192	18	1,236	3.0	182.0	228.0
Montenegro	94	92	..	..	2	423	5.0	30.0	300.0
Morocco	570	68	210	149	143	1,745	12.0	40.0	108.0
Mozambique	..	..	..	..	..	380	11.0	..	..
Namibia	..	..	..	..	..	..	3.0	..	..
New Zealand	7,405	7,121	15	..	269	3,921	36.0	22.0	23.0
Norway	15,238	12,516	..	182	2,540	8,600	28.0	190.0	240.0
Pakistan	73,391	25,498	43,421	..	4,472	2,775	6.0	50.0	240.0
Panama	..	..	..	..	..	222	6.0	..	..
Peru	37,741	30,577	..	5,027	2,137	6,157	42.0	5.0	75.0
Philippines	22,028	17,014	..	269	4,745	8,052	31.0	48.0	..
Portugal	17,385	14,607	230	2,277	271	3,433	28.0	120.0	150.0
Republic of Korea	183,560	146,863	..	36,697	..	161,520	131.0	165.0	312.0
Republic of Moldova	1,878	1,279	240	204	155	2,266	34.0	11.0	241.0
Romania	6,646	5,528	..	852	266	3,460	24.0	7.0	150.0
Russian Federation	61,355	54,342	..	6,530	483	35,917	196.0	224.1	239.0
Rwanda	..	..	..	..	..	8	1.0	..	..
Saint Lucia	..	..	..	..	..	..	2.0	..	..
Saint Vincent and the Grenadines	60	50	10	..	..	136	3.0	..	..
Samoa	177	147	22	8	..	40	2.0	15.0	30.0
Sao Tome and Principe	..	..	..	..	..	32	8.0	..	..
Seychelles	..	..	..	..	..	42	5.0	..	..
Sierra Leone	..	..	..	..	..	..	5.0	..	..
Slovakia	2,865	2,502	21	342	..	738	8.0	27.0	120.0
South Africa	..	..	..	..	..	..	13.0	7.0	..
Spain	25,139	22,584	..	1,911	644	27,148	45.0	20.0	116.0
Sri Lanka	11,656	5,189	..	3,457	3,010	4,492	20.0	142.0	192.0
Sudan	1,820	1,580	12	224	4	631	20.0	3.0	10.0
Suriname	..	..	..	..	..	546	2.0	..	..
Sweden	9,290	7,085	86	335	1,784	2,181	25.0	84.0	159.0
Thailand	100,721	27,817	..	51,920	20,984	100,112	19.0	80.0	402.0
Tonga	..	..	..	..	..	6	5.0	..	..
Trinidad and Tobago	..	..	..	..	..	..	7.0	..	..
Tunisia	..	..	..	..	..	..	1.0	..	..
Turkey	124,476	105,996	10,844	6,470	1,166	111,812	87.0	4.0	24.0
Ukraine	25,157	18,123	..	1,791	5,243	37,783	86.0	256.0	512.0
United Kingdom	79,507	72,101	..	3,115	4,291	1,054	93.0	9.0	9.0
United Republic of Tanzania	570	..	128	407	35	42	5.0	14.0	20.0
United States of America	360,671	272,693	..	..	87,978	592,857	584.0	96.0	289.0
Uzbekistan	5,446	2,314	2,161	205	766	2,331	11.0	195.0	240.0
Viet Nam	138	50	..	45	43	98,707	51.0	607.2	661.6

Note: FTE is full time equivalent. WIPO collects data from IP offices using a common questionnaire and methodology. Every effort has been made to compile procedural data based on common definitions and concepts, but procedural differences make it extremely difficult to fully harmonize such data. Therefore caution should be exercised when making comparisons across offices. The total number of applications processed for a given office may be incomplete due to the omission of one or several elements by the office.

.. indicates not available.

Source: WIPO Statistics Database, August 2019.

Industrial designs

Highlights

Applications filed worldwide reached 1 million

An estimated 1.02 million applications were filed worldwide in 2018. This represents an increase of 8.4% on 2017 (figure 3.1). The number of industrial design applications filed globally doubled between 2007 and 2018. Filing activity in China alone explains 88.4% of this growth.

The number of designs contained in applications (design count) totaled 1.31 million in 2018 (figure 3.2). Compared to 2017, the number of designs in applications grew by 5.7%. This increase is largely due to growth in China, which offset declines at several offices, including those of the Islamic Republic of Iran, Spain and Turkey.

For a second consecutive year, designs in applications filed in the U.K. grew sharply

The office of China received applications containing 54% of all designs in applications filed worldwide in 2018, representing 708,799 designs. The office of China was followed by the European Union Intellectual Property Office (EUIPO) (108,174), the offices of the Republic of Korea (68,054), of the United States of America (U.S.) (47,137) and of Germany (44,460) (figure 3.3).

Combined, the top 20 offices accounted for 93.5% of all designs in applications. Of the top 20 offices, 12 saw increases in their application design count (figure C11). The five offices to experience double-digit growth were those of the United Kingdom (U.K.) (+42.4%), the Russian Federation (+21%), Italy (+16.6%), India (+13.6%) and China (+12.7%). In contrast, the offices of the Islamic Republic of Iran (−17.8%), Spain (−16.6%) and Switzerland (−11%) saw the sharpest decreases among the top 20 offices in 2018, after having each experienced double-digit growth in 2017.

In 2018, 10 of the top 20 offices saw an increase in the number of designs contained in resident applications; for six of them, the number of designs in non-resident filings grew also. Increases in resident design were particularly high at the offices of China, India, Italy and the U.K. An increase in non-resident design count was the main or sole driver of growth at four offices, namely the offices of Canada, the Republic of Korea, the Russian Federation and the U.S.

Among offices located in low- and middle-income countries, annual growth in 2018 was especially high for Madagascar (+61.3%) and African Regional Intellectual Property Organization (ARIPO) (+23.3%) – albeit from a low base. Bangladesh (+18%), Colombia (+14.7%) and the Philippines (+12.1%) likewise witnessed double-digit growth. Conversely, the offices of Georgia (−53.7%), the Syrian Arab Republic (−43.7%), Romania (−34%) and Serbia (−27.9%) all saw sharp falls (figure C13).

An estimated 1.02 million industrial design applications were filed worldwide
3.1. Industrial design applications worldwide, 2004–2018

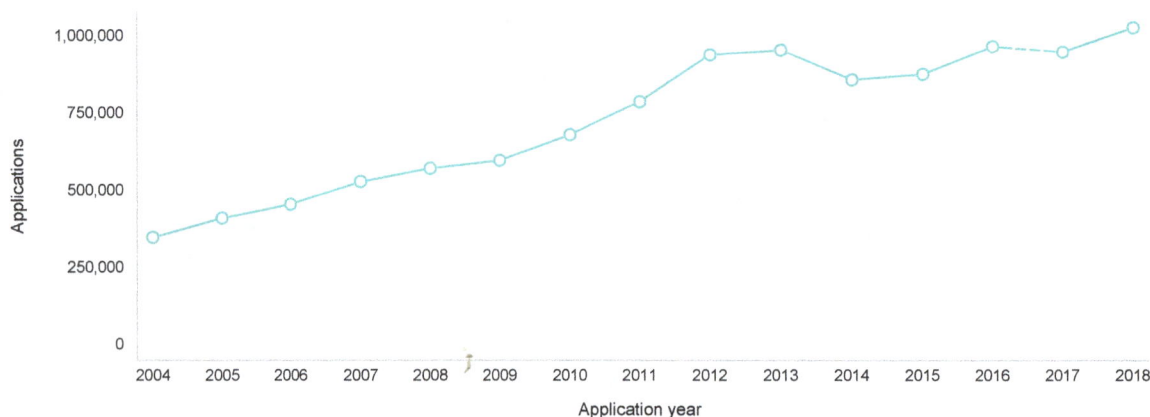

Source: Figure C1.

The number of designs contained in applications totaled 1.31 million

3.2. Number of designs in industrial design applications worldwide, 2004–2018

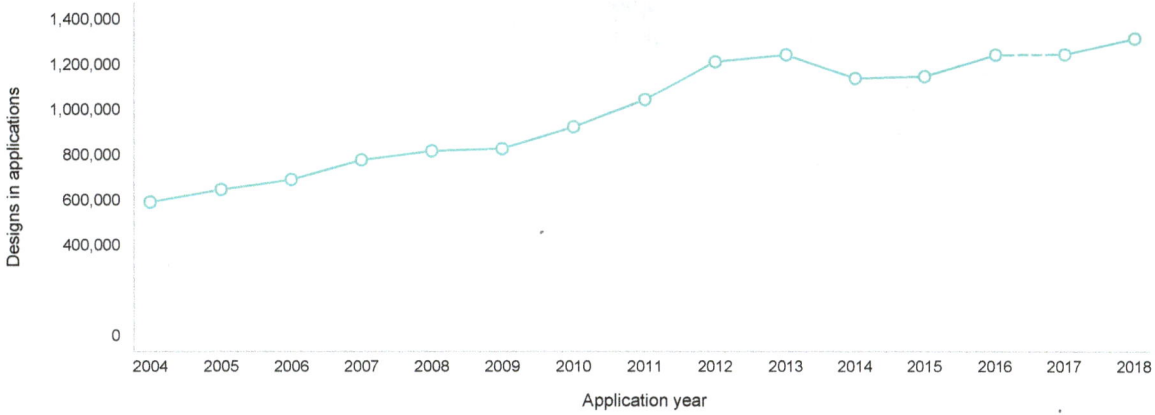

Source: Figure C2.

China received 54% of all designs contained in applications filed worldwide

3.3. Application design counts for the top 10 offices, 2018

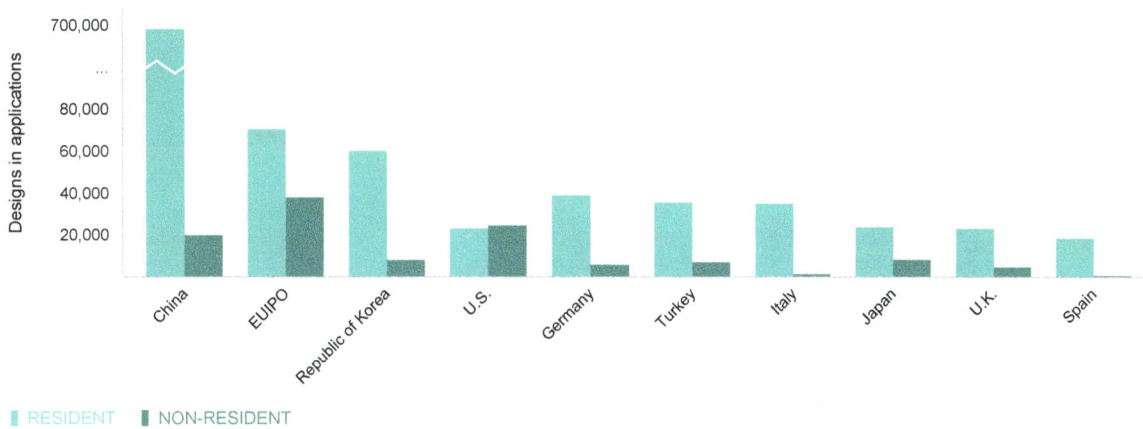

RESIDENT   NON-RESIDENT

Source: Figure C10.

Designs contained in resident applications accounted for 84.8% of the world total design count in 2018. The particularly high resident design share in China (97.2%) largely accounts for the significant proportion of resident designs at world level. However, resident design counts also accounted for a majority of filing activity in 15 of the top 20 offices (figure C10). The exceptions were Canada (11.4%), Switzerland (29.6%), Australia (38.5%), the Russian Federation (42.7%) and the U.S. (48.4%).

Design count

Some offices allow industrial design applications to contain more than one design for the same good or in the same class; others allow only one design per application. To capture the differences in application filing systems across offices, one needs to compare their respective application and registration design counts.

Equivalent design count

Designs in applications filed at regional offices are equivalent to multiple designs in applications filed in the respective member states of those offices. To calculate the number of equivalent designs for the African Intellectual Property Organization (OAPI) which has 17 member states, the Benelux Office for Intellectual Property (BOIP) which has three, and the EUIPO (28), each design is multiplied by the corresponding number of member states. However, the African Regional Intellectual Property Organization (ARIPO) does not register industrial designs with automatic region-wide applicability. Therefore, for this office, each application is counted as one application abroad if the applicant does not reside in a member state or as one resident application and one application abroad if the applicant resides in a member state.

Combined, the offices of upper middle-income countries received 61.6% of all designs contained in applications filed in 2018 (table C7). China accounted for a vast majority of this share, with the other upper middle-income countries receiving only 7.6% of the world total. The combined share of the high-income countries stood at 34.6%. Offices of lower middle-income countries received 3.6% of the total, and those of low-income countries only 0.2%. Between 2008 and 2018, average annual growth in design counts was 7.6% for upper middle-income countries. Over the same period, offices in high-income (+1.8%) and lower middle-income (+0.8%) economies had much lower growth rates in comparison.

Asia accounted for 69.7% of all designs in applications filed worldwide in 2018 (figure 3.4). It was followed by Europe (23%) and North America (4.1%). Four of the six geographical regions experienced growth between 2008 and 2018, with Asia (+6.6%) and North America (+5%) seeing the largest average increases; Africa (−0.7%) and Latin America and the Caribbean (LAC) (−0.4%) were the two exceptions.

Offices located in Asia accounted for almost 70% of total filing activity

3.4. Application design counts by region, 2008 and 2018

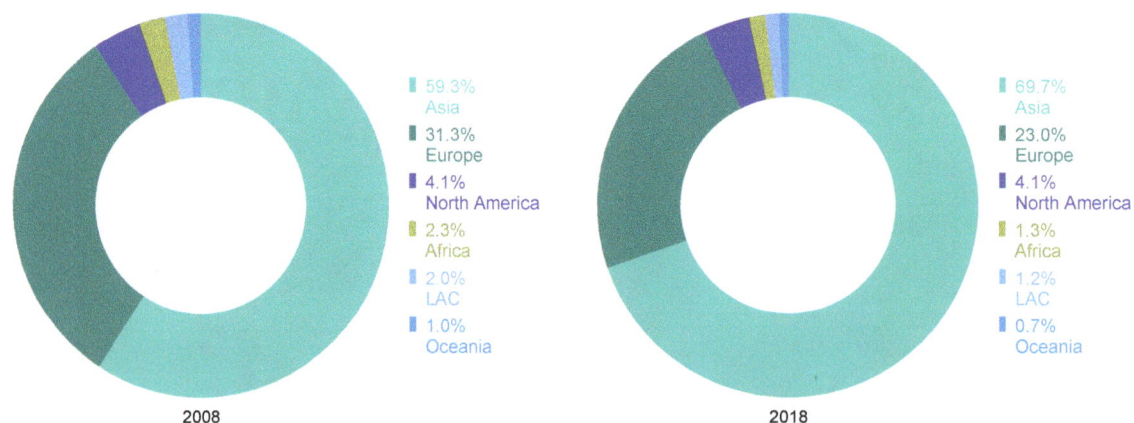

2008

- 59.3% Asia
- 31.3% Europe
- 4.1% North America
- 2.3% Africa
- 2.0% LAC
- 1.0% Oceania

2018

- 69.7% Asia
- 23.0% Europe
- 4.1% North America
- 1.3% Africa
- 1.2% LAC
- 0.7% Oceania

Source: Table C8.

Industrial design applications filed since 1883

Between 1883 and the early 1950s, the offices of Japan and the U.S. averaged similar numbers of applications, rarely exceeding 10,000. The office of Japan received the largest number of applications per year from the 1950s to the late 1990s, reaching approximately 50,000 annual filings at its peak. The office of China began receiving applications in 1985 and has seen unprecedented growth: from 640 in 1985 to 660,000 in 2013. The office of the Republic of Korea surpassed the office of Japan in 2004 and has remained in second position since. In 2012, the office of the U.S. moved ahead of the office of Japan to become the third largest. Ranked fifth is the EUIPO, which began receiving applications in 2003. Unlike the other four offices, the EUIPO has a multiple design system. Applications filed at the EUIPO contained 108,196 designs in 2018.

Trend in industrial design applications for the top five offices, 1883–2018

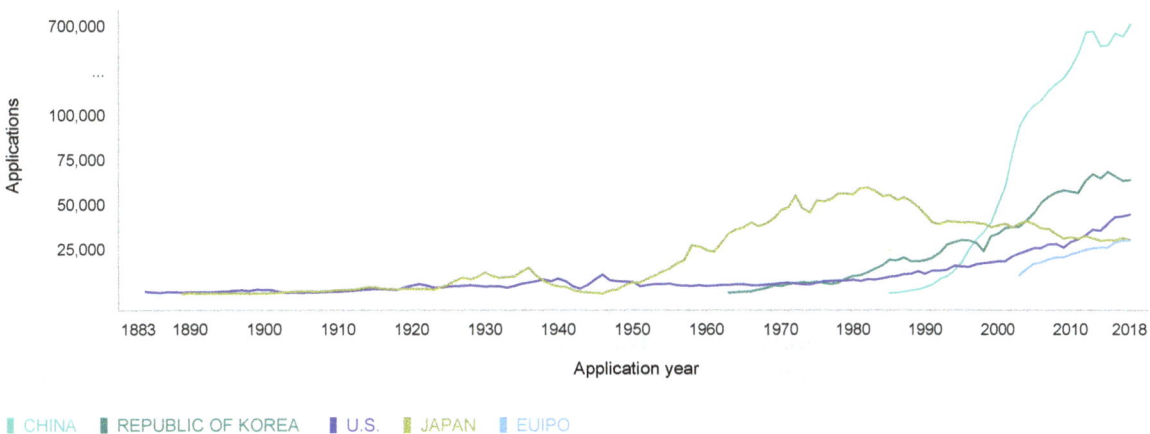

■ CHINA ■ REPUBLIC OF KOREA ■ U.S. ■ JAPAN ■ EUIPO

Source: Figure C8.

Applicants from Germany had over 580,000 equivalent designs in applications filed abroad

Applications received by offices from resident and non-resident applicants are referred to as office data, whereas applications filed by applicants at their home office (resident applications) or at foreign offices (applications abroad) are referred to as origin data. Here, industrial design statistics based on the origin of residence of the first named applicant are reported in order to complement the picture of industrial design activity worldwide.

Applicants from China had the highest equivalent application design count in 2018, nearing the 1 million mark, with a total of 957,241 (map 3.5). They were followed by applicants residing in Germany (643,987), the U.S. (390,996) and Italy (361,977). Equivalent designs in applications filed abroad accounted for between 82% and 98% of the total for applicants from all of the top 20 origins, except for those from China (28%), Turkey (35.7%) and the Republic of Korea (47.5%).

Among the top 10 origins, the largest increases in equivalent design counts were experienced in China (+11%), Italy (+9.7%), Japan (+5%) and in the U.S. (+3.9%). In contrast, applicants from Germany (–11.6%), the U.K. (–7%) and the Republic of Korea (–6.2%) saw the sharpest decreases in equivalent design count compared to 2017 (figure C17).

European countries dominate the top 20 origins with a total of 13, followed by five origins located in Asia and one each in Oceania and North America. In terms of income categories, 18 of the top 20 origins belong to the high-income group, while two upper middle-income countries – China and Turkey – also feature.

Applicants from Germany (584,288), the U.S. (368,172) and Italy (315,828) had the highest number of equivalent designs in applications filed abroad in 2018. Of the top 10 origins of equivalent designs in applications filed abroad, applicants from Italy (+8.6%), Japan (+7%) and China (+6.5%) saw the most pronounced increases; in contrast, applicants from Germany (–12.2%) and the U.K. (–10.8%) experienced a double-digit drop in numbers.

Applicants from China had by far the highest equivalent design count
3.5. Equivalent design counts by origin, 2018

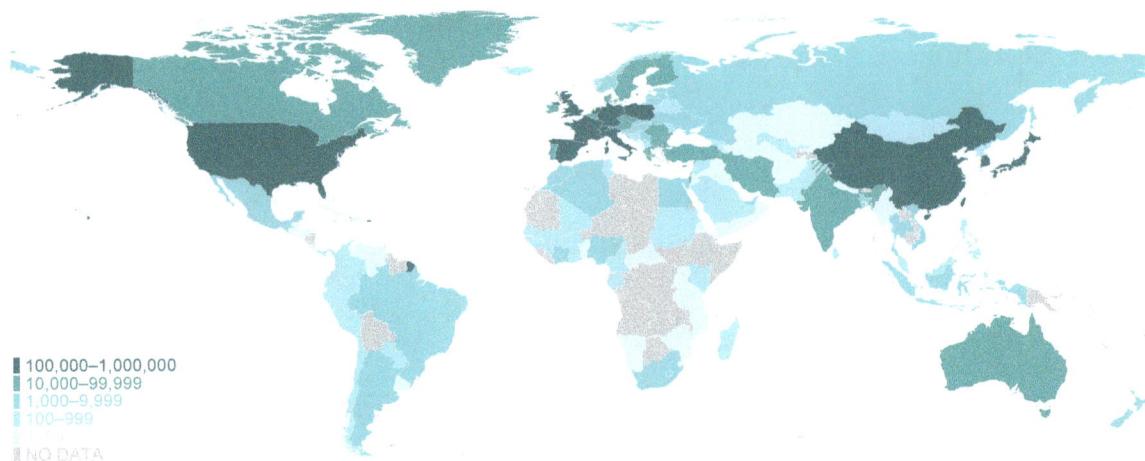

■ 100,000–1,000,000
■ 10,000–99,999
■ 1,000–9,999
■ 100–999
▨ NO DATA

Source: Map C16.

The Republic of Korea tops the ranking when adjusting for GDP and population

The Republic of Korea (3,164) had the highest resident design count per 100 billion US dollars (USD) of gross domestic product (GDP) in 2018 (figure 3.6). It was followed by China (3,057) and Italy (2,137). Germany, Turkey and Ukraine each had ratios between 1,500 and 1,800. In contrast, India (96), the Russian Federation (102), Brazil (124) and the U.S. (125) had much lower ratios.

The Republic of Korea (1,163) was also the country with by far the highest resident design count per million population in 2018 (figure C26). It was followed by Italy (764) and Germany (720). Compared to the 2008 ratios, those for 2018 increased sharply for China (+270) and Spain (+134). In contrast, the ratios for Switzerland (–115), France (–55) and Japan (–46) decreased drastically. Even though residents of Japan and the U.S. ranked among the top five in terms of industrial design filing activity, their 2018 ratios of resident design count per million population were relatively low, with ratios of 185 and 70, respectively.

Furnishing and clothing remained the most recorded classes

The Locarno classification includes 32 classes of industrial designs. In 2018, the classes that accounted for the largest shares of the world total remained furnishings (10.5%), clothing (8.3%) and packages and containers (7.7%). Combined, these three classes accounted for slightly more than one-quarter of all designs in applications (figure C22).

Grouping the Locarno classes into 12 industry sectors highlights the most important sectors for designs contained in industrial design applications filed in each country. For all of the top 10 offices for which data were available, at least one-third of their total design count was concentrated in just three sectors, although these top three sectors varied from office to office (figure 3.7).

Advertising, furniture and household goods, and textiles and accessories accounted for 72.3% of the total design count at the office of France and 63.1% at the office of Germany. Construction, furniture and household goods, and textiles and accessories were the top three sectors at the office of the Republic of Korea and represented 46.8% of the total design count. At the EUIPO, ICT and audiovisual, furniture and household goods, and textiles and accessories accounted for 43.8% of the total design count.

All of the top 10 countries of origin had more than 40% of designs in applications filed among their top three sectors, with applicants residing in Switzerland (70.3%) and Italy (62.1%) recording the highest level of concentration among their top three sectors (figure C24). The textiles and accessories sector was a top three sector for nine of the top 10 origins, whereas furniture and household goods featured in the top three sectors for seven of them.

For the first time, designs in applications registered worldwide exceeded 1 million

An estimated 812,800 industrial design applications were registered worldwide in 2018. This represents a sharp increase of 14.3% on 2017 (figure C4). Growth was mainly due to a considerable rise in the number of registrations issued by the offices of China (+93,255), the U.K. (+7,110) and Brazil (+2,505) compared to 2017.

Nearly 1.08 million designs were contained in applications registered in 2018, up 9.3%. This represents 91,300 more designs in applications registered compared to 2017. The office of China accounted for half (49.8%) of all designs in applications registered worldwide, and the top 20 offices combined comprised 92.7% of the total. Among these offices, nine saw annual growth, including the U.K. (+43.6%), Brazil (+40.3%), the Russian Federation (+39.4%), Italy (+27.6%) and China (+21.1%). In contrast, the offices of Ukraine (–24.5%),

The Republic of Korea had the highest number of designs per unit of GDP

3.6. Resident application design count per USD 100 billion GDP for selected origins, 2008 and 2018

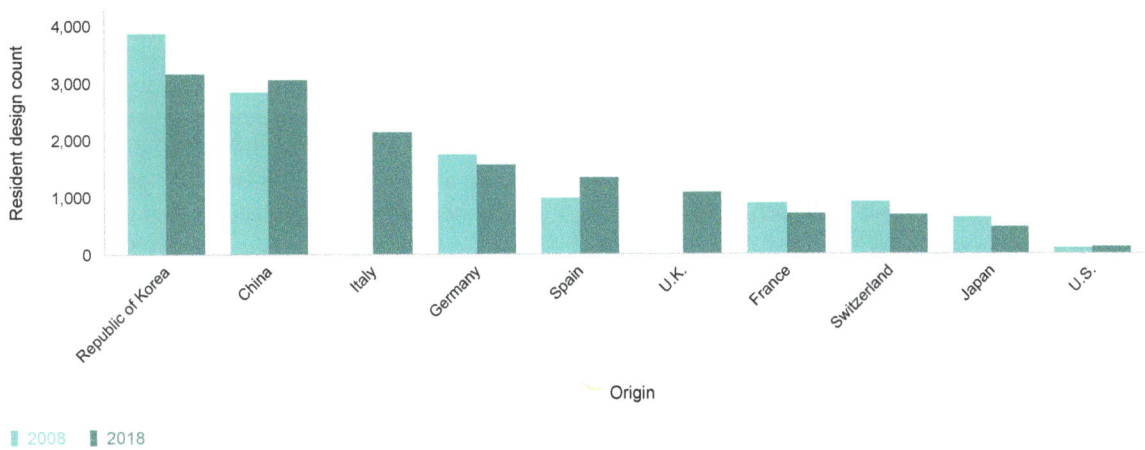

2008   2018

Source: Figure C25.

The top three sectors accounted for nearly half of designs in applications in the Republic of Korea

3.7. Distribution of application design counts by the top three sectors and for selected offices, 2018

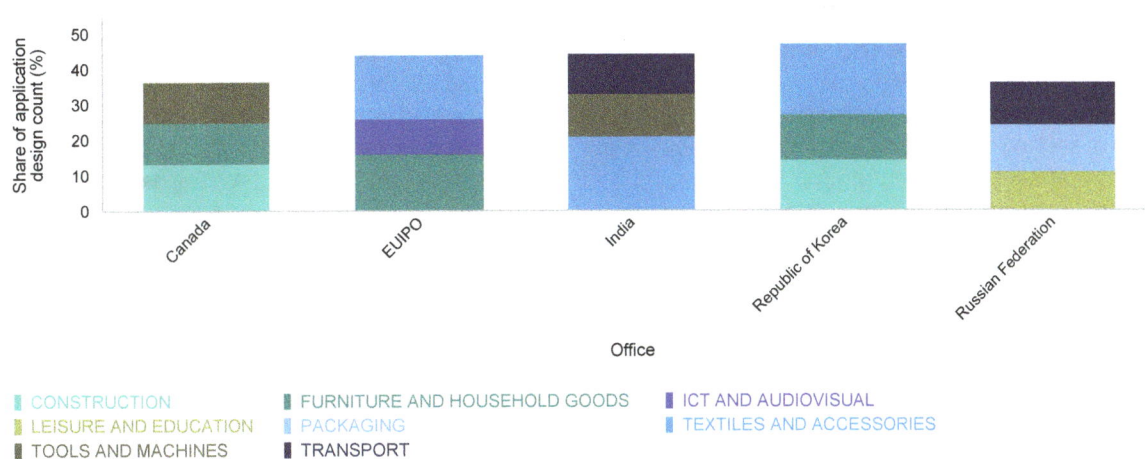

CONSTRUCTION   FURNITURE AND HOUSEHOLD GOODS   ICT AND AUDIOVISUAL
LEISURE AND EDUCATION   PACKAGING   TEXTILES AND ACCESSORIES
TOOLS AND MACHINES   TRANSPORT

Source: Figure C23.

Industrial designs

India (–19.5%), Spain (–18.7%) and Switzerland (–18.4%) saw sharp falls in the number of designs registered (figure C14).

Almost 4 million industrial design registrations were in force worldwide

Industrial design rights generally last for up to 15 years from the date an application is filed. In 2018, there were an estimated 3.99 million active industrial design registrations at 122 offices worldwide. This represents an increase of 6.5% on 2017 (figure C27). The number of registrations in force in China increased by 10.4% to reach 1.61 million, representing 40.4% of the world total in 2018. China was followed by the Republic of Korea (344,560), the U.S. (336,116), Japan (257,157) and the EUIPO (223,492). Combined, the top five offices represented more than two-thirds (69.5%) of active industrial design registrations globally.

About 3.3 million of the active industrial design registrations in force at 81 offices in 2018 can be distributed according to the year in which they were first registered (figure C29). A quarter of the industrial design applications registered in 2005 were still in force in 2018. Half of those registered in 2009 remained in force in 2018, as well as two-thirds of those registered in 2013.

The average age of active industrial design registrations varied across offices. For example, in 2018, the average age of all industrial design registrations in force in Spain was 8.5 years, and 2.8 years in China. Together with Spain, Turkey (8.3), Germany (7.3), Brazil (7.2) and Malaysia (7.1) have industrial designs in force dating back at least seven years on average (figure C30).

German and Swiss applicants remained the largest users of the Hague System

The Hague System offers applicants an advantageous way of seeking industrial design protection internationally as an alternative to using the Paris Convention for the Protection of Industrial Property. For further information and statistics on the System, see the *Hague Yearly Review 2019*.

The number of Hague international applications grew by 3.6% in 2018, to reach 5,443 applications. However, the number of designs contained in Hague applications decreased by 1.8% to 19,387 in 2018, ending 11 years of uninterrupted growth (figure C31).

This decrease in the number of designs in applications – despite an increase in the number of applications filed – was due to recent Hague members, such as Japan and the Republic of Korea, averaging fewer designs per application when compared to long-term members, such as Germany and Switzerland.

Germany remained the top user of the Hague System in 2018, with 710 international applications filed containing 3,942 designs (figure C33). It was followed by Switzerland (2,441 designs), the Republic of Korea (1,535), France (1,436) and the U.S, (1,359). Recent members Japan (1,257), the Republic of Korea and the U.S. were among the top 10 largest users of the Hague System, while the U.K. – which joined the System in 2018 – was in eleventh position, with 370 designs. Combined, the top 10 origins accounted for 79.8% of all designs in 2018.

Of the top 10 origins, the Netherlands (+66.9%) was the one to experience the fastest growth in 2018. It was followed by Japan (+47.7%), Turkey (+33.2%) and Italy (+19%). In contrast, the U.S. (–21.4%), Switzerland (–17%), the Republic of Korea (–12.6%) and Germany (–7.7%) saw declines.

The European Union (EU) remained the most designated Hague member in international applications since 2010, with 3,659 designations containing 14,848 designs in 2018 (figure C34). It was followed by Switzerland (8,802 designs), Turkey (5,734), the U.S. (5,026) and Norway (3,192). Of the five top designated members, the U.S. (+8.8%) was the only one to see an increase in the number of designs in designations; conversely, Turkey (–14.3%) and Norway (–11.5%) saw the sharpest declines.

Industrial design statistics

Industrial designs

Industrial designs

Industrial design applications and registrations worldwide

C1. Trend in industrial design applications worldwide, 2004–2018

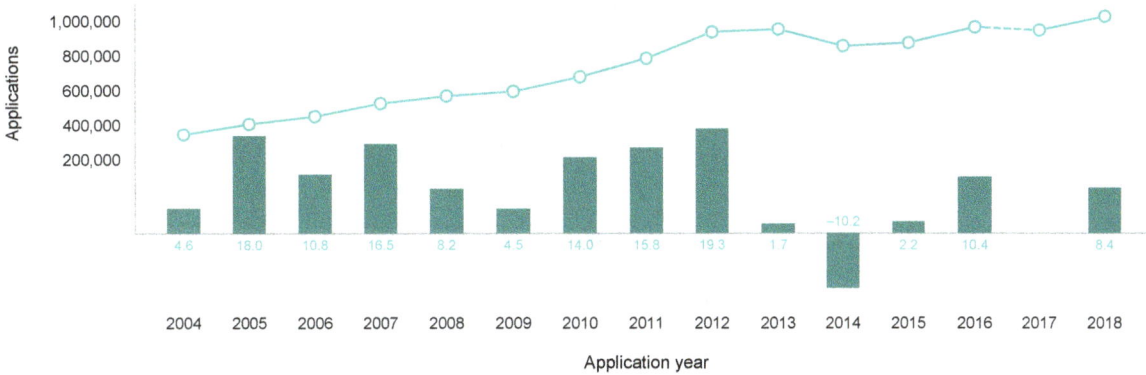

■ APPLICATIONS   ■ GROWTH RATE (%)

Note: China's 2017 data are not comparable with its previous year's data due to the new way in which the IP office of China counts its applications data. Prior to 2017, it included all applications received; however, starting in 2017, China's application count data include only those applications for which the office has received the necessary application fees. As China accounts for the bulk of the global total, it is not possible to report the 2017 worldwide application growth rate. World totals are WIPO estimates using data covering 152 IP offices. These totals include the numbers of applications filed directly with national and regional offices (known as the "Paris route") as well as the numbers of designations received via the Hague System (where applicable).

Source: WIPO Statistics Database, August 2019.

C2. Trend in application design counts worldwide, 2004–2018

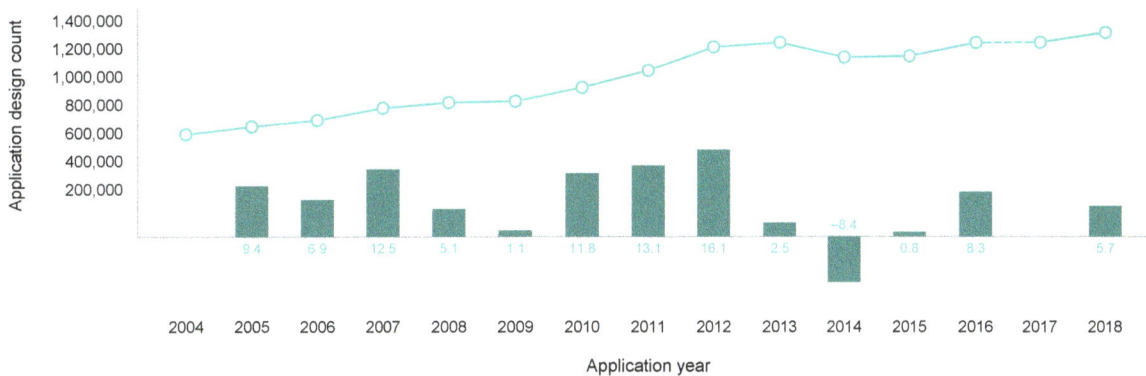

■ APPLICATION DESIGN COUNT   ■ GROWTH RATE (%)

Note: China's 2017 data are not comparable with its previous year's data due to the new way in which the IP office of China counts its applications data. Prior to 2017, it included all applications received; however, starting in 2017, China's application count data include only those applications for which the office has received the necessary application fees. As China accounts for the bulk of the global total, it is not possible to report the 2017 worldwide application growth rate. World totals are WIPO estimates using data covering 148 IP offices. These totals include design counts in applications filed directly with national and regional offices (known as the "Paris route") as well as design counts in designations received via the Hague System (where applicable). See the glossary for the definition of design count.

Source: WIPO Statistics Database, August 2019.

C3. Resident and non-resident application design counts worldwide, 2004–2018

NON-RESIDENT SHARE (%)

| 29.4 | 25.1 | 23.3 | 22.1 | 20.1 | 16.2 | 15.3 | 15.0 | 14.2 | 14.6 | 15.5 | 15.7 | 14.8 | 16.3 | 15.2 |

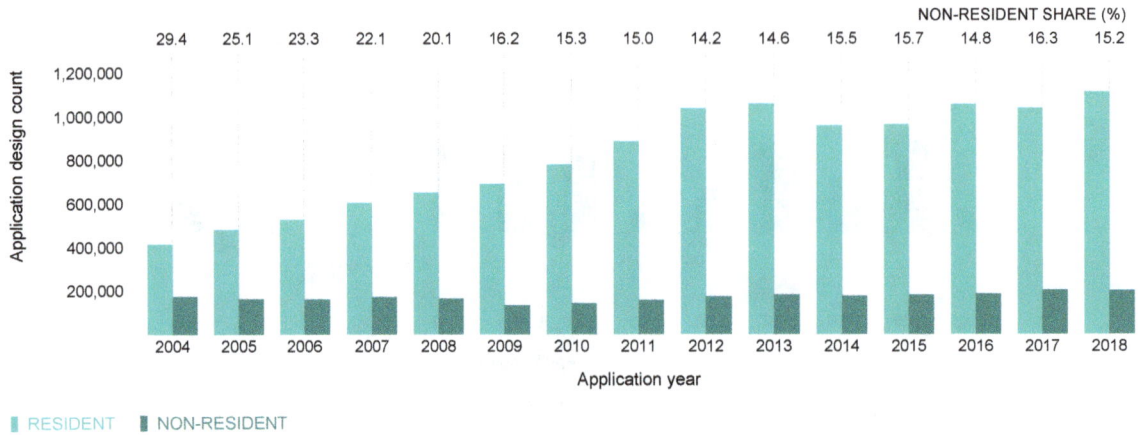

RESIDENT   NON-RESIDENT

Note: World totals are WIPO estimates using data covering 148 IP offices. These totals include design counts in applications filed directly with national and regional offices (known as the "Paris route") as well as design counts in designations received via the Hague System (where applicable). See the glossary for the definition of design count.

Source: WIPO Statistics Database, August 2019.

C4. Trend in industrial design registrations worldwide, 2004–2018

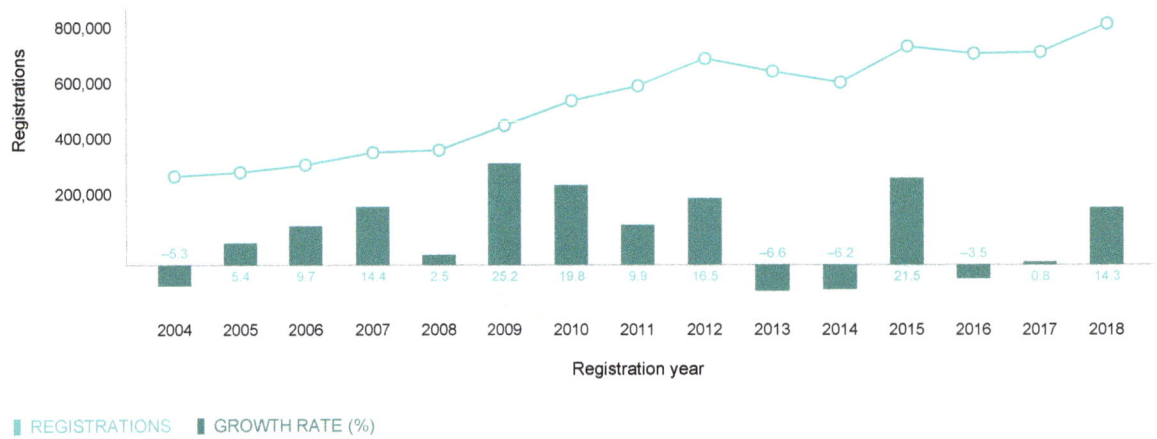

| | –5.3 | 5.4 | 9.7 | 14.4 | 2.5 | 25.2 | 19.8 | 9.9 | 16.5 | –6.6 | –6.2 | 21.5 | –3.5 | 0.8 | 14.3 |

REGISTRATIONS   GROWTH RATE (%)

Note: World totals are WIPO estimates using data covering 142 IP offices. These totals include the numbers of registrations issued by national and regional offices for applications filed directly with offices (known as the "Paris route") as well as for designations received via the Hague System (where applicable).

Source: WIPO Statistics Database, August 2019.

C5. Trend in registration design counts worldwide, 2004–2018

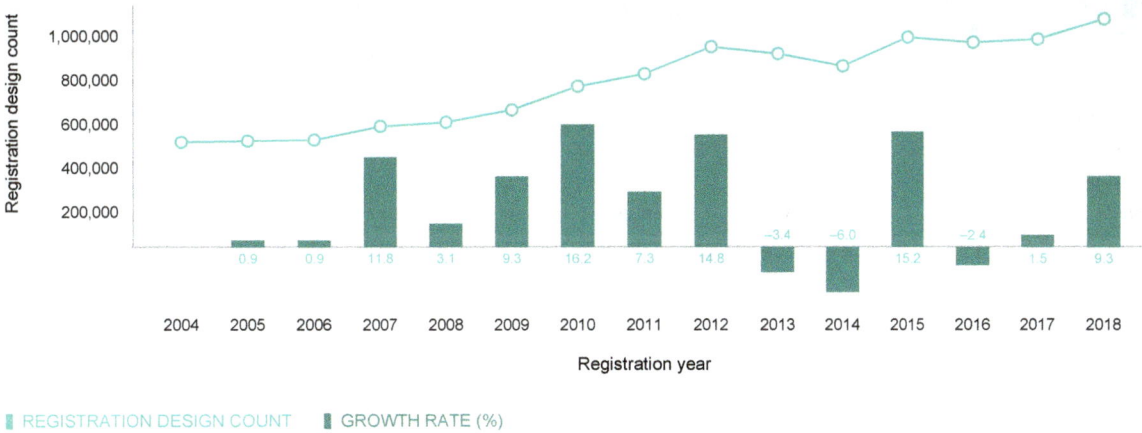

Growth rate (%) values shown: 2005: 0.9, 2006: 0.9, 2007: 11.8, 2008: 3.1, 2009: 9.3, 2010: 16.2, 2011: 7.3, 2012: 14.8, 2013: −3.4, 2014: −6.0, 2015: 15.2, 2016: −2.4, 2017: 1.5, 2018: 9.3

▌ REGISTRATION DESIGN COUNT   ▌ GROWTH RATE (%)

Note: World totals are WIPO estimates using data covering 142 IP offices. These totals include design counts in registrations issued by national and regional offices for applications filed directly with offices (known as the "Paris route") as well as for designations received via the Hague System (where applicable). See the glossary for the definition of design count.

Source: WIPO Statistics Database, August 2019.

C6. Resident and non-resident registration design counts worldwide, 2004–2018

NON-RESIDENT SHARE (%)

| 30.8 | 27.7 | 27.8 | 27.2 | 25.3 | 20.4 | 17.8 | 16.8 | 16.0 | 17.6 | 19.0 | 17.3 | 17.2 | 19.0 | 17.0 |

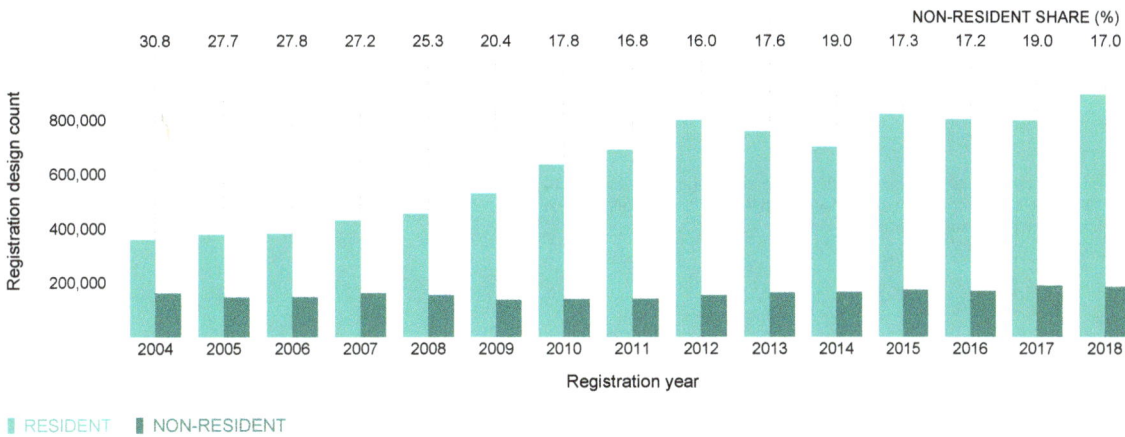

▌ RESIDENT   ▌ NON-RESIDENT

Note: World totals are WIPO estimates using data covering 142 IP offices. These totals include design counts in registrations issued by national and regional offices for applications filed directly with offices (known as the "Paris route") as well as for designations received via the Hague System (where applicable). See the glossary for the definition of design count.

Source: WIPO Statistics Database, August 2019.

Industrial design applications and registrations by office

C7. Application design counts by income group, 2008 and 2018

Income group	Number of designs in applications		Resident share (%)		Share of world total (%)		Average growth (%)
	2008	2018	2008	2018	2008	2018	2008–2018
High-income	379,200	454,100	64.4	70.7	46.5	34.6	1.8
Upper middle-income	389,300	808,400	88.5	93.9	47.8	61.6	7.6
Upper middle-income without China	*76,396*	*99,601*	*60.1*	*70.3*	*9.4*	*7.6*	*2.7*
Lower middle-income	44,100	47,900	35.6	65.3	5.4	3.6	0.8
Low-income	2,200	2,200	13.5	45.4	0.3	0.2	0.0
World	**814,800**	**1,312,600**	**74.2**	**84.7**	**100.0**	**100.0**	**4.9**

Note: Totals by income group are WIPO estimates using data covering 148 IP offices. Each category includes the following number of offices: high-income countries/economies (52), upper middle-income (48), lower middle-income (33) and low-income (15). Data for the European Union Intellectual Property Office are allocated to the high-income group because most EU member states are high-income countries. For similar reasons, data for the African Regional Intellectual Property Organization and the African Intellectual Property Organization are allocated to the low-income group. For information on income group classification, see the Data description section.

Source: WIPO Statistics Database, August 2019.

C8. Application design counts by region, 2008 and 2018

Region	Number of designs in applications		Resident share (%)		Share of world total (%)		Average growth (%)
	2008	2018	2008	2018	2008	2018	2008–2018
Africa	18,600	17,400	42.0	61.4	2.3	1.3	−0.7
Asia	483,500	914,900	88.6	92.8	59.3	69.7	6.6
Europe	255,300	301,300	56.2	72.3	31.3	23.0	1.7
Latin America and the Caribbean	16,000	15,300	40.7	48.9	2.0	1.2	−0.4
North America	33,100	54,000	48.7	43.7	4.1	4.1	5.0
Oceania	8,300	9,700	32.9	37.1	1.0	0.7	1.6
Total	**814,800**	**1,312,600**	**74.2**	**84.7**	**100.0**	**100.0**	**4.9**

Note: Totals by geographical region are WIPO estimates using data covering 148 IP offices. Each region includes the following number of offices: Africa (29), Asia (42), Europe (41), Latin America and the Caribbean (29), North America (2) and Oceania (5). For information on geographical region classification, see the Data description section.

Source: WIPO Statistics Database, August 2019.

Industrial designs

C9. Trend in industrial design applications for the top five offices, 1883–2018

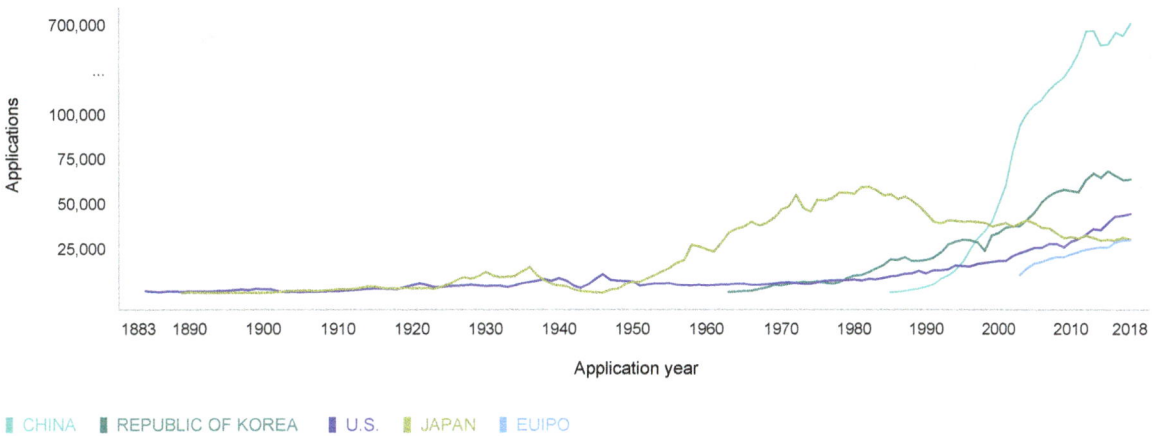

■ CHINA   ■ REPUBLIC OF KOREA   ■ U.S.   ■ JAPAN   ■ EUIPO

Note: The decrease in applications at the IP office of China in 2017 is most likely explained by the new way in which the office counts its applications data. Prior to 2017, it included all applications received; however, starting in 2017, China's application count data include only those applications for which the office has received the necessary application fees. EUIPO is the European Union Intellectual Property Office. Data are based on the numbers of applications filed; that is, differences between single-design and multiple-design filing systems across IP offices are not taken into account. The top five offices were selected based on their 2018 totals.

Source: WIPO Statistics Database, August 2019.

C10. Application design counts for the top 20 offices, 2018

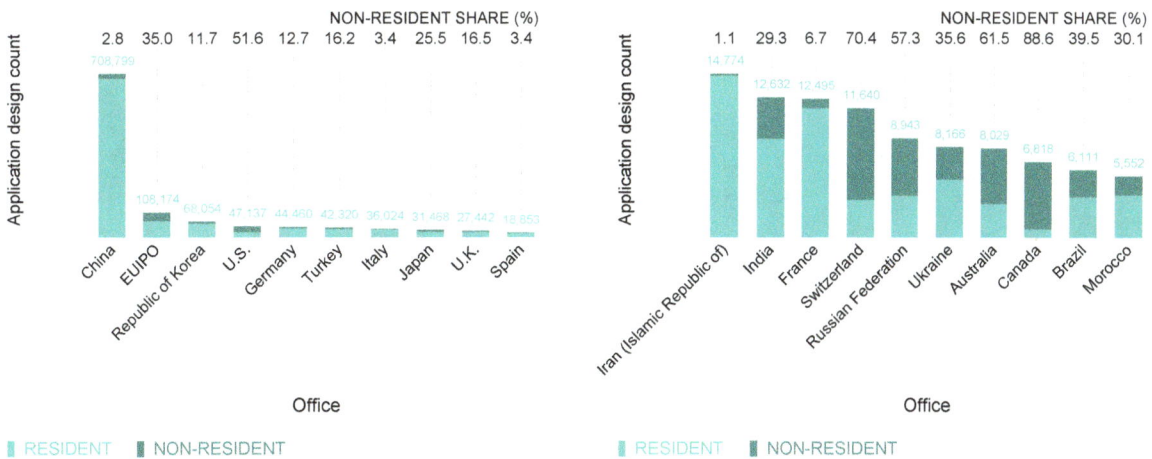

■ RESIDENT   ■ NON-RESIDENT

Note: EUIPO is the European Union Intellectual Property Office.
Source: WIPO Statistics Database, August 2019.

Industrial designs

C11. Contribution of resident and non-resident application design counts to total growth for the top 20 offices, 2017–2018

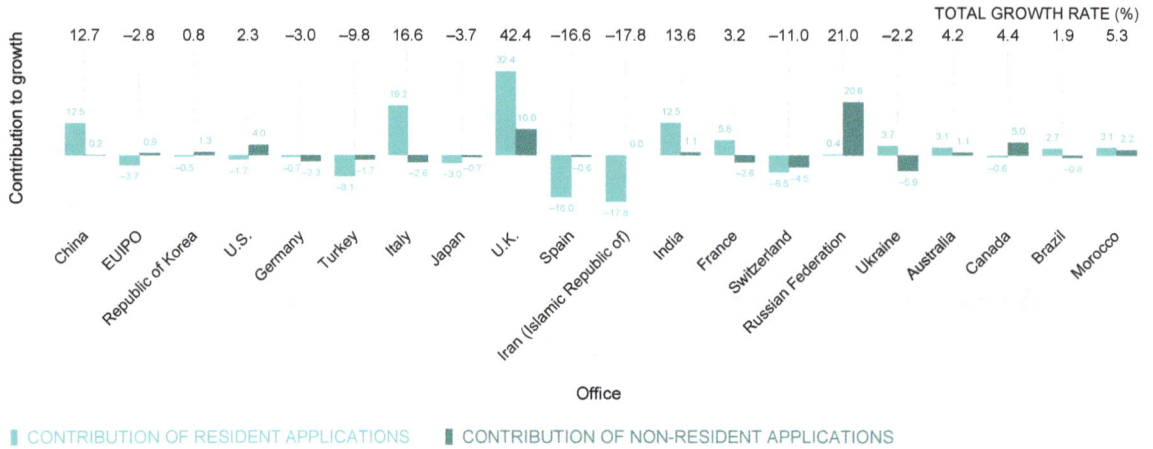

TOTAL GROWTH RATE (%)

| 12.7 | −2.8 | 0.8 | 2.3 | −3.0 | −9.8 | 16.6 | −3.7 | 42.4 | −16.6 | −17.8 | 13.6 | 3.2 | −11.0 | 21.0 | −2.2 | 4.2 | 4.4 | 1.9 | 5.3 |

Contribution to growth

Office: China, EUIPO, Republic of Korea, U.S., Germany, Turkey, Italy, Japan, U.K., Spain, Iran (Islamic Republic of), India, France, Switzerland, Russian Federation, Ukraine, Australia, Canada, Brazil, Morocco

Bar values: 12.5, 0.2 / −3.7 / 0.9, −0.5 / 1.3, −1.7 / 4.0, −0.7, −3.3 / −0.1, −1.7 / 19.2, −2.6 / −3.0, −0.7 / 32.4, 10.0 / −18.0, −0.6 / 0.0, −17.8 / 12.5, 1.1 / 5.8, −2.6 / −6.5, −4.5 / 20.6, 0.4 / 3.7, −5.9 / 3.1, 1.1 / 5.0, −0.6 / 2.7, −0.8 / 3.1, 2.2

■ CONTRIBUTION OF RESIDENT APPLICATIONS   ■ CONTRIBUTION OF NON-RESIDENT APPLICATIONS

Note: EUIPO is the European Union Intellectual Property Office. This figure shows total growth in application design counts, broken down by the respective contributions of resident and non-resident filings. For example, total design counts in the U.K. grew by 42.4%, with resident applicants contributing 32.4 percentage points to this overall growth.

Source: WIPO Statistics Database, August 2019.

C12. Application design counts for offices of selected low- and middle-income countries, 2018

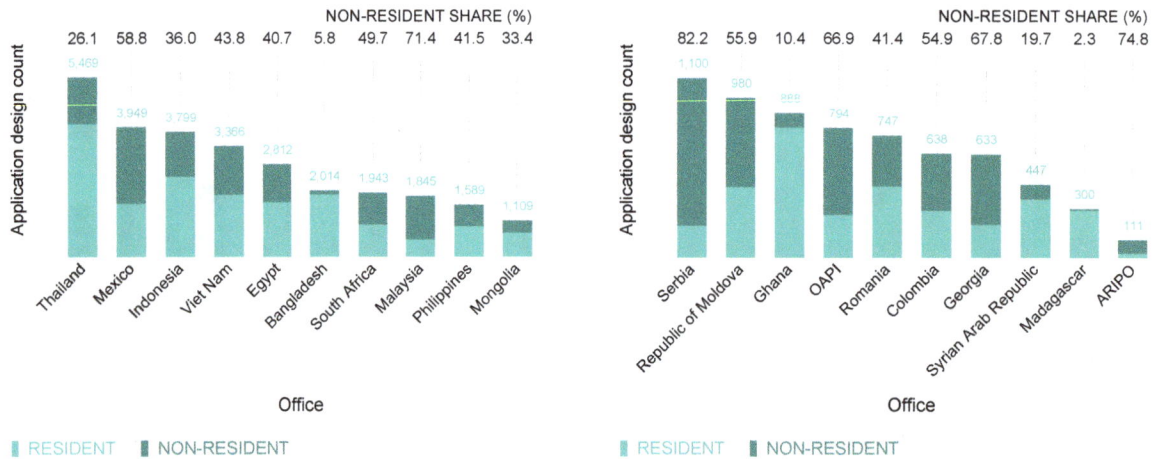

NON-RESIDENT SHARE (%)

| 26.1 | 58.8 | 36.0 | 43.8 | 40.7 | 5.8 | 49.7 | 71.4 | 41.5 | 33.4 |

Application design count

Office: Thailand 5,469, Mexico 3,949, Indonesia 3,799, Viet Nam 3,366, Egypt 2,812, Bangladesh 2,014, South Africa 1,943, Malaysia 1,845, Philippines 1,589, Mongolia 1,109

NON-RESIDENT SHARE (%)

| 82.2 | 55.9 | 10.4 | 66.9 | 41.4 | 54.9 | 67.8 | 19.7 | 2.3 | 74.8 |

Application design count

Office: Serbia 1,100, Republic of Moldova 980, Ghana 888, OAPI 794, Romania 747, Colombia 638, Georgia 633, Syrian Arab Republic 447, Madagascar 300, ARIPO 111

■ RESIDENT   ■ NON-RESIDENT

■ RESIDENT   ■ NON-RESIDENT

Note: ARIPO is the African Regional Intellectual Property Organization and OAPI is the African Intellectual Property Organization. The selected offices are from different world regions and income groups (low-income, lower middle-income and upper middle-income). Where available, data for all offices are presented in the statistical table at the end of this section.

Source: WIPO Statistics Database, August 2019.

C13. Contribution of resident and non-resident application design counts to total growth for offices of selected low- and middle-income countries, 2017–2018

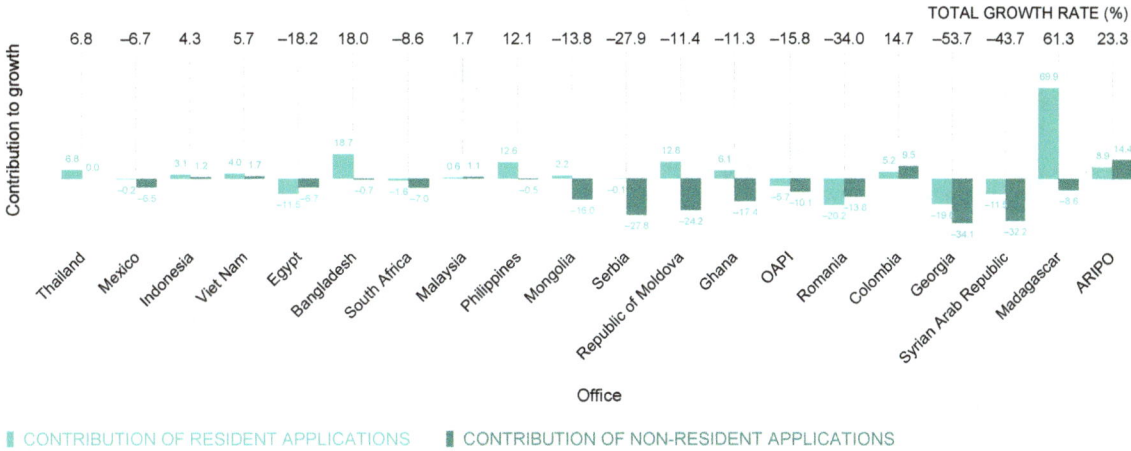

TOTAL GROWTH RATE (%)

| 6.8 | −6.7 | 4.3 | 5.7 | −18.2 | 18.0 | −8.6 | 1.7 | 12.1 | −13.8 | −27.9 | −11.4 | −11.3 | −15.8 | −34.0 | 14.7 | −53.7 | −43.7 | 61.3 | 23.3 |

Contribution to growth

6.8 0.0 −0.2 −8.5 3.1 1.2 4.0 1.7 −11.9 −5.7 18.7 −0.7 −1.8 −7.0 0.6 1.1 12.6 −0.5 2.2 −16.0 −27.8 12.8 −24.2 6.1 −17.4 −6.7 −10.1 −20.2 −13.8 5.2 9.5 −19.9 −34.1 −11.8 −32.2 69.9 −8.6 8.9 14.4

Thailand · Mexico · Indonesia · Viet Nam · Egypt · Bangladesh · South Africa · Malaysia · Philippines · Mongolia · Serbia · Republic of Moldova · Ghana · OAPI · Romania · Colombia · Georgia · Syrian Arab Republic · Madagascar · ARIPO

Office

▌ CONTRIBUTION OF RESIDENT APPLICATIONS   ▌ CONTRIBUTION OF NON-RESIDENT APPLICATIONS

Note: ARIPO is the African Regional Intellectual Property Organization and OAPI is the African Intellectual Property Organization. The selected offices are from different world regions and income groups (low-income, lower middle-income and upper middle-income). Where available, data for all offices are in the statistical table at the end of this section. This figure shows total growth in design counts, broken down by the respective contributions of resident and non-resident filings. For example, the total design count at ARIPO grew by 23.3%, with resident applicants contributing 8.9 percentage points to this overall growth.

Source: WIPO Statistics Database, August 2019.

Industrial designs

C14. Registration design counts for the top 20 offices, 2018

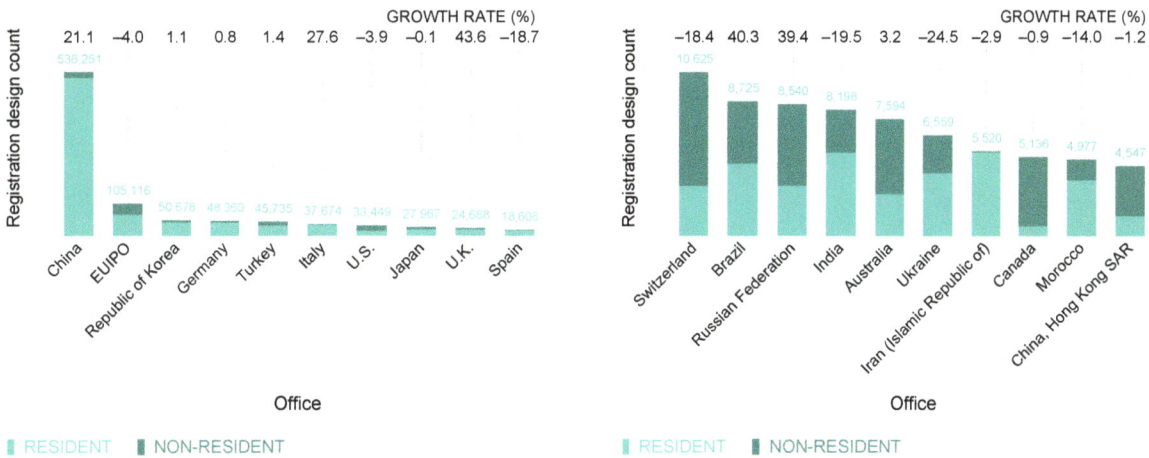

GROWTH RATE (%)

| 21.1 | −4.0 | 1.1 | 0.8 | 1.4 | 27.6 | −3.9 | −0.1 | 43.6 | −18.7 |

Registration design count

536,251 · 105,116 · 50,678 · 48,360 · 45,735 · 37,674 · 33,449 · 27,967 · 24,688 · 18,605

China · EUIPO · Republic of Korea · Germany · Turkey · Italy · U.S. · Japan · U.K. · Spain

Office

GROWTH RATE (%)

| −18.4 | 40.3 | 39.4 | −19.5 | 3.2 | −24.5 | −2.9 | −0.9 | −14.0 | −1.2 |

Registration design count

10,625 · 8,725 · 8,540 · 8,198 · 7,594 · 6,559 · 5,520 · 5,196 · 4,977 · 4,547

Switzerland · Brazil · Russian Federation · India · Australia · Ukraine · Iran (Islamic Republic of) · Canada · Morocco · China, Hong Kong SAR

Office

▌ RESIDENT   ▌ NON-RESIDENT

Note: EUIPO is the European Union Intellectual Property Office. Registration design count data for France are not available.

Source: WIPO Statistics Database, August 2019.

C15. Registration design counts for offices of selected low- and middle-income countries, 2018

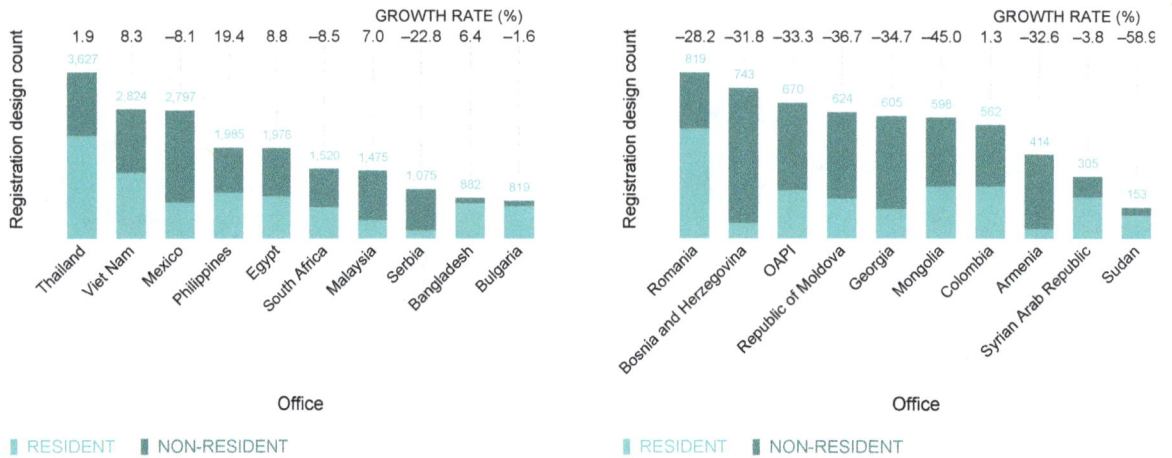

GROWTH RATE (%)

1.9	8.3	−8.1	19.4	8.8	−8.5	7.0	−22.8	6.4	−1.6

Registration design count

- Thailand 3,627
- Viet Nam 2,824
- Mexico 2,797
- Philippines 1,985
- Egypt 1,976
- South Africa 1,520
- Malaysia 1,475
- Serbia 1,075
- Bangladesh 882
- Bulgaria 819

Office

■ RESIDENT ■ NON-RESIDENT

GROWTH RATE (%)

−28.2	−31.8	−33.3	−36.7	−34.7	−45.0	1.3	−32.6	−3.8	−58.9

Registration design count

- Romania 819
- Bosnia and Herzegovina 743
- OAPI 670
- Republic of Moldova 624
- Georgia 605
- Mongolia 598
- Colombia 562
- Armenia 414
- Syrian Arab Republic 305
- Sudan 153

Office

■ RESIDENT ■ NON-RESIDENT

Note: OAPI is the African Intellectual Property Organization. The selected offices are from different world regions and income groups (low-income, lower middle-income and upper middle-income). Where available, data for all offices are presented in the statistical table at the end of this section.

Source: WIPO Statistics Database, August 2019.

Industrial designs

Application design counts by origin

C16. Equivalent application design counts by origin, 2018

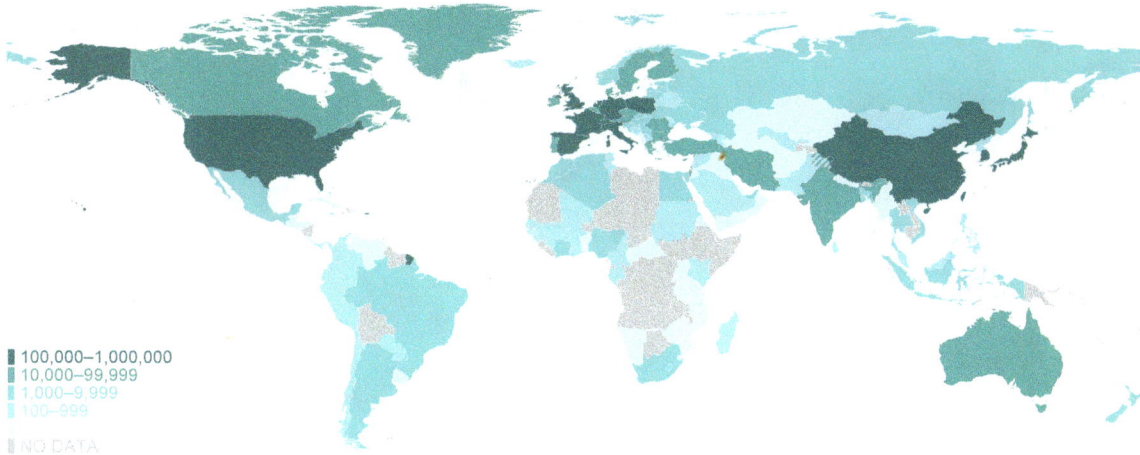

- ■ 100,000–1,000,000
- ■ 10,000–99,999
- ■ 1,000–9,999
- ■ 100–999
- ▯ NO DATA

Note: Equivalent application design count includes resident applications and applications filed abroad. The origin of an industrial design application is determined by the residence of the first named applicant. Applications filed at some regional offices are considered equivalent to multiple applications in the member states of those offices. See the glossary for the full definition of equivalent application and design count.

Source: WIPO Statistics Database, August 2019.

C17. Equivalent application design counts for the top 20 origins, 2018

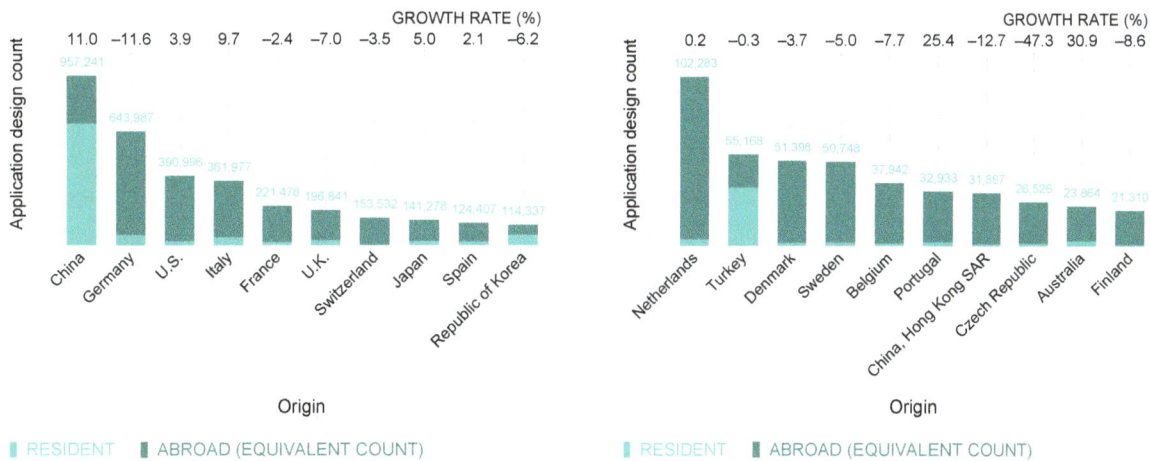

GROWTH RATE (%)

11.0 −11.6 3.9 9.7 −2.4 −7.0 −3.5 5.0 2.1 −6.2

957,241
643,987
390,996 361,977
221,478 196,841 153,532 141,278 124,487 114,337

China, Germany, U.S., Italy, France, U.K., Switzerland, Japan, Spain, Republic of Korea

GROWTH RATE (%)

0.2 −0.3 −3.7 −5.0 −7.7 25.4 −12.7 −47.3 30.9 −8.6

102,283
55,168 51,398 50,748 37,942 32,933 31,887 26,526 23,664 21,310

Netherlands, Turkey, Denmark, Sweden, Belgium, Portugal, China, Hong Kong SAR, Czech Republic, Australia, Finland

■ RESIDENT   ■ ABROAD (EQUIVALENT COUNT)

Note: The origin of an industrial design application is determined by the residence of the first named applicant. An application filed at a regional office is considered to be a resident filing if the applicant is a resident of one of that office's member states. Applications filed at some regional offices are considered equivalent to multiple applications in the member states of those offices. See the glossary for the definition of equivalent application and design count.

Source: WIPO Statistics Database, August 2019.

Industrial designs

C18. Application design counts for the top 20 origins, 2018

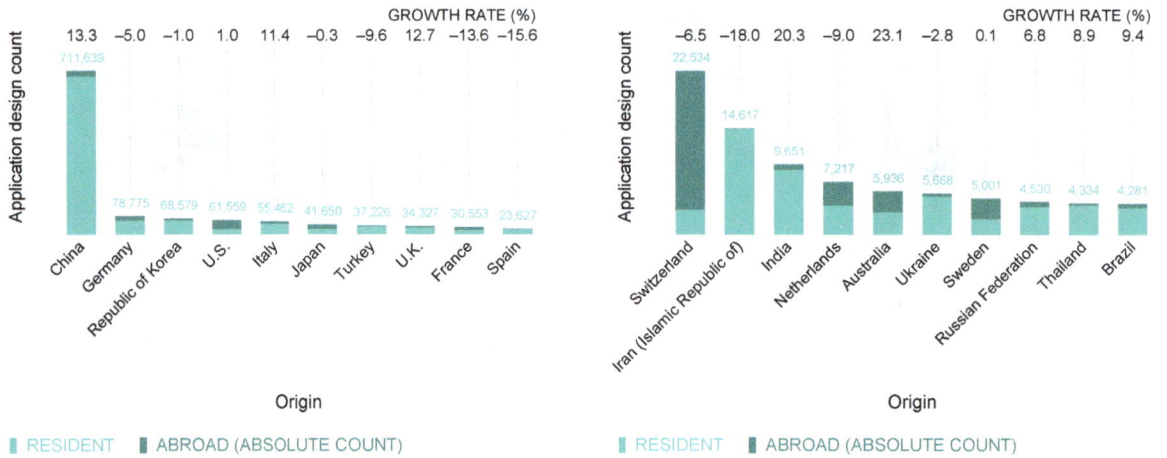

GROWTH RATE (%)

| 13.3 | –5.0 | –1.0 | 1.0 | 11.4 | –0.3 | –9.6 | 12.7 | –13.6 | –15.6 |

Application design count

China	Germany	Republic of Korea	U.S.	Italy	Japan	Turkey	U.K.	France	Spain
711,639	78,775	68,579	61,559	55,462	41,650	37,226	34,327	30,553	23,627

Origin

■ RESIDENT ■ ABROAD (ABSOLUTE COUNT)

GROWTH RATE (%)

| –6.5 | –18.0 | 20.3 | –9.0 | 23.1 | –2.8 | 0.1 | 6.8 | 8.9 | 9.4 |

Application design count

Switzerland	Iran (Islamic Republic of)	India	Netherlands	Australia	Ukraine	Sweden	Russian Federation	Thailand	Brazil
22,534	14,617	9,651	7,217	5,936	5,668	5,001	4,530	4,334	4,281

Origin

■ RESIDENT ■ ABROAD (ABSOLUTE COUNT)

Note: Data are based on absolute count, not equivalent count. The origin of an industrial design application is determined by the residence of the first named applicant. An application filed at a regional office is considered to be a resident filing if the applicant is a resident of one of that office's member states.

Source: WIPO Statistics Database, August 2019.

C19. Application design counts for selected low- and middle-income origins, 2018

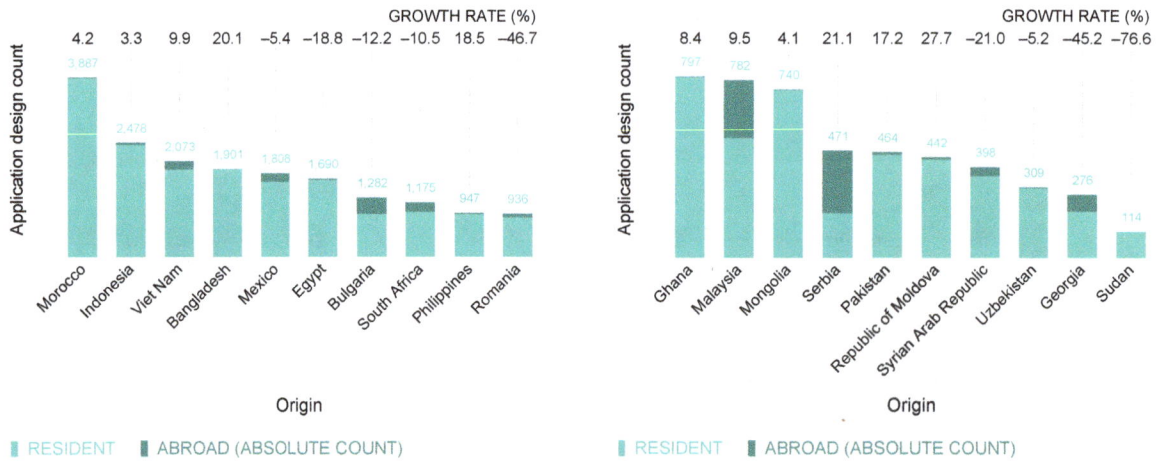

GROWTH RATE (%)

| 4.2 | 3.3 | 9.9 | 20.1 | –5.4 | –18.8 | –12.2 | –10.5 | 18.5 | –46.7 |

Application design count

Morocco	Indonesia	Viet Nam	Bangladesh	Mexico	Egypt	Bulgaria	South Africa	Philippines	Romania
3,687	2,478	2,073	1,901	1,808	1,690	1,282	1,175	947	936

Origin

■ RESIDENT ■ ABROAD (ABSOLUTE COUNT)

GROWTH RATE (%)

| 8.4 | 9.5 | 4.1 | 21.1 | 17.2 | 27.7 | –21.0 | –5.2 | –45.2 | –76.6 |

Application design count

Ghana	Malaysia	Mongolia	Serbia	Pakistan	Republic of Moldova	Syrian Arab Republic	Uzbekistan	Georgia	Sudan
797	782	740	471	464	442	398	309	276	114

Origin

■ RESIDENT ■ ABROAD (ABSOLUTE COUNT)

Note: Data are based on absolute count, not equivalent count. The selected origins are from different world regions and income groups (low-income, lower middle-income and upper middle-income). Where available, data for all origins are presented in the statistical table at the end of this section. The origin of an industrial design application is determined by the residence of the first named applicant.

Source: WIPO Statistics Database, August 2019.

C20. Flows of non-resident application design counts for the top five origins and the top 10 offices of high-income economies, 2018

Origin

Office

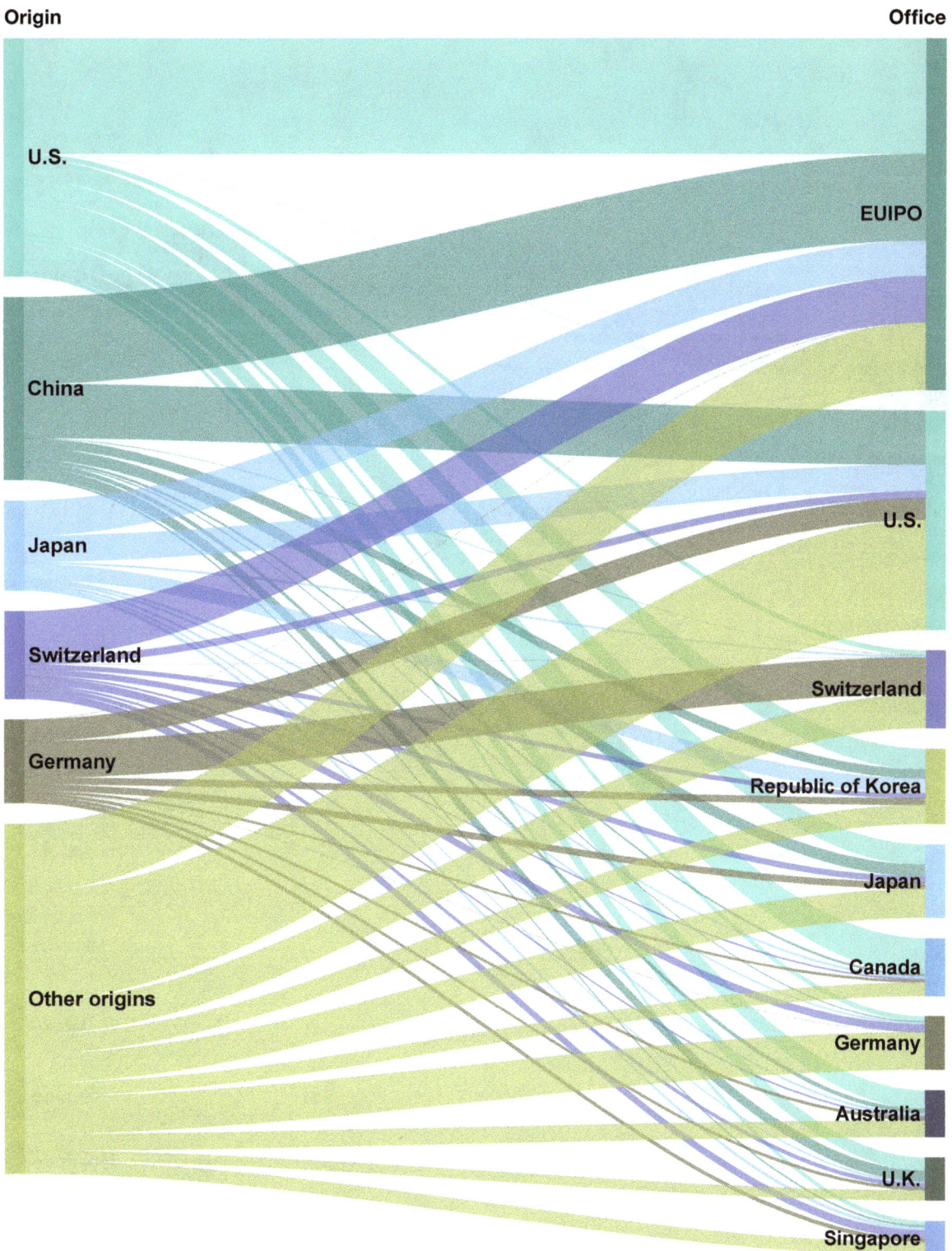

Note: EUIPO is the European Union Intellectual Property Office.

Source: WIPO Statistics Database, August 2019.

Industrial designs

C21. Flows of non-resident application design counts for the top five origins and the top 10 offices of low- and middle-income economies, 2018

Origin
Office

Industrial designs

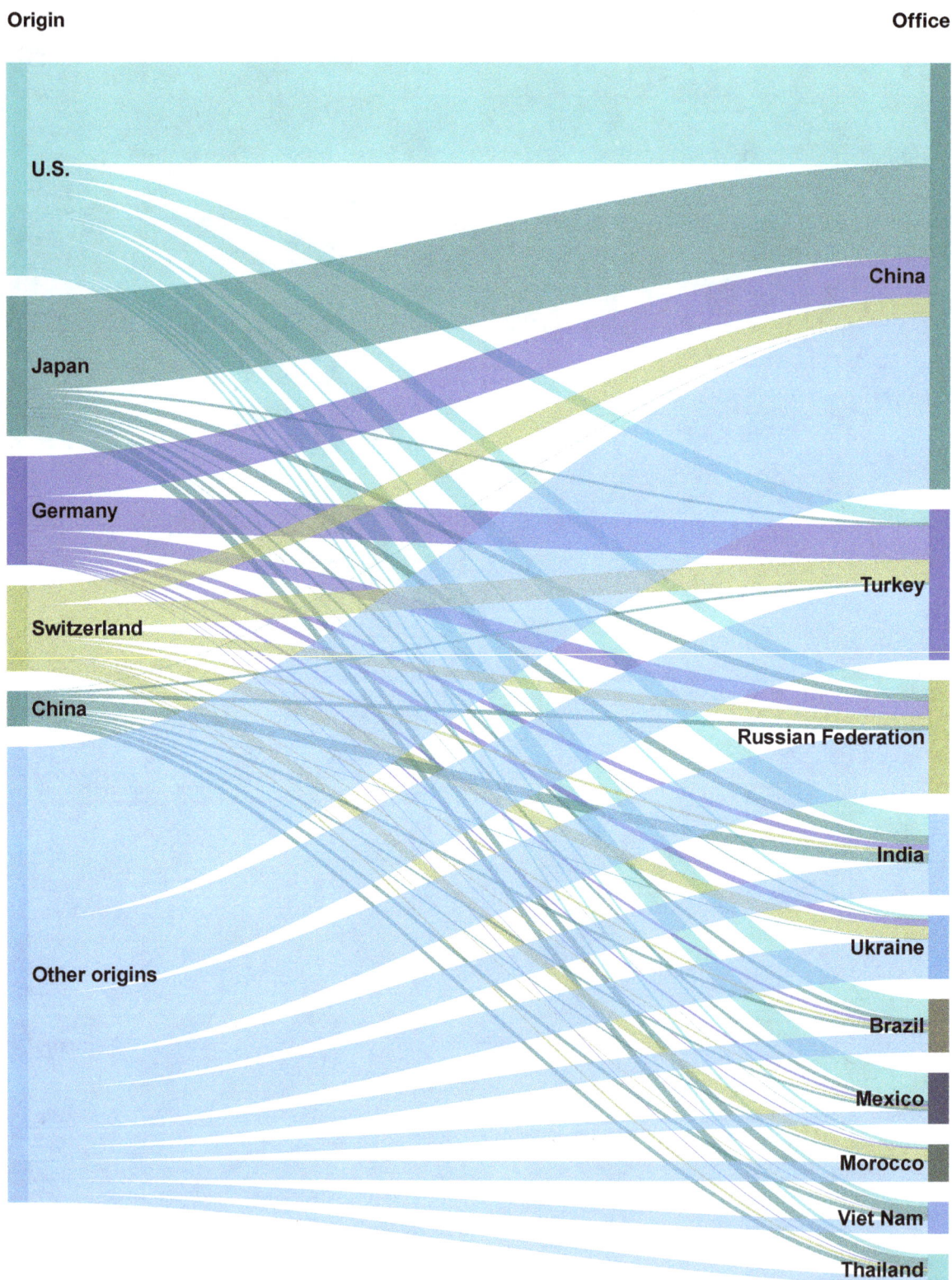

U.S.

Japan

Germany

Switzerland

China

Other origins

China

Turkey

Russian Federation

India

Ukraine

Brazil

Mexico

Morocco

Viet Nam

Thailand

Source: WIPO Statistics Database, August 2019.

Application design counts by Locarno class and industry sector

C22. Application design counts by Locarno class, 2018

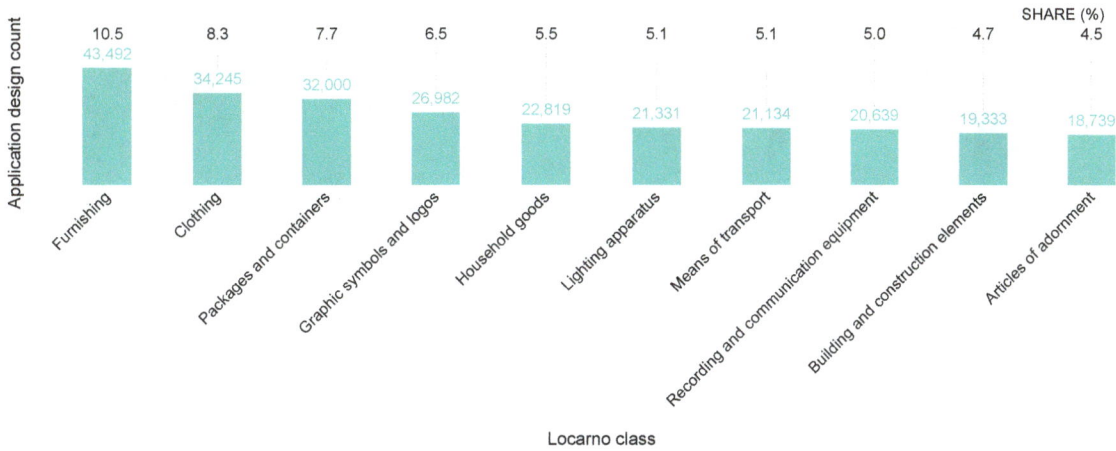

SHARE (%)

	10.5	8.3	7.7	6.5	5.5	5.1	5.1	5.0	4.7	4.5

Application design count

| 43,492 | 34,245 | 32,000 | 26,982 | 22,819 | 21,331 | 21,134 | 20,639 | 19,333 | 18,739 |

Locarno classes: Furnishing, Clothing, Packages and containers, Graphic symbols and logos, Household goods, Lighting apparatus, Means of transport, Recording and communication equipment, Building and construction elements, Articles of adornment

Locarno class

Note: See annex C for class numbers. These figures are based on data from 112 IP offices. Data for several large offices are not available or are incomplete, including the offices of China, Japan and the U.S.

Source: WIPO Statistics Database, August 2019.

C23. Distribution of application design counts by the top three sectors and for the top 10 offices, 2018

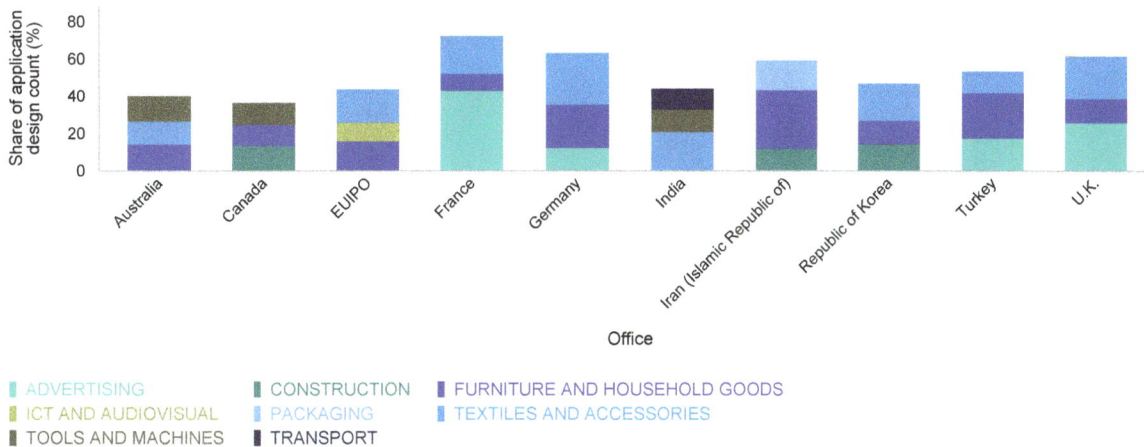

Share of application design count (%)

Offices: Australia, Canada, EUIPO, France, Germany, India, Iran (Islamic Republic of), Republic of Korea, Turkey, U.K.

Office

Legend:
- ADVERTISING
- CONSTRUCTION
- FURNITURE AND HOUSEHOLD GOODS
- ICT AND AUDIOVISUAL
- PACKAGING
- TEXTILES AND ACCESSORIES
- TOOLS AND MACHINES
- TRANSPORT

Note: EUIPO is the European Union Intellectual Property Office. A concordance table produced by the Organisation for Economic Co-operation and Development (OECD) was used to convert the 32 classes into 12 industry sectors (see annex C for definitions). The top three sectors and top 10 offices were selected based on their 2018 totals. Data for several large offices are not available or are incomplete, including the offices of China, Japan and the U.S.

Source: WIPO Statistics Database, August 2019.

C24. Distribution of application design counts by the top three sectors for the top 10 origins, 2018

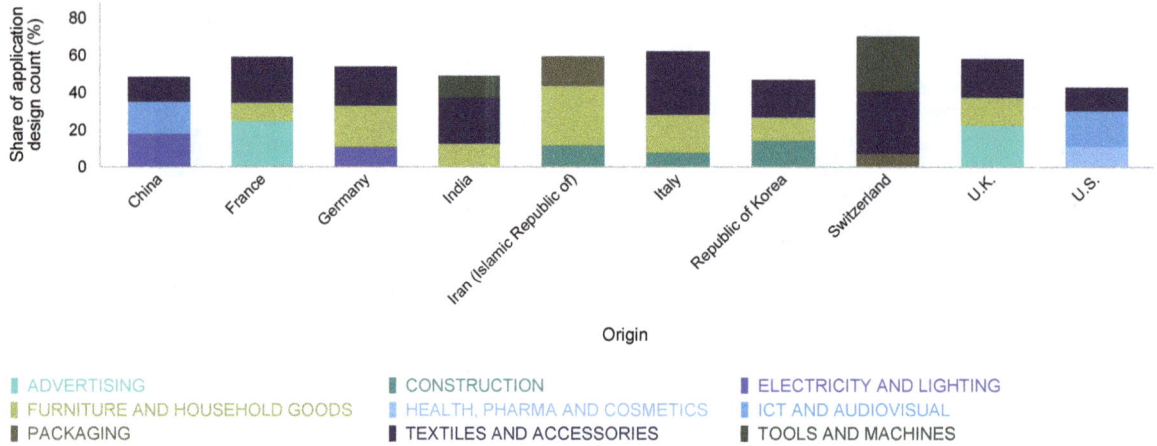

Legend:
- ADVERTISING
- CONSTRUCTION
- ELECTRICITY AND LIGHTING
- FURNITURE AND HOUSEHOLD GOODS
- HEALTH, PHARMA AND COSMETICS
- ICT AND AUDIOVISUAL
- PACKAGING
- TEXTILES AND ACCESSORIES
- TOOLS AND MACHINES

Note: A concordance table produced by the Organisation for Economic Co-operation and Development (OECD) was used to convert the 32 classes into 12 industry sectors (see annex C for definitions). These figures are based on data from 112 IP offices. Data for several large offices are not available or are incomplete, including the offices of China, Japan and the U.S.

Source: WIPO Statistics Database, August 2019.

Industrial designs

Application design count in relation to GDP and population

C25. Resident application design count per USD 100 billion of GDP for the top 20 origins, 2008 and 2018

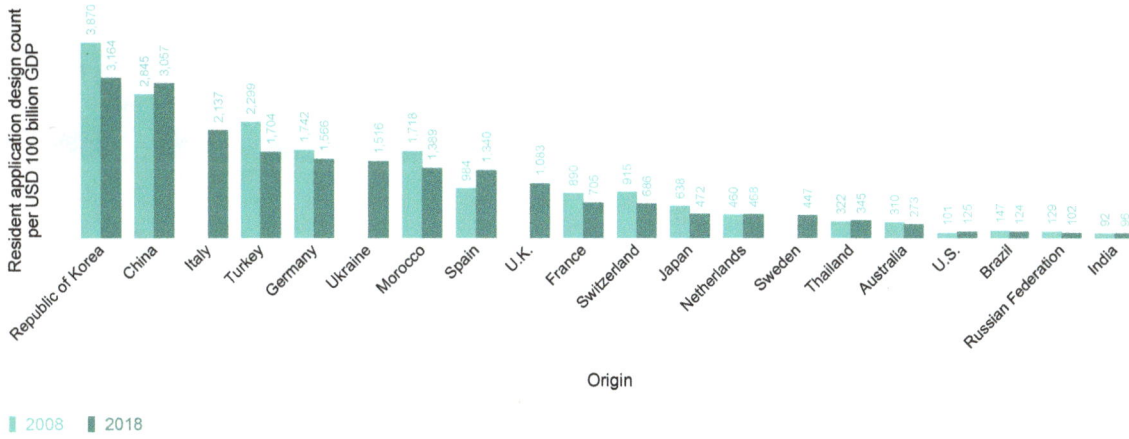

■ 2008   ■ 2018

Note: GDP data are in constant 2011 US PPP dollars. Origins were selected based on the top origins list in terms of application design count and on GDP data availability.

Sources: WIPO Statistics Database and World Bank, August 2019.

C26. Resident application design count per million population for the top 20 origins, 2008 and 2018

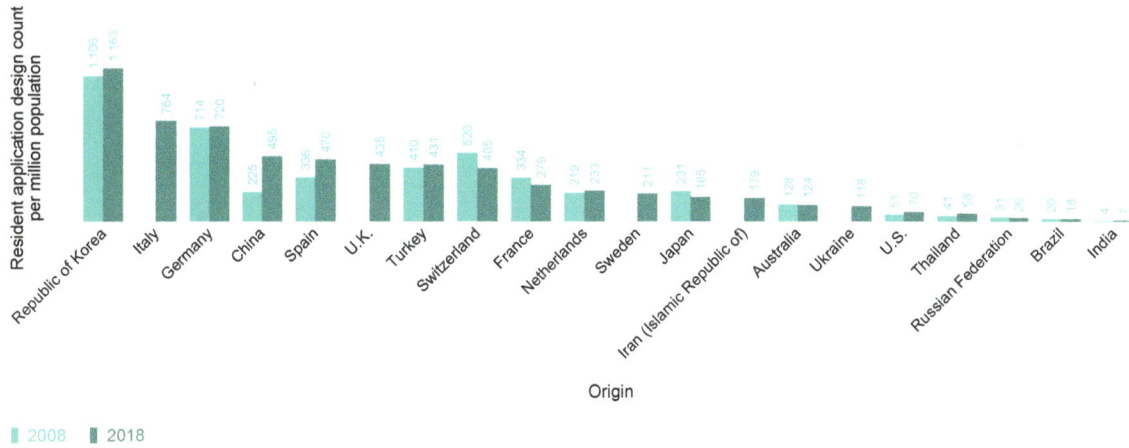

■ 2008   ■ 2018

Note: Origins were selected based on the top origins list in terms of application design count and on population data availability.

Sources: WIPO Statistics Database and World Bank, August 2019.

Industrial design registrations in force

C27. Trend in industrial design registrations in force worldwide, 2010–2018

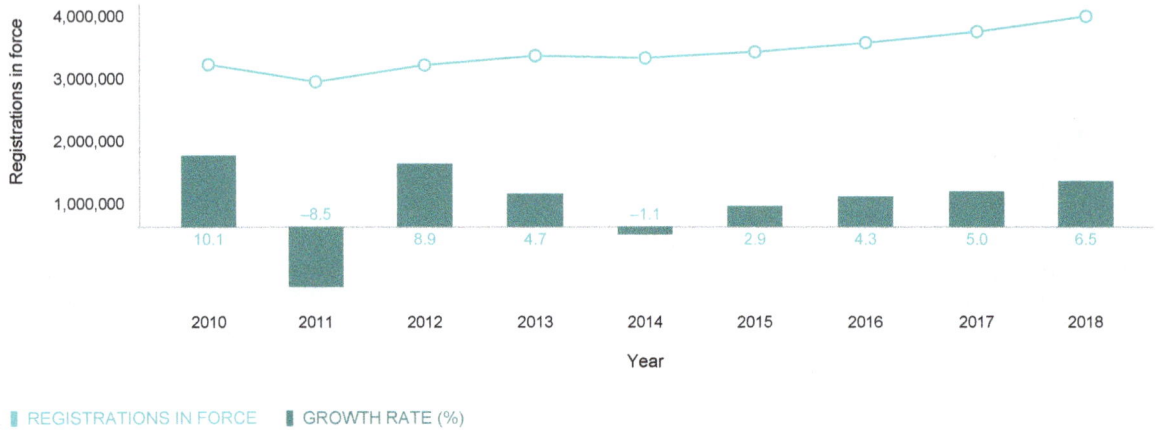

| | REGISTRATIONS IN FORCE | | GROWTH RATE (%) |

Note: WIPO estimates cover 122 IP offices and include direct national and regional applications as well as designations received via the Hague System. Data refer to the number of industrial design registrations in force and not the number of designs contained in registrations in force.

Source: WIPO Statistics Database, August 2019.

C28. Industrial design registrations in force for the top 20 offices, 2018

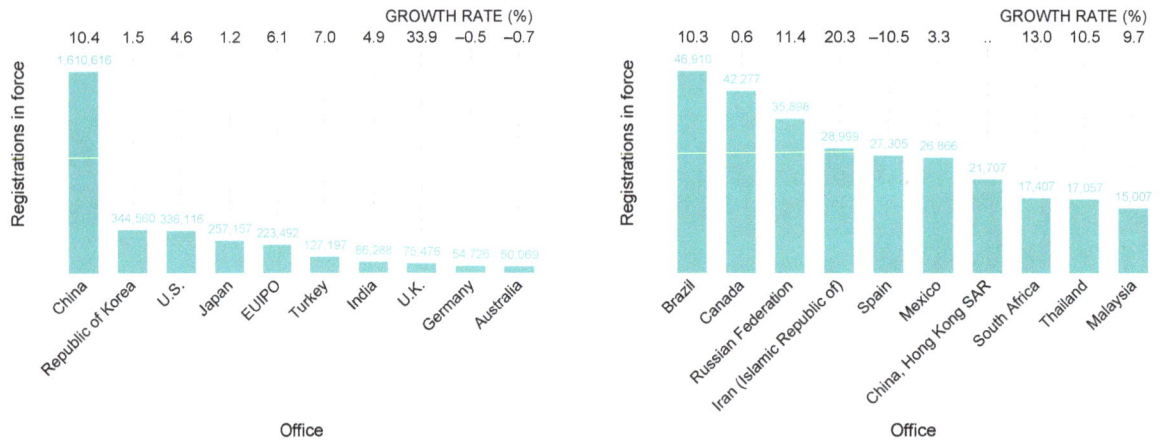

Note: EUIPO is the European Union Intellectual Property Office. Data refer to the number of industrial design registrations in force and not the number of designs contained in registrations in force. Registrations in force data are not available for France.

.. indicates not available.

Source: WIPO Statistics Database, August 2019.

Industrial designs

C29. Industrial design registrations in force in 2018 as a percentage of total registrations

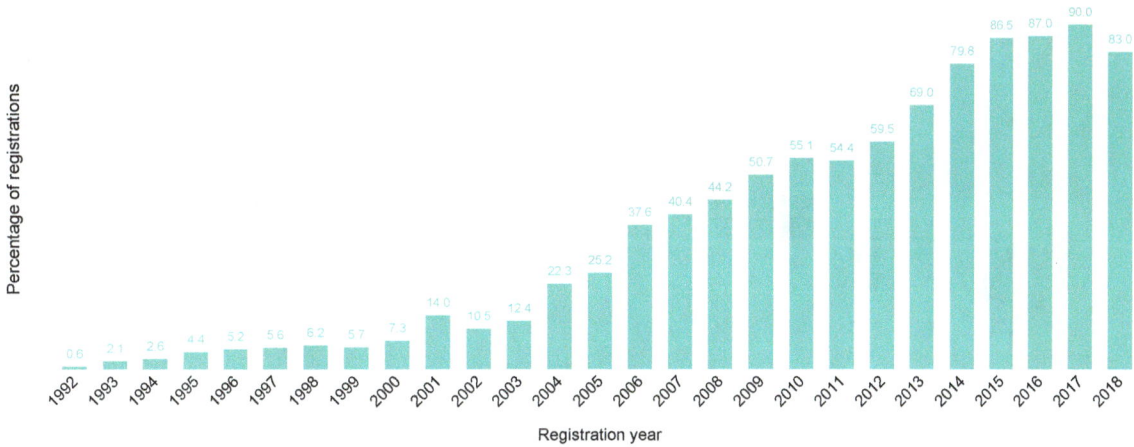

Percentage of registrations

1992	0.6
1993	2.1
1994	2.6
1995	4.4
1996	5.2
1997	5.6
1998	8.2
1999	5.7
2000	7.3
2001	14.0
2002	10.5
2003	12.4
2004	22.3
2005	25.2
2006	37.6
2007	40.4
2008	44.2
2009	50.7
2010	55.1
2011	54.4
2012	59.5
2013	69.0
2014	79.8
2015	86.5
2016	87.0
2017	90.0
2018	83.0

Registration year

Note: Percentages are calculated using the number of industrial designs registered in year *t* and in force in 2018 divided by the total number of industrial designs registered in year *t*. The graph is based on data from 81 offices (including most large offices, with the exception of France, Italy and Japan) for which a breakdown of industrial design registrations in force by year of registration was available.

Source: WIPO Statistics Database, August 2019.

Industrial designs

C30. Average age of industrial design registrations in force at selected offices, 2013 and 2018

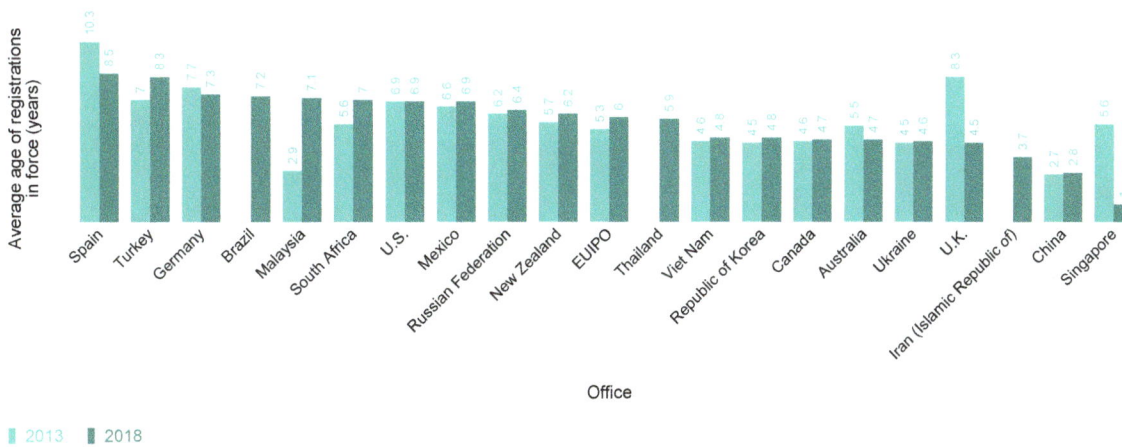

Average age of registrations in force (years)

Office

█ 2013   █ 2018

Note: EUIPO is the European Union Intellectual Property Office.
Source: WIPO Statistics Database, August 2019.

151

Industrial design applications through the Hague System

C31. Trend in designs contained in Hague international applications, 2004–2018

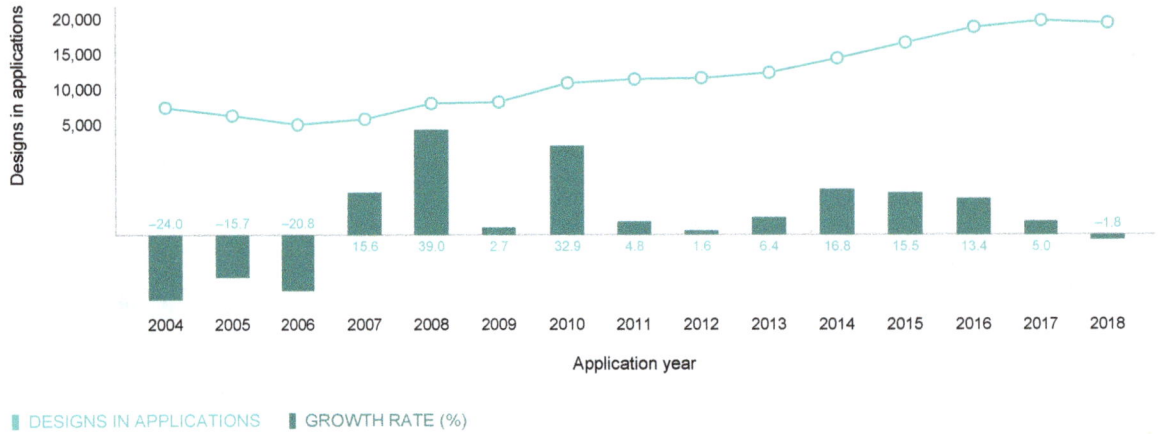

DESIGNS IN APPLICATIONS GROWTH RATE (%)

Source: WIPO Statistics Database, August 2019.

C32. Designs contained in Hague international applications by origin, 2018

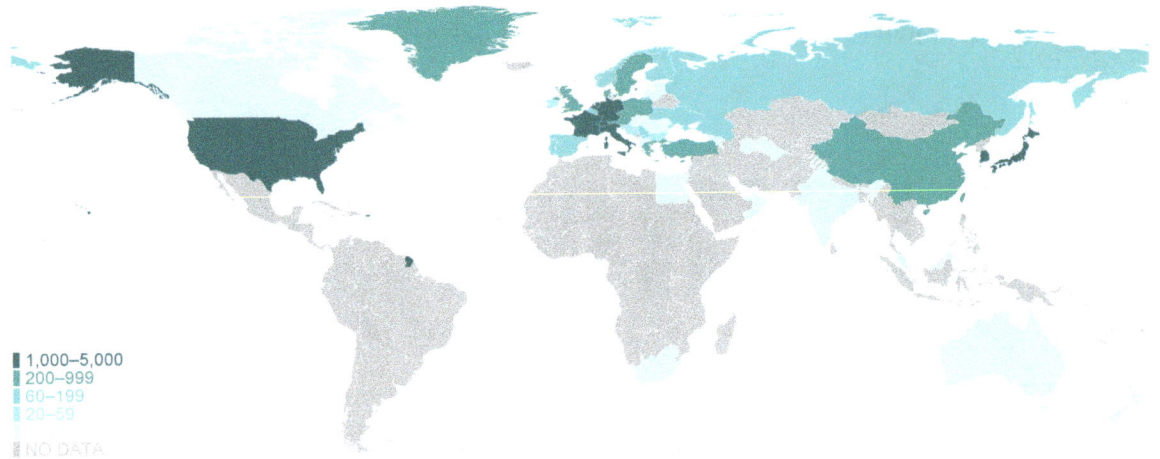

- 1,000–5,000
- 200–999
- 60–199
- 20–59
- NO DATA

Note: Applicants residing in a non-member country can file applications for international registrations if they have a real and effective industrial or commercial establishment within the jurisdiction of a Hague member.

Source: WIPO Statistics Database, August 2019.

Industrial designs

C33. Designs contained in Hague international applications for the top 20 origins, 2018

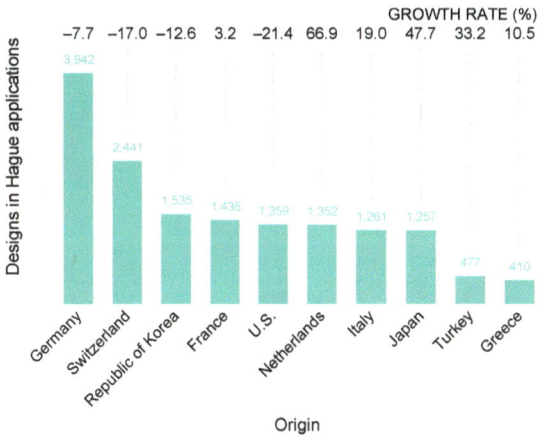

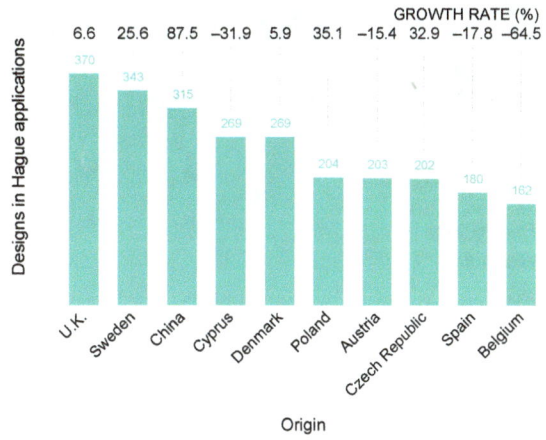

GROWTH RATE (%)

–7.7	–17.0	–12.6	3.2	–21.4	66.9	19.0	47.7	33.2	10.5

Designs in Hague applications

- Germany: 3,942
- Switzerland: 2,441
- Republic of Korea: 1,535
- France: 1,436
- U.S.: 1,359
- Netherlands: 1,352
- Italy: 1,261
- Japan: 1,257
- Turkey: 477
- Greece: 410

Origin

GROWTH RATE (%)

6.6	25.6	87.5	–31.9	5.9	35.1	–15.4	32.9	–17.8	–64.5

Designs in Hague applications

- U.K.: 370
- Sweden: 343
- China: 315
- Cyprus: 269
- Denmark: 269
- Poland: 204
- Austria: 203
- Czech Republic: 202
- Spain: 180
- Belgium: 162

Origin

Source: WIPO Statistics Database, August 2019.

C34. Designs contained in designations in Hague international applications for the top 20 designated Hague members, 2018

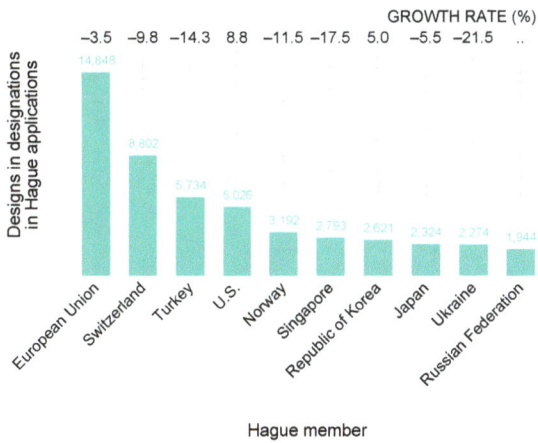

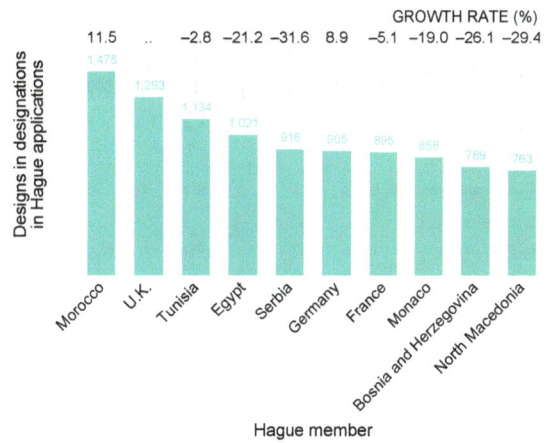

GROWTH RATE (%)

–3.5	–9.8	–14.3	8.8	–11.5	–17.5	5.0	–5.5	–21.5	..

Designs in designations in Hague applications

- European Union: 14,648
- Switzerland: 8,802
- Turkey: 5,734
- U.S.: 5,026
- Norway: 3,192
- Singapore: 2,793
- Republic of Korea: 2,621
- Japan: 2,324
- Ukraine: 2,274
- Russian Federation: 1,944

Hague member

GROWTH RATE (%)

11.5	..	–2.8	–21.2	–31.6	8.9	–5.1	–19.0	–26.1	–29.4

Designs in designations in Hague applications

- Morocco: 1,478
- U.K.: 1,293
- Tunisia: 1,134
- Egypt: 1,021
- Serbia: 916
- Germany: 905
- France: 895
- Monaco: 858
- Bosnia and Herzegovina: 789
- North Macedonia: 763

Hague member

.. indicates not available.

Source: WIPO Statistics Database, August 2019.

Industrial designs

153

Statistical tables

C35. Industrial design applications by office and origin, 2018

Name	Application design count by office			Application design count by origin	Equivalent application design count by origin	Hague international application design count	
	Total	Resident	Non-resident	Total [a]	Total [a]	Origin [c]	Designated Hague member
Afghanistan (b)	..	..	..	4	4	..	n.a.
African Intellectual Property Organization	794	263	531	n.a.	n.a.	n.a.	483
African Regional Intellectual Property Organization	111	28	83	n.a.	n.a.	n.a.	n.a.
Albania (b)	..	..	..	4	31	1	666
Algeria	1,418	1,033	385	1,053	1,269	..	n.a.
Andorra (b)	..	..	..	3	84	..	n.a.
Argentina	1,607	932	675	1,017	1,422	..	n.a.
Armenia	498	61	437	167	680	19	441
Australia	8,029	3,095	4,934	5,936	23,864	4	n.a.
Austria (b)	..	..	..	3,951	64,362	203	n.a.
Azerbaijan	589	54	535	54	54	..	510
Bahamas (b)	..	..	..	106	619	19	n.a.
Bahrain	84	5	79	5	5	..	n.a.
Bangladesh	2,014	1,897	117	1,901	1,901	..	n.a.
Barbados (b)	..	..	..	344	1,802	..	n.a.
Belarus	448	183	265	255	552	..	n.a.
Belgium	n.a.	n.a.	n.a.	2,885	37,942	162	n.a.
Belize	215	2	213	3	3	..	213
Benelux Office for Intellectual Property	1,248	809	439	n.a.	n.a.	n.a.	460
Benin (b,d)	n.a.	n.a.	n.a.	3	51	..	28
Bermuda (b)	..	..	..	9	9	..	n.a.
Bosnia and Herzegovina	869	76	793	194	842	44	789
Botswana (b)	..	..	..	..	..	..	82
Brazil	6,111	3,696	2,415	4,281	9,211	..	n.a.
Brunei Darussalam	89	0	89	..	..	..	75
Bulgaria	545	433	112	1,282	14,862	33	107
Burkina Faso (b,d)	n.a.	n.a.	n.a.	7	119	..	n.a.
Cabo Verde	38	31	7	31	31	..	n.a.
Cambodia (b)	..	..	..	..	..	..	75
Cameroon (b,d)	n.a.	n.a.	n.a.	36	612	..	n.a.
Canada	6,818	774	6,044	2,899	19,277	15	250
Central African Republic (b,d)	n.a.	n.a.	n.a.	5	85	..	n.a.
Chile	602	49	553	140	140	..	n.a.
China	708,799	689,097	19,702	711,639	957,241	315	n.a.
China, Hong Kong SAR	4,435	1,247	3,188	3,494	31,887	..	n.a.
China, Macao SAR	208	67	141	199	1,360	..	n.a.
Colombia	638	288	350	336	417	..	n.a.
Cook Islands (b)	..	..	..	1	1	..	n.a.
Costa Rica	70	8	62	20	20	..	n.a.
Côte d'Ivoire (b,d)	n.a.	n.a.	n.a.	92	1,564	..	29
Croatia	826	367	459	554	2,271	40	448
Cuba	21	11	10	12	39	..	n.a.
Curaçao (b)	..	..	..	1	28	1	n.a.
Cyprus	86	86	0	1,680	10,617	269	n.a.
Czech Republic	718	627	91	2,367	26,526	202	n.a.

Name	Application design count by office			Application design count by origin	Equivalent application design count by origin	Hague international application design count	
	Total	Resident	Non-resident	Total [a]	Total [a]	Origin [c]	Designated Hague member
Democratic People's Republic of Korea (b)	..	..	..	19	235	..	106
Denmark	452	177	275	3,149	51,398	269	274
Dominican Republic	31	5	26	5	5	..	n.a.
Ecuador	353	246	107	247	247	..	n.a.
Egypt	2,812	1,668	1,144	1,690	1,868	2	1,021
El Salvador	46	19	27	25	25	..	n.a.
Eritrea (b)	..	..	..	1	1	..	n.a.
Estonia	142	62	80	326	5,186	13	74
Eswatini (b)	..	..	..	37	37	..	n.a.
European Union Intellectual Property Office	108,174	70,320	37,854	n.a.	n.a.	n.a.	14,848
Finland	262	157	105	1,568	21,310	71	94
France	12,495	11,661	834	30,553	221,478	1,436	895
Gabon (b,d)	n.a.	n.a.	n.a.	6	102	..	19
Georgia	633	204	429	276	276	15	411
Germany	44,460	38,815	5,645	78,775	643,987	3,942	905
Ghana	888	796	92	797	797	..	92
Greece	1,023	541	482	2,194	18,889	410	482
Guatemala	258	35	223	39	41	..	n.a.
Guinea (b,d)	n.a.	n.a.	n.a.	39	663	..	n.a.
Guinea-Bissau (b,d)	n.a.	n.a.	n.a.	8	120	..	n.a.
Guyana	9	0	9	..	..	..	n.a.
Honduras	29	4	25	4	4	..	n.a.
Hungary	689	595	94	868	7,510	6	70
Iceland (b)	..	..	..	44	989	..	265
India	12,632	8,928	3,704	9,651	15,211	1	n.a.
Indonesia	3,799	2,432	1,367	2,478	2,667	..	n.a.
Iran (Islamic Republic of)	14,774	14,610	164	14,617	14,617	..	n.a.
Iraq	89	81	8	94	94	..	n.a.
Ireland	555	88	467	817	12,022	27	n.a.
Israel	1,688	981	707	2,101	11,200	1	n.a.
Italy	36,024	34,812	1,212	55,462	361,977	1,261	467
Jamaica	121	114	7	115	115	..	n.a.
Japan	31,468	23,459	8,009	41,650	141,278	1,257	2,324
Jordan	49	26	23	42	42	..	n.a.
Kazakhstan	253	83	170	95	95	..	n.a.
Kenya	177	170	7	170	170	..	n.a.
Kuwait (b)	..	..	..	1	1	..	n.a.
Kyrgyzstan (b)	..	..	..	6	6	..	298
Latvia	193	154	39	344	3,260	19	36
Lebanon (b)	..	..	..	20	133	3	n.a.
Liechtenstein	973	261	712	772	4,768	45	722
Lithuania	531	160	371	320	3,506	3	362
Luxembourg	n.a.	n.a.	n.a.	1,269	14,894	118	n.a.
Madagascar	300	293	7	293	293	..	n.a.
Malaysia	1,845	528	1,317	782	971	8	n.a.

Industrial designs

Name	Application design count by office			Application design count by origin	Equivalent application design count by origin	Hague international application design count	
	Total	Resident	Non-resident	Total [a]	Total [a]	Origin [c]	Designated Hague member
Maldives (b)	..	..	..	2	2	..	n.a.
Mali (b,d)	n.a.	n.a.	n.a.	15	223	..	3
Malta (b)	..	..	..	150	2,720	2	n.a.
Mauritius	99	75	24	94	191	..	n.a.
Mexico	3,949	1,627	2,322	1,808	3,185	..	n.a.
Monaco	927	74	853	230	2,309	60	858
Mongolia	1,109	739	370	740	740	..	332
Montenegro	738	1	737	1	1	..	719
Morocco	5,552	3,879	1,673	3,887	4,010	..	1,478
Mozambique	69	5	64	5	5	..	n.a.
Myanmar (b)	..	..	..	10	10	..	n.a.
Namibia (b)	..	..	..	2	2	..	79
Nepal (b)	..	..	..	2	2	..	n.a.
Netherlands	n.a.	n.a.	n.a.	7,217	102,283	1,352	n.a.
New Zealand	1,581	463	1,118	1,427	6,881	4	n.a.
Niger (b,d)	n.a.	n.a.	n.a.	..	..	..	5
Nigeria	1,172	1,146	26	1,148	1,148	..	n.a.
North Macedonia	846	63	783	70	151	1	763
Norway	4,201	555	3,646	1,413	8,373	142	3,192
Oman (b)	..	..	..	10	53	1	651
Pakistan	588	453	135	464	518	..	n.a.
Panama	68	0	68	33	600	..	n.a.
Paraguay	221	159	62	159	159	..	n.a.
Peru	381	134	247	141	141	..	n.a.
Philippines	1,589	929	660	947	947	..	n.a.
Poland (b)	..	..	..	4,960	117,739	204	244
Portugal	1,350	1,288	62	2,610	32,933	105	n.a.
Qatar (b)	..	..	..	4	4	..	n.a.
Republic of Korea	68,054	60,075	7,979	68,579	114,337	1,535	2,621
Republic of Moldova	980	432	548	442	604	2	481
Romania	747	438	309	936	12,249	13	276
Russian Federation	8,943	3,822	5,121	4,530	8,310	107	1,944
Rwanda	68	5	63	5	5	..	63
Saint Kitts and Nevis (b)	..	..	..	1	1	..	n.a.
Saint Vincent and the Grenadines (b)	..	..	..	1	28	..	n.a.
Samoa	44	44	0	52	160	..	n.a.
San Marino	21	17	4	603	981	..	n.a.
Sao Tome and Principe	105	0	105	..	..	..	53
Saudi Arabia	917	345	572	368	368	..	n.a.
Senegal (b,d)	n.a.	n.a.	n.a.	52	884	..	24
Serbia	1,100	196	904	471	1,947	64	916
Seychelles (b)	..	..	..	26	188	9	n.a.
Singapore	4,047	342	3,705	1,319	6,454	33	2,793
Slovakia	330	272	58	584	6,221	10	n.a.
Slovenia	532	40	492	583	5,687	54	486
South Africa	1,943	977	966	1,175	2,809	2	n.a.

Industrial designs

Name	Application design count by office			Application design count by origin	Equivalent application design count by origin	Hague international application design count	
	Total	Resident	Non-resident	Total [a]	Total [b]	Origin [c]	Designated Hague member
Spain	18,853	18,219	634	23,627	124,407	180	507
Sri Lanka	288	228	60	270	486	..	n.a.
Sudan	161	114	47	114	114	..	n.a.
Suriname (b)	..	..	..	..	..	..	31
Sweden	579	457	122	5,001	50,748	343	n.a.
Switzerland	11,640	3,446	8,194	22,534	153,532	2,441	8,802
Syrian Arab Republic	447	359	88	398	473	..	82
Tajikistan (b)	..	..	..	..	..	..	99
Thailand	5,469	4,044	1,425	4,334	5,063	..	n.a.
Togo (b,d)	n.a.	n.a.	n.a.	3	51	..	n.a.
Trinidad and Tobago	174	160	14	164	164	..	n.a.
Tunisia	1,328	164	1,164	173	173	..	1,134
Turkey	42,320	35,461	6,859	37,226	55,168	477	5,734
Turkmenistan (b)	..	..	..	15	15	1	85
Tuvalu (b)	..	..	..	1	1	..	n.a.
Uganda	29	29	0	29	29	..	n.a.
Ukraine	8,166	5,261	2,905	5,668	7,395	69	2,274
United Arab Emirates (b)	..	..	..	135	1,663	1	n.a.
United Kingdom	27,442	22,904	4,538	34,327	196,841	370	1,293
United Republic of Tanzania (b)	..	..	..	1	1	..	n.a.
United States of America	47,137	22,824	24,313	61,559	390,996	1,359	5,026
Uruguay (b)	..	..	..	2	2	..	n.a.
Uzbekistan	333	307	26	309	309	..	n.a.
Vanuatu (b)	..	..	..	1	1	..	n.a.
Venezuela (Bolivarian Republic of) (b)	..	..	..	4	4	..	n.a.
Viet Nam	3,366	1,891	1,475	2,073	2,316	..	n.a.
Yemen	17	17	0	18	18	..	n.a.
Zimbabwe (b)	..	..	..	6	6	..	n.a.
Others/Unknown	..	..	..	4,946	34,020	212	n.a.
Total (2018 estimates)	**1,312,600**	**1,113,300**	**199,300**	**1,312,600**	**n.a.**	**19,387**	**71,469**

(a) Design count by origin data are incomplete because some offices do not report the origin of applications.

(b) Only Hague designation data are available and/or the office has not reported the origin of applications therefore design count by office and origin data may be incomplete.

(c) Origin is defined as the country of the stated address of residence of the first named applicant in an international application.

(d) The African Intellectual Property Organization (OAPI) is the competent office for processing applications.

(e) Origin is defined as the country/territory of the stated residence of the applicant in an international application.

n.a. indicates not applicable.

.. indicates not available.

Source: WIPO Statistics Database, August 2019.

Industrial designs

C36. Industrial design registrations by office and origin, and industrial designs in force, 2018

Name	Registration design count by office			Registration design count by origin	Equivalent registration design count by origin	Hague international registration design count	In force by office
	Total	Resident	Non-resident	Total [a]	Total [a]	Origin [c]	Total
Afghanistan (b)	..	..	..	6	6	..	..
African Intellectual Property Organization	670	238	432	n.a.	n.a.	n.a.	..
African Regional Intellectual Property Organization	67	7	60	n.a.	n.a.	n.a.	864
Albania (b)	..	..	..	5	32	1	33
Algeria	620	432	188	452	668	..	3,091
Andorra (b)	..	..	..	3	84	..	..
Antigua and Barbuda (b)	..	..	..	..	..	..	28
Argentina	1,314	709	605	787	1,165	..	..
Armenia	414	48	366	137	731	22	101
Australia	7,594	2,725	4,869	4,972	24,036	3	50,069
Austria (b)	..	..	..	3,758	64,925	167	8,844
Azerbaijan	467	27	440	27	27	..	150
Bahamas (b)	..	..	..	12	12	..	..
Bahrain	71	13	58	14	14	..	299
Bangladesh	882	772	110	777	777	..	..
Barbados (b)	..	..	..	346	1,939	..	..
Belarus	371	109	262	193	679	..	1,368
Belgium	n.a.	n.a.	n.a.	2,744	37,961	214	n.a.
Belize	145	1	144	1	1	..	1
Benelux Office for Intellectual Property	1,314	896	418	n.a.	n.a.	n.a.	4,171
Benin (b,d)	n.a.	n.a.	n.a.	3	51	..	..
Bermuda (b)	..	..	..	1	1	..	..
Bosnia and Herzegovina	743	77	666	259	1,501	62	430
Botswana (b)	..	..	..	..	..	..	403
Brazil	8,725	4,728	3,997	5,154	9,814	..	46,910
Brunei Darussalam	87	0	87	..	..	..	58
Bulgaria	819	707	112	1,629	15,560	41	2,156
Burkina Faso (b,d)	n.a.	n.a.	n.a.	13	125	..	..
Cambodia (b)	..	..	..	..	..	..	..
Cameroon (b,d)	n.a.	n.a.	n.a.	31	527	..	..
Canada	5,136	656	4,480	2,239	15,766	1	42,277
Chile	340	35	305	130	157	..	3,509
China	536,251	517,693	18,558	534,209	774,005	259	1,610,616
China, Hong Kong SAR	4,547	1,282	3,265	3,174	30,633	..	21,707
China, Macao SAR	207	13	194	112	1,030	..	1,222
Colombia	562	258	304	309	390	..	4,472
Cook Islands (b)	..	..	..	6	6	..	..
Costa Rica	61	5	56	5	5	..	697
Côte d'Ivoire (b,d)	n.a.	n.a.	n.a.	79	1,343	..	..
Croatia	676	283	393	551	3,553	29	3,939
Cuba	12	5	7	6	33	..	53
Cyprus	84	84	0	1,355	7,430	182	37
Czech Republic	327	295	32	2,143	25,930	164	2,760
Democratic People's Republic of Korea (b)	..	..	..	1	1	..	..
Denmark	389	119	270	2,842	47,365	247	855

Name	Registration design count by office			Registration design count by origin	Equivalent registration design count by origin	Hague international registration design count	In force by office
	Total	Resident	Non-resident	Total [a]	Total [a]	Origin [c]	Total
Dominican Republic	23	5	18	5	5	..	291
Ecuador	255	182	73	190	190	..	..
Egypt	1,976	925	1,051	960	1,311	..	5,374
El Salvador	37	13	24	13	13	..	333
Estonia	84	48	36	269	4,886	10	1,532
Eswatini (b)	..	..	..	49	49	..	..
European Union Intellectual Property Office	105,116	68,801	36,315	n.a.	n.a.	n.a.	223,492
Finland	184	117	67	1,654	23,313	73	..
France (b)	..	..	..	18,009	211,306	1,407	..
Gabon (b,d)	n.a.	n.a.	n.a.	6	102	..	..
Georgia	605	147	458	208	208	11	2,685
Germany	48,360	42,772	5,588	82,791	646,390	3,773	54,726
Ghana (b)	..	..	..	..	..	..	..
Greece	1,168	755	413	3,044	21,895	460	1,417
Guatemala	202	40	162	44	46	..	573
Guinea (b,d)	n.a.	n.a.	n.a.	38	646	..	..
Guinea-Bissau (b,d)	n.a.	n.a.	n.a.	9	137	..	..
Honduras	32	9	23	9	9	..	378
Hungary	561	490	71	776	7,148	5	3,564
Iceland	263	14	249	50	995	..	1,027
India	8,198	5,422	2,776	5,958	11,934	..	86,288
Indonesia	3,300	1,955	1,345	1,991	2,153	..	..
Iran (Islamic Republic of)	5,520	5,441	79	5,444	5,471	..	28,999
Iraq	55	53	2	60	60	..	280
Ireland	588	120	468	868	13,153	32	1,630
Israel	1,019	635	384	1,572	9,834	..	..
Italy	37,674	36,587	1,087	56,658	349,890	1,066	9,599
Jamaica	123	116	7	117	117	..	1,406
Japan	27,967	21,338	6,629	38,821	133,023	962	257,157
Jordan	58	42	16	55	55	..	2,061
Kazakhstan	219	67	152	70	70	..	938
Kenya	135	125	10	125	125	..	..
Kuwait (b)	..	..	..	..	..	..	350
Kyrgyzstan	289	12	277	20	20	1	85
Latvia	148	113	35	220	2,623	4	369
Lebanon (b)	..	..	..	13	126	3	..
Lesotho (b)	..	..	..	..	..	..	39
Liberia (b)	..	..	..	2	2	..	..
Liechtenstein (b)	..	..	..	592	5,938	67	..
Lithuania	478	175	303	336	3,630	3	293
Luxembourg	n.a.	n.a.	n.a.	1,765	16,895	150	n.a.
Madagascar	173	167	6	167	167	..	964
Malaysia	1,475	405	1,070	620	944	7	15,007
Maldives (b)	..	..	..	2	2	..	..
Mali (b,d)	n.a.	n.a.	n.a.	16	208	..	..
Malta (b)	..	..	..	94	1,179	2	..

Industrial designs

Name	Registration design count by office			Registration design count by origin	Equivalent registration design count by origin	Hague international registration design count	In force by office
	Total	Resident	Non-resident	Total [a]	Total [a]	Origin [c]	Total
Mauritius	23	7	16	14	111	..	143
Mexico	2,797	787	2,010	988	2,446	..	26,866
Monaco	781	72	709	220	2,299	59	309
Mongolia	598	258	340	258	258		..
Montenegro	641	1	640	2	2	..	84
Morocco	4,977	3,644	1,333	3,658	3,808	1	..
Mozambique	69	5	64	5	5	..	1,342
Myanmar (b)	..	..	..	2	2	..	..
Namibia (b)	..	..	..	4	4	..	..
Nepal (b)	..	..	..	1	1	..	..
Netherlands	n.a.	n.a.	n.a.	7,406	90,354	953	n.a.
Netherlands Antilles (b)	..	..	..	3	3	..	..
New Zealand	1,326	311	1,015	1,040	5,981	1	11,570
Niger (b,d)	n.a.	n.a.	n.a.	..	..	..	..
Nigeria	1,160	1,138	22	1,142	1,142	..	..
North Macedonia	802	89	713	97	178	1	2,239
Norway	3,758	551	3,207	1,370	7,196	111	10,342
Oman (b)	..	..	..	4	4	..	..
Pakistan	421	316	105	327	381	..	6,881
Panama	106	0	106	9	90	..	720
Paraguay	55	7	48	10	10	..	..
Peru	453	138	315	140	140	..	2,991
Philippines	1,985	1,002	983	1,028	1,028	..	..
Poland (b)	..	..	..	4,484	109,703	147	8,476
Portugal	1,137	1,105	32	2,296	29,379	76	4,038
Qatar (b)	..	..	..	25	25	..	..
Republic of Korea	50,678	44,171	6,507	52,222	98,785	1,478	344,560
Republic of Moldova	624	197	427	223	385	1	3,109
Romania	819	545	274	1,111	12,829	14	3,578
Russian Federation	8,540	3,284	5,256	3,859	6,073	37	35,898
Rwanda	85	3	82	3	3	..	5
Saint Kitts and Nevis (b)	..	..	..	1	1	..	..
Saint Lucia (b)	..	..	..	1	1	..	..
Saint Vincent and the Grenadines (b)	..	..	..	1	28	..	1
Samoa	23	23	0	31	139	..	43
San Marino	9	8	1	474	852	..	..
Sao Tome and Principe	85	0	85	..	..	..	178
Saudi Arabia	786	279	507	315	315	..	4,545
Senegal (b,d)	n.a.	n.a.	n.a.	51	867	..	..
Serbia	1,075	179	896	377	1,583	49	6,567
Seychelles (b)	..	..	..	26	215	9	..
Singapore	3,704	347	3,357	1,175	6,310	23	14,142
Slovakia	355	216	139	526	6,055	10	915
Slovenia	429	35	394	436	5,224	46	558
South Africa	1,520	687	833	862	2,384	..	17,407
Spain	18,606	18,065	541	23,016	120,783	157	27,305

Name	Registration design count by office			Registration design count by origin	Equivalent registration design count by origin	Hague international registration design count	In force by office
	Total	Resident	Non-resident	Total [a]	Total [a]	Origin [c]	Total
Sri Lanka	124	86	38	119	308	..	1,632
Sudan	153	116	37	116	116	..	153
Suriname (b)	..	..	..	..	..	..	..
Sweden	461	350	111	4,959	52,272	358	4,414
Switzerland	10,625	3,274	7,351	21,998	148,534	2,234	9,530
Syrian Arab Republic	305	205	100	224	299	..	210
Tajikistan (b)	..	..	..	..	..	..	..
Thailand	3,627	2,250	1,377	2,479	3,235	..	17,057
Togo (b,d)	n.a.	n.a.	n.a.	3	51	..	..
Trinidad and Tobago	179	166	13	169	169	..	48
Tunisia	1,150	162	988	164	164	..	..
Turkey	45,735	33,806	11,929	35,859	53,208	431	127,197
Turkmenistan (b)	..	..	..	..	..	..	..
Tuvalu (b)	..	..	..	1	1	..	..
Uganda	29	29	0	29	29	..	..
Ukraine	6,559	4,093	2,466	4,500	6,367	70	14,383
United Arab Emirates (b)	..	..	..	120	1,621	1	3,053
United Kingdom	24,688	20,995	3,693	32,557	190,505	320	75,476
United Republic of Tanzania (b)	..	..	..	1	1	..	..
United States of America	33,449	16,731	16,718	51,689	361,644	1,193	336,116
Uruguay (b)	..	..	..	3	3	..	..
Uzbekistan	259	237	22	242	242	..	566
Vanuatu (b)	..	..	..	1	1	..	..
Venezuela (Bolivarian Republic of) (b)	..	..	..	4	4	..	..
Viet Nam	2,824	1,433	1,391	1,535	1,778	..	12,264
Yemen	22	21	1	22	22	..	83
Zimbabwe (b)	..	..	..	1	1	..	..
Others/Unknown	..	..	..	3,414	30,619	4	..
Total (2018 estimates)	**1,077,100**	**894,300**	**182,800**	**1,077,100**	**n.a.**	**17,212**	**3,988,900**

(a) Design count by origin data are incomplete because some offices do not report the origin of registrations.

(b) Only Hague designation data are available and/or the office has not reported the origin of registrations therefore design count by office and origin data may be incomplete.

(c) Origin is defined as the country of the stated address of residence of the holder in an international registration.

(d) The African Intellectual Property Organization (OAPI) is the competent office for registering applications.

(e) Origin is defined as the country/territory of the stated residence of the holder of an international registration.

n.a. indicates not applicable.

.. indicates not available.

Source: WIPO Statistics Database, August 2019.

Industrial designs

Plant varieties

Highlights

Plant variety applications surpass 20,000

Around 20,210 plant variety applications were filed worldwide in 2018, up 8.9% on 2017 – the third year in a row of positive growth and the first time plant varieties have exceeded 20,000 applications in a single year (figure 4.1). The offices of China, Colombia, the Community Plant Variety Office of the European Union (CPVO), Spain, Ukraine and the United Kingdom (U.K.) accounted for most of this growth.

China received 28.5% of all plant variety applications filed worldwide

China remained the top filing office in 2018, receiving 5,760 applications. The China office now accounts for over a quarter of the plant varieties filed worldwide. The CPVO received 3,554 applications, accounting for 17.6% of global filings. The CPVO was followed by the national offices of the United States of America (U.S.) (1,609), Ukraine (1,575) and Japan (880) (figure 4.2). Filings in China represent a 29% year-on-year growth, driven almost entirely by resident filings. Among the other top five offices, the CPVO (+3.9%), the U.S. (+3.3%) and Ukraine (+17.1%) experienced growth, while Japan (–13.6%) was the only one to experience a decline. Resident filings drove growth in China and the U.S., whereas an increase in non-resident filings drove growth in Ukraine. The decline in filings at the Japan office was the result of a sharp fall in non-resident filings, in addition to a relatively smaller decrease in resident filings.

The combined share of applications received at the top five offices worldwide increased, from 63.7% in 2017 to 66.2% in 2018, due to the pronounced growth experienced by China and Ukraine.

Seven of the top 10 offices received more applications from residents than from non-residents. China's resident share (90.7%) was the highest among these offices. In contrast, Australia, Canada and Ukraine received more than half their filings from non-resident applicants.

Offices of high-income economies accounted for the largest proportion (47.4%) of plant variety applications received in 2018. However, this figure is down markedly from 72.7% a decade earlier in 2008 (figure 4.3). Offices in the upper middle-income group have, on the other hand, seen their combined share increase from 24.7% in 2007 to 42.0% in 2018, mostly driven by an increase of filings in China. The share held by the lower middle-income group has likewise increased, from 2.6% in 2008 to 10.5% in 2018, led by Morocco, Ukraine and Viet Nam.

For the first time, offices in Asia received the most filings, representing 39.4% of all plant variety applications in 2018. Filings at Asian offices more than doubled as compared to 2008, when their share was 23.6% (figure 4.4). Despite its total filings actually increasing over this period, Europe has seen its share decrease from 45.1% in 2008 to 38.7% in 2018. Latin America and the Caribbean (LAC) (7.3%) and Africa (2.5%) also experienced growth in total filings between 2008 and 2018, but not at the same pace as Asia; shares for both declined slightly as a result. North America (9.6%) and Oceania (2.5%) experienced small decreases in their total filings in 2018 as compared to 2008; this is reflected in their shares, which fell by 5.8 and 1.7 percentage points respectively.

Applications grew by 8.9%

4.1. Plant variety applications worldwide, 2004–2018

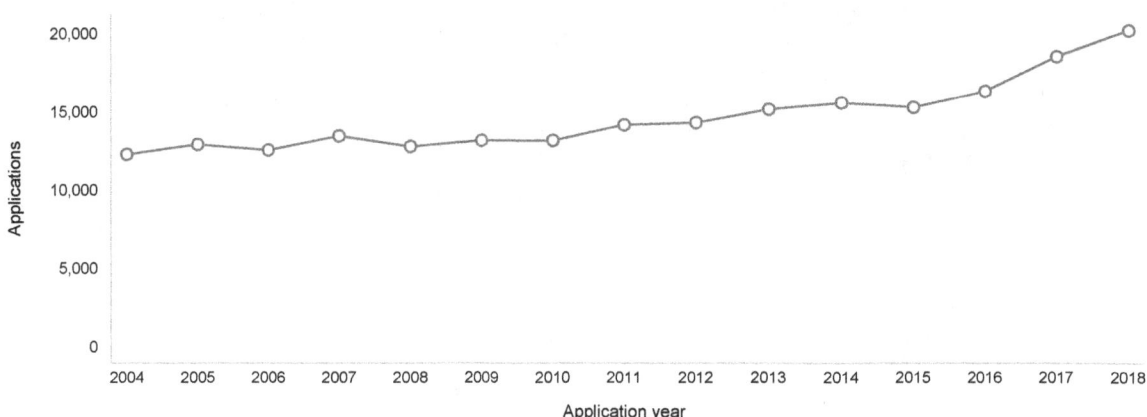

Source: Figure D1.

China is the top destination for plant variety applications
4.2. Plant variety applications for the top 10 offices, 2018

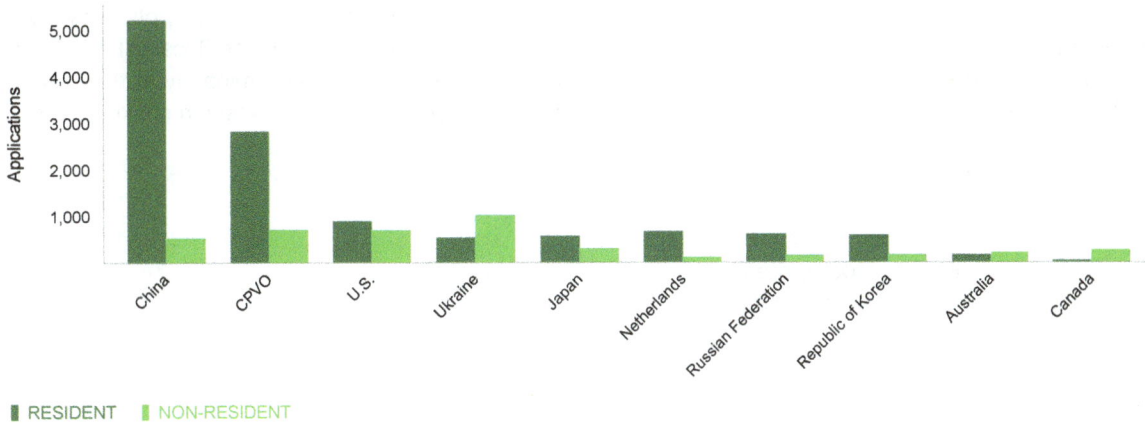

■ RESIDENT   ■ NON-RESIDENT

Source: Figure D5.

Offices of high-income economies received 47.4% of all applications filed worldwide
4.3. Plant variety applications by income group, 2008 and 2018

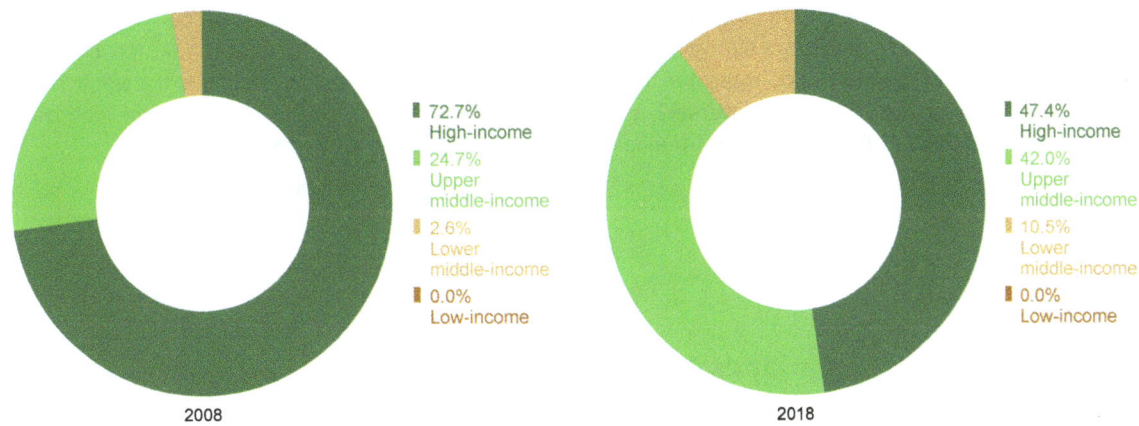

2008

■ 72.7% High-income
■ 24.7% Upper middle-income
■ 2.6% Lower middle-income
■ 0.0% Low-income

2018

■ 47.4% High-income
■ 42.0% Upper middle-income
■ 10.5% Lower middle-income
■ 0.0% Low-income

Source: Figure D3.

Asia overtook Europe as top region with 39.4% of all applications
4.4. Plant variety applications by region 2008 and 2018

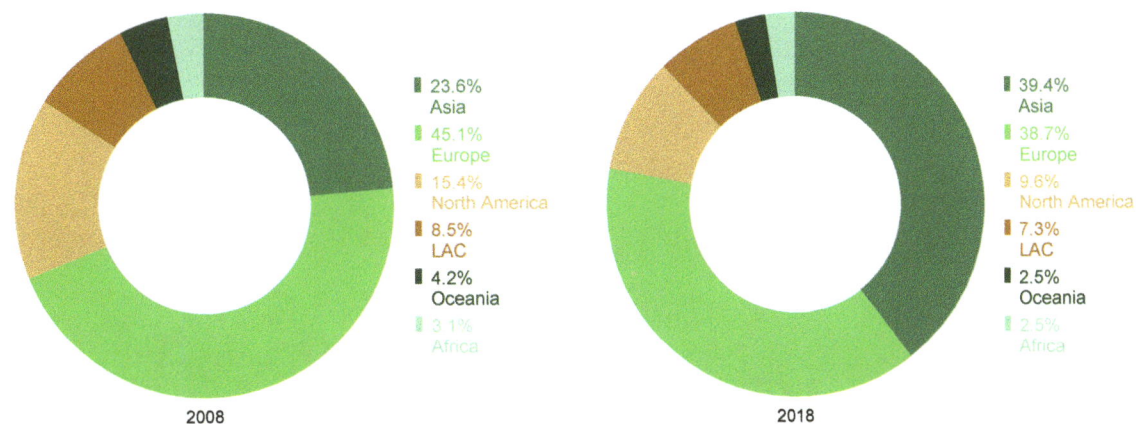

2008

■ 23.6% Asia
■ 45.1% Europe
■ 15.4% North America
■ 8.5% LAC
■ 4.2% Oceania
■ 3.1% Africa

2018

■ 39.4% Asia
■ 38.7% Europe
■ 9.6% North America
■ 7.3% LAC
■ 2.5% Oceania
■ 2.5% Africa

Source: Figure D4.

Plant varieties

165

Applicants from China filed the most worldwide

Applications received by offices from resident and non-resident applicants are referred to as office data, whereas applications filed by applicants at a national/ regional office (resident applications) or at a foreign office (applications abroad) are referred to as origin data. Here, plant variety statistics based on the origin of residence are reported in order to complement the global picture. Note that for applicants domiciled in European Union (EU) member states, filing at the CPVO regional office is regarded as a resident filing.

Applicants from China were the most active applicants in the world in 2018, filing 5,254 plant variety applications. This represents a 30.0% growth on the previous year – the fastest recorded among the top 10 origins. Chinese applicants were followed by applicants from the Netherlands, who filed 3,616 applications. The U.S. (2,308), France (1,066) and Germany (1,046) were the next three largest origins, respectively. Germany (+20.4%), the U.S. (+9.5%) and the Netherlands (+7.5%) all saw growth, whereas France declined by 1.8%. Germany's rapid growth was driven by a strong increase (32.8%) in resident filings that accounted for three quarters of its total growth. France, conversely, saw its resident filings fall by –5.8%, while its non-resident filings rose by a similar amount (5.3%).

Whereas applicants from four of the top five origins filed most of their applications either abroad or at the regional office, only those from China filed almost exclusively at home. Like China, applicants from Japan, the Republic of Korea, the Russian Federation and Ukraine also filed predominantly at their home offices, reflecting a lesser interest in seeking protection internationally.

Equivalent count

Origin data are compiled using two different counting methods – absolute counts and equivalent counts. The difference between the two lies in the treatment of regional offices data (the CPVO and the African Intellectual Property Organization (OAPI)). For absolute counts, an application received by a regional office is counted only once. For the equivalent count, a single application filed at a regional office is equivalent to multiple applications. To calculate the number of equivalent applications at a regional office in 2018, each application has been multiplied by the corresponding number of member states for the regional office. For CPVO applications, if the applicant resided in one of the 28 EU member states, the application was counted as one resident filing and 27 filings abroad. If the applicant did not reside in a EU member state, the application was counted as 28 filings abroad. The same methodology was applied to OAPI member states.

Applicants from the Netherlands were first by equivalent count

4.5. Equivalent plant variety applications by origin, 2018

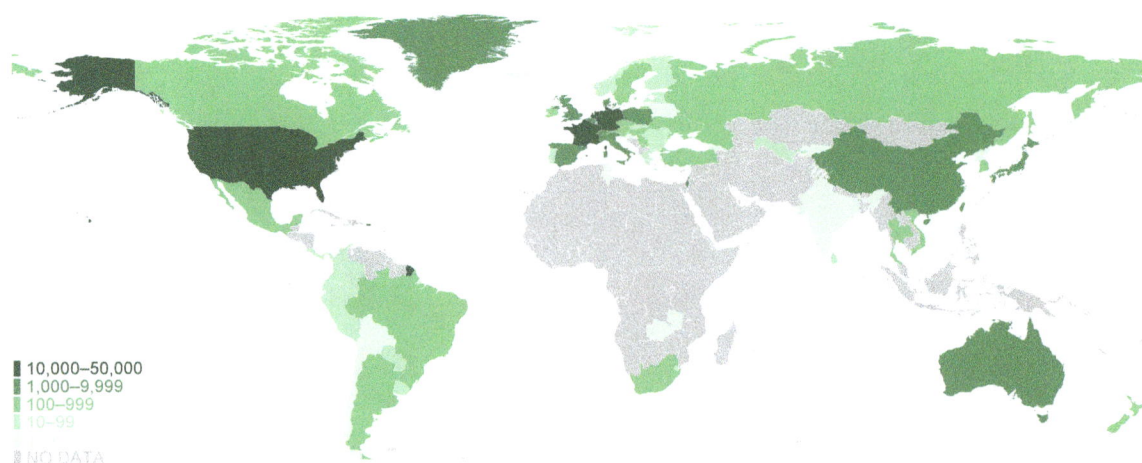

10,000–50,000
1,000–9,999
100–999
10–99
NO DATA

Source: Figure D9.

Plant variety titles issued increased by 3.5%
4.6. Plant variety titles issued worldwide, 2004–2018

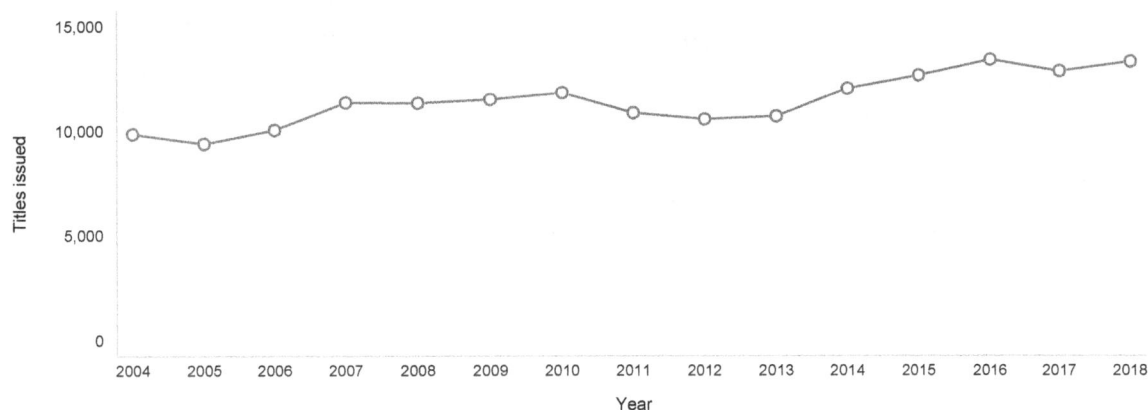

Source: Figure D2.

Equivalent counts take multiple members of the regional office into account. One would expect to see those country origins whose applicants filed intensively at the CPVO move up the ranking when this counting method is applied (Figure 4.5). Not surprisingly, therefore, European countries and the U.S. topped the list of origins based on equivalent counts. Applicants from the Netherlands once again ranked first, with 39,850 equivalent applications filed worldwide. They were followed by applicants from Germany (12,791), France (12,784) and the U.S. (11,576). Rounding out the top five origins by equivalent count was China, with 5,310 applications.

Apart from Japan (in 8th place, with 2,988 applicants), China was the only other non-European country to be found among the top 10 origins, despite only 1.7% of its applicants' filings being equivalent filings abroad. This is in marked contrast to the Netherlands, for which the abroad share was 95%.

The number of titles issued returns to growth

The total number of plant variety titles issued increased by 3.5% in 2018, reversing last year's contraction. With 13,300 plant variety titles issued, the total for 2018 was only just below the highest number ever recorded, which was in 2016 (13,390 titles) (figure 4.6). The CPVO issued the most titles, with 2,757, despite a modest year-on-year decline of 3.8%. China, the primary driver of global growth, issued 2,395 titles, up 45.5% from a year earlier. The CPVO and the China office were followed by the offices of the U.S. (1,424), Ukraine (1,021) and Japan (758). The offices of both the U.S. (–11.2%) and Japan (–6.7%) experienced an overall decline in titles issued. In contrast, the Ukrainian office increased the number of titles it issued by 15.1% in 2018.

The grant or registration process takes time, so fluctuations in the volumes of plant variety titles granted may reflect changes in processing capacities or procedural delays.

Steady growth in plant varieties in force

Around 133,190 plant variety titles were in force at the end of 2018, up 5.4% on 2017. The CPVO (26,896) and the U.S. (25,787) were the two offices with the highest number of active titles. Other offices maintaining at least 5,000 active titles included China (9,989), Ukraine (9,039), Japan (8,681), the Netherlands (8,552), the Republic of Korea (5,325) and the Russian Federation (5,313).

Plant variety statistics

Plant varieties

Plant variety applications and titles issued worldwide

D1. Trend in plant variety applications worldwide, 2004–2018

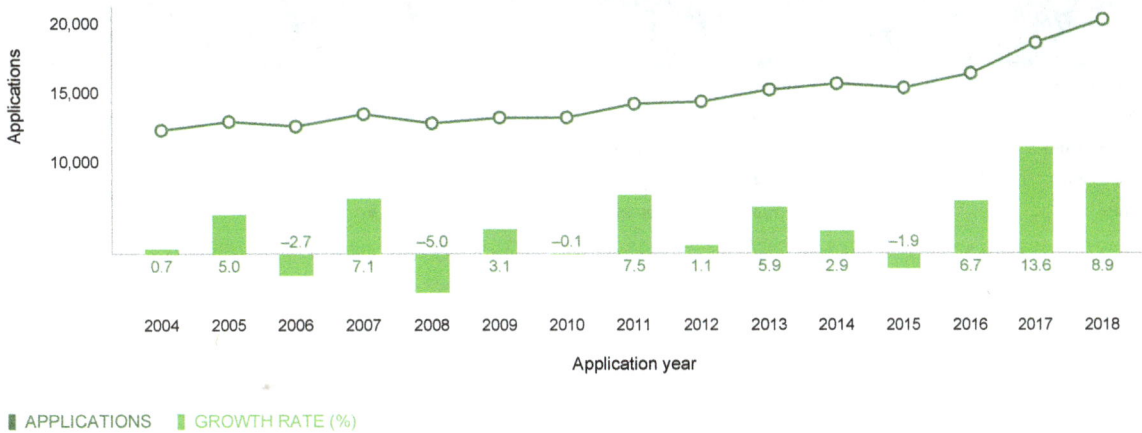

Note: World totals are WIPO estimates using data covering 70 offices.
Source: WIPO Statistics Database, September 2019.

D2. Trend in plant variety titles issued worldwide, 2004–2018

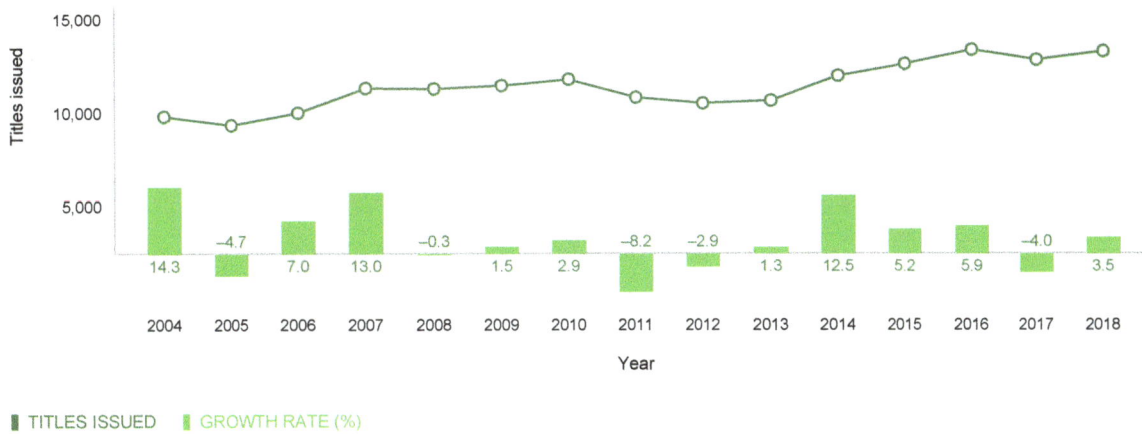

Note: World totals are WIPO estimates using data covering 70 offices.
Source: WIPO Statistics Database, September 2019.

Plant variety applications and titles issued by office

D3. Plant variety applications by income group, 2008 and 2018

Income group	Number of applications		Resident share (%)		Share of world total (%)		Average growth (%)
	2008	2018	2008	2018	2008	2018	2008–2018
High-income	9,296	9,571	64.6	66.3	72.7	47.4	0.3
Upper middle-income	3,153	8,498	67.2	78.2	24.7	42.0	10.4
Lower middle-income	327	2,132	43.4	39.2	2.6	10.5	20.6
Low-income	4	9	0.0	0.0	0.0	0.0	8.4
World	**12,780**	**20,210**	**64.7**	**68.4**	**100.0**	**100.0**	**4.7**

Note: Totals by income group are WIPO estimates using data covering 70 offices. Each category includes the following number of offices: high-income countries/economies (37), upper middle-income (21), lower middle-income (10) and low-income (2). The EU's Community Plant Variety Office (CPVO) data are allocated to the high-income group, because a majority of EU member states are high-income countries. For information on income group classification, see the Data description section.

Source: WIPO Statistics Database, September 2019.

D4. Plant variety applications by region, 2008 and 2018

Region	Number of applications		Resident share (%)		Share of world total (%)		Average growth (%)
	2008	2018	2008	2018	2008	2018	2008–2018
Africa	397	502	27.2	16.1	3.1	2.5	2.4
Asia	3,022	7,967	73.7	85.0	23.6	39.4	10.2
Europe	5,767	7,824	74.6	66.8	45.1	38.7	3.1
Latin America and the Caribbean	1,091	1,482	44.0	39.7	8.5	7.3	3.1
North America	1,972	1,939	45.3	49.1	15.4	9.6	−0.2
Oceania	531	496	49.2	41.7	4.2	2.5	−0.7
World	**12,780**	**20,210**	**64.7**	**68.4**	**100.0**	**100.0**	**4.7**

Note: Totals by geographical region are WIPO estimates using data covering 70 offices. Each region includes the following number of offices: Africa (6), Asia (12), Europe (33), Latin America and the Caribbean (14), North America (3) and Oceania (2).

Source: WIPO Statistics Database, September 2019.

Plant varieties

D5. Plant variety applications for the top 20 offices, 2018

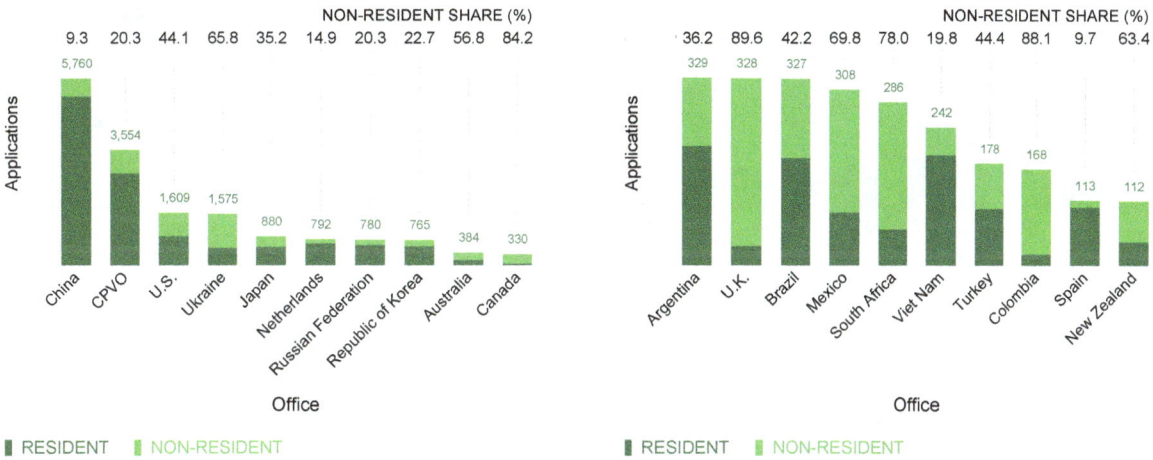

NON-RESIDENT SHARE (%)

| 9.3 | 20.3 | 44.1 | 65.8 | 35.2 | 14.9 | 20.3 | 22.7 | 56.8 | 84.2 |

Applications

China 5,760; CPVO 3,554; U.S. 1,609; Ukraine 1,575; Japan 880; Netherlands 792; Russian Federation 780; Republic of Korea 765; Australia 384; Canada 330

Office

■ RESIDENT ■ NON-RESIDENT

NON-RESIDENT SHARE (%)

| 36.2 | 89.6 | 42.2 | 69.8 | 78.0 | 19.8 | 44.4 | 88.1 | 9.7 | 63.4 |

Applications

Argentina 329; U.K. 328; Brazil 327; Mexico 308; South Africa 286; Viet Nam 242; Turkey 178; Colombia 168; Spain 113; New Zealand 112

Office

■ RESIDENT ■ NON-RESIDENT

Note: CPVO is the Community Plant Variety Office. In general, national offices of CPVO member states receive lower volumes of applications, because applicants may apply via the CPVO to seek protection within any CPVO member state.

Source: WIPO Statistics Database, September 2019.

D6. Contribution of resident and non-resident applications to total growth for the top 20 offices, 2017–2018

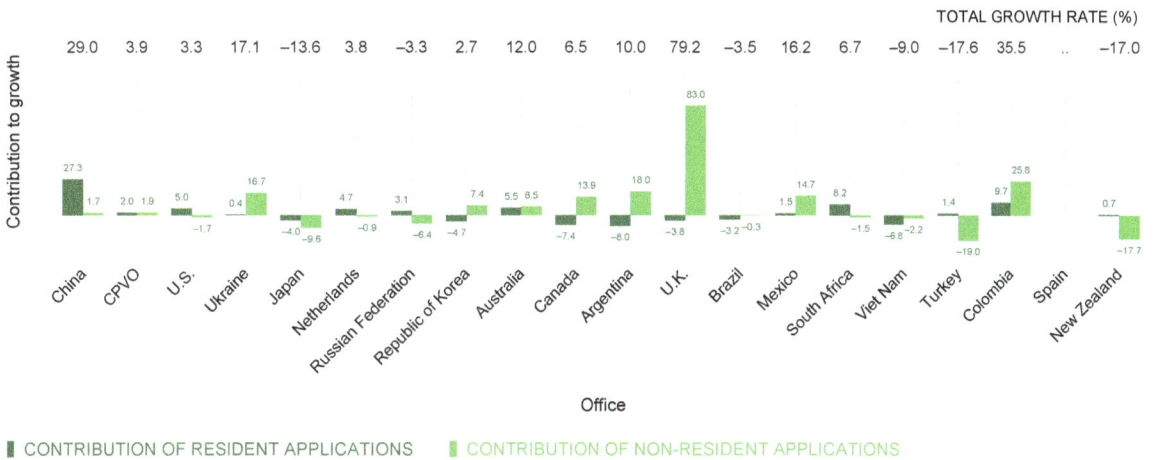

TOTAL GROWTH RATE (%)

| 29.0 | 3.9 | 3.3 | 17.1 | −13.6 | 3.8 | −3.3 | 2.7 | 12.0 | 6.5 | 10.0 | 79.2 | −3.5 | 16.2 | 6.7 | −9.0 | −17.6 | 35.5 | .. | −17.0 |

Contribution to growth

China 27.3, 1.7; CPVO 2.0, 1.9; U.S. 5.0, −1.7; Ukraine 0.4, 16.7; Japan −4.0, −9.6; Netherlands 4.7, −0.9; Russian Federation 3.1, −6.4; Republic of Korea −4.7, 7.4; Australia 5.5, 8.5; Canada 13.9, −7.4; Argentina 18.0, −8.0; U.K. −3.8, 83.0; Brazil −3.2, −0.3; Mexico 1.5, 14.7; South Africa 8.2, −1.5; Viet Nam −6.8, −2.2; Turkey 1.4, −19.0; Colombia 9.7, 25.8; Spain 0.7; New Zealand −17.7

Office

■ CONTRIBUTION OF RESIDENT APPLICATIONS ■ CONTRIBUTION OF NON-RESIDENT APPLICATIONS

Note: CPVO is the Community Plant Variety Office. This figure shows total growth in plant variety applications broken down by the respective contributions of resident and non-resident filings. For example, applications in the Ukraine grew by 17.1%, and resident applications contributed 0.4 percentage points to this total growth, while non-resident applications accounted for the other 16.7 percentage points.

.. indicates not available.

Source: WIPO Statistics Database, September 2019.

Plant varieties

D7. Plant variety applications for offices of selected low- and middle-income countries, 2018

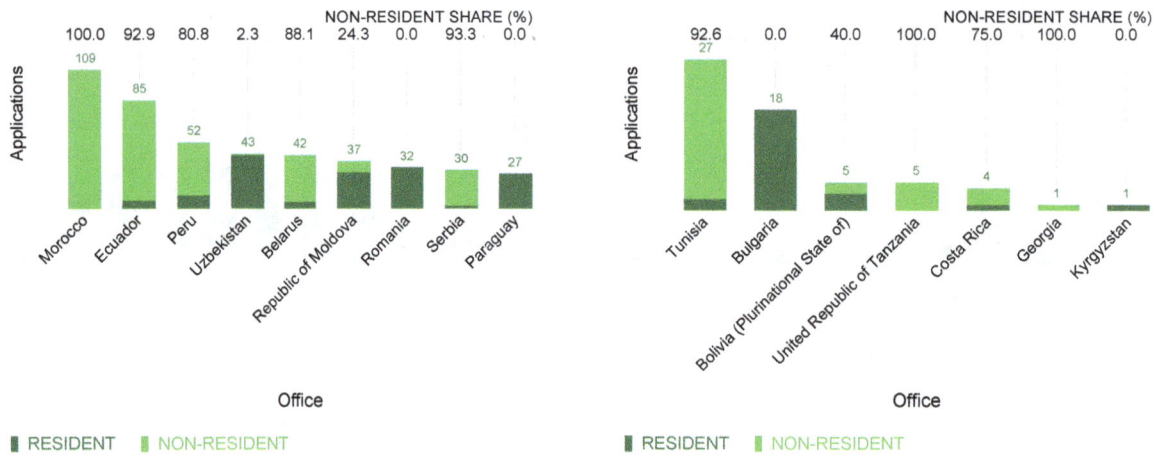

NON-RESIDENT SHARE (%)

| 100.0 | 92.9 | 80.8 | 2.3 | 88.1 | 24.3 | 0.0 | 93.3 | 0.0 |

Applications

- Morocco — 109
- Ecuador — 85
- Peru — 52
- Uzbekistan — 43
- Belarus — 42
- Republic of Moldova — 37
- Romania — 32
- Serbia — 30
- Paraguay — 27

Office

NON-RESIDENT SHARE (%)

| 92.6 | 0.0 | 40.0 | 100.0 | 75.0 | 100.0 | 0.0 |

Applications

- Tunisia — 27
- Bulgaria — 18
- Bolivia (Plurinational State of) — 5
- United Republic of Tanzania — 5
- Costa Rica — 4
- Georgia — 1
- Kyrgyzstan — 1

Office

RESIDENT NON-RESIDENT

RESIDENT NON-RESIDENT

Note: The selected offices are from different world regions and income groups. Where available, data for all offices are in the statistical table at the end of this section.

Source: WIPO Statistics Database, September 2019.

D8. Plant variety titles issued by the top 20 offices, 2018

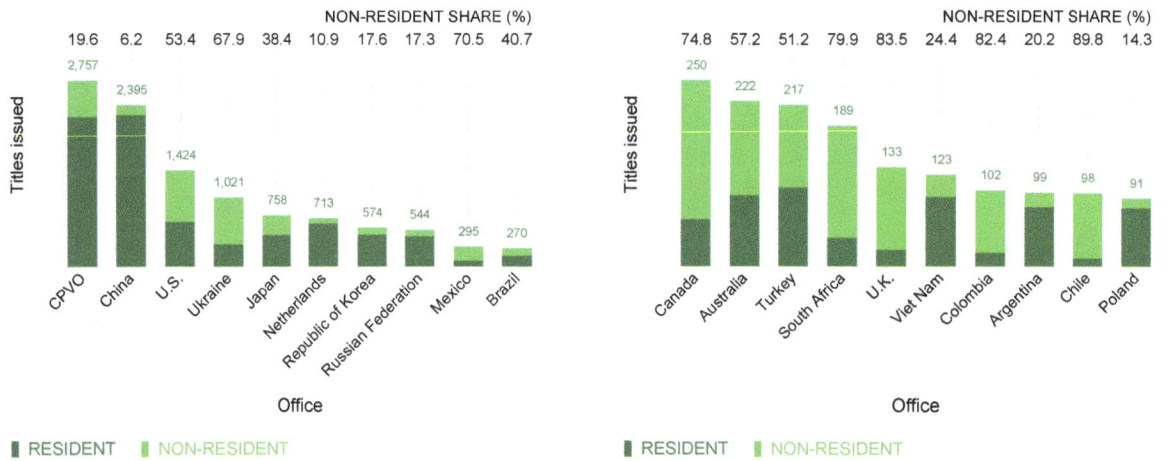

NON-RESIDENT SHARE (%)

| 19.6 | 6.2 | 53.4 | 67.9 | 38.4 | 10.9 | 17.6 | 17.3 | 70.5 | 40.7 |

Titles issued

- CPVO — 2,757
- China — 2,395
- U.S. — 1,424
- Ukraine — 1,021
- Japan — 758
- Netherlands — 713
- Republic of Korea — 574
- Russian Federation — 544
- Mexico — 295
- Brazil — 270

Office

NON-RESIDENT SHARE (%)

| 74.8 | 57.2 | 51.2 | 79.9 | 83.5 | 24.4 | 82.4 | 20.2 | 89.8 | 14.3 |

Titles issued

- Canada — 250
- Australia — 222
- Turkey — 217
- South Africa — 189
- U.K. — 133
- Viet Nam — 123
- Colombia — 102
- Argentina — 99
- Chile — 98
- Poland — 91

Office

RESIDENT NON-RESIDENT

RESIDENT NON-RESIDENT

Note: CPVO is the Community Plant Variety Office. The procedure for issuing titles varies across offices, and differences in the numbers of titles issued between offices depend on factors such as examination capacity and procedural delays, therefore there is a time lag between application and title issue dates. For this reason, data on applications for a given year should not be compared with data on titles issued for the same year.

Source: WIPO Statistics Database, September 2019.

Plant varieties

Plant variety applications and titles issued by origin

D9. Equivalent plant variety applications by origin, 2018

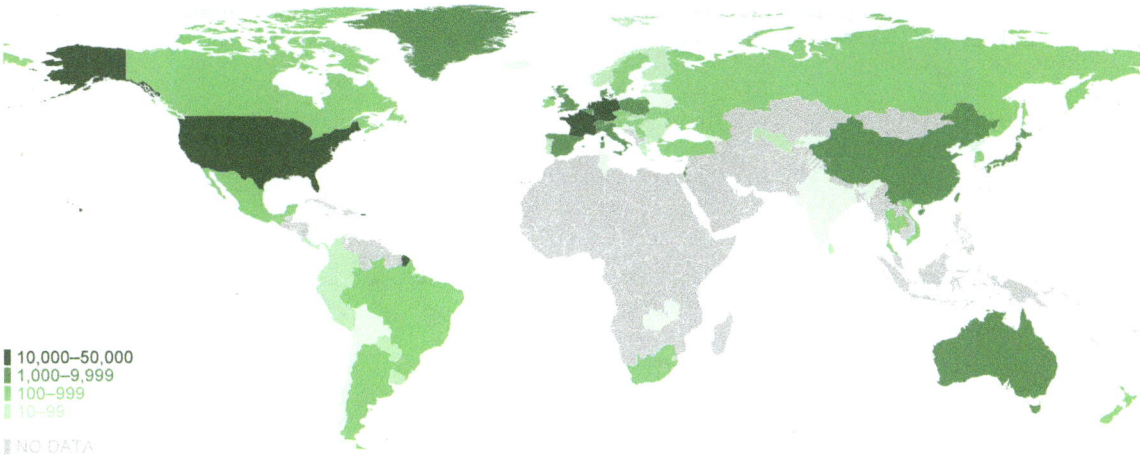

- 10,000–50,000
- 1,000–9,999
- 100–999
- 10–99
- NO DATA

Note: Equivalent plant variety applications by origin include resident applications and applications filed abroad. The origin of an application is determined by the residence of the applicant. Applications filed at regional offices are considered equivalent to multiple applications in the relevant member states. See the glossary for the definition of equivalent application.

Source: WIPO Statistics Database, September 2019.

D10. Plant variety applications for the top 20 origins, 2018

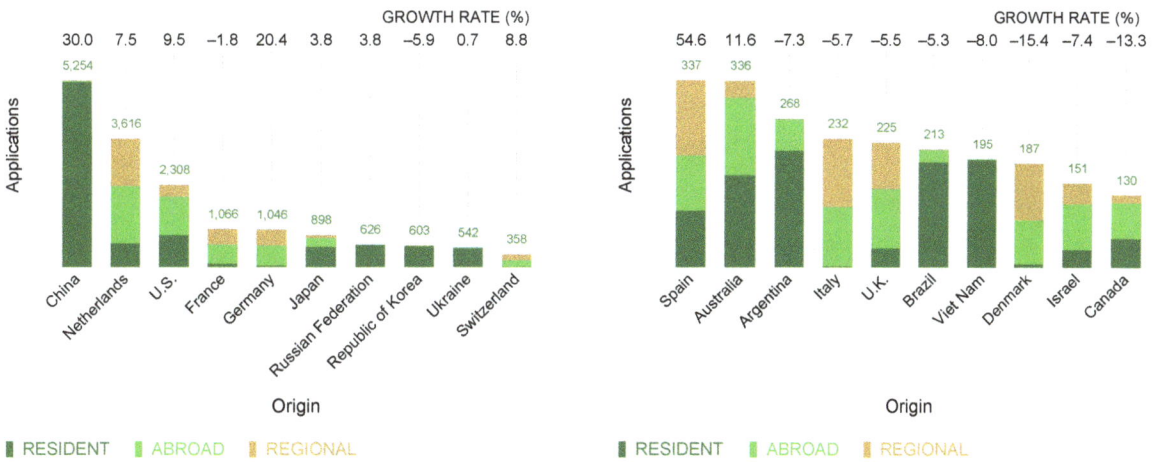

GROWTH RATE (%)
30.0 7.5 9.5 −1.8 20.4 3.8 3.8 −5.9 0.7 8.8

China 5,254; Netherlands 3,616; U.S. 2,308; France 1,066; Germany 1,046; Japan 898; Russian Federation 626; Republic of Korea 603; Ukraine 542; Switzerland 358

GROWTH RATE (%)
54.6 11.6 −7.3 −5.7 −5.5 −5.3 −8.0 −15.4 −7.4 −13.3

Spain 337; Australia 336; Argentina 268; Italy 232; U.K. 225; Brazil 213; Viet Nam 195; Denmark 187; Israel 151; Canada 130

■ RESIDENT ■ ABROAD ■ REGIONAL

Note: Data are based on absolute count, not equivalent count. Applications by origin include resident applications and applications filed abroad. The origin of an application is determined by the residence of the applicant. Regional refers to applications filed at the EU's Community Plant Variety Office.

Source: WIPO Statistics Database, September 2019.

D11. Plant variety applications abroad for the top 20 origins, 2018

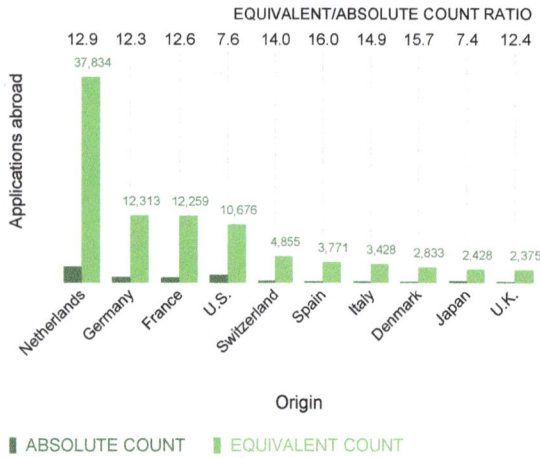

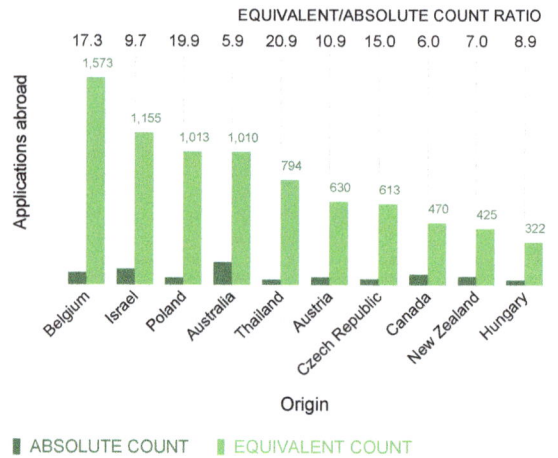

EQUIVALENT/ABSOLUTE COUNT RATIO

| 12.9 | 12.3 | 12.6 | 7.6 | 14.0 | 16.0 | 14.9 | 15.7 | 7.4 | 12.4 |

Applications abroad

- Netherlands: 37,834
- Germany: 12,313
- France: 12,259
- U.S.: 10,676
- Switzerland: 4,855
- Spain: 3,771
- Italy: 3,428
- Denmark: 2,833
- Japan: 2,428
- U.K.: 2,375

Origin

■ ABSOLUTE COUNT ■ EQUIVALENT COUNT

EQUIVALENT/ABSOLUTE COUNT RATIO

| 17.3 | 9.7 | 19.9 | 5.9 | 20.9 | 10.9 | 15.0 | 6.0 | 7.0 | 8.9 |

Applications abroad

- Belgium: 1,573
- Israel: 1,155
- Poland: 1,013
- Australia: 1,010
- Thailand: 794
- Austria: 630
- Czech Republic: 613
- Canada: 470
- New Zealand: 425
- Hungary: 322

Origin

■ ABSOLUTE COUNT ■ EQUIVALENT COUNT

Note: The origin of an application is determined by the residence of the applicant. Applications filed at regional offices are considered equivalent to multiple applications in the relevant member states. See the glossary for the definition of equivalent applications.

Source: WIPO Statistics Database, September 2019.

D12. Plant variety titles issued for the top 20 origins, 2018

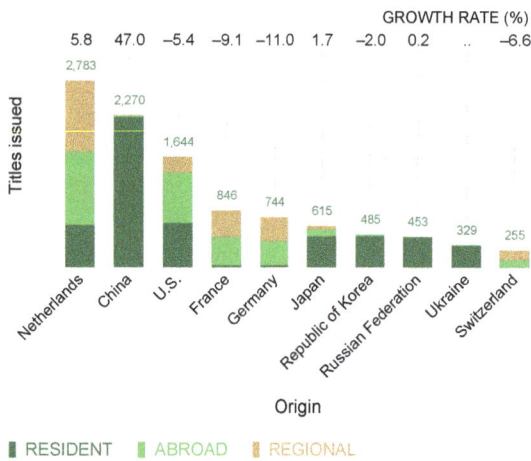

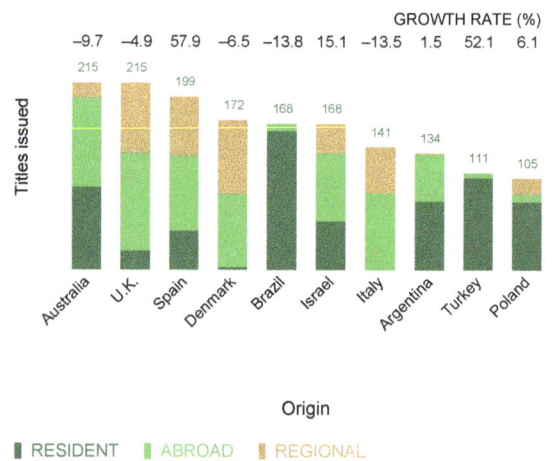

GROWTH RATE (%)

| 5.8 | 47.0 | −5.4 | −9.1 | −11.0 | 1.7 | −2.0 | 0.2 | .. | −6.6 |

Titles issued

- Netherlands: 2,783
- China: 2,270
- U.S.: 1,644
- France: 846
- Germany: 744
- Japan: 615
- Republic of Korea: 485
- Russian Federation: 453
- Ukraine: 329
- Switzerland: 255

Origin

■ RESIDENT ■ ABROAD ■ REGIONAL

GROWTH RATE (%)

| −9.7 | −4.9 | 57.9 | −6.5 | −13.8 | 15.1 | −13.5 | 1.5 | 52.1 | 6.1 |

Titles issued

- Australia: 215
- U.K.: 215
- Spain: 199
- Denmark: 172
- Brazil: 168
- Israel: 168
- Italy: 141
- Argentina: 134
- Turkey: 111
- Poland: 105

Origin

■ RESIDENT ■ ABROAD ■ REGIONAL

Note: Data are based on absolute count, not equivalent count. The origin of titles issued is determined by the residence of the applicant. Regional refers to titles issued by the EU's Community Plant Variety Office.

.. indicates not available.

Source: WIPO Statistics Database, September 2019.

Plant varieties

D13. Plant variety titles issued abroad for the top 20 origins, 2018

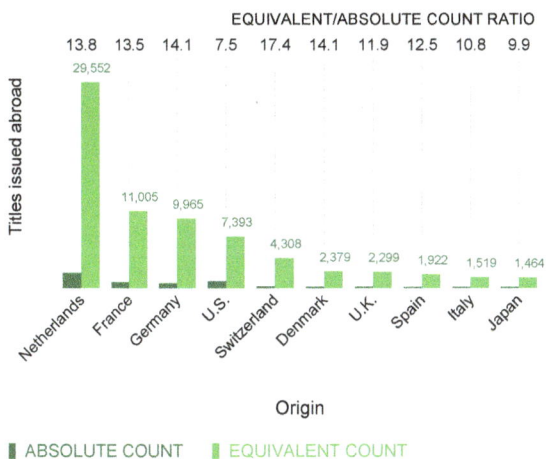

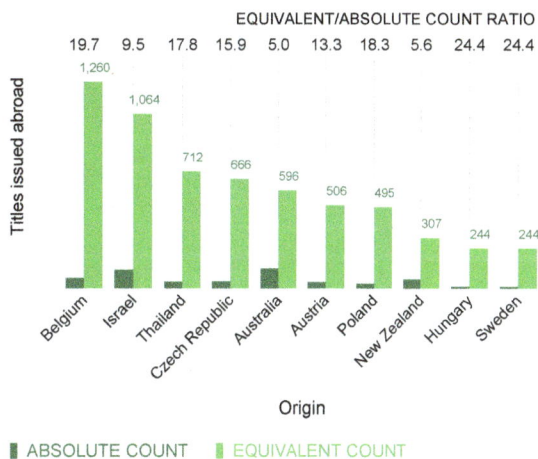

EQUIVALENT/ABSOLUTE COUNT RATIO

13.8	13.5	14.1	7.5	17.4	14.1	11.9	12.5	10.8	9.9

Titles issued abroad

- Netherlands: 29,552
- France: 11,005
- Germany: 9,965
- U.S.: 7,393
- Switzerland: 4,308
- Denmark: 2,379
- U.K.: 2,299
- Spain: 1,922
- Italy: 1,519
- Japan: 1,464

Origin

■ ABSOLUTE COUNT   ■ EQUIVALENT COUNT

EQUIVALENT/ABSOLUTE COUNT RATIO

19.7	9.5	17.8	15.9	5.0	13.3	18.3	5.6	24.4	24.4

Titles issued abroad

- Belgium: 1,260
- Israel: 1,064
- Thailand: 712
- Czech Republic: 666
- Australia: 596
- Austria: 506
- Poland: 495
- New Zealand: 307
- Hungary: 244
- Sweden: 244

Origin

■ ABSOLUTE COUNT   ■ EQUIVALENT COUNT

Note: The origin of titles issued is determined by the residence of the applicant. Titles issued by regional offices are considered equivalent to multiple titles in the relevant member states. See the glossary for the definition of equivalent count.

Source: WIPO Statistics Database, September 2019.

Plant varieties

Plant varieties in force

D14. Trend in plant varieties in force worldwide, 2004–2018

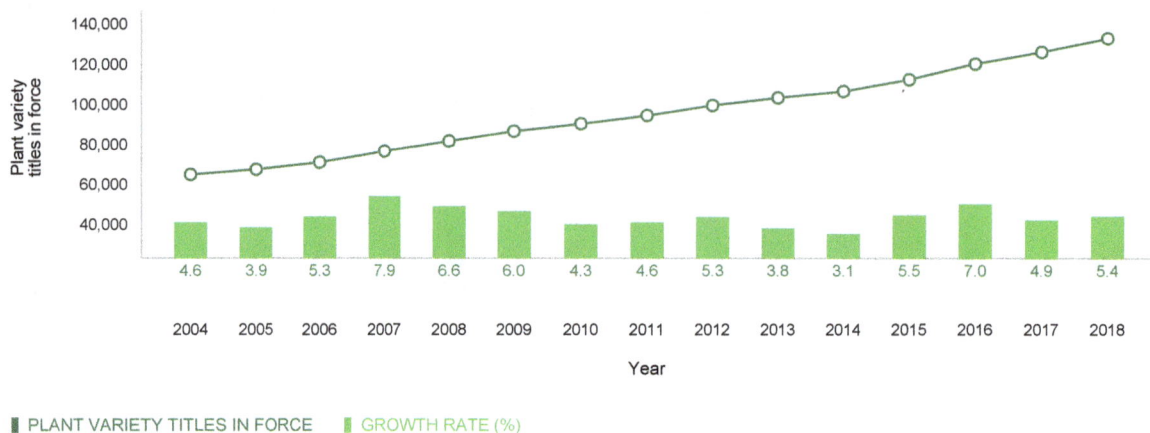

Note: World totals are WIPO estimates using data covering 70 offices.
Source: WIPO Statistics Database, September 2019.

D15. Plant varieties in force at selected offices, 2018

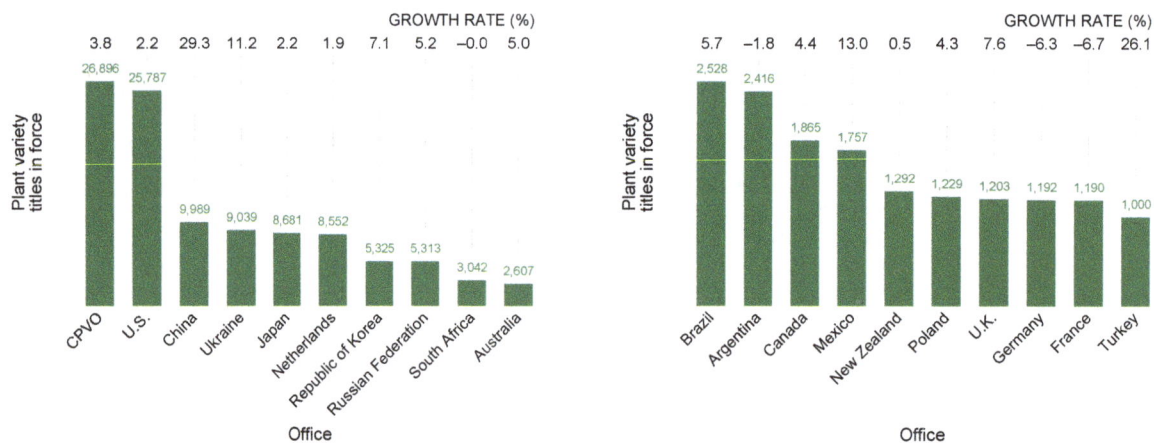

Note: CPVO is the Community Plant Variety Office.
Source: WIPO Statistics Database, September 2019.

Plant varieties

Statistical table

D16. Plant variety applications and titles issued by office and origin, and plant variety titles in force by office, 2018

Name	Total	Applications by office		Applications by origin	Equivalent applications by origin	Grants by office			Plant varieties in force
		Resident	Non-resident	Total	Total	Total	Resident	Non-resident	Office
Argentina	329	210	119	268	296	99	79	20	2,416
Australia	384	166	218	336	1,176	222	95	127	2,607
Austria (a)	..	..	..	58	652	..	..	..	18
Belarus	42	5	37	9	9	18	8	10	234
Belgium	1	1	0	92	1,631	..	..	..	43
Bolivia (Plurinational State of)	5	3	2	3	3	5	3	2	59
Brazil	327	189	138	213	241	270	160	110	2,528
Bulgaria	18	18	0	26	26	47	47	0	419
Canada	330	52	278	130	522	250	63	187	1,865
Chile	99	4	95	9	9	98	10	88	875
China	5,760	5,222	538	5,254	5,310	2,395	2,247	148	9,989
Colombia	168	20	148	25	53	102	18	84	578
Community Plant Variety Office	3,554	2,831	723	n.a.	4	2,757	2,218	539	26,896
Costa Rica	4	1	3	5	61	2	0	2	14
Croatia	9	9	0	9	9	8	8	0	62
Czech Republic	70	65	5	106	700	68	61	7	780
Democratic People's Republic of Korea (b)	..	..	..	1	1	..	..	..	..
Denmark	7	6	1	187	2,941	4	3	1	69
Ecuador	85	6	79	13	69	60	17	43	304
Estonia	5	3	2	5	59	4	3	1	97
Eswatini (b)	..	..	..	41	41	..	..	..	..
Finland	7	6	1	13	40	7	7	0	195
France	98	91	7	1,066	12,784	41	33	8	1,190
Georgia	1	0	1	1	1	4	0	4	213
Germany	57	43	14	1,046	12,791	42	35	7	1,192
Greece (b)	..	..	..	12	39	..	..	..	..
Hungary	6	5	1	41	338	16	16	0	162
Iceland (a)	..	..	..	1	1	..	..	..	..
India (b)	..	..	..	2	2	..	..	..	..
Ireland (a)	..	..	..	23	212	..	..	..	..
Israel	68	32	36	151	1,187	82	56	26	822
Italy	3	2	1	232	3,553	..	..	..	..
Japan	880	570	310	898	2,998	758	467	291	8,681
Kyrgyzstan	1	1	0	1	1	1	0	1	5
Latvia	16	12	4	13	13	12	9	3	194
Lithuania	7	4	3	4	4	12	8	4	103
Luxembourg (b)	..	..	..	59	86	..	..	..	..
Mauritius (b)	..	..	..	10	10	..	..	..	..
Mexico	308	93	215	99	127	295	87	208	1,757
Morocco	109	0	109	..	..	73	2	71	408
Netherlands	792	674	118	3,616	39,850	713	635	78	8,552
New Zealand	112	41	71	102	466	76	39	37	1,292
Nicaragua (a)	..	..	..	..	..	3	0	3	15
Norway	14	2	12	4	32	11	1	10	198
Panama (a)	..	..	..	1	29	..	..	..	19

Name	Applications by office			Applications by origin	Equivalent applications by origin	Grants by office			Plant varieties in force
	Total	Resident	Non-resident	Total	Total	Total	Resident	Non-resident	Office
Paraguay	27	27	0	28	28	27	27	0	501
Peru	52	10	42	12	12	53	8	45	217
Poland	103	60	43	111	1,110	91	78	13	1,229
Portugal (a)	..	..	..	3	57	..	..	..	11
Republic of Korea	765	591	174	603	631	574	473	101	5,325
Republic of Moldova	37	28	9	47	47	32	30	2	210
Romania	32	32	0	47	47	45	45	0	410
Russian Federation	780	622	158	626	626	544	450	94	5,313
Serbia	30	2	28	34	314	25	4	21	355
Singapore	8	1	7	1	1	2	0	2	5
Slovakia	8	5	3	10	64	9	7	2	373
Slovenia (a)	..	..	..	6	168	..	..	..	..
South Africa	286	63	223	124	320	189	38	151	3,042
Spain	113	102	11	337	4,009	48	45	3	339
Sri Lanka (b)	..	..	..	2	58	..	..	..	..
Sweden	2	1	1	10	118	1	1	0	106
Switzerland	57	11	46	358	4,866	64	7	57	699
Thailand (b)	..	..	..	38	794	..	..	..	..
Tunisia	27	2	25	2	2	25	3	22	178
Turkey	178	99	79	115	115	217	106	111	1,000
Ukraine	1,575	539	1,036	542	542	1,021	328	693	9,039
United Kingdom	328	34	294	225	2,493	133	22	111	1,203
United Republic of Tanzania	5	0	5	..	..	4	0	4	116
United States of America (PPA) (c)	1,079	439	640	n.a.	..	1,208	493	715	18,266
United States of America (PVPA)	530	461	69	2,308	11,576	216	170	46	7,521
Uruguay	48	8	40	11	11	37	7	30	568
Uzbekistan	43	42	1	42	42	45	45	0	124
Viet Nam	242	194	48	195	195	123	93	30	452
Zambia (b)	..	..	..	1	1	..	..	..	..
Others/Unknown	..	..	..	4	88	..	..	..	..
Total (2018 estimates)	**20,210**	**13,900**	**6,310**	**20,210**	**n.a.**	**13,300**	**8,300**	**3,710**	**133,190**

(a) This office did not report data; therefore, applications by origin data may be incomplete.

(b) Is not a member of the International Union for the Protection of New Varieties of Plants (UPOV).

(c) Applications by origin are reported under United States of America (PVPA).

n.a. indicates not applicable.

.. indicates not available.

Sources: WIPO Statistics Database, September 2019.

Geographical indications

Introduction

A geographical indication (GI) is a sign identifying a good as originating from a specific geographical area and possessing a given quality, reputation or other characteristic that is essentially attributable to that geographical origin. Thus, the main function of a GI is to indicate a connection between that quality, reputation or characteristic of that good and its territory of origin.

GIs can be protected through a variety of legal means (e.g., *sui generis* systems, trademark laws, international agreements, other national legal means, etc.). In addition, the protection of GIs at a national level is often shared among several agencies. WIPO has made major efforts to gather data from all sources. Notwithstanding the improvements mentioned above, in many instances it has not been possible to obtain data from every source. Nonetheless, these statistics offer valuable insight into how this form of IP is used in different parts of the world.

How many GIs are in force worldwide?

Data received from the 92 national/regional authorities that shared their 2018 data with WIPO reveals that 65,900 protected GIs are in existence. Furthermore, to minimize double counting, the 4,968 European Union (EU) GIs in force in each of the EU member states are counted once only rather than multiplied by the 28 member states.

The offices of the upper middle-income countries account for 43% of the total GIs in force in 2018, followed in turn by the offices of the high-income (42.3%) and lower middle-income countries (14.7%). In terms of regional distribution, Europe had the largest number of GIs in force across all regions, accounting for 57.4%, followed by Asia (28.3%) and Latin America and the Caribbean (8.4%).

Figure 5.1 shows the total number of GIs in force for each selected national/regional authority, while figure 5.2 reports data on GIs in force for the EU member states. Germany had the largest number of GIs in force (15,566) in 2018, followed by China (7,247), Hungary (6,683), Czech Republic (6,285), Bulgaria (6,038), Italy (6,015) and Portugal (5,998). There are several middle-income countries with a large number of GIs in force within their respective jurisdictions; for example, in 2018, 4,732 were in force in the Republic of Moldova, 4,499 in Bosnia and Herzegovina and 4,426 GIs in force in Georgia. In contrast, India (330) and Brazil (68) – two of the larger middle-income countries – had considerably fewer GIs in force.

GIs in force relating to "wines and spirits" accounted for 51.1% of the 2018 total, followed by agricultural products and foodstuffs (29.9%) (figure 5.3). Handicrafts accounted for 2.7% of the total. China, Hungary, India and Viet Nam each had more than 100 GIs for handicrafts in force within their jurisdictions in 2018. Indications relating to services amounted to 34 GIs in 2018, mainly reported by the United States of America (U.S.) (17 GIs) and Viet Nam (12 GIs).

China had more than 7,200 GIs in force in 2018

5.1. Geographical indications in force for selected national/regional authorities, 2018

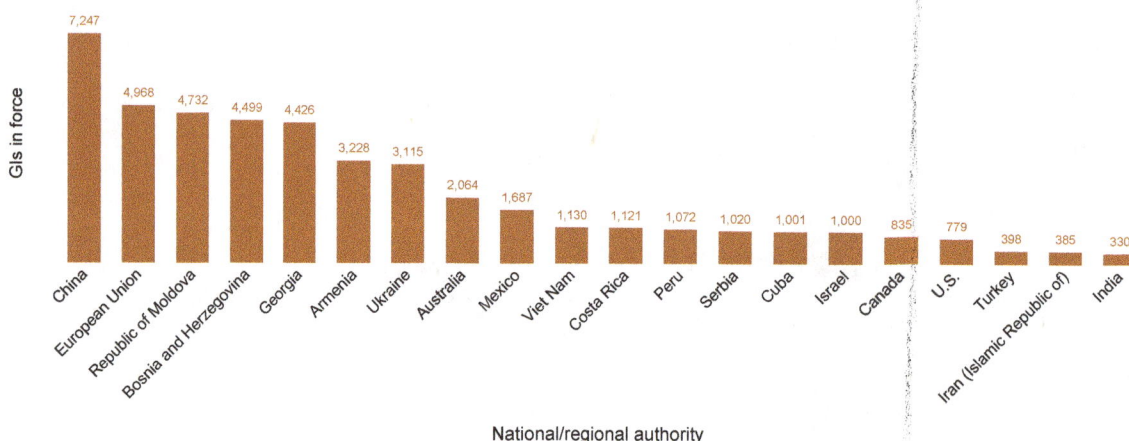

Source: WIPO Statistics Database, August 2019.

GIs in force based on national systems accounted for 68.1% of total GIs in Germany

5.2. Geographical indications in force for EU member states, 2018

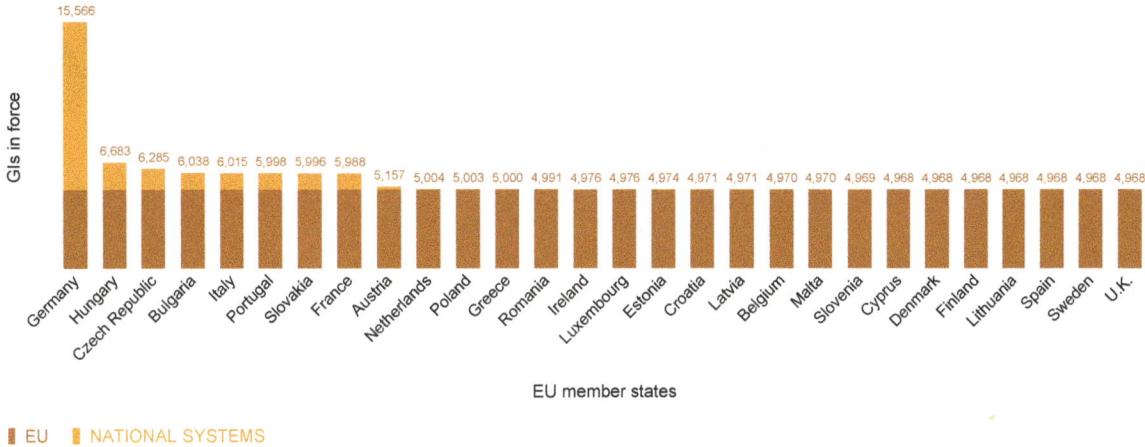

EU member states

■ EU   ■ NATIONAL SYSTEMS

Note: This figure shows the total number of geographical indications in force in the EU member states, broken down by GIs in force based on the EU regional systems and agreements and on national systems. The EU has regional systems for the protection of GIs covering agricultural and foodstuff products, wines and spirits.

Source: WIPO Statistics Database, August 2019.

Wines and spirits accounted for 51.1% of GIs in force

5.3. Geographical indications in force by product categories, 2018

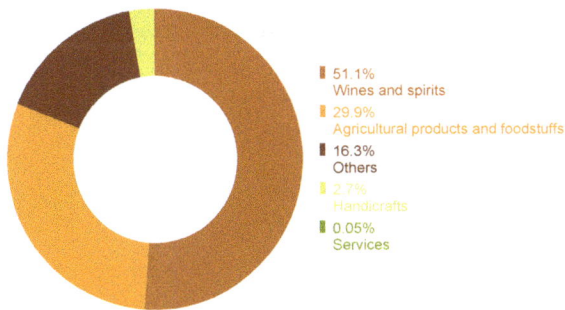

■ 51.1%
Wines and spirits
■ 29.9%
Agricultural products and foodstuffs
■ 16.3%
Others
■ 2.7%
Handicrafts
■ 0.05%
Services

Note: GIs in force through the EU regional systems are counted once rather than 28 times as they are in force in all EU member states. This is done to minimize double counting. The distribution is based on data from 74 jurisdictions for which 2018 data by product category are available.

Source: WIPO Statistics Database, August 2019.

The GIs in force data reported here are partial and incomplete and therefore should be interpreted with caution. The questionnaire underlying the data collection asked for information regarding GIs protected through *sui generis* systems, trademark systems, other national legal means, regional systems and international agreements (including GIs in force under the Lisbon System and the Madrid System). As can be seen from table 5.4, many countries were unable to provide statistics on the number of GIs protected through trademark systems, a reflection of the difficulty in identifying such GIs among all trademarks (most commonly, collective and certification trademarks). In addition, several countries could not provide data on the number of GIs protected through international agreements.

Use of the Lisbon System to protect appellations of origin

As of 2018, the Lisbon System consists of 28 member countries, seven of who are EU members. In 2018, there were 1,012 appellations of origin in force via the Lisbon System (figure 5.5). This represents a 2.1% increase on the previous year, mostly driven by strong growth from Italy and the Islamic Republic of Iran. France remains the largest user of the System. It accounted for 50.3% of the 2018 total, followed by Italy (17.3%), Czech Republic (7.4%), the Islamic Republic of Iran (6%) and Bulgaria (3.9%).

5.4. Geographical indications in force in 2018

National/regional authority	Total	*Sui generis*	Trademarks	Other national legal means	Regional system	Agreements	Unknown
Andorra	7	4	2	..	..	1	..
Albania	13	..	..	13	..	..	..
Argentina	108	108	..	..	..	..	..
Armenia	3,228	8	..	..	..	3,220	..
Australia	2,064	116	76	..	..	1,872	..
Austria	5,157	..	..	..	3,434	1,723	..
Azerbaijan	35	..	..	..	..	..	35
Bahamas (a)	..	..	..	..	..	..	..
Bangladesh	3	3	..	..	..	..	..
Barbados	..	..	..	..	..	..	..
Belarus	33	31	2	..	..	..	..
Belgium	4,970	2	..	..	3,434	1,534	..
Bhutan	11	..	11	..	..	..	..
Bosnia and Herzegovina	4,499	13	..	..	..	4,486	..
Botswana	1	..	..	1	..	..	..
Brazil	68	68	..	..	..	..	..
Brunei Darussalam	..	..	..	..	..	..	..
Bulgaria	6,038	111	..	..	3,434	2,493	..
Cambodia	1	1	..	..	..	..	..
Canada	835	651	..	..	..	184	..
Chile (a)	283	167	..	..	..	116	..
China	7,247	2,380	4,867	..	..	..	..
China, Hong Kong SAR	43	..	43	..	..	..	..
China, Macao SAR	11	2	9	..	..	..	..
Colombia	151	151	..	..	..	..	..
Costa Rica	1,121	4	..	..	..	1,117	..
Côte d'Ivoire (a)	..	..	..	..	..	..	..
Croatia	4,971	3	..	..	3,434	1,534	..
Cuba	1,001	25	5	..	..	971	..
Cyprus	4,968	..	..	..	3,434	1,534	..
Czech Republic	6,285	62	..	..	3,434	2,789	..
Denmark	4,968	..	..	..	3,434	1,534	..
Dominica	..	..	..	..	..	..	..
Ecuador	53	5	..	..	..	48	..
El Salvador	139	96	30	..	..	13	..
Estonia	4,974	6	..	..	3,434	1,534	..
European Union	4,968	3,434	..	..	..	1,534	..
Finland	4,968	..	..	..	3,434	1,534	..
France	5,988	7	..	4	3,434	2,543	..
Gambia	..	..	..	..	..	..	..
Georgia	4,426	48	..	..	..	4,378	..
Germany	15,566	7,276	1	..	4,537	3,752	..
Greece	5,000	16	..	16	3,434	1,534	..
Guatemala	116	3	..	..	..	113	..
Honduras	45	..	45	..	..	..	..
Hungary	6,683	25	..	..	3,434	3,224	..
Iceland	1	1	..	..	..	..	..
India	330	330	..	..	..	..	..
Indonesia	74	74	..	..	..	..	..
Iran (Islamic Republic of)	385	30	..	..	..	355	..
Ireland	4,976	8	..	..	3,434	1,534	..
Israel	1,000	1	..	..	..	999	..
Italy	6,015	36	..	..	3,434	2,545	..
Jamaica	3	2	1	..	..	..	..
Japan	90	73	..	10	..	7	..
Jordan	5	..	5	..	..	..	..
Kazakhstan	47	47	..	..	..	..	..
Kenya	..	..	..	..	..	..	..
Lao People's Democratic Republic	2	..	..	..	..	..	2
Latvia	4,971	3	..	..	3,434	1,534	..
Lithuania	4,968	..	..	..	3,434	1,534	..
Luxembourg	4,976	..	..	8	3,434	1,534	..
Malaysia	84	84	..	..	..	..	..
Maldives (a)	..	..	..	..	..	..	..

Geographical indications

National/regional authority	Total	Sui generis	Trademarks	Other national legal means	Regional system	Agreements	Unknown
Malta	4,970	..	2	..	3,434	1,534	..
Mauritius	..	..	..	..	..	..	..
Mexico	1,687	16	..	..	..	1,671	..
Mongolia	1	1	..	..	..	..	..
Morocco	121	66	54	..	..	1	..
Netherlands	5,004	..	..	..	3,434	1,570	..
New Zealand	21	21	..	..	..	..	..
Norway	29	29	..	..	..	..	..
Pakistan	..	..	..	..	..	..	..
Peru	1,072	10	..	..	..	1,062	..
Philippines (a)	..	..	..	..	..	..	..
Poland	5,003	35	..	..	3,434	1,534	..
Portugal	5,998	20	..	..	3,434	2,544	..
Republic of Moldova	4,732	18	..	..	..	4,714	..
Romania	4,991	23	..	..	3,434	1,534	..
Russian Federation	285	184	..	..	..	101	..
Saint Vincent and Grenadines	..	..	..	..	..	..	..
Serbia	1,020	81	3	..	..	936	..
Singapore	..	..	..	..	..	..	..
Slovakia	5,996	20	..	..	3,434	2,542	..
Slovenia	4,969	1	..	..	3,434	1,534	..
Spain	4,968	..	..	..	3,434	1,534	..
Sri Lanka	4	..	4	..	..	..	..
Sweden	4,968	..	..	..	3,434	1,534	..
Thailand	119	119	..	..	..	..	..
Togo (a)	..	..	..	..	..	..	..
Trinidad and Tobago	1	1	..	..	..	..	..
Turkey	398	395	..	..	..	3	..
Uganda	..	..	..	..	..	..	..
Ukraine	3,115	25	..	..	..	3,090	..
United Kingdom	4,968	..	..	..	3,434	1,534	..
United States of America	779	..	779	..	..	..	..
Uzbekistan (a)	..	..	..	..	..	..	..
Viet Nam	1,130	69	1,061	..	..	..	..
Yemen (a)	..	..	..	..	..	..	..

(a) 2017 data.

.. indicates zero.

Source: WIPO Statistics Database, August 2019.

France remains the largest user of the Lisbon System

5.5. Appellations of origin in force by origin, 2018

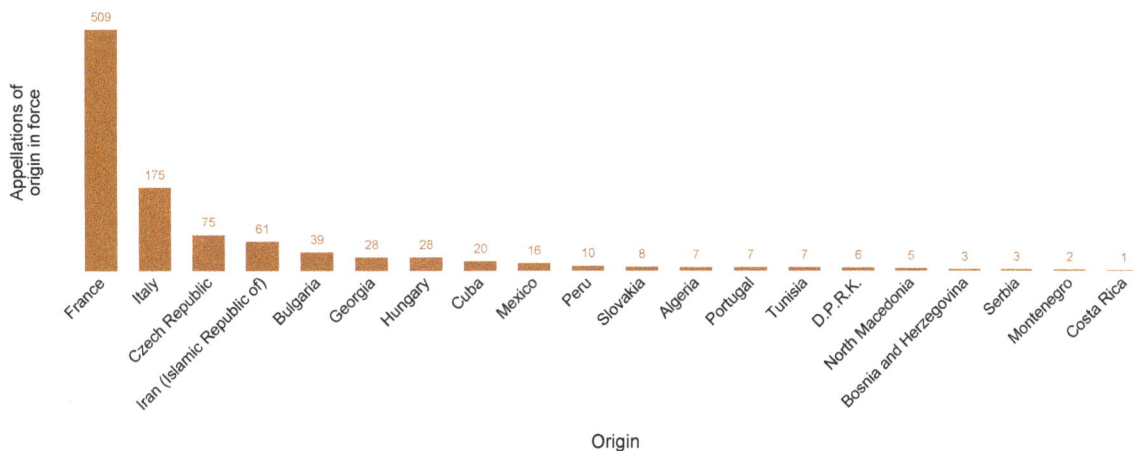

Note: D.P.R.K. is the Democratic People's Republic of Korea.

Source: WIPO Statistics Database, August 2019.

Creative economy

Highlights

In 2017, the International Publishers Association (IPA) and the World Intellectual Property Organization (WIPO) launched a new survey to compile statistics on the creative economy. In all, 35 national publishers' associations and copyright authorities shared their 2016 data covering the publishing industry. The following year, in 2017, 53 countries shared their data with WIPO. Based on additional feedback received by WIPO, the questionnaire was simplified and methodological guidance refined. Moreover, WIPO started to collect additional data to validate and/or supplement the data compiled through the IPA–WIPO questionnaire.

This section presents the following data covering the publishing industry: (a) IPA–WIPO survey data, (b) legal deposits data compiled by WIPO through a simple questionnaire, and (c) data provided by the Nielsen Company. Publishing industry data are not unified under a single authority. Therefore it is necessary to compile data from different sources so as to provide a broader perspective on the publishing industry in any particular country. Readers should be aware that the IPA–WIPO survey data and the Nielsen Book data differ due to differences in methodology and market coverage.

IPA–WIPO publishing survey

The first IPA–WIPO publishing survey was launched in 2017, covering three sectors: trade, educational and scientific, technological and medical (STM). Recipients of and respondents to the survey were national publishers' associations and copyright authorities. A number of respondents indicated that data for the STM sector was not available. Furthermore, because STM sector publishing is dominated by multinational firms located around the world, it is extremely difficult to track the requested data. The survey is now focused on the collection of data for the trade and the educational sectors and excludes the STM sector entirely. At the same time, additional data sources were identified with which to validate and complement the IPA–WIPO survey data; for example, data from legal deposits, International Standard Book Identifier (ISBN), data provided by private entities, etc. Cooperation with the Federation of European Publishers (FEP) and the Centro Regional para al Fomento del Libro en América Latina y el Caribe (CERLALC) was strengthened so as to reduce the burden on respondents and increase the geographical coverage of the survey. We are grateful to the FEP and the CERLALC for sharing their data. The ISBN agency shared aggregate data for 20 countries that serves as a benchmark for the number of titles published in each of these countries. Although an ISBN is not the only book identifier used in some countries, it is nonetheless the largest standardized identification system in most. WIPO would also like to register its appreciation for the cooperation given it by the Nielsen Company in sharing aggregate sales and revenue data for 10 countries.

The scope of the IPA–WIPO survey is limited to published materials (i.e., books monographs, and so on) that have been issued with an ISBN number, a Digital Object Identifier (DOI) or any other book identifier.

IPA–WIPO publishing survey data

The IPA-WIPO questionnaire resulted in publishing industry data from 58 countries. In total, 49 national publishers' associations and copyright authorities shared their 2018 data, while a further nine associations/authorities shared their 2016/2017 data. Moreover, a number of respondents indicated a willingness to share their 2018 data when available.

U.S. publishing industry revenue reached over 23 billion USD in 2018

The 2018 total sales and licensing revenue generated by both the trade and the educational sectors are available for 14 countries. These 14 countries generated USD 42.5 billion revenue in 2018. The United States of America (U.S.) (USD 23.3 billion) reported the largest net revenue, followed by Germany (USD 6.1 billion), the U.K. (USD 5.4 billion) and France (USD 3 billion) (figure 6.1). Trade sector revenue accounted for 50% or more of total revenue in nine of the countries – ranging from 56.6% in Finland to 93.3% in the Czech Republic. Educational sector revenue accounted for over 50% of total revenue in Brazil (67.8%) and Turkey (50.5%).

The total revenue generated from sales of "children's books", a subcategory of the trade sector, is available for five countries and amounted to USD 5.1 billion in 2018. The share of children's books revenue as a percentage of total trade sector revenue was largest for the U.S. (27.5%) and Sweden (21.5%) (figure F2).

The online sales channel generated 51.5% of trade sector revenue in the U.K.

The 2018 trade sector revenue is available for 14 countries. The U.S., with USD 16.2 billion, reported the largest revenue, followed by Japan (USD 8.4 billion), the U.K. (USD 3.2 billion) and France (USD 2.1 billion) (figure F1). Eight countries provided their 2018 trade sector revenue broken down by format, that is, printed, digital and other format categories. For each of these eight countries, print editions generated more than three-quarters of trade sector revenue, whereas digital editions accounted for the largest revenue share in Japan (24.5%), Sweden (23.2%) and the U.S. (19.4%) (figure F3).

The 2018 trade sector revenue broken down by destination market is available for 10 countries. Domestic sales accounted for the bulk of total revenue for all observed countries, ranging from 60.6% in Belgium to 99.9% in Japan. The share of revenue from foreign sales and licensing represents a relatively high proportion of trade revenue in Belgium (39.4%) and the U.K. (33%) (figure F4).

The online sales channel generated more than half of total trade sector revenue in the U.K. The U.S. (41.6%), Brazil (25.5%) and Sweden (23.5%) also had a large proportion of their total trade sector revenue generated by the online sales channel. However, the brick and mortar channel continues to generate the largest share of total trade sector revenue for all reported countries, except for Slovenia, the U.K. and the U.S. (figure F5).

6.1. Total net publishing industry revenue (USD million), 2018

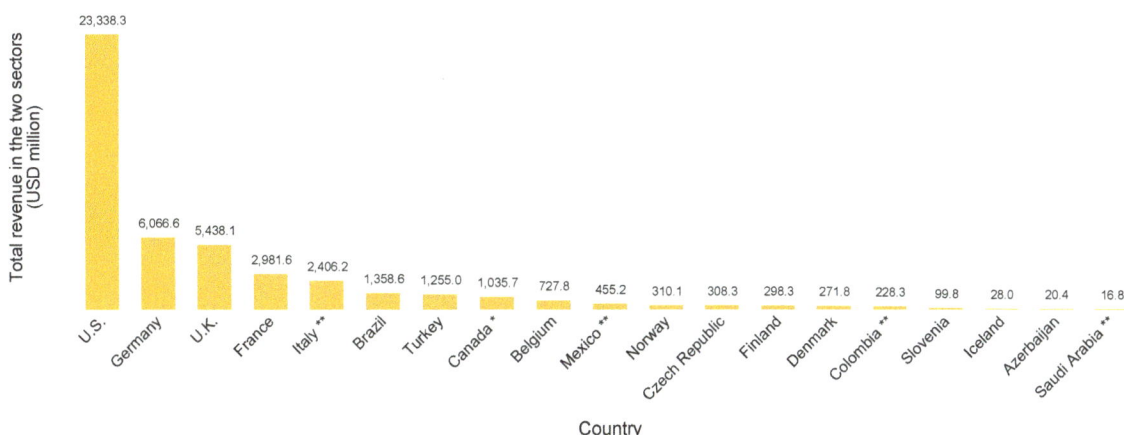

* indicates 2016 data.
** indicates 2017 data.
Source: Table F22.

Foreign sales accounted for 55.9% of educational sector revenue in the U.K.

Revenue generated by the educational sector is available for 11 countries. The U.S. with USD 7.1 billion reported the largest total revenue, followed by the U.K. (USD 2.3 billion) and Brazil (USD 0.9 billion) (figure F14). For all reported countries, print editions accounted for the bulk of total educational sector revenue, ranging from 67.4% in Denmark to 96.9% in France, while digital editions accounted for 32.6% in Denmark, 28.8% in Norway and 19.6% in the U.K. (figure F15). Breakdown of the total educational sector revenue by domestic and foreign markets shows that the U.K. (55.9%) and Belgium (24.9%) had the largest shares of total revenue generated from the foreign market. Revenue generated from the domestic market accounted for almost all the educational sector revenue in Denmark, Finland, Norway and the U.S. (figure F16).

In 2018, the U.K. published 188,000 titles covering the trade and educational sectors

Data on the total number of titles published in 2018 covering both the trade and educational sectors are available for 43 countries. The U.K. reported a combined total of 188,000 published titles in 2018, followed by the Russian Federation (116,915) and France (106,799) (figure 6.2). The trade sector accounted for more than half of all titles published in most of those countries where a breakdown according to sector was

available – ranging from 50.5% (Belarus and Brazil) to 97.7% (Estonia).

Children's books accounted for 27.9% of trade sector titles published in Slovenia in 2018

Data on children's books published in 2018 is available for 13 countries. France reported the most children's books published, amounting to 18,477 titles, followed by the Russian Federation (14,556) and Turkey (9,294). Children's books accounted for the largest share of trade sector titles published in Slovenia (27.9%), Sweden (24.3%) and France (23.9%) (figure F7).

Digital editions accounted for 48.7% of trade sector titles published in Sweden

Data on the number of titles published by the trade sector are available for 28 countries. Spain had by far the highest number of titles published in 2018 (81,228), followed by France (77,221), Japan (71,661) and Turkey (56,991) (figure F6). In total, 12 countries were able to disaggregate the number of titles published by the trade sector between printed editions, digital editions and other formats. Print editions accounted for more than half of all titles published by the trade sector in most countries. The largest share of digital editions was reported by Sweden (48.7%), followed by Norway (43.5%), Estonia (30.7%) and Ecuador (25.4%) (figure F8).

6.2. Total number of titles published, 2018

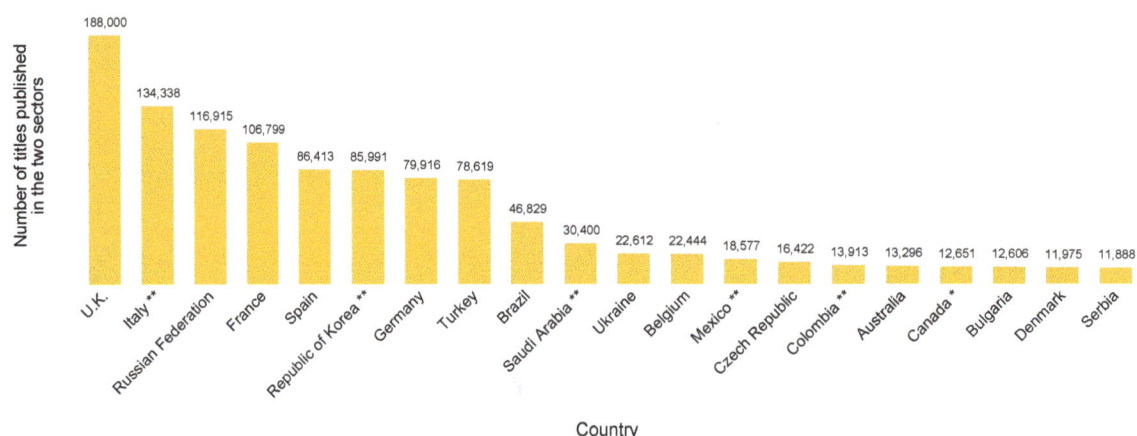

* indicates 2016 data.
** indicates 2017 data.
Source: Table F23.

Brazil and Turkey published the highest number of titles in the educational sector

Data on the number of titles published by the educational sector are available for 25 countries. Brazil had the highest number of titles published (23,160), followed by Turkey (21,628) and France (9,934) (figure F18). The majority of titles in the educational sector were published in print format for all reporting countries. Spain (36.6%) reported the largest share of digital educational titles, followed by Finland (31.6%) and Guatemala (29.5%) (figure F19).

The U.S. sold 2,597 million copies of published titles in 2018

Ten countries were able to report data on the total number of copies sold covering the two sectors. The U.S. sold 2,597 million copies in 2018, followed by the U.K. (652 million), France (419 million) and Turkey (400 million) (figure 6.3). The trade sector accounted for more than 80% of total copies sold in France, Norway and the U.S., whereas the educational sector had the largest share of total copies sold in Uzbekistan (80.8%), Brazil (57.2%) and Turkey (53.8%).

Data on the number of copies sold by the trade sector alone in 2018 are available for 13 countries. The U.S. accounts for the highest number of copies sold in this sector (2,483 million), followed by Japan (571 million) and the U.K. (508 million) (figure F9). Data on the number of copies sold by the educational sector in 2018 are available for nine countries. Turkey (215 million) reported the highest number of copies sold in this sector, followed by Brazil (201 million), the U.K. (144 million) and the U.S. (114 million) (figure F20).

6.3. Total number of copies sold, 2018

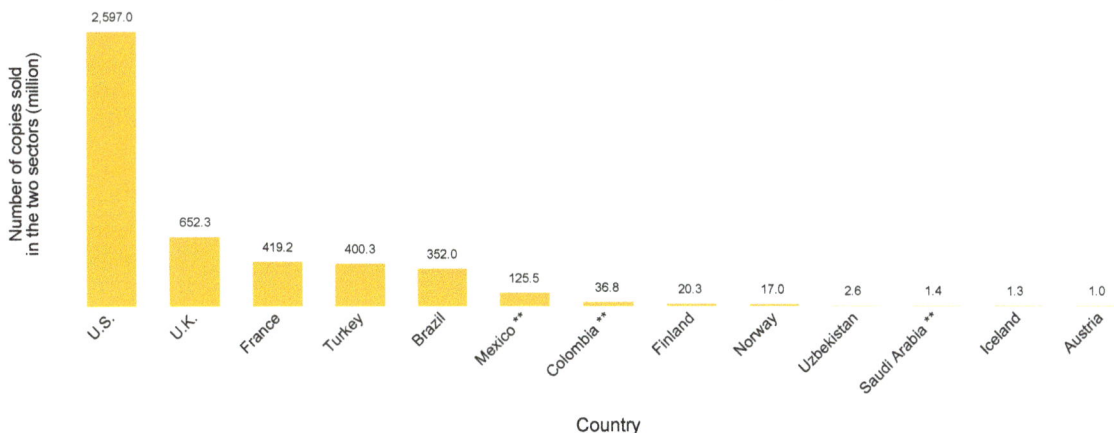

* indicates 2016 data.

** indicates 2017 data.

Source: Table F24.

Legal deposits

More than 40 countries responded to a WIPO survey of legal deposits, of which 39 shared their 2018 legal deposits data (table F25). The highest number of books published and deposited in a national repository in 2018 was recorded by the U.K. (210,628), followed by the Republic of Korea (90,620), France (82,313), Turkey (71,074), Spain (67,884) and Italy (60,058) (figure 6.4). It should be noted, however, that several large book markets like those of the U.S., China and the Russian Federation did not participate in this survey.

Disaggregated data in terms of format is available for 17 countries. The largest shares of digital books in national legal deposits are in the U.K. (61.8%), Colombia (59.1%) and Finland (59%), followed by Costa Rica (37.3%), Poland (35.1%), New Zealand (33.4%) and Estonia (30.8%) (table F25). In Belgium, the share of digital books in legal deposit accounts for 12% and represents only submissions made on a voluntary basis.

Legal deposits

Legal deposit is a statutory obligation at the national level requiring publishers to deposit a certain number of copies of their published documents at a repository, that is, a recognized place of legal deposit. Ordinarily, national legal provisions require that at least two copies are submitted, although this varies across countries. It should be noted that in some countries legal deposits are required only for printed books, while in others there is a legal requirement to deposit digital publications and other formats also. In some countries, there is no legal obligation to deposit e-books, although it may be done so on a voluntary basis. For this reason, care should be exercised when making cross-country comparisons.

6.4. Number of books in legal repositories, 2018

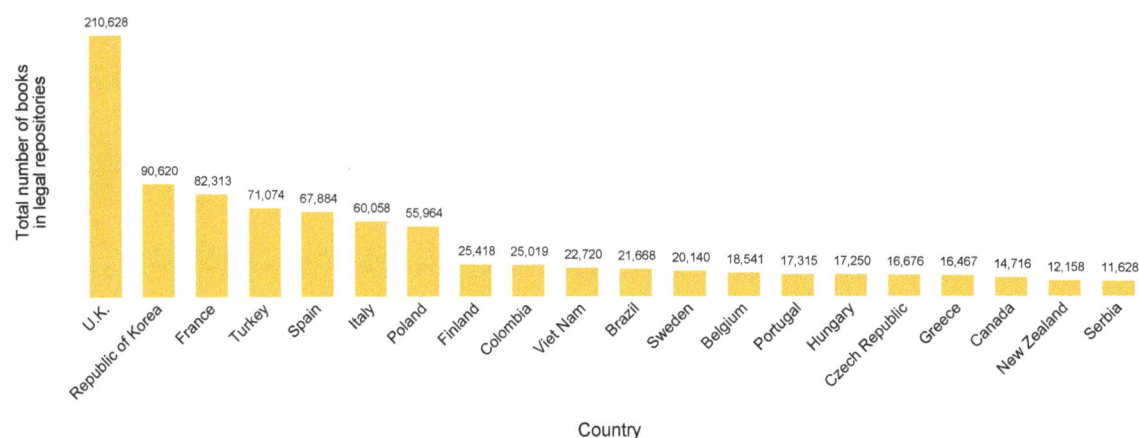

Source: Table F25.

Nielsen BookScan data

Nielsen BookScan collects transactional data at the point of sale, directly from the tills and dispatch systems of all major book retailers. It operates in a number of countries, including Brazil, India and the UK; for example, in the U.K., Nielsen tracks sales through around 6,500 retailers. That said, the market coverage of the Nielsen BookScan data varies across countries, ranging from 90% in Australia and the U.K. to around 60% in Mexico. WIPO is grateful to the Nielsen Company for sharing its revenue and sales data for 10 countries. Table 6.5 presents data on units sold and revenue generated. The U.K. had the highest number of copies sold in 2018, amounting to 190.9 million copies. It was followed by Italy (85.6 million), Spain (64 million) and Australia (61.2 million). The children's books sub-category accounted for over 40% of total sales in Australia, New Zealand and Spain. The total revenue generated at the point of sale amounted to USD 2.2 billion in the U.K., followed by Italy (USD 1.5 billion), Spain (USD 1.2 billion) and Australia (USD 0.9 billion).

6.5. Total number of copies sold and sales revenue, 2018

	Total number of books sold (million)	Distribution (%)			Total Sales revenue (USD, million)	Distribution (%)		
		Fiction	Children's	Non Fiction		Fiction	Children's	Non Fiction
Australia	61.2	22.3	44.3	33.4	880.8	22.0	27.8	50.3
Brazil	44.4	26.6	23.3	50.2	510.1	20.8	22.5	56.7
India	21.0	19.7	20.1	60.2	93.6	16.8	17.5	65.6
Ireland	11.8	26.0	37.9	36.1	165.9	24.2	30.1	45.7
Italy	85.6	34.3	29.4	36.3	1,502.3	33.3	25.9	40.7
Mexico*	8.4	16.5	17.1	66.3	90.4	20.5	17.3	62.1
New Zealand	6.2	21.0	43.6	35.4	95.3	22.4	28.2	49.5
South Africa	9.2	19.8	36.7	43.5	118.7	20.4	26.3	53.3
Spain	64.0	26.3	42.4	31.3	1,168.1	26.3	39.4	34.3
U.K.	190.9	26.8	33.2	40.1	2,173.4	22.0	23.6	54.3

Note: Total consumer book (print) market coverage by Nielsen BookScan is: Australia (90%), Brazil (more than 65%), India (significant part of the organized market), Ireland (more than 70%), Italy (60%), Mexico (60%), New Zealand (70%), South Africa (68%), Spain (around 80%), and the U.K. (90%). Post 16 education books (textbooks and study guides) are included within the non fiction category. Coverage for all education books varies from country to country.

* Data from March to December (i.e. not full year).

Source: Nielsen BookScan, September 2019.

Creative economy

Creative economy statistics

Creative economy

Trade sector

F1. Trade sector revenue (USD million), 2018

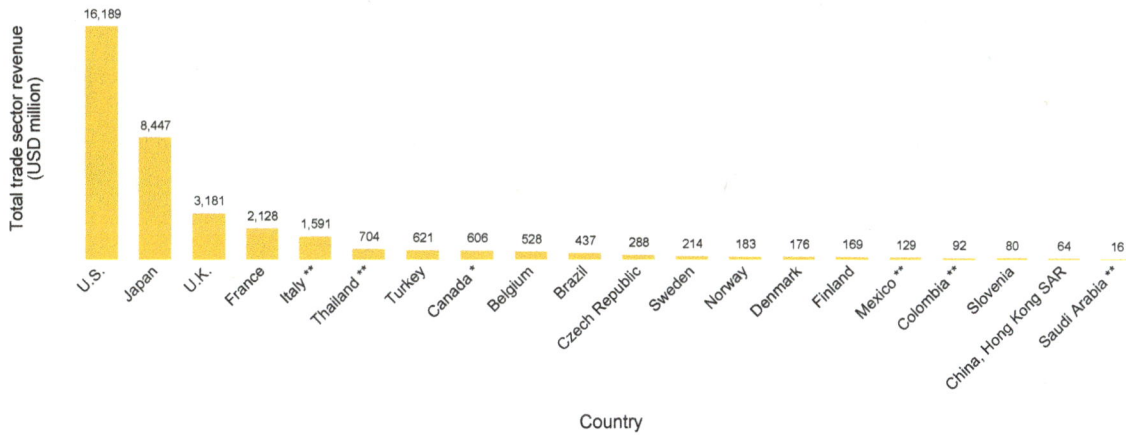

Note: Caution should be exercised when interpreting the data shown here due to data being incomplete and partial. The share of the total publishing industry represented by national publishers' associations (NPA) varies between countries. There are also methodological differences that make it a challenge to make comparisons between countries. For all reported countries, the data source is the NPA, except for Canada (Statistics Canada) and Japan (Japan Copyright Office).

* indicates 2016 data.

** indicates 2017 data.

Source: WIPO Statistics Database, September 2019.

F2. Share of children's books within trade sector revenue, 2018

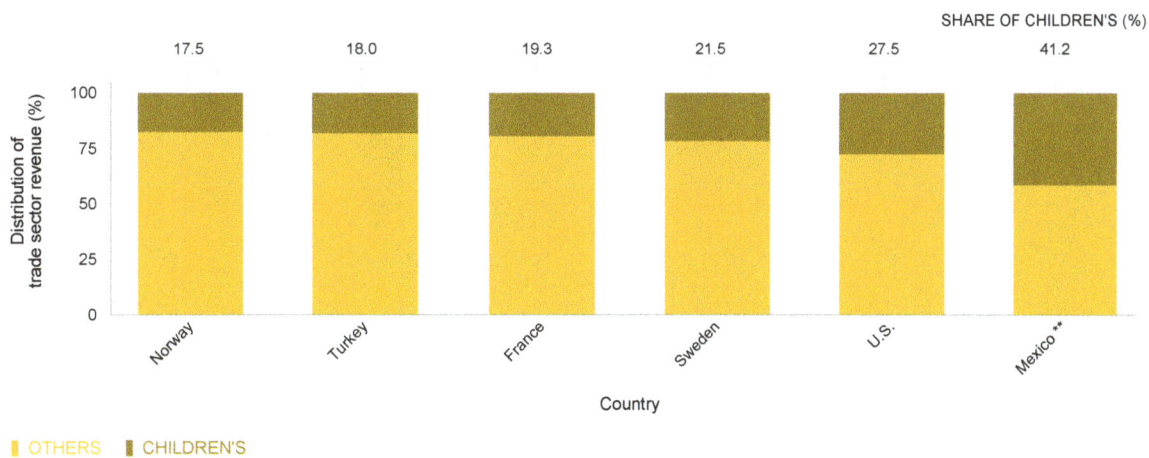

OTHERS   CHILDREN'S

Note: Caution should be exercised when interpreting the data shown here due to data being incomplete and partial. The share of the total publishing industry represented by national publishers' associations (NPA) varies between countries. There are also methodological differences which mean that it is difficult to make comparisons between countries. For all reported countries, the data source is the NPA, except for Canada (Statistics Canada) and Japan (Japan Copyright Office).

** indicates 2017 data.

Source: WIPO Statistics Database, September 2019.

Creative economy

F3. Distribution of trade sector revenue by format, 2018

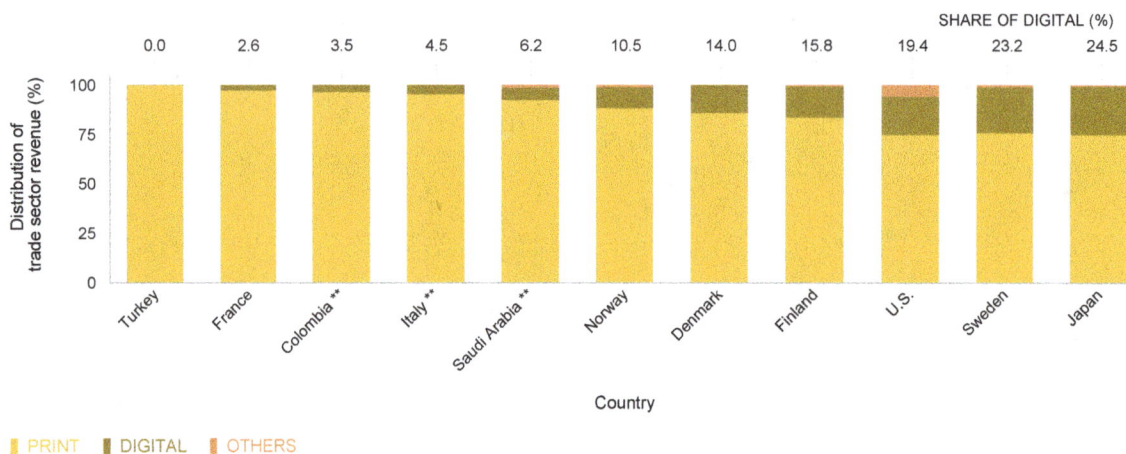

SHARE OF DIGITAL (%)

| 0.0 | 2.6 | 3.5 | 4.5 | 6.2 | 10.5 | 14.0 | 15.8 | 19.4 | 23.2 | 24.5 |

Distribution of trade sector revenue (%)

Country: Turkey, France, Colombia **, Italy **, Saudi Arabia **, Norway, Denmark, Finland, U.S., Sweden, Japan

PRINT   DIGITAL   OTHERS

Note: Caution should be exercised when interpreting the data shown here due to data being incomplete and partial. The share of the total publishing industry represented by national publishers' associations (NPA) varies between countries. There are also methodological differences which mean that it is difficult to make comparisons between countries. For all reported countries, the data source is the NPA, except for Canada (Statistics Canada) and Japan (Japan Copyright Office).

** indicates 2017 data.

Source: WIPO Statistics Database, September 2019.

F4. Distribution of trade sector revenue by destination, 2018

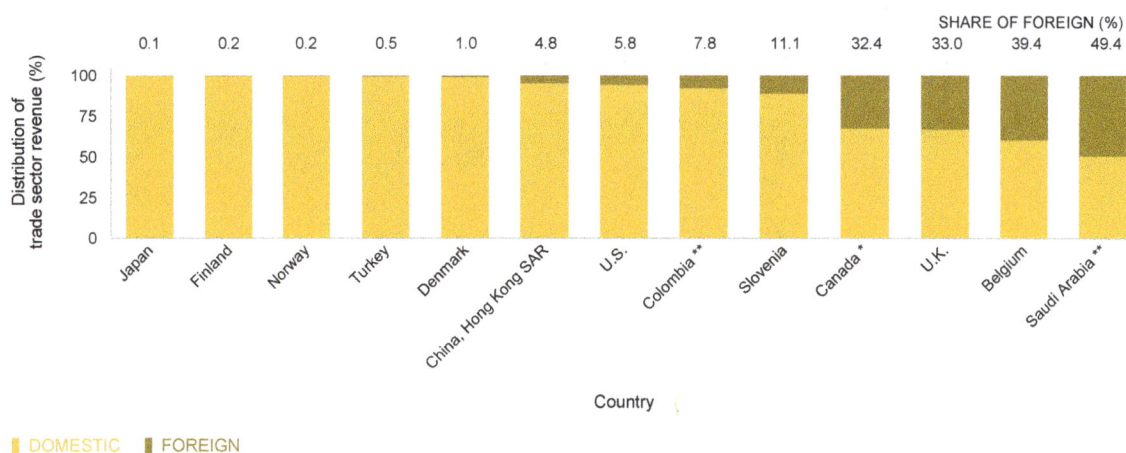

SHARE OF FOREIGN (%)

| 0.1 | 0.2 | 0.2 | 0.5 | 1.0 | 4.8 | 5.8 | 7.8 | 11.1 | 32.4 | 33.0 | 39.4 | 49.4 |

Distribution of trade sector revenue (%)

Country: Japan, Finland, Norway, Turkey, Denmark, China, Hong Kong SAR, U.S., Colombia **, Slovenia, Canada *, U.K., Belgium, Saudi Arabia **

DOMESTIC   FOREIGN

Note: Caution should be exercised when interpreting the data shown here due to data being incomplete and partial. The share of the total publishing industry represented by national publishers' associations (NPA) varies between countries. There are also methodological differences which mean that it is difficult to make comparisons between countries. For all reported countries, the data source is the NPA, except for Canada (Statistics Canada) and Japan (Japan Copyright Office).

* indicates 2016 data.

** indicates 2017 data.

Source: WIPO Statistics Database, September 2019.

Creative economy

F5. Distribution of trade sector revenue by sales channel, 2018

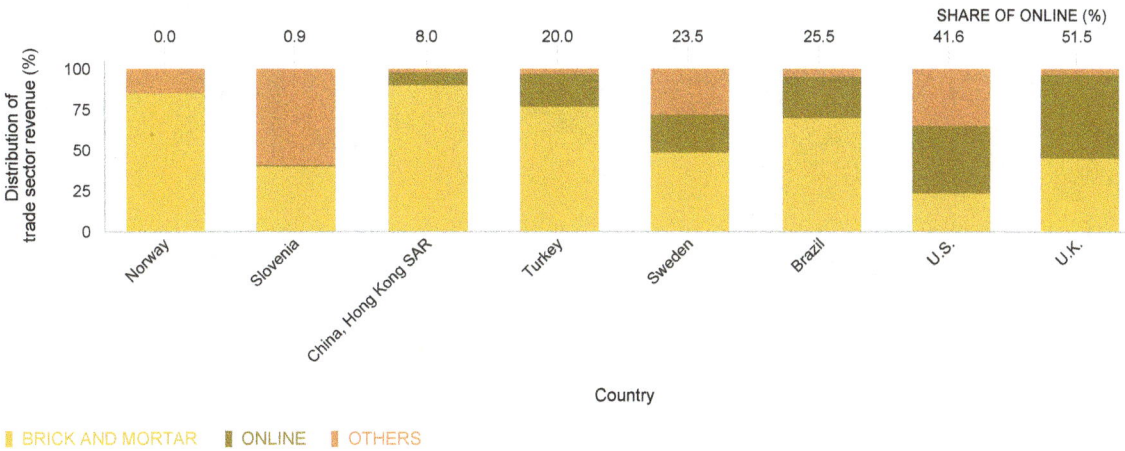

SHARE OF ONLINE (%)

| | 0.0 | 0.9 | 8.0 | 20.0 | 23.5 | 25.5 | 41.6 | 51.5 |

Distribution of trade sector revenue (%)

Country

▌ BRICK AND MORTAR   ▌ ONLINE   ▌ OTHERS

Note: Caution should be exercised when interpreting the data shown here due to data being incomplete and partial. The share of the total publishing industry represented by national publishers' associations (NPA) varies between countries. There are also methodological differences which mean that it is difficult to make comparisons between countries. For all reported countries, the data source is the NPA, except for Canada (Statistics Canada) and Japan (Japan Copyright Office).

Source: WIPO Statistics Database, September 2019.

F6. Number of titles published by the trade sector, 2018

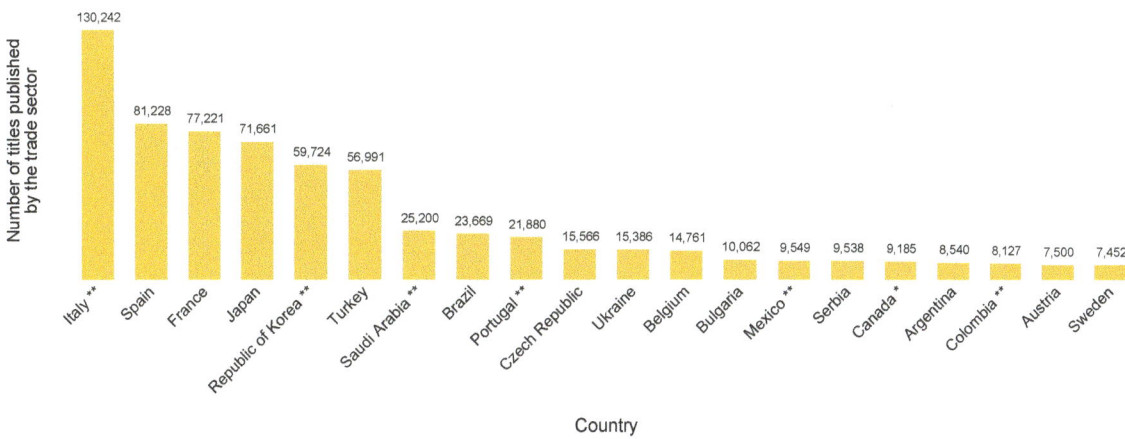

Number of titles published by the trade sector

130,242 — Italy **
81,228 — Spain
77,221 — France
71,661 — Japan
59,724 — Republic of Korea **
56,991 — Turkey
25,200 — Saudi Arabia **
23,669 — Brazil
21,880 — Portugal **
15,566 — Czech Republic
15,386 — Ukraine
14,761 — Belgium
10,062 — Bulgaria
9,549 — Mexico **
9,538 — Serbia
9,185 — Canada *
8,540 — Argentina
8,127 — Colombia **
7,500 — Austria
7,452 — Sweden

Country

Note: Caution should be exercised when interpreting the data shown here due to data being incomplete and partial. The share of the total publishing industry represented by national publishers' associations (NPA) varies between countries. There are also methodological differences which mean that it is difficult to make comparisons between countries. For all reported countries, the data source is the NPA, except for Canada (Statistics Canada) and Japan (Japan Copyright Office).

* indicates 2016 data.

** indicates 2017 data.

Source: WIPO Statistics Database, September 2019.

F7. Share of children's books in the number of titles published by the trade sector, 2018

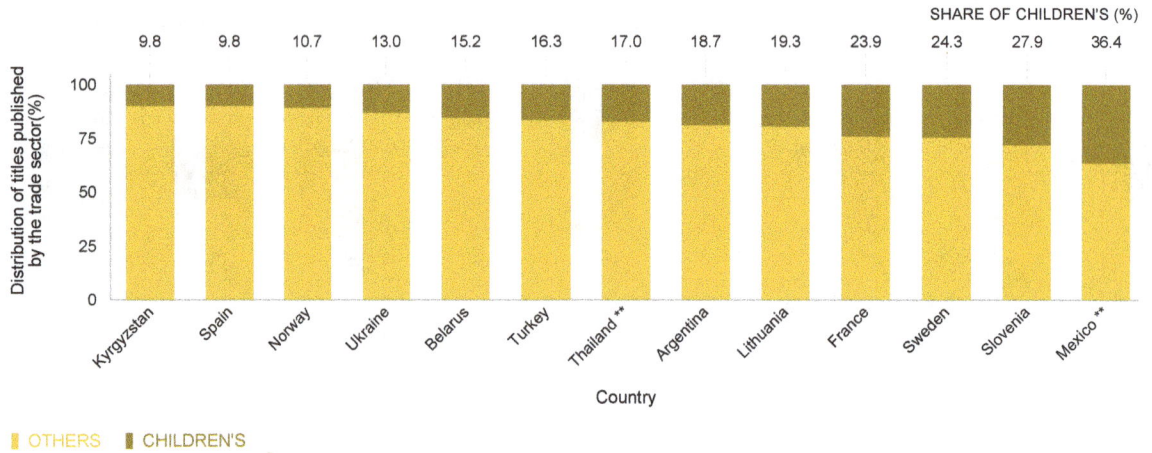

SHARE OF CHILDREN'S (%)

| 9.8 | 9.8 | 10.7 | 13.0 | 15.2 | 16.3 | 17.0 | 18.7 | 19.3 | 23.9 | 24.3 | 27.9 | 36.4 |

Distribution of titles published by the trade sector(%)

Country: Kyrgyzstan, Spain, Norway, Ukraine, Belarus, Turkey, Thailand **, Argentina, Lithuania, France, Sweden, Slovenia, Mexico **

Country

▮ OTHERS ▮ CHILDREN'S

Note: Caution should be exercised when interpreting the data shown here due to data being incomplete and partial. The share of the total publishing industry represented by national publishers' associations (NPA) varies between countries. There are also methodological differences which mean that it is difficult to make comparisons between countries. For all reported countries, the data source is the NPA, except for Canada (Statistics Canada) and Japan (Japan Copyright Office).

** indicates 2017 data.

Source: WIPO Statistics Database, September 2019.

F8. Distribution of titles published by the trade sector by format, 2018

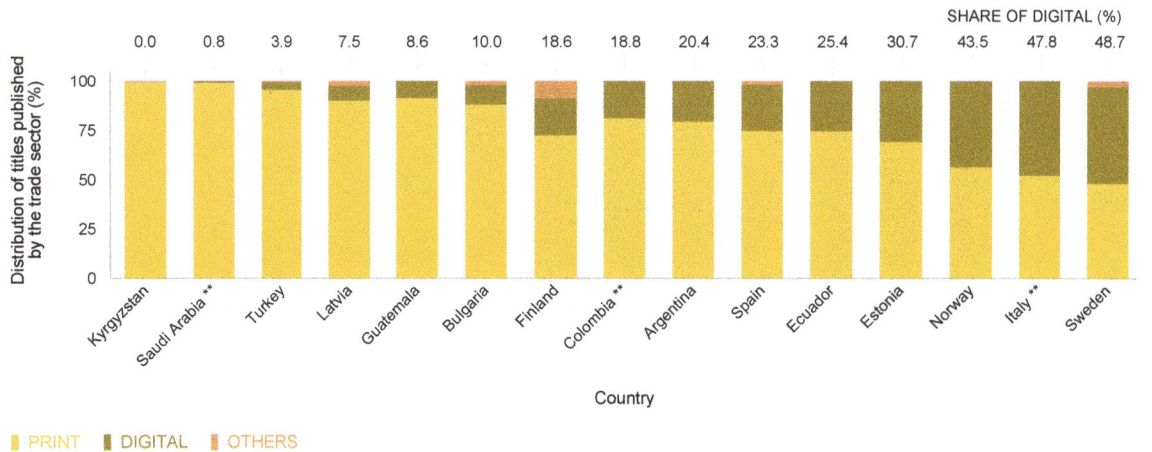

SHARE OF DIGITAL (%)

| 0.0 | 0.8 | 3.9 | 7.5 | 8.6 | 10.0 | 18.6 | 18.8 | 20.4 | 23.3 | 25.4 | 30.7 | 43.5 | 47.8 | 48.7 |

Distribution of titles published by the trade sector (%)

Country: Kyrgyzstan, Saudi Arabia **, Turkey, Latvia, Guatemala, Bulgaria, Finland, Colombia **, Argentina, Spain, Ecuador, Estonia, Norway, Italy **, Sweden

Country

▮ PRINT ▮ DIGITAL ▮ OTHERS

Note: Caution should be exercised when interpreting the data shown here due to data being incomplete and partial. The share of the total publishing industry represented by national publishers' associations (NPA) varies between countries. There are also methodological differences which mean that it is difficult to make comparisons between countries. For all reported countries, the data source is the NPA, except for Canada (Statistics Canada) and Japan (Japan Copyright Office).

** indicates 2017 data.

Source: WIPO Statistics Database, September 2019.

Creative economy

F9. Number of copies sold by the trade sector, 2018

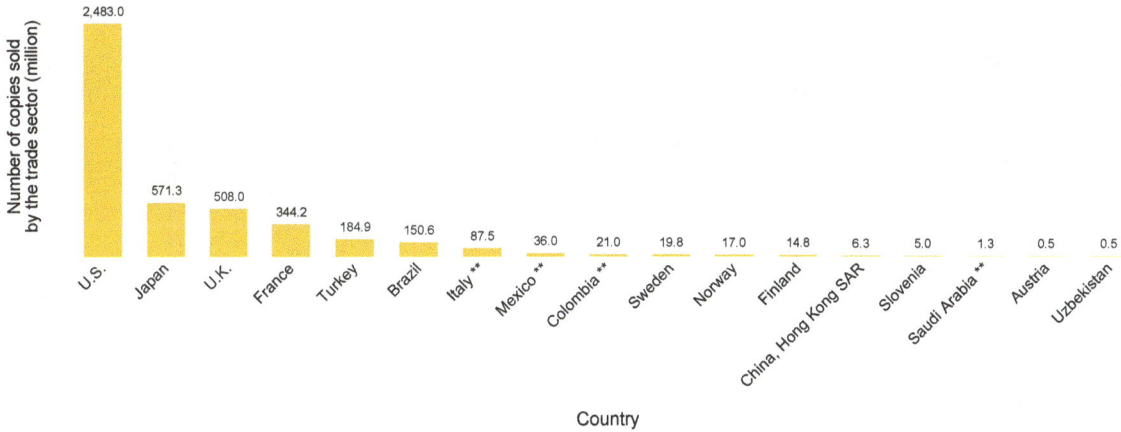

Number of copies sold by the trade sector (million)

Country	Value
U.S.	2,483.0
Japan	571.3
U.K.	508.0
France	344.2
Turkey	184.9
Brazil	150.6
Italy **	87.5
Mexico **	36.0
Colombia **	21.0
Sweden	19.8
Norway	17.0
Finland	14.8
China, Hong Kong SAR	6.3
Slovenia	5.0
Saudi Arabia **	1.3
Austria	0.5
Uzbekistan	0.5

Note: Caution should be exercised when interpreting the data shown here due to data being incomplete and partial. The share of the total publishing industry represented by national publishers' associations (NPA) varies between countries. There are also methodological differences which mean that it is difficult to make comparisons between countries. For all reported countries, the data source is the NPA, except for Canada (Statistics Canada) and Japan (Japan Copyright Office).

** indicates 2017 data.

Source: WIPO Statistics Database, September 2019.

F10. Share of children's books in the number of copies sold by the trade sector, 2018

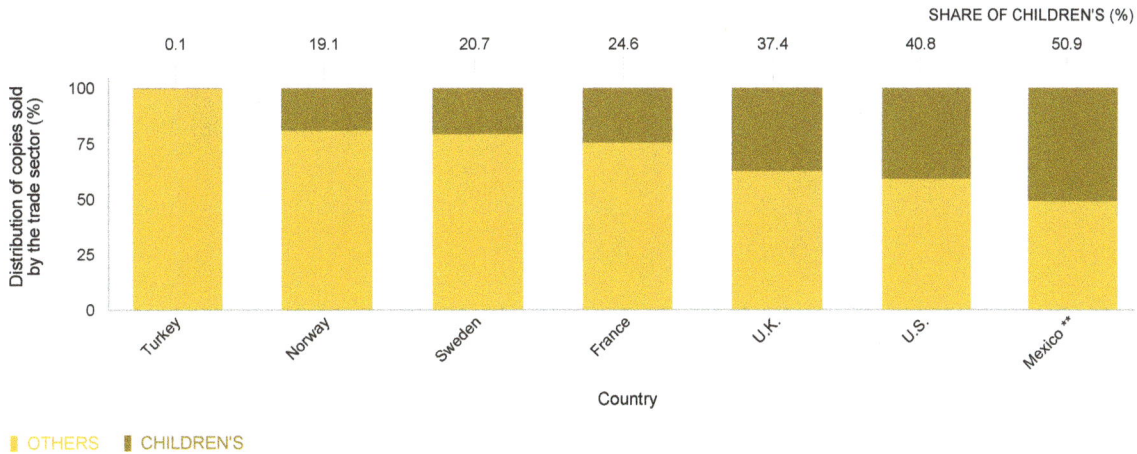

SHARE OF CHILDREN'S (%)

Country	Share
Turkey	0.1
Norway	19.1
Sweden	20.7
France	24.6
U.K.	37.4
U.S.	40.8
Mexico **	50.9

OTHERS CHILDREN'S

Note: Caution should be exercised when interpreting the data shown here due to data being incomplete and partial. The share of the total publishing industry represented by national publishers' associations (NPA) varies between countries. There are also methodological differences which mean that it is difficult to make comparisons between countries. For all reported countries, the data source is the NPA, except for Canada (Statistics Canada) and Japan (Japan Copyright Office).

** indicates 2017 data.

Source: WIPO Statistics Database, September 2019.

Creative economy

197

F11. Distribution of copies sold by sales channel for the trade sector, 2018

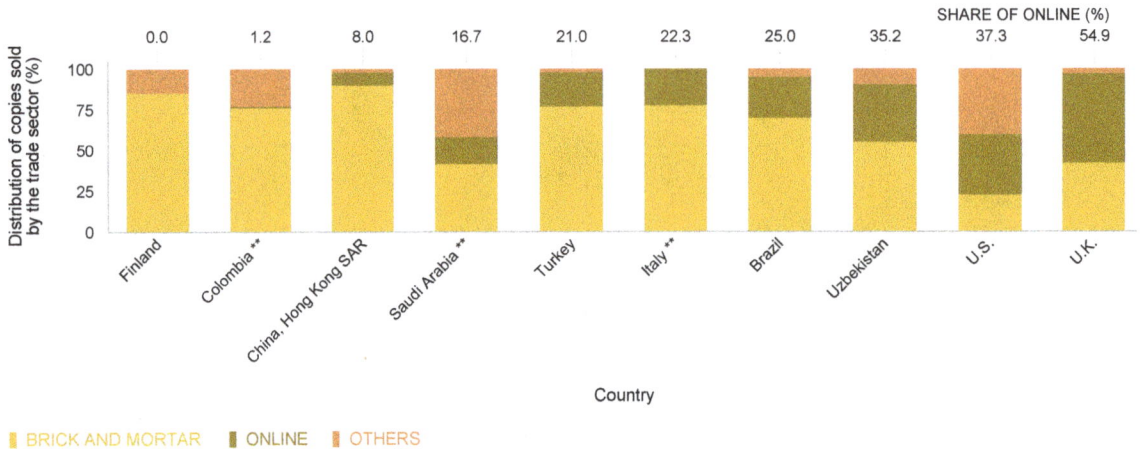

SHARE OF ONLINE (%)

| | 0.0 | 1.2 | 8.0 | 16.7 | 21.0 | 22.3 | 25.0 | 35.2 | 37.3 | 54.9 |

Distribution of copies sold by the trade sector (%)

Countries: Finland, Colombia **, China, Hong Kong SAR, Saudi Arabia **, Turkey, Italy **, Brazil, Uzbekistan, U.S., U.K.

Country

■ BRICK AND MORTAR   ■ ONLINE   ■ OTHERS

Note: Caution should be exercised when interpreting the data shown here due to data being incomplete and partial. The share of the total publishing industry represented by national publishers' associations (NPA) varies between countries. There are also methodological differences which mean that it is difficult to make comparisons between countries. For all reported countries, the data source is the NPA, except for Canada (Statistics Canada) and Japan (Japan Copyright Office).

** indicates 2017 data.

Source: WIPO Statistics Database, September 2019.

F12. Distribution of copies sold by format in the trade sector, 2018

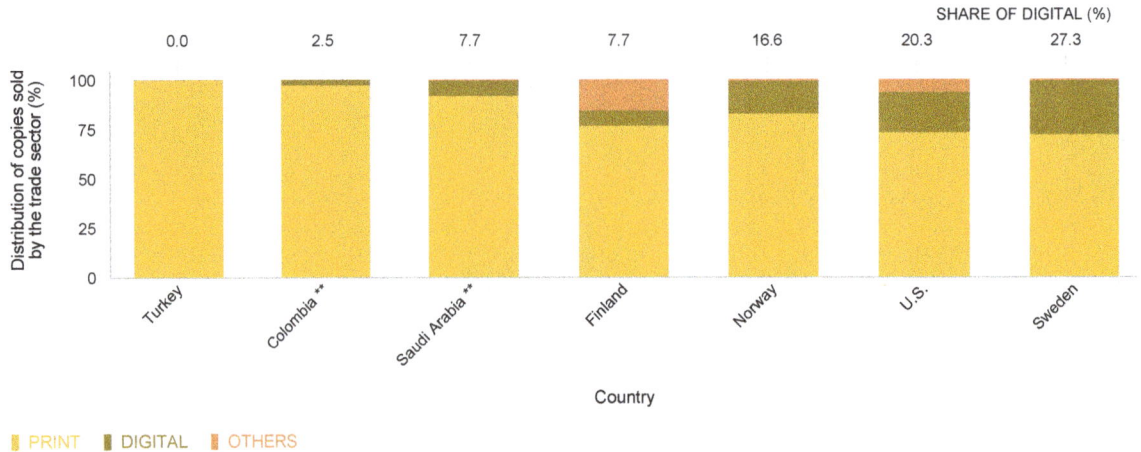

SHARE OF DIGITAL (%)

| | 0.0 | 2.5 | 7.7 | 7.7 | 16.6 | 20.3 | 27.3 |

Distribution of copies sold by the trade sector (%)

Countries: Turkey, Colombia **, Saudi Arabia **, Finland, Norway, U.S., Sweden

Country

■ PRINT   ■ DIGITAL   ■ OTHERS

Note: Caution should be exercised when interpreting the data shown here due to data being incomplete and partial. The share of the total publishing industry represented by national publishers' associations (NPA) varies between countries. There are also methodological differences which mean that it is difficult to make comparisons between countries. For all reported countries, the data source is the NPA, except for Canada (Statistics Canada) and Japan (Japan Copyright Office).

** indicates 2017 data.

Source: WIPO Statistics Database, September 2019.

Creative economy

F13. Distribution of copies sold by destination in the trade sector, 2018

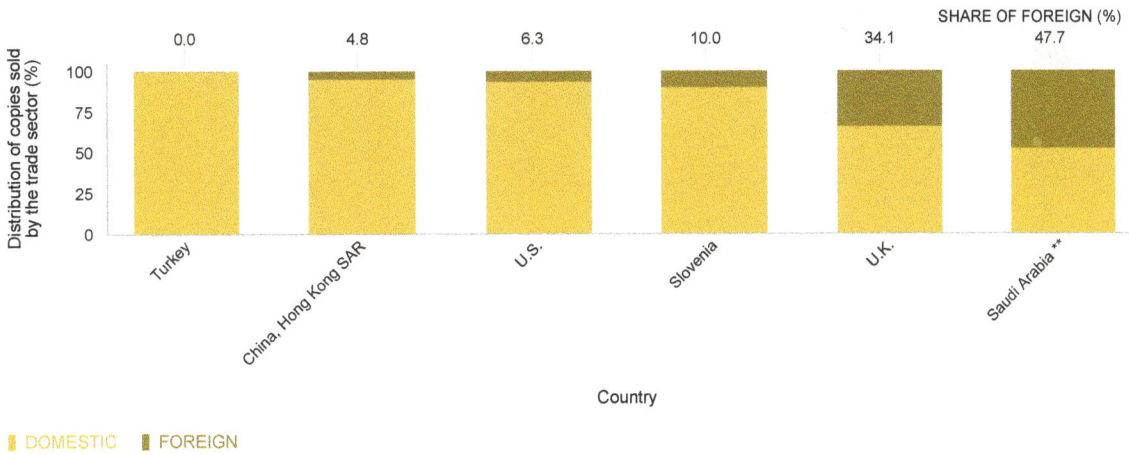

SHARE OF FOREIGN (%)

| | 0.0 | 4.8 | 6.3 | 10.0 | 34.1 | 47.7 |

Distribution of copies sold by the trade sector (%)

Turkey · China, Hong Kong SAR · U.S. · Slovenia · U.K. · Saudi Arabia **

Country

DOMESTIC   FOREIGN

Note: Caution should be exercised when interpreting the data shown here due to data being incomplete and partial. The share of the total publishing industry represented by national publishers' associations (NPA) varies between countries. There are also methodological differences which mean that it is difficult to make comparisons between countries. For all reported countries, the data source is the NPA, except for Canada (Statistics Canada) and Japan (Japan Copyright Office).

** indicates 2017 data.

Source: WIPO Statistics Database, September 2019.

Creative economy

Educational sector

F14. Educational sector revenue (USD million), 2018

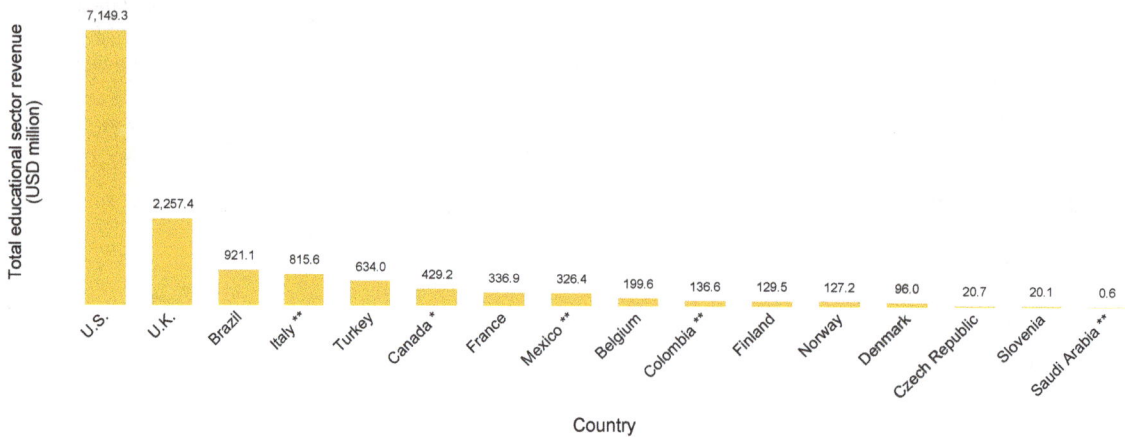

Note: Caution should be exercised when interpreting the data shown here due to data being incomplete and partial. The share of the total publishing industry represented by national publishers' associations (NPA) varies between countries. There are also methodological differences which mean that it is difficult to make comparisons between countries. For all reported countries, the data source is the NPA, except for Canada (Statistics Canada) and Japan (Japan Copyright Office).

* indicates 2016 data.

** indicates 2017 data.

Source: WIPO Statistics Database, September 2019.

F15. Distribution of educational sector revenue by format, 2018

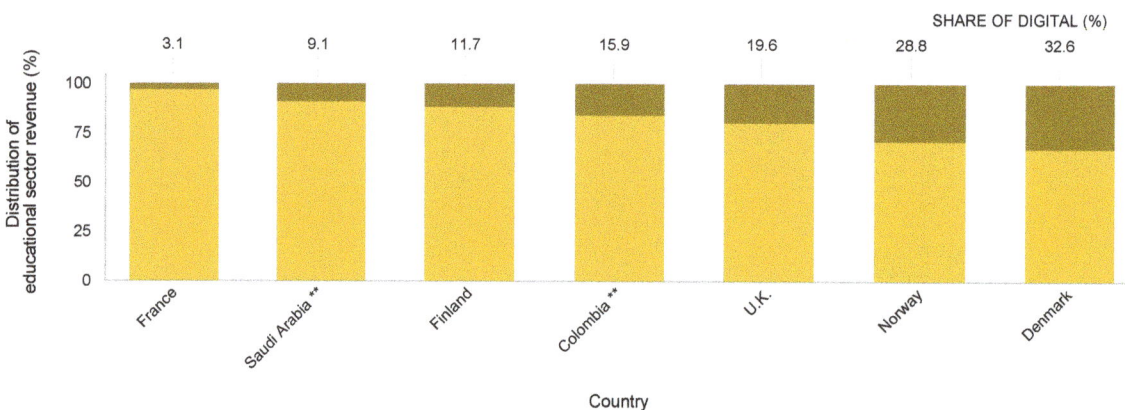

PRINT   DIGITAL

Note: Caution should be exercised when interpreting the data shown here due to data being incomplete and partial. The share of the total publishing industry represented by national publishers' associations (NPA) varies between countries. There are also methodological differences which mean that it is difficult to make comparisons between countries. For all reported countries, the data source is the NPA, except for Canada (Statistics Canada) and Japan (Japan Copyright Office).

** indicates 2017 data.

Source: WIPO Statistics Database, September 2019.

Creative economy

F16. Distribution of educational sector revenue by destination, 2018

SHARE OF FOREIGN (%)

	0.1	0.9	1.6	1.8	5.6	20.0	24.9	55.9

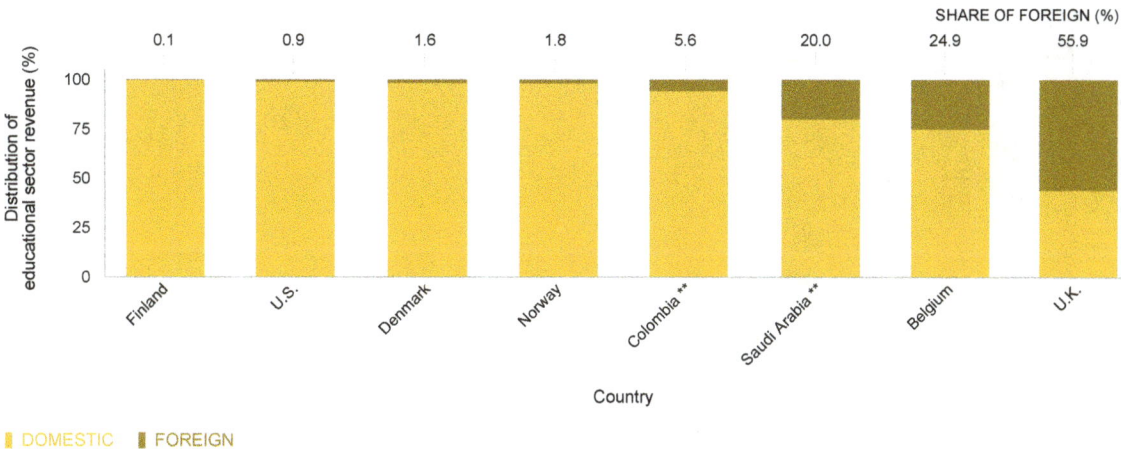

Distribution of educational sector revenue (%)

Finland U.S. Denmark Norway Colombia ** Saudi Arabia ** Belgium U.K.

Country

DOMESTIC   FOREIGN

Note: Caution should be exercised when interpreting the data shown here due to data being incomplete and partial. The share of the total publishing industry represented by national publishers' associations (NPA) varies between countries. There are also methodological differences which mean that it is difficult to make comparisons between countries. For all reported countries, the data source is the NPA, except for Canada (Statistics Canada) and Japan (Japan Copyright Office).

** indicates 2017 data.

Source: WIPO Statistics Database, September 2019.

F17. Distribution of educational sector revenue by sales channel, 2018

SHARE OF ONLINE (%)

	0.0	7.9	16.0	16.2

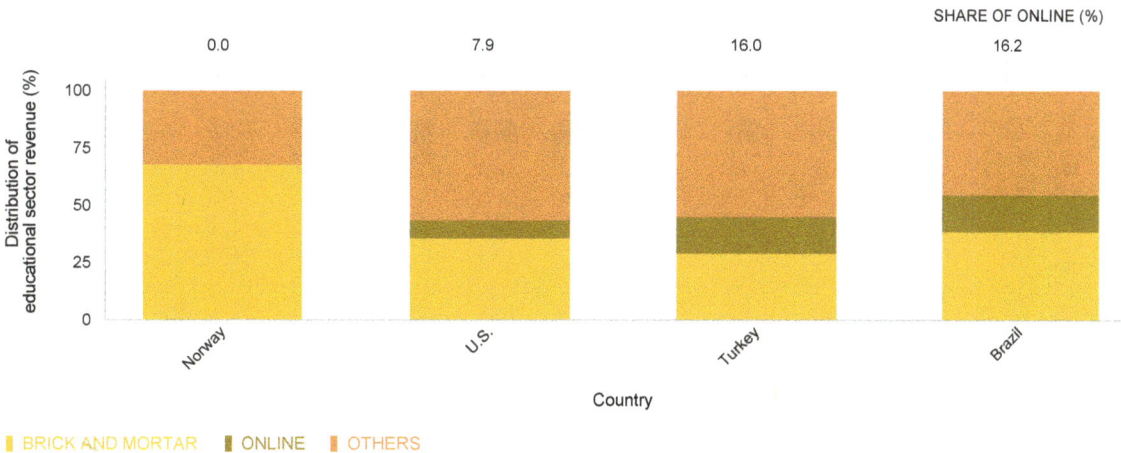

Distribution of educational sector revenue (%)

Norway U.S. Turkey Brazil

Country

BRICK AND MORTAR   ONLINE   OTHERS

Note: Caution should be exercised when interpreting the data shown here due to data being incomplete and partial. The share of the total publishing industry represented by national publishers' associations (NPA) varies between countries. There are also methodological differences which mean that it is difficult to make comparisons between countries. For all reported countries, the data source is the NPA, except for Canada (Statistics Canada) and Japan (Japan Copyright Office).

Source: WIPO Statistics Database, September 2019.

Creative economy

F18. Number of titles published by the educational sector, 2018

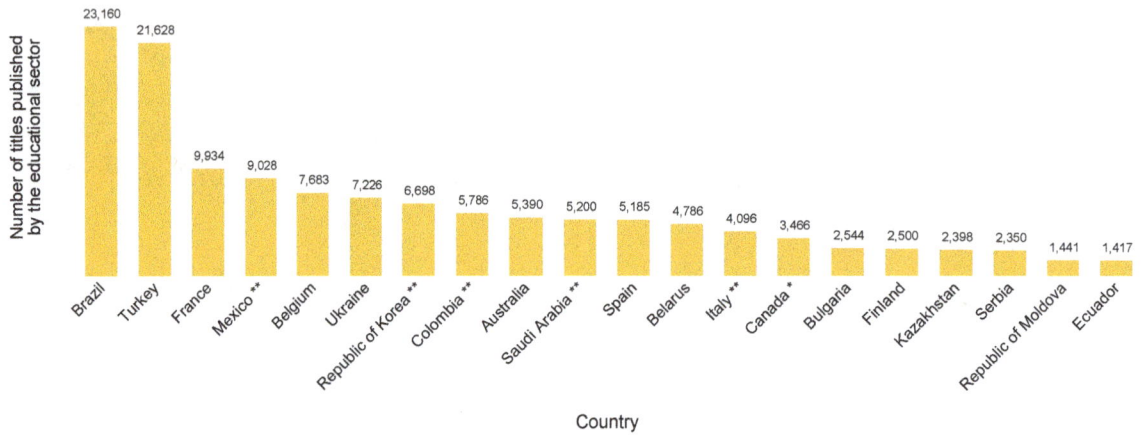

Number of titles published by the educational sector

Country	Value
Brazil	23,160
Turkey	21,628
France	9,934
Mexico **	9,028
Belgium	7,683
Ukraine	7,226
Republic of Korea **	6,698
Colombia **	5,786
Australia	5,390
Saudi Arabia **	5,200
Spain	5,185
Belarus	4,786
Italy **	4,096
Canada *	3,466
Bulgaria	2,544
Finland	2,500
Kazakhstan	2,398
Serbia	2,350
Republic of Moldova	1,441
Ecuador	1,417

Country

Note: Caution should be exercised when interpreting the data shown here due to data being incomplete and partial. The share of the total publishing industry represented by national publishers' associations (NPA) varies between countries. There are also methodological differences which mean that it is difficult to make comparisons between countries. For all reported countries, the data source is the NPA, except for Canada (Statistics Canada) and Japan (Japan Copyright Office).

* indicates 2016 data.

** indicates 2017 data.

Source: WIPO Statistics Database, September 2019.

F19. Distribution of titles published by the educational sector by format, 2018

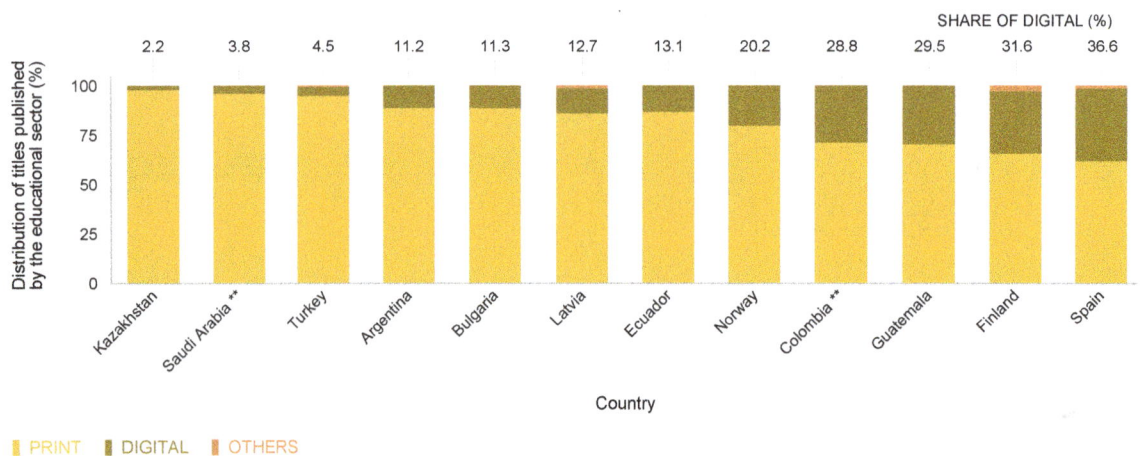

SHARE OF DIGITAL (%)

Country	Share
Kazakhstan	2.2
Saudi Arabia **	3.8
Turkey	4.5
Argentina	11.2
Bulgaria	11.3
Latvia	12.7
Ecuador	13.1
Norway	20.2
Colombia **	28.8
Guatemala	29.5
Finland	31.6
Spain	36.6

Distribution of titles published by the educational sector (%)

Country

▌ PRINT ▌ DIGITAL ▌ OTHERS

Note: Caution should be exercised when interpreting the data shown here due to data being incomplete and partial. The share of the total publishing industry represented by national publishers' associations (NPA) varies between countries. There are also methodological differences which mean that it is difficult to make comparisons between countries. For all reported countries, the data source is the NPA, except for Canada (Statistics Canada) and Japan (Japan Copyright Office).

** indicates 2017 data.

Source: WIPO Statistics Database, September 2019.

Creative economy

F20. Number of copies sold by the educational sector, 2018

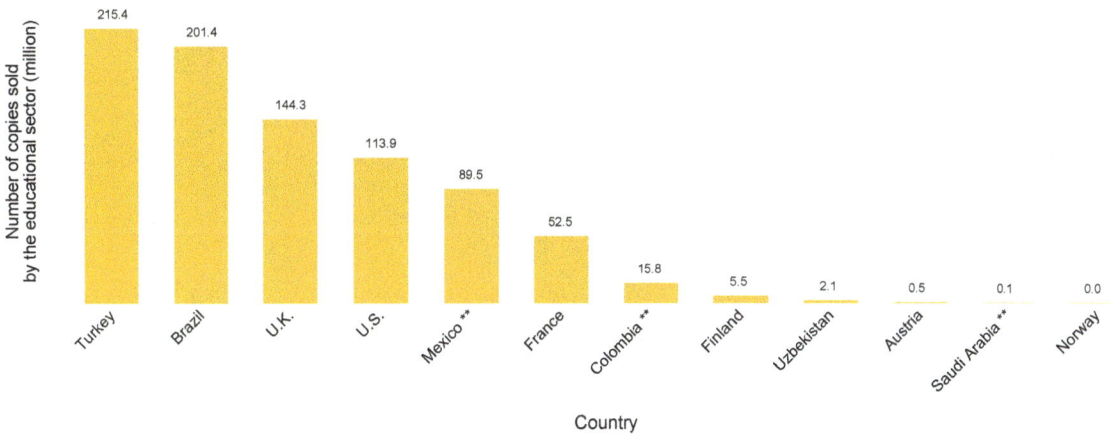

Number of copies sold by the educational sector (million)

Country	Value
Turkey	215.4
Brazil	201.4
U.K.	144.3
U.S.	113.9
Mexico **	89.5
France	52.5
Colombia **	15.8
Finland	5.5
Uzbekistan	2.1
Austria	0.5
Saudi Arabia **	0.1
Norway	0.0

Country

Note: Caution should be exercised when interpreting the data shown here due to data being incomplete and partial. The share of the total publishing industry represented by national publishers' associations (NPA) varies between countries. There are also methodological differences which mean that it is difficult to make comparisons between countries. For all reported countries, the data source is the NPA, except for Canada (Statistics Canada) and Japan (Japan Copyright Office).

** indicates 2017 data.

Source: WIPO Statistics Database, September 2019.

F21. Distribution of copies sold by sales channel for the educational sector, 2018

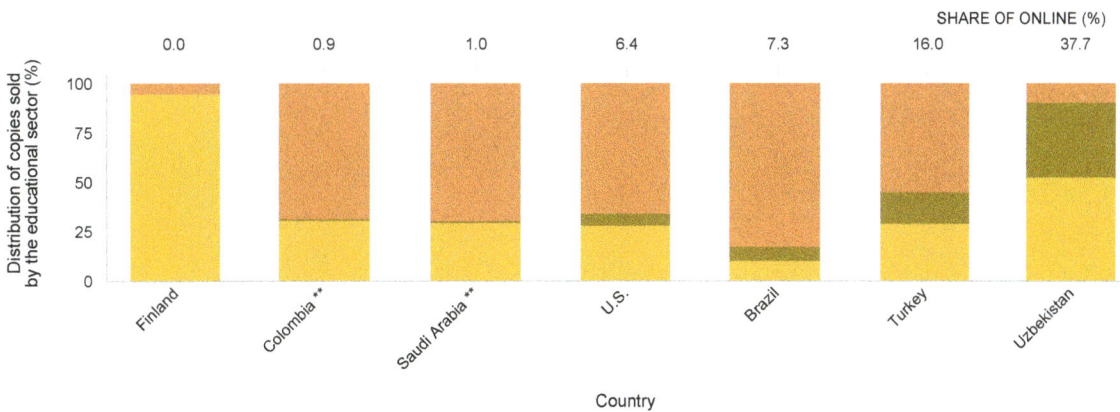

Distribution of copies sold by the educational sector (%)

SHARE OF ONLINE (%)

Country	Share
Finland	0.0
Colombia **	0.9
Saudi Arabia **	1.0
U.S.	6.4
Brazil	7.3
Turkey	16.0
Uzbekistan	37.7

Country

▌ BRICK AND MORTAR   ▌ ONLINE   ▌ OTHERS

Note: Caution should be exercised when interpreting the data shown here due to data being incomplete and partial. The share of the total publishing industry represented by national publishers' associations (NPA) varies between countries. There are also methodological differences which mean that it is difficult to make comparisons between countries. For all reported countries, the data source is the NPA, except for Canada (Statistics Canada) and Japan (Japan Copyright Office).

** indicates 2017 data.

Source: WIPO Statistics Database, September 2019.

Creative economy

Statistical tables

F22. Total net publishing industry revenue by sector (USD million), 2018

Country	Total	Trade	Educational
Azerbaijan	20.4	..	..
Belgium	727.8	528.2	199.6
Brazil	1,358.6	437.5	921.1
Canada (a)	1,035.7	606.4	429.2
China, Hong Kong SAR	..	64.3	..
Colombia (b)	228.3	91.8	136.6
Czech Republic	308.3	287.6	20.7
Denmark	271.8	175.9	96.0
Finland	298.3	168.8	129.5
France (c)	2,981.6	2,128.3	336.9
Germany	6,066.6	..	..
Iceland	28.0	..	..
Italy (b)	2,406.2	1,590.6	815.6
Japan	..	8,446.6	..
Mexico (b)	455.2	128.8	326.4
Nicaragua	..	..	..
Norway	310.1	182.9	127.2
Panama	..	..	..
Saudi Arabia (b)	16.8	16.2	0.6
Serbia	..	..	..
Slovenia	99.8	79.7	20.1
Sweden	..	214.4	..
Thailand (b)	..	704.2	..
Turkey	1,255.0	621.0	634.0
U.K.	5,438.1	3,180.7	2,257.4
U.S.	23,338.4	16,189.0	7,149.3

Note: Caution should be exercised when interpreting the data shown here due to data being incomplete and partial. The share of the total publishing industry represented by national publishers' associations (NPA) varies between countries. There are also methodological differences which mean that it is difficult to make comparisons between countries. For all reported countries, the data source is the NPA, except for Canada (Statistics Canada) and Japan (Japan Copyright Office). For Italy, the revenue is at market value at retail prices.

(a) indicates 2016 data.

(b) indicates 2017 data.

(c) data includes additional sectors beyond the trade sector and educational sector.

.. indicates not available.

Source: WIPO Statistics Database, September 2019.

F23. Total number of titles published by sector, 2018

Country	Total	Trade	Educational
Argentina	9,931	8,540	1,391
Australia (c)	13,296	6,441	5,390
Austria	8,466	7,500	966
Belarus	9,665	4,879	4,786
Belgium	22,444	14,761	7,683
Bolivia (Plurinational State of)	1,578	..	..
Brazil	46,829	23,669	23,160
Bulgaria	12,606	10,062	2,544
Canada (a)	12,651	9,185	3,466
Chile	8,152	..	..
China, Hong Kong SAR	..	5,510	..
Colombia (b)	13,913	8,127	5,786
Costa Rica	2,158	..	..
Cuba	992	..	..
Czech Republic	16,422	15,566	856
Denmark	11,975	..	..
Dominican Republic	1,866	..	..
Ecuador	5,253	3,836	1,417

Country	Total	Trade	Educational
El Salvador	661	..	..
Estonia	5,420	5,297	123
Finland	9,368	6,868	2,500
France (c)	106,799	77,221	9,934
Germany	79,916	..	..
Guatemala	1,042	723	319
Honduras	102	79	23
Iceland	1,726	..	..
Italy (b)	134,338	130,242	4,096
Japan	..	71,661	..
Kazakhstan	6,515	4,117	2,398
Kyrgyzstan	1,455	1,029	426
Latvia (c)	2,910	2,400	79
Lebanon	4,585	..	..
Lithuania	3,075	2,713	362
Mexico (b)	18,577	9,549	9,028
Nicaragua	27	..	..
Norway	6,724	5,971	753
Panama	940	..	..
Paraguay	1,007	..	..
Peru	7,111	..	..
Portugal (b)	..	21,880	..
Republic of Korea (b, c)	85,991	59,724	6,698
Republic of Moldova	3,941	2,500	1,441
Russian Federation	116,915	..	..
Saudi Arabia (b)	30,400	25,200	5,200
Serbia	11,888	9,538	2,350
Slovenia	4,898	4,301	597
Spain	86,413	81,228	5,185
Sweden	..	7,452	..
Thailand (b)	..	6,750	..
Turkey	78,619	56,991	21,628
U.K.	188,000	..	..
Ukraine	22,612	15,386	7,226
Uruguay	3,231	..	..
Venezuela (Bolivarian Republic of)	2,275	..	..

Note: Caution should be exercised when interpreting the data shown here due to data being incomplete and partial. The share of the total publishing industry represented by national publishers' associations (NPA) varies between countries. There are also methodological differences which mean that it is difficult to make comparisons between countries. For all reported countries, the data source is the NPA, except for Canada (Statistics Canada) and Japan (Japan Copyright Office).

(a) indicates 2016 data.

(b) indicates 2017 data.

(c) data includes additional sectors beyond the trade sector and educational sector.

.. indicates not available.

Source: WIPO Statistics Database, September 2019.

Creative economy

F24. Total number of copies sold by sector (million), 2018

Country	Total	Trade	Educational
Austria	1.0	0.5	0.5
Brazil	352.0	150.6	201.4
China, Hong Kong SAR	..	6.3	..
Colombia (a)	36.8	21.0	15.8
Finland	20.3	14.8	5.5
France (b)	419.2	344.2	52.5
Iceland	1.3	..	..
Italy (a)	..	87.5	..
Japan	..	571.3	..
Mexico (a)	125.5	36.0	89.5
Norway	17.0	17.0	0.0
Saudi Arabia (a)	1.4	1.3	0.1
Slovenia	..	5.0	..
Sweden	..	19.8	..
Turkey	400.3	184.9	215.4
U.K.	652.3	508.0	144.3
U.S.	2,597.0	2,483.0	113.9
Uzbekistan	2.6	0.5	2.1

Note: Caution should be exercised when interpreting the data shown here due to data being incomplete and partial. The share of the total publishing industry represented by national publishers' associations (NPA) varies between countries. There are also methodological differences which mean that it is difficult to make comparisons between countries. For all reported countries, the data source is the NPA, except for Canada (Statistics Canada) and Japan (Japan Copyright Office).

(a) indicates 2017 data.

(b) data includes additional sectors beyond the trade sector and educational sector.

.. indicates not available.

Source: WIPO Statistics Database, September 2019.

Legal deposits

F25. Total number of books deposited in a recognized repository, 2018

Country	Repository	Total number of deposits	Share of total (%)		
			Print	Digital	Other formats
Belgium (c)	Royal Library of Belgium	18,541	88.0	12.0	..
Belize	Belize National Library Service and Information System	42	..	..	..
Brazil	National Library of Brazil (Fundação Biblioteca Nacional)	21,668	..	..	..
Canada (a)	Library and Archives Canada	14,716	..	..	..
Chile	Biblioteca Nacional de Chile	7,025	..	..	..
China, Hong Kong SAR	Leisure and Cultural Services Department	12,880	..	..	..
Colombia	Dirección Nacional de Derecho de Autor, Biblioteca Nacional de Colombia	25,019	40.9	59.1	...
Costa Rica	Sistema Nacional de Bibliotecas	2,158	62.7	37.3	...
Croatia (d)	Croatian National Bibliography	7,875	86.9	0.0	13.1
Cuba	Biblioteca Nacional de Cuba José Martí	1,679	96.1	3.9	...
Cyprus	The Cyprus Library	30	..	..	
Czech Republic	National Library of the Czech Republic	16,676	..	..	
Estonia	National Library of Estonia	4,785	69.2	30.8	...
Finland	National Library of Finland	25,418	40.8	59.0	0.2
France	Bibliothèque nationale de France	82,313	..	..	..
Ghana	George Padmore Research Library on African Affairs	1,411	99.9	0.1	...
Greece	National Library of Greece	16,467	98.1	1.7	0.1
Hungary	National Széchényi Library	17,250	..	..	..
Ireland	National Library of Ireland	1,602	..	..	..
Italy	National Library in Rome	60,058	..	..	..
Kenya (a)	Kenya National Library	2,105	..	..	..
Lithuania	Martynas Mažvydas National Library of Lithuania	4,838	..	..	..
Maldives	National Library	62	..	..	..
Malta	Malta Libraries, National Bibliographic Office	510	..	..	..
Mauritius	National Library of Mauritius	2,268	..	..	..
Nepal (b)	Nepal National Library	3,612	..	..	..
New Zealand (a)	National Library of New Zealand	12,158	66.5	33.4	0.1
Panama	Biblioteca Nacional "Ernesto J. Castillero R."	491	..	..	..
Poland	National Library of Poland	55,964	64.9	35.1	...
Portugal	Biblioteca Nacional de Portugal	17,315	..	..	..
Republic of Korea	National Library of Korea	90,620	76.0	24.0	..
Serbia	Intellectual Property Office	11,628	99.3	0.7	..
Slovakia	Slovak National Library	6,043	..	..	
Slovenia	National and University Library	7,375	90.2	9.8	..
Spain	Biblioteca Nacional de España	67,884	..	..	..
Sweden	National Library of Sweden	20,140	..	..	..
Thailand	National Library of Thailand	9,153	91.4	8.6	..
Turkey	National Library of Turkey	71,074	..	..	..
U.K. (a)	The British Library	210,628	38.2	61.8	..
Viet Nam	National Library of Viet Nam	22,720	99.8	0.2	..

(a) data reported for the national fiscal year 2017/2018.

(b) voluntary deposit system where the majority of publishers make deposits.

(c) digital deposits are collected on a voluntary basis.

(d) other category includes e-books in other formats.

.. indicates not available.

Source: WIPO Statistics Database, September 2019.

Creative economy

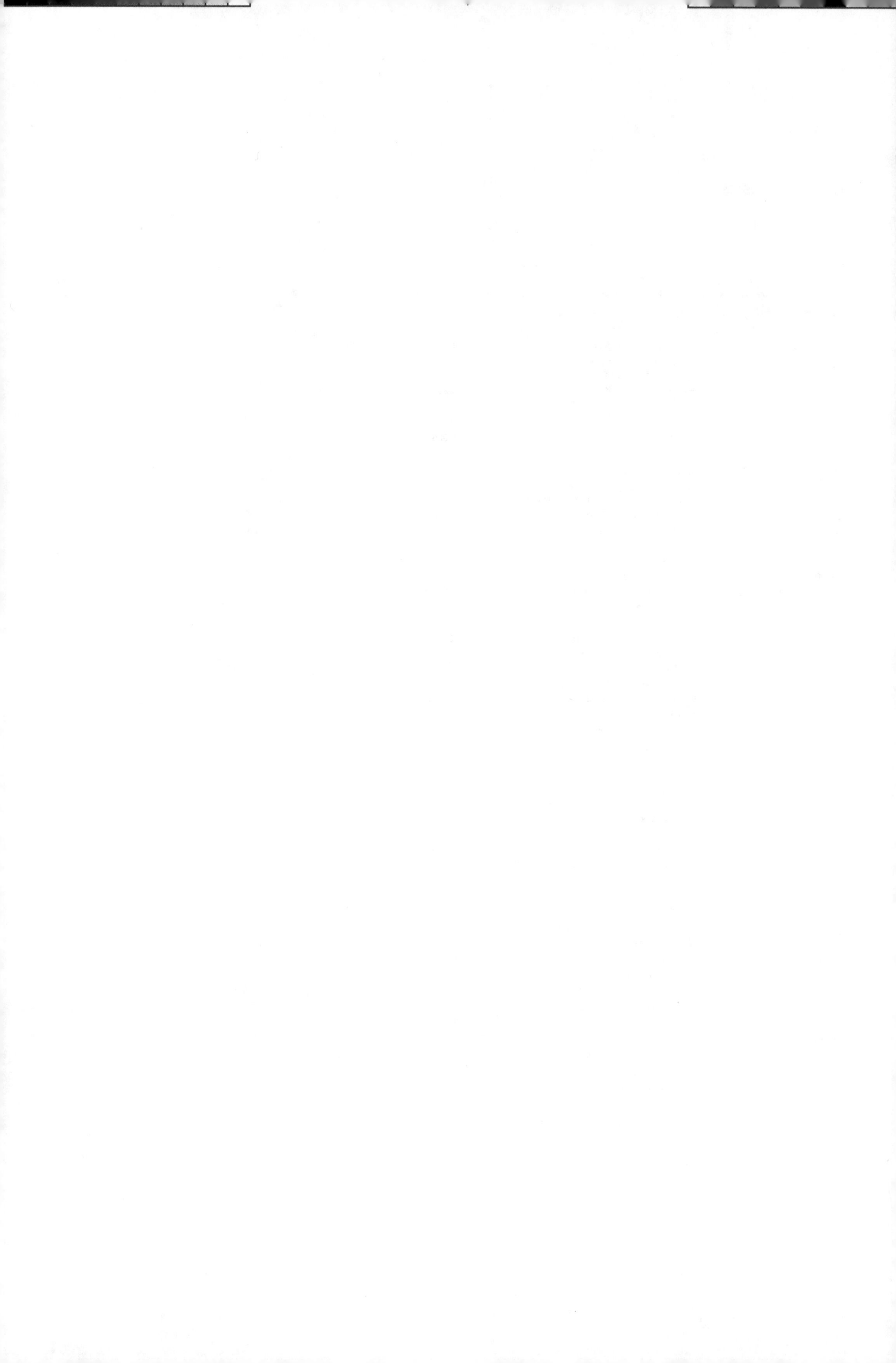

Additional information

Data description

Data sources

Intellectual property (IP) data are taken from the WIPO Statistics Database and based primarily on WIPO's annual IP statistics surveys (see below) and on data compiled by WIPO in processing international applications/registrations through the Patent Cooperation Treaty (PCT) and the Madrid and Hague Systems.

Data are available from WIPO's Statistics Data Center at *www.wipo.int/ipstats*.

Patent family and technology data are extracted from the WIPO Statistics Database and from the 2019 spring edition of the European Patent Office's PATSTAT database.

Gross domestic product and population data are from the World Bank's World Development Indicators database.

This report uses the World Bank's income classifications. Economies are classified according to 2018 gross national income per capita, calculated using the World Bank Atlas method. These classifications are low-income (USD 1,025 or less), lower middle-income (USD 1,026 to USD 3,995), upper middle-income (USD 3,996 to USD 12,375) and high-income (over USD 12,375).

This report uses United Nations (UN) definitions of regions and sub-regions, whereas the geographical terms used may differ slightly from those defined by the UN.

WIPO's annual IP statistics surveys

WIPO collects data from national/regional IP offices, other competent authorities and publishers' associations from around the world through annual surveys consisting of multiple questionnaires. These data are then entered into the WIPO Statistics Database. Where possible, data published on IP offices' websites or in their annual reports are used to supplement the questionnaire responses in cases where IP offices/countries do not provide statistics. Continuous efforts are being made to improve the quality and availability of IP statistics and to gather data from as many IP offices and countries as possible.

WIPO's long-established and regular IP survey covers patents, utility models, trademarks, industrial designs and plant varieties. It consists of 28 questionnaires, all of which are available in English, French and Spanish at *www.wipo.int/ipstats/en/data_collection/questionnaire*.

The geographical indications (GI) questionnaire seeks to collect data on GIs in force through a simple questionnaire. In 2017, for the first time, WIPO published statistics on GIs in force covering data for 54 jurisdictions. The 2018 edition of this report included GIs in force data covering 82 authorities. This 2019 edition reports data for 92 authorities – a considerable improvement upon the 54 responses that WIPO received only two years ago.

In 2017, in collaboration with the International Publishers Association (IPA), WIPO launched a new survey of the global publishing industry. This survey covers trade publishing and educational publishing only. Its scope is limited to published materials (i.e., books, monographs, etc.) that have been issued with an International Standard Book Number (ISBN), a Digital Object Identifier (DOI) or any other national/international book identifier (e.g., ASIN, etc.). Last year's edition reported data for the 28 associations/authorities that shared their 2017 data with the IPA and WIPO. This edition includes publishing industry data for the 49 associations/authorities who shared their 2018 data. Although the data coverage has improved this year, further efforts will be made over the coming years to enhance the quality and coverage of publishing industry data.

To validate the data collected through the global publishing survey, WIPO has started to collect data on legal deposit. Legal deposit is a statutory obligation at the national level requiring publishers to deposit a certain number of copies of their published documents at a repository, that is, a recognized place of legal deposit. WIPO conducted a pilot survey among national legal repositories. Over 40 countries participated in this survey. The data presented in this report does not cover all the countries that participated, but is available for 39. Two countries, namely Switzerland and the Netherlands, reported that they had no legal deposit system in place. In Nepal, there is a "voluntary" deposit system, with a majority of publications deposited at the Nepal National Library.

IP office survey coverage

IP offices are requested to report data by the origin (country or territory) of applications, grants or registrations. However, some offices are unable to provide a detailed breakdown. Instead, these offices report either an aggregate total or a simple breakdown by total resident and total non-resident counts. For this reason, the totals for each origin are underreported. However, the unknown origin shares of the 2018 totals are low – only 0.5% for patent applications, 1.1% for trademark application class counts and 0.4% for application design counts.

IP applications data coverage by IP type

IP type	Number of offices on which 2018 world totals are based	Number of offices for which 2018 data are available	Data coverage (%)
Patents	160	130	99.9
Utility models	75	72	100.0
Trademarks (a)	166	127	98.9
Industrial designs (b)	148	137	99.7
Plant varieties	70	58	99.1

(a) Refers to the number of trademark applications based on class count (that is, the number of classes specified in applications).

(b) Refers to the number of industrial design applications based on design count (that is, the number of designs contained in applications).

Estimating world totals

World totals for applications for, and grants/registrations of, patents, utility models, trademarks, industrial designs and plant varieties are WIPO estimates. Data are not available for all IP offices for every year. Missing data are estimated using methods such as linear extrapolation and averaging adjacent data points. The estimation method used depends on the year and office in question. When an office provides data which are not broken down by origin, WIPO estimates the resident and non-resident counts using the historical shares of that office. Data are available for most of the larger offices; only small shares of world totals are estimated. For example, the estimate of the total number of patent applications worldwide covers 160 offices; data are available for 130 of them, which together account for 99.9% of the estimated world total.

National and international data

Application and grant/registration data include data on both direct filings and filings made through WIPO-administered international systems (where applicable). For patents and utility models, data include direct filings at national patent offices, as well as PCT national phase entries. For trademarks, data include filings at national and regional offices and designations received by relevant offices through the Madrid System. For industrial designs, data include national and regional applications combined with designations received by relevant offices through the Hague System.

International comparability of indicators

Every effort has been made to compile IP statistics based on the same definitions and to facilitate international comparability. Although data are collected from offices using questionnaires from WIPO's harmonized annual IP survey, national laws and regulations for filing IP applications or for issuing IP rights, as well as statistical reporting practices, may vary between jurisdictions. Due to the continual updating of data and the revision of historical statistics, data in this report may differ from data in previous editions and from data available on WIPO's website.

Change in method of counting IP applications by CNIPA in 2017

Due to a change in the method by which the National Intellectual Property Administration of the People's Republic of China (CNIPA) calculates the number of patent, utility model and industrial design applications filed, data on the number of such applications filed in China in 2017 and 2018 are not comparable with data for previous years. Prior to 2017, these data included all applications received; from 2017 onwards, however, they include only those applications for which the office has received the necessary application fees. As a result, it is not meaningful to report growth rates in the number of patent, utility model and industrial design applications filed in China in 2017 compared to 2016. Moreover, since China represents such a large share of IP applications globally, it is not meaningful to report growth rates in the number of such applications filed worldwide in 2017 compared to 2016. For the reason of this break in the data series, figure A1 (page 24), figure A53 (page 56), figure C1 (page 135) and figure C2 (page 135) do not report 2017 growth.

IP systems at a glance

The patent system

A patent is a set of exclusive rights granted by law to applicants for an invention that meets the standards of novelty, non-obviousness and industrial applicability. It is valid for a limited period (generally 20 years), during which time the patent holder can commercially exploit the invention on an exclusive basis. In return, applicants are obliged to disclose their inventions to the public, so that others skilled in the art may replicate them. The patent system is designed to encourage innovation by providing innovators with time-limited exclusive legal rights, thus enabling them to appropriate the returns from their innovative activity.

The procedures for acquiring patent rights are governed by the rules and regulations of national and regional patent offices. These offices are responsible for issuing patents and the rights are limited to the jurisdiction of the issuing authority. To obtain patent rights, applicants must file an application describing the invention with a national or regional office.

Applicants can also file an international application through the Patent Cooperation Treaty (PCT) System, an international treaty administered by WIPO that facilitates the acquisition of patent rights in multiple jurisdictions. The PCT System simplifies the process of multiple national patent filings by delaying the requirement to file a separate application in each jurisdiction in which protection is sought. However, the decision on whether to grant a patent remains the prerogative of national or regional patent offices and patent rights are limited to the jurisdiction of each patent-granting authority.

The PCT application process begins with the international phase, during which an international search and optional preliminary examination and supplementary international search are performed. It concludes with the national phase, during which national (or regional) patent offices decide on the patentability of an invention according to national law. Further information about the PCT System is available at *www.wipo.int/pct*.

The utility model system

Like a patent, a utility model (UM) confers a set of rights to an invention for a limited period, during which

the UM rights holder can commercially exploit their invention on an exclusive basis. The terms and conditions for granting a UM differ from those for granting a traditional patent. For example, UMs are issued for a shorter period (6–10 years) and at most offices protection is granted without substantive examination. As with patents, procedures for granting UM rights are governed by the rules and regulations of national intellectual property (IP) offices and rights are limited to the jurisdiction of the issuing authority.

Approximately 75 countries provide protection for UMs. In this report, the term "utility model" refers to UMs and other types of protection similar to UMs, such as innovation patents in Australia and short-term patents in Ireland.

Microorganisms under the Budapest Treaty

The Budapest Treaty on the International Recognition of the Deposit of Microorganisms for the Purposes of Patent Procedure plays an important role in relation to biotechnological inventions. Disclosing an invention is a generally recognized requirement for receiving a patent. When an invention involves microorganisms, national laws in most countries require the applicant to deposit a sample at a designated International Depositary Authority (IDA).

To eliminate the need to deposit a microorganism in every country in which patent protection is sought, the Budapest Treaty provides that depositing a microorganism with any IDA will suffice for the purposes of patent procedures at the national patent offices of all contracting states and at regional patent offices that recognize the Treaty. An IDA is a scientific institution – typically a "culture collection" – capable of storing microorganisms. Currently, there are 47 IDAs around the world. Further information about the Budapest Treaty is available at *www.wipo.int/treaties/en/registration/budapest*.

The trademark system

A trademark is a distinctive sign that identifies certain goods or services as those produced or provided by a specific person or enterprise. Trademarks can be registered for both goods and services. In the latter case, the term "service mark" is sometimes used. For simplicity, this report uses "trademark" regardless of whether the registration concerns goods or services. The holder of a registered trademark has the exclusive right to use the mark in relation to the goods or services for which it is registered and can block unauthorized use of the trademark, or a confusingly similar mark, to prevent consumers from being misled. Unlike patents, trademark registrations can be maintained indefinitely, provided that the trademark holder pays the required renewal fees.

The procedures for registering trademarks are governed by the rules and regulations of national and regional IP offices. Therefore, trademark rights are limited to the jurisdiction of the authority in which a trademark is registered. Trademark applicants can file an application with the relevant national or regional IP office or an international application through the Madrid System. However, when an applicant files internationally via the Madrid System, the decision to issue a trademark registration remains the prerogative of the national or regional IP office concerned and trademark rights remain limited to the jurisdiction of the authority issuing that registration.

Originally, two treaties administered by WIPO governed the Madrid System for the International Registration of Marks. These treaties are the Madrid Agreement Concerning the International Registration of Marks and the Protocol Relating to the Madrid Agreement, and are jointly referred to as the Madrid System. The Madrid Agreement was concluded in 1891 and the Madrid Protocol came into operation in 1996. With Algeria's accession to the Madrid Protocol in October 2015, the last remaining member to be a party only to the Madrid Agreement joined the Protocol, effectively making Madrid a one-treaty system. The Madrid System offers many advantages to both trademark holders and IP offices over the alternative method of obtaining international protection for marks called the Paris route or the "direct route". The Paris route involves filing separate applications in a number of countries or regions using rights established under the Paris Convention for the Protection of Industrial Property. In comparison, the Madrid System allows trademark holders to submit a single application in one language and pay a single set of fees in one currency.

The Madrid System also simplifies the subsequent management of the trademark, since it is possible to centrally request and record further changes or renew the registration through a single procedure. A registration recorded in the International Register yields the same effect as a registration made directly with each designated Contracting Party (Madrid member) if the competent authority of that jurisdiction has not issued a refusal within a specified time period. Further information about the Madrid System is available at *www.wipo.int/madrid*.

The industrial design system

Industrial designs are applied to a wide variety of industrial products and handicrafts.[1] They refer to the ornamental or aesthetic aspects of a useful article, including compositions of lines or colors or three-dimensional forms that give a special appearance to a product or handicraft. The holder of a registered industrial design has exclusive rights over the design and can prevent unauthorized copying or imitation of the design by others.

The procedures for registering industrial designs are governed by national or regional laws. An industrial design can be protected if it is new or original and rights are limited to the jurisdiction of the issuing authority. Registrations can be obtained by filing an application with a relevant national or regional IP office or by filing an international application through the Hague System. Once a design is registered, the term of protection is generally five years and may be renewed for additional five-year periods up to a total of 15 years in most cases. In some countries, industrial designs are protected through the delivery of a design patent rather than design registration.

The Hague System comprises two international treaties – the Hague Act and the Geneva Act. The System makes it possible for an applicant to register industrial designs in multiple countries by filing a single application with the International Bureau of WIPO, thus simplifying the multinational registration process. Moreover, by allowing the filing of up to 100 different designs per application, the System offers considerable opportunities for efficiency gains. It also streamlines the subsequent management of industrial design registration, since it is possible to record changes or renew a registration through a single procedure. Further information about the Hague System is available at at *www.wipo.int/hague*.

Plant variety protection

To obtain protection, a plant breeder must file an individual application with each authority entrusted with granting breeders' rights. A breeder's right is granted only when a variety is new, distinct, uniform and stable, and has a suitable denomination.

In the United States of America (U.S.), two legal frameworks protect new plant varieties: the Plant Patent Act (PPA) and the Plant Variety Protection Act (PVPA). Under the PPA, whoever invents or discovers and asexually reproduces any distinct and new variety of plant –

including cultivated sports, mutants, hybrids and newly found seedlings, other than a tuber-propagated plant (in practice, Irish potato and Jerusalem artichoke) or a plant found in an uncultivated state – may obtain a patent. Under the PVPA, the U.S. protects all sexually reproduced plant varieties and tuber-propagated plant varieties, excluding fungi and bacteria.

Protection of geographical indications

A geographical indication (GI) is a sign identifying a good as originating in a specific geographical area and possessing a given quality, reputation or other characteristic that is essentially attributable to that geographical origin. Thus, the main function of a GI is to indicate a connection between that quality, characteristic or reputation of the good and its territory of origin.

World-renowned examples of GIs include Café de Colombia (Colombia), Bordeaux (France), Kampot Pepper (Cambodia), Penja Pepper (Cameroon) and Scotch Whisky (U.K.).

GIs are mainly used for agricultural and food products, which typically tend to have a close natural link with their place of origin. There are, however, also many GIs for other kinds of products. The specific qualities of the product may derive from traditional manufacturing skills or from a combination of local know-how and natural resources. Examples of such GIs include Bohemia Crystal (Czech Republic), Solingen Cutlery (Germany), Isfahan Handmade Carpet (Islamic Republic of Iran), Swiss Watches (Switzerland) and Yangzhou Lacquerware (China).

Although GIs are commonly names of places, under many systems they may consist of non-geographical terms with a traditional geographical connotation; for example, Reblochon (France) and Argane (Morocco) serve as GIs, although neither are geographical names.

GIs can only be used by producers whose goods conform to the applicable requirements concerning the area of origin, processing method and typicity of the product. Production sites located outside the area of origin and goods that do not meet the applicable requirements are prevented from using the protected indication.

Appellations of origin

An appellation of origin is a special kind of geographical indication. It generally consists of a geographical name or a traditional denomination which serves to designate a product as originating therein, where the quality or characteristics of the product are due exclusively or essentially to the geographical environment, including natural and human factors, and which have given the good its reputation. The most important difference between appellations of origin and other GIs is that the link with the place of origin should be stronger in the case of an appellation of origin; in other words, appellations of origin are a more restrictive sub-category of GIs.

Protection of GIs

At the national and regional levels, GIs are protected through a variety of legal means. These include *sui generis* systems – laws specifically designed to protect geographical indications,[2] often based on a registration procedure. *Sui generis* systems generally provide protection against any direct and indirect commercial use of the GI, as well as against its imitation. *Sui generis* systems for GI protection are used in many countries and also by two regional intergovernmental organizations: the African Intellectual Property Organization (OAPI) and the European Union (EU).

GIs are also protected on the basis of trademark law, commonly through the use of collective and certification marks. Because trademarks incorporating geographical terms are typically not recorded by IP offices as a separate category of trademarks, and because not all trademarks incorporating geographical terms can be considered to be GIs, it may be difficult to determine the exact number of registered GIs within those jurisdictions. It is also worth noting that GI protection via trademark and *sui generis* systems are not mutually exclusive but often coexist, under many legal frameworks, and are available to the benefit of GI holders.

Finally, GIs are typically also protected under unfair competition regulation, consumer protection laws and administrative and judicial decisions, as well as under specific laws or decrees recognizing individual GIs.

The effects of a GI right obtained in a particular jurisdiction are limited to the territory of that jurisdiction. Thus, where a right over a GI is obtained in one jurisdiction, it is protected there but not abroad. In order to obtain protection in a foreign jurisdiction, GI holders must, in principle, seek protection under the relevant national laws prevailing in the jurisdiction in question. However, international agreements can facilitate the acquisition of GI rights abroad. In particular, many bilateral and regional trade agreements have incorporated lists of GIs that are to be protected in the relevant parties to the agreement. The listed GIs may relate to existing or

Additional information

subsequent registrations of GI rights, but protection may also emanate from the trade agreements themselves.

Another way of obtaining protection for GIs abroad is through two international registration systems administered by WIPO: the Lisbon System and the Madrid System.

The Lisbon System

The Lisbon System was established in 1958 to facilitate the international protection of appellations of origin through a single registration procedure.[3] Registration with the WIPO International Bureau ensures protection in all Lisbon contracting parties, without the need for renewal and for as long as the appellation of origin remains protected in its contracting party of origin. However, the decision as to whether to protect a newly registered appellation of origin at the national level remains the prerogative of each contracting party and each Lisbon member can refuse protection based on any ground within one year of being notified of a new appellation of origin by the WIPO International Bureau. The Lisbon System is flexible with regard to the means by which countries may provide protection for the registered appellation of origin (e.g., *sui generis* systems, trademark laws or specific ad hoc decrees, as well as judicial and administrative decisions).

Globally-renowned examples of appellations of origin protected under the Lisbon System include Tequila (Mexico), Chianti for wines (Italy), Habanos for cigars (Cuba) and handicrafts such as Chulucanas for ceramics (Peru), Herend for porcelain (Hungary) and Kraslice musical instruments (Czech Republic). The scope of the System extends to non-geographical traditional names, such as Reblochon (France) and Vinho Verde (Portugal).

In 2015, with the adoption of the Geneva Act of the Lisbon Agreement on Appellations of Origin and Geographical Indications, which will enter into force after five ratifications or accessions, Lisbon contracting parties modernized the System to attract a wider membership, while preserving its principles and objectives. The Geneva Act formally extends the scope of the Lisbon System to the general category of GIs in addition to appellations of origin. The new Act also opens the Lisbon System to accession by intergovernmental organizations, such as the EU and OAPI.

Protection of GIs abroad through the Madrid System

GIs can also be protected in several countries as trademarks (most commonly collective and certification marks) through the Madrid System, an international registration system legally governed by the Madrid Agreement (1891) and the Madrid Protocol (1989) and administered by WIPO.[4] Famous examples of collective and certification marks registered under the Madrid System include Napa Valley for wine (U.S.) and Parmigiano Reggiano for cheese (Italy). As at June 2017, there were more than 1,200 collective and certification marks registered under the Madrid System. However, collective and certification marks protecting GIs are not separately recorded, so it is difficult to determine their exact number.

1   The products and handicrafts to which industrial designs are applied range from technical and medical instruments to watches, jewelry and other luxury items, and from housewares, electrical appliances, vehicles and construction materials to textile designs and leisure goods.

2   The terminology used at national and regional levels to refer to *sui generis* rights over GIs is not uniform. Different terms, such as appellations of origin, controlled appellations of origin, protected designations of origin, protected geographical indications, (qualified) indications of source or simply geographical indications are used in different legislations. Despite the different terminology, however, the common denominator remains the link between the specific quality, characteristics or reputation of the product and its territory of origin. For simplicity, the present text generally uses "geographical indication (GI)" regardless of the different national and regional terminology.

3   The Lisbon System is administered by WIPO and comprises the Lisbon Agreement for the Protection of Appellations of Origin and their International Registration (1958), as revised at Stockholm in 1967 and amended in 1979, and the Geneva Act of the Lisbon Agreement on Appellations of Origin and Geographical Indications (2015), which has not yet entered into force.

4   For more information about the Madrid System, please see the *Madrid Yearly Review 2019*.

Glossary

This glossary provides definitions of key technical terms and concepts. Many of these terms are defined generically (for example, "application") but apply to several or all of the various forms of intellectual property (IP) covered in this report.

Applicant

An individual or other legal entity that files an application for a patent, utility model, trademark or industrial design. There may be more than one applicant in an application. For the statistics in this publication, the name of the first named applicant is used to determine the origin of the application.

Application

The procedure for requesting IP rights at an office, which then examines the application and decides whether to grant protection. Also refers to a set of documents submitted to an office by the applicant.

Application abroad

For statistical purposes, an application filed by a resident of a given state or jurisdiction with the IP office of another state or jurisdiction. For example, an application filed by an applicant domiciled in France with the Japan Patent Office (JPO) is considered an application abroad from the perspective of France. This differs from a "non-resident application," which describes an application filed by a resident of a foreign state or jurisdiction from the perspective of the office receiving the application: the example above would be a non-resident application from the JPO's point of view.

Application date

The date on which the IP office receives an application that meets the minimum requirements. Also referred to as the filing date.

Budapest Treaty

Disclosure of an invention is a requirement for granting a patent. Normally, an invention is disclosed by means of a written description. Where an invention involves a microorganism or the use of a microorganism, disclosure is not always possible in writing but can sometimes only be effected by depositing a sample of the microorganism with a specialized institution. To eliminate the need to deposit a microorganism in each country in which patent protection is sought, the Budapest Treaty provides that the deposit of a microorganism with any International Depositary Authority (IDA) suffices for the purposes of patent procedure at the national patent offices of all contracting states and at any regional patent office that recognizes the Treaty.

Certification trademark

Certification marks are usually given for compliance with defined standards but are not confined to any membership. They may be used by anyone who can certify that the products involved meet certain established standards. In many countries, the main difference between collective marks and certification marks is that collective marks may only be used by a specific group of enterprises, for example, members of an association, while certification marks may be used by anybody who complies with the standards defined by the owner of the certification mark.

Class

May refer to the classes defined in either the Locarno Classification or the Nice Classification. Classes indicate the categories of goods and services (where applicable) for which industrial design or trademark protection is requested. See "Locarno Classification" and "Nice Classification."

Class count

The number of classes specified in a trademark application or registration. In the international trademark system and at certain national and regional offices, an applicant can file a trademark application that specifies one or more of the 45 goods and services classes of the Nice Classification. Offices use a single or multi-class filing system. For example, the offices of Japan, the Republic of Korea and the United States of America (U.S.), as well as many European IP offices, have multi-class filing systems. The offices of Brazil, Mexico and South Africa follow a single-class filing system, requiring a separate application for each class in which an applicant seeks trademark protection. To capture the differences in application and registration numbers across offices, it is useful to compare their respective application and registration class counts.

Collective trademark

Collective marks are usually defined as signs which distinguish the geographical origin, material, mode of manufacture or other common characteristics of goods or services of different enterprises using the collective mark. The owner may be either an association of which those enterprises are members or any other entity, including a public institution or a cooperative.

Community Plant Variety Office (CPVO) of the European Union (EU)

An EU agency that manages a system of plant variety rights covering all EU member states.

Design count

The number of designs contained in an industrial design application or registration. Under the Hague System for the International Registration of Industrial Designs, it is possible for an applicant to obtain protection for up to 100 industrial designs for products belonging to one and the same class by filing a single application. Some national or regional IP offices allow applications to contain more than one design for the same product or within the same class, while others allow only one design per application. In order to capture the differences in application and registration numbers across offices, it is useful to compare their respective application and registration design counts.

Designation

The request, in an international application or registration, by which the applicant/international registration holder specifies the jurisdiction(s) in which they seek to protect their industrial designs (Hague System) or trademarks (Madrid System).

Direct filing

See "National route."

Equivalent application

Applications at regional offices are equivalent to multiple applications, one in each of the states that is a member of those offices. To calculate the number of equivalent applications for the Benelux Office for Intellectual Property (BOIP), the Eurasian Patent Organization (EAPO), the African Intellectual Property Organization (OAPI), the Patent Office of the Cooperation Council for the Arab States of the Gulf (GCC Patent Office) and the European Union Intellectual Property Office (EUIPO), each application is multiplied by the corresponding number of member states. For European Patent Office (EPO) and African Regional Intellectual Property Organization (ARIPO) data, each application is counted as one application abroad if the applicant does not reside in a member state or as one resident application and one application abroad if the applicant resides in a member state. The equivalent application concept is used for reporting data by origin.

Equivalent grant (registration)

Grants (registrations) at regional offices are equivalent to multiple grants (registrations), one in each of the states that is a member of those offices. To calculate the number of equivalent grants (registrations) for BOIP, EAPO, the EUIPO, the GCC Patent Office or OAPI, each grant (registration) is multiplied by the corresponding number of member states. For EPO and ARIPO data, each grant is counted as one grant abroad if the applicant does not reside in a member state or as one resident grant and one grant abroad if the applicant resides in a member state. The equivalent grant (registration) concept is used for reporting data by origin.

European Patent Office (EPO)

The EPO is the regional patent office created under the European Patent Convention (EPC), in charge of granting European patents for EPC member states. Under Patent Cooperation Treaty (PCT) procedures, the EPO acts as a receiving office, an International Searching Authority and an International Preliminary Examining Authority.

European Union Intellectual Property Office (EUIPO)

The EUIPO is the office responsible for managing the EU trademark and the registered community design. The validity of these two intellectual property rights extends across the jurisdictions of the EU's 28 member states.

Filing

See "Application."

Foreign-oriented patent families

A special subset of patent families that comprises foreign-oriented patent families: this includes only patent families that have at least one filing office which differs from the office of the applicant's country of origin. Some foreign-oriented patent families include only one filing office, because applicants may choose to file directly with a foreign office. For example, if a Canadian applicant files a patent application directly with the United States Patent and Trademark Office (USPTO) without previously filing with the patent office of Canada, that application and applications filed subsequently with the USPTO will form a foreign-oriented patent family.

Geographical indication

A geographical indication (GI) is a sign identifying a good as originating in a specific geographical area and possessing a given quality, reputation or other characteristic that is essentially attributable to that geographical origin. Thus, the main function of a GI is to indicate a connection between that quality, characteristic or reputation of the good and its territory of origin.

Grant

A set of exclusive rights legally accorded to the applicant when a patent or utility model is granted or issued.

Gross domestic product (GDP)

The total unduplicated output of economic goods and services produced within a country as measured in monetary terms.

Hague international application

An application for the international registration of an industrial design filed under the WIPO-administered Hague System.

Hague international registration

An international registration issued via the Hague

System, which facilitates the acquisition of industrial design rights in multiple jurisdictions. An application for international registration of an industrial design leads to its recording in the International Register and the publication of the registration in the *International Designs Bulletin*. If the registration is not refused by the IP office of a designated Hague member, the international registration will have the same effect as a registration made in that jurisdiction.

Hague member (Contracting Party)

A state or intergovernmental organization that is a member of the Hague System. Includes any state or intergovernmental organization which is party to the Geneva Act of 1999 and/or the Hague Act of 1960. Entitlement to file an international application under the Hague Agreement is limited to natural persons or legal entities having a real and effective industrial or commercial establishment, or a domicile, in at least one of the Contracting Parties to the Agreement, or being a national of one of those Contracting Parties or of a member state of an intergovernmental organization that is a Contracting Party. In addition – but only under the 1999 Act – an international application may be filed on the basis of habitual residence in the jurisdiction of a Contracting Party.

Hague route

An alternative to the Paris route (i.e., the direct national or regional route), the Hague route enables an application for international registration of industrial designs to be filed using the Hague System.

Hague System

The abbreviated form of the Hague System for the International Registration of Industrial Designs. This System comprises two international treaties: the Hague Act of 1960 and the Geneva Act of 1999. The Hague System makes it possible for an applicant to register up to 100 industrial designs in multiple jurisdictions by filing a single application with the International Bureau of WIPO. It simplifies multinational registration by reducing the requirement to file separate applications with each IP office. The System also simplifies the subsequent management of the industrial design, since it is possible to record changes or renew a registration through a single procedural step.

Industrial design

Industrial designs are applied to a wide variety of industrial products and handicrafts. They refer to the ornamental or aesthetic aspects of a useful article, including compositions of lines or colors or any three-dimensional forms that give a special appearance to a product or handicraft. The holder of a registered industrial design has exclusive rights against unauthor-ized copying or imitation of the design by third parties. Industrial design registrations are valid for a limited period. The term of protection is usually 15 years in most jurisdictions. However, differences in legislation exist, notably in China (which provides for a 10-year term from the application date).

In force

Refers to IP rights that are currently valid or, in the case of trademarks, active. To remain in force, IP protection must be maintained.

Intellectual property (IP)

Refers to creations of the mind: inventions, literary and artistic works, and symbols, names, images and designs used in commerce. IP is divided into two categories: industrial property – which includes patents, utility models, trademarks, industrial designs and geographical indications of source – and copyright, which includes literary and artistic works (such as novels, poems, plays, films), musical works, artistic works (such as drawings, paintings, photographs and sculptures) and architectural designs. Rights related to copyright include those of performing artists in their performances, those of producers of sound recordings in their recordings and those of broadcasters in their radio and television programs.

International Depositary Authority (IDA)

A scientific institution – typically a culture collection – capable of storing microorganisms that has acquired the status of an International Depositary Authority under the Budapest Treaty and provides for the receipt, acceptance and storage of microorganisms and the furnishing of samples thereof. Currently, 47 such authorities exist around the world.

International Patent Classification (IPC)

An internationally recognized patent classification system, the IPC has a hierarchical structure of language-independent symbols and is divided into sections, classes, sub-classes and groups. IPC symbols are assigned according to the technical features in patent applications. A patent application that relates to multiple technical features can be assigned several IPC symbols.

International Union for the Protection of New Varieties of Plants (UPOV)

An intergovernmental organization established by the International Convention for the Protection of New Varieties of Plants (the UPOV Convention), which was adopted on December 2, 1961. UPOV provides and promotes an effective system of plant variety protection aim at encouraging the development of new varieties of plants for the benefit of society.

Additional information

Invention

A new solution to a technical problem. To qualify for patent protection, the invention must be novel, involve an inventive step and be industrially applicable, as judged by a person skilled in the art.

Lisbon System

The Lisbon System was established in 1958 to facilitate the international protection of appellations of origin through a single registration procedure. Registration with the WIPO International Bureau ensures protection in all Lisbon contracting parties, without need for renewal and for as long as the appellation of origin remains protected in its contracting party of origin. However, the decision on whether to protect a newly registered appellation of origin at the national level remains the prerogative of each contracting party, and each Lisbon member can refuse protection based on any ground within one year of being notified of a new appellation of origin by the WIPO International Bureau. The Lisbon System is flexible with regard to the means by which countries may provide protection for the registered appellation of origin (e.g., *sui generis* systems, trademark laws or specific ad hoc decrees, as well as judicial and administrative decisions).

Locarno Classification

The abbreviated form of the International Classification for Industrial Designs under the Locarno Agreement, used for registering industrial designs. The Locarno Classification consists of 32 classes and their respective subclasses with explanatory notes plus an alphabetical list of the goods in which industrial designs are incorporated and an indication of the classes and subclasses into which they fall.

Madrid international application

An application for international registration under the Madrid System, which is a request for protection of a trademark in one or more Madrid members' jurisdictions. An international application must be based on a basic mark, that is, prior application or registration of a mark in a Madrid member jurisdiction.

Madrid international registration

An application for international registration of a mark leads to its recording in the International Register and the publication of the international registration in the *WIPO Gazette of International Marks*. If the international registration is not refused protection by a designated Madrid member, it will have the same effect as a national or regional trademark registration made under the law applicable in that Madrid member's jurisdiction.

Madrid member (Contracting Party)

A state or intergovernmental organization – for example, the African Intellectual Property Organization (OAPI) or the European Union (EU) – that is party to the Madrid Agreement and/or the Madrid Protocol.

Madrid route

The Madrid route (the Madrid System) is an alternative to the direct national or regional route (also called the Paris route).

Madrid System

An abbreviation describing two procedural treaties for the international registration of trademarks, namely, the Madrid Agreement Concerning the International Registration of Marks and the Protocol Relating to the Madrid Agreement. Following the decision by the Madrid Union Assembly in October 2016, the Protocol is the sole governing treaty of the Madrid System. The Madrid System is administered by the International Bureau of WIPO.

Maintenance

An act by the applicant to keep an IP grant/registration valid (in force), primarily by paying the required fee to the IP office of the state or jurisdiction providing protection. That fee is also known as a "maintenance fee." A trademark can be maintained indefinitely by paying renewal fees; however, patents, utility models and industrial designs can be maintained for only a limited number of years.

Microorganism deposit

The transmittal of a microorganism to an International Depositary Authority (IDA), which receives and accepts it, the storage of such a microorganism by the IDA, or both transmittal and storage.

National phase under the PCT

The phase that follows the international phase of the PCT procedure and that consists of the entry and processing of the international application in the individual countries or regions in which the applicant seeks protection for an invention.

National route

Applications for IP protection filed directly with the national office of, or acting for, the relevant state or jurisdiction (see also "Hague route," "Madrid route" and "PCT route"). The national route is also called the "direct route" or "Paris route."

Nice Classification

The abbreviated form of the International Classification of Goods and Services for the Purposes of Registering Marks, an international classification established under the Nice Agreement. The Nice Classification consists of 45 classes, which are divided into 34 classes for goods and 11 for services. (See "Class.")

Non-resident

For statistical purposes, a "non-resident" application refers to an application filed with the IP office of, or acting for, a state or jurisdiction in which the first named applicant in the application is not domiciled. For example, an application filed with the Japan Patent Office (JPO) by an applicant residing in France is considered to be a non-resident application from the perspective of the JPO. Non-resident applications are sometimes referred to as foreign applications. A non-resident grant or registration is an IP right issued on the basis of a non-resident application.

Origin (country or region)

For statistical purposes, the origin of an application means the country or territory of residence of the first named applicant in the application. In some cases (notably in the U.S.), the country of origin is determined by the residence of the assignee rather than that of the applicant.

Paris Convention

The Paris Convention for the Protection of Industrial Property, signed on March 20, 1883, is one of the most important treaties, as it establishes general principles applicable to all IP rights. It establishes the "right of priority" enabling an IP applicant, when filing an application in countries other than the original country of filing, to claim priority of an earlier application filed up to 12 months previously for patents and utility models, and up to six months previously for trademarks and industrial designs.

Paris route

An alternative to the Hague, Madrid or PCT routes, the Paris route (also called the "direct route" or "national route") enables individual IP applications to be filed directly with an IP office of a country/territory that is a signatory to the Paris Convention.

Patent

A set of exclusive rights granted by law to applicants for inventions that are new, non-obvious and commercially applicable. A patent is valid for a limited period of time (generally 20 years), during which patent holders can commercially exploit their inventions on an exclusive basis. In return, applicants are obliged to disclose their inventions to the public in a manner that enables others skilled in the art to replicate the invention. The patent system is designed to encourage innovation by providing innovators with time-limited exclusive legal rights, thus enabling them to appropriate the returns from their innovative activity.

Patent Cooperation Treaty (PCT)

An international treaty administered by WIPO, the PCT allows applicants to seek patent protection for an invention simultaneously in a large number of countries (PCT contracting states) by filing a single PCT international application. The granting of patents, which remains under the control of national or regional patent offices, is carried out in what is called the "national phase under the PCT."

Patent family

Applicants often file patent applications in multiple jurisdictions, so some inventions are recorded more than once. To take this into account, WIPO has indicators related to patent families, defined as patent applications interlinked by one or more of: priority claim, Patent Cooperation Treaty national phase entry, continuation, continuation-in-part, internal priority and addition or division. WIPO's patent family definition includes only those associated with patent applications for inventions and excludes patent families associated with utility model applications.

PCT application

A patent application filed through the WIPO-administered PCT, also known as an international application.

PCT-patent prosecution highway (PCT-PPH) pilots

A number of bilateral agreements signed between patent offices that enable applicants to request an accelerated examination procedure, because of positive patentability findings made by the international searching and/or international preliminary examining authority, in the written opinion of an international searching authority, the written opinion of an international preliminary examining authority or the international preliminary report on patentability.

PCT route

The procedure outlined in the PCT, as opposed to the Paris route.

PCT System

The PCT, an international treaty administered by WIPO, facilitates the acquisition of patent rights in a large number of jurisdictions. The PCT System simplifies the process of multiple national patent filings by reducing the requirement to file a separate application in each jurisdiction. However, the decision on whether to grant patent rights remains in the hands of national and regional patent offices, and patent rights remain limited to the jurisdiction of the patent-granting authority. The PCT application process starts with the international phase, during which an international search and, possibly, a preliminary examination are performed, and concludes with the national phase, during which a national or regional patent office decides on the patentability of an invention according to national law.

Additional information

Pending patent application

In general, this refers to a patent application filed with a patent office for which no patent has yet been either granted or refused, and for which the application has not been withdrawn. In jurisdictions where a request for examination is required to start the examination process, a pending application may refer to an application for which a request for examination has been received or one for which no patent has been granted or refused, and for which the application has not been withdrawn.

Plant Patent Act (PPA) of the U.S.

Under the law commonly known as the "Plant Patent Act," whoever invents or discovers and asexually reproduces any distinct and new variety of plant, including cultivated sports, mutants, hybrids and newly found seedlings, other than a tuber-propagated plant or a plant found in an uncultivated state, may obtain a patent therefor.

Plant variety

According to the UPOV Convention, plant variety means a plant grouping within a single botanical taxon of the lowest known rank which, irrespective of whether the conditions for the granting of a breeder's right are fully met, can be defined by the expression of the characteristics resulting from a given genotype or combination of genotypes, distinguished from any other plant grouping by the expression of at least one of the said characteristics and considered as a unit with regard to its suitability for being propagated unchanged.

Plant variety grant

Under the UPOV Convention, the breeder's right is granted (title of protection is issued) only when the variety is new, distinct, uniform, stable and has a suitable denomination.

Plant Variety Protection Act (PVPA) of the U.S.

Under the PVPA, the U.S. protects all sexually reproduced plant varieties and tuber-propagated plant varieties, excluding fungi and bacteria.

Prior art

All information disclosed to the public about an invention, in any form, before a given date. Information on prior art can assist in determining whether the claimed invention is new and involves an inventive step (i.e., is non-obvious) for the purposes of international searches and international preliminary examination.

Priority date

The filing date of the application on the basis of which priority is claimed. (See "Paris Convention.")

Publication date

The date on which an IP application is disclosed to the public. On that date, the subject matter of the application becomes prior art.

Regional application/grant (registration)

An application filed with or granted (registered) by an IP office having regional jurisdiction over more than one country. There are currently seven regional offices: the African Intellectual Property Organization (OAPI), the African Regional Intellectual Property Organization (ARIPO), the Benelux Office for Intellectual Property (BOIP), the Eurasian Patent Organization (EAPO), the European Patent Office (EPO), the European Union Intellectual Property Office (EUIPO) and the Patent Office of the Cooperation Council for the Arab States of the Gulf (GCC Patent Office).

Registered Community Design

A registration issued by the EUIPO based on a single application filed directly with the office by an applicant seeking protection within the EU as a whole.

Registration

An exclusive set of rights legally accorded to the applicant when an industrial design or trademark is registered or issued. See "Industrial design" or "Trademark." Registrations are issued to applicants to make use of and exploit their industrial designs or trademarks for a limited period of time and can, in some cases (particularly in the case of trademarks), be renewed indefinitely.

Renewal

The process by which the protection of an IP right is maintained (kept in force). This usually consists of paying renewal fees to an IP office at regular intervals. If renewal fees are not paid, the registration may lapse. See also "Maintenance."

Resident

For statistical purposes, a resident application refers to an application filed with the IP office of, or acting for, the state or jurisdiction in which the first named applicant in the application has residence. For example, an application filed with the JPO by a resident of Japan is considered a resident application from the perspective of the JPO. Resident applications are sometimes referred to as "domestic applications." A resident grant/registration is an IP right issued on the basis of a resident application.

Trademark

A sign used to distinguish the goods or services of one undertaking from those of others. A trademark may consist of words and combinations of words (for instance, names or slogans), logos, figures and images, letters, numbers, sounds, or, in rare instances, smells or moving images, or a combination thereof. The procedures for registering trademarks are governed by the legislation and procedures of national and regional IP offices and WIPO. Trademark rights are limited to the jurisdiction of the IP office that registers the trademark. Trademarks can be registered by filing an application at the relevant national or regional office(s), or by filing an international application through the Madrid System.

Utility model

A special form of patent right granted by a state or jurisdiction to an inventor or the inventor's assignee for a fixed period of time. The terms and conditions for granting a utility model are slightly different from those for normal patents (including a shorter term of protection and less stringent patentability requirements). The term can also describe what are known in certain countries as "petty patents," "short-term patents" or "innovation patents."

World Intellectual Property Organization (WIPO)

A United Nations specialized agency dedicated to the promotion of innovation and creativity for the economic, social and cultural development of all countries through a balanced and effective international IP system. WIPO was established in 1967 with a mandate to promote the protection of IP throughout the world through cooperation between states and in collaboration with other international organizations.

Abbreviations

ARIPO	African Regional Intellectual Property Organization
BOIP	Benelux Office for Intellectual Property
CNIPA	National Intellectual Property Administration of the People's Republic of China
CPVO	Community Plant Variety Office of the European Union
EAPO	Eurasian Patent Organization
EPO	European Patent Office
EU	European Union
EUIPO	European Union Intellectual Property Office
GCC Patent Office	Patent Office of the Cooperation Council for the Arab States of the Gulf
GDP	gross domestic product
GI	geographical indication
IDA	International Depositary Authority
IP	intellectual property
IPA	International Publishers Association
IPC	International Patent Classification
JPO	Japan Patent Office
KIPO	Korean Intellectual Property Office
NPA	national publishers' association
OAPI	African Intellectual Property Organization
PCT	Patent Cooperation Treaty
PPA	Plant Patent Act of the United States of America
PVPA	Plant Variety Protection Act of the United States of America
R&D	research and development
U.K.	United Kingdom
UM	utility model
UN	United Nations
UPOV	International Union for the Protection of New Varieties of Plants
U.S.	United States of America
USPTO	United States Patent and Trademark Office
WIPO	World Intellectual Property Organization

Annexes

Annex A. Definitions for selected energy-related technology fields

Energy-related technologies	International patent classification (IPC) symbols
Solar energy technology	E04D 1/30, E04D 13/18, F24J 2/00, F24J 2/02, F24J 2/04, F24J 2/05, F24J 2/06, F24J 2/07, F24J 2/08, F24J 2/10, F24J 2/12, F24J 2/13, F24J 2/14, F24J 2/15, F24J 2/16, F24J 2/18, F24J 2/23, F24J 2/24, F24J 2/36, F24J 2/38, F24J 2/42, F24J 2/46, F03G 6/06, G02B 5/10, H01L 31/052, H01L 31/04, H01L 31/042, H01L 31/18, G02F 1/136, G05F 1/67, H01L 25/00, H01L 31/00, H01L 31/048, H01L 33/00, H02J 7/35, H02N 6/00
Fuel cell technology	H01M 4/00, H01M 4/86, H01M 4/88, H01M 4/90, H01M 8/00, H01M 8/02, H01M 8/04, H01M 8/06, H01M 8/08, H01M 8/10, H01M 8/12, H01M 8/14, H01M 8/16, H01M 8/18, H01M 8/20, H01M 8/22, H01M 8/24
Wind energy	F03D 1/00, F03D 3/00, F03D 5/00, F03D 7/00, F03D 9/00, F03D 11/00, B60L 8/00
Geothermal energy	F24J 3/08, F03G 4/00, F03G 7/05

Note: For definitions of IPC symbols, see *www.wipo.int/classifications/ipc*. The correspondence between IPC symbols and technology fields is not always clear-cut, therefore it is difficult to capture all patents in a specific technology field. Nonetheless, the IPC-based definitions of the four technologies presented above are likely to capture the vast majority of related patents.

Source: WIPO.

Annex B. Composition of industry sectors by Nice goods and services classes

Industry sector	Abbreviation (where applicable)	Nice classes
Agricultural products and services	Agriculture	29, 30, 31, 32, 33, 43
Management, communications, real estate and financial services	Business services	35, 36
Chemicals	..	1, 2, 4
Textiles – clothing and accessories	Clothing and accessories	14, 18, 22, 23, 24, 25, 26, 27, 34
Construction, infrastructure	Construction	6, 17, 19, 37, 40
Pharmaceuticals, health, cosmetics	Health	3, 5, 10, 44
Household equipment	..	8, 11, 20, 21
Leisure, education, training	Leisure & Education	13, 15, 16, 28, 41
Scientific research, information and communication technology	Research & Technology	9, 38, 42, 45
Transportation and logistics	Transportation	7, 12, 39

Source: Edital®.

Annex C. Industry sectors by Locarno classes

Sector	Locarno classes
Advertising	20, 32
Agricultural products and food preparation	1, 27, 31
Construction	23, 25, 29
Electricity and lighting	13, 26
Furniture and household goods	6, 7, 30
Health, pharma and cosmetics	24, 28
ICT and audiovisual	14, 16, 18
Leisure and education	17, 19, 21, 22
Packaging	9
Textiles and accessories	2, 3, 5, 11
Tools and machines	4, 8, 10, 15
Transport	12

Source: Organisation for Economic Co-operation and Development (OECD).